Navigating Mergers, Acquisitions, and Organizational Redesign

Ricardo Marcão
https://orcid.org/0000-0003-3277-3078

ISLA Santarem, Portugal & NECE, University of Beira Interior, Portugal

Vasco Santos
https://orcid.org/0000-0002-3535-9377

Institute Polytechnic of Tomar, Portugal & NECE, University of Beira Interior, Portugal

IGI Global
Scientific Publishing
Publishing Tomorrow's Research Today

Vice President of Editorial	Melissa Wagner
Director of Acquisitions	Mikaela Felty
Director of Book Development	Jocelynn Hessler
Production Manager	Mike Brehm
Cover Design	Jose Rosado

Published in the United States of America by
IGI Global Scientific Publishing
701 East Chocolate Avenue
Hershey, PA, 17033, USA
Tel: 717-533-8845 | Fax: 717-533-7115
Website: https://www.igi-global.com E-mail: cust@igi-global.com

Library of Congress Cataloging-in-Publication Data

LCCN: 2025034455 (CIP Data Pending)
ISBN13: 979-8-3373-5233-6
Isbn13Softcover: 979-8-3373-5234-3
EISBN13: 979-8-3373-5235-0
British Cataloguing in Publication Data
A Cataloguing in Publication record for this book is available from the British Library.

This book is dedicated to our daughters, *Caetana Santos* and *Camila Monteiro e Marcão*.

May you grow up in a world shaped by curiosity, knowledge, and integrity. May you always have the courage to ask questions, the determination to pursue your ambitions, and the wisdom to build bridges between people, ideas, and cultures.

You remind us every day that the future is not something we simply inherit. It is something we build together.

Ricardo Marcão
ISLA Santarem, Portugal & NECE, University of Beira Interior, Portugal

Vasco Santos
Institute Polytechnic of Tomar, Portugal

Table of Contents

Detailed Table of Contents

The connection between Artificial Intelligence (AI) and ESG (Environmental, Social and Governance) criteria is transforming management practices in digital and traditional organizations. This article examines, from theoretical and empirical perspectives, how Artificial Intelligence contributes to enhanced organizational performance and ESG criteria. It presents practical applications in management, the methodology of the studies, limitations, and opportunities for future research. It concludes by interconnecting all the topics covered, such as: AI capabilities, digital transformation, data-driven management practices, and improvements in ESG metrics. Finally, it demonstrates the most effective and impactful measures for the management area.

Cultural synergy is a key success factor in a merger and acquisition that can affect the involvement of employees, the rate of integration, and the sustainability of the organization. Whereas the conventional M&A initiatives aimed at financial and operational measures, the cultural fit has come out as strategic requirement to create value. The chapter reviews discussion of cultural collisions in terms of trust, motivation, and performance, and identifies assessment tools which can be used to support cultural due diligence. Such strategies as inclusive leadership, focused HR practice, open communication, and participatory structures are discussed as ways to create shared meaning and entire identity. The examples of cross-border and technology mergers demonstrate the importance of planned integration in changing cultural diversity into innovation and long-term development. The chapter concludes that cultural synergy is not by chance and it is the result of intentional planning and flexible management.

This chapter examines the critical role of ethical governance and anti-corruption within the mergers and acquisitions (M&A) lifecycle, aligning corporate conduct with United Nations Sustainable Development Goal 16. While M&A frameworks traditionally prioritize financial and operational performance, it argues proactive, value-based decision-making to mitigate systemic risks such as insider trading and successor liability. The chapter reviews international regulatory landscapes, including the FCPA, UK Bribery Act, and India's Companies Act 2013, alongside high-profile cases like Siemens and Enron. It proposes a three-pillar framework consisting of Integrity Assurance Systems, Institutional Accountability Structures, and Stakeholder Inclusivity to operationalize integrity. By integrating ethical due diligence from deal origination through post-merger integration, organizations can transform M&A into a strategic mechanism for building institutional trust and advancing global justice.

Digital transformation has increased the strategic importance of technological capabilities and knowledge-intensive services, leading firms to use mergers and acquisitions to accelerate digital capability development. This chapter examines how strategic value may emerge during digital post-merger integration through the acquisition of Devoteam Middle East by solutions by stc. Using a qualitative case-based analytical approach drawing on publicly available corporate and industry sources, the analysis identifies the mechanisms through which acquired digital capabilities are integrated and expanded. The findings suggest that value creation depends on stabilizing specialized human capital, aligning technological and organizational structures, and scaling capabilities through hybrid organizational arrangements.

This chapter explores how legal and regulatory frameworks for mergers and acquisitions (M&A) act as critical enablers of economic resilience in emerging markets. It analyzes the interplay between competition law, corporate governance, and foreign direct investment (FDI) controls, highlighting their role in fostering investor confidence, regulatory transparency, and sustainable growth. Through comparative analysis of key jurisdictions—such as the U.S., EU, India, Brazil, and ASEAN—and landmark case studies like Microsoft–Activision and Grab–Uber, the chapter demonstrates how legal clarity and institutional maturity shape M&A outcomes. It further emphasizes the importance of integrating ESG standards and enhancing cross-border legal coordination. The study positions legal infrastructure not just as a compliance mechanism but as a strategic foundation for inclusive and resilient economic development.

This study explores how structural, cultural, and technological redesign initiatives influence the outcomes of post-merger integration (PMI) across diverse sectors in India, including banking, IT, pharmaceuticals, manufacturing, and telecom. Using a mixed-method approach, the research draws insights from interviews with senior executives, surveys from mid-level employees, and secondary data such as post-merger reports and industry case studies. The findings suggest that companies that invest in thoughtful, phased, and inclusive redesign—covering areas like leadership realignment, cultural harmonization, employee engagement, and digital standardization—are significantly more likely to achieve synergy realization, operational efficiency, and talent retention. Conversely, the absence of strategic redesign often leads to resistance, confusion, and integration failure.

In today's volatile business environment, organizational redesign is essential for sustaining competitiveness amidst technological disruptions, market shifts, and structural transformations. This chapter explores the strategic role of competitive intelligence (CI) in facilitating effective redesign, particularly during mergers, acquisitions, and restructuring. CI provides actionable insights into industry dynamics, market trends, competitor behavior, and internal capabilities. Using frameworks like the McKinsey 7S and Nadler-Tushman Congruence Model, the chapter illustrates how CI informs structural alignment and strategic decisions. Practical tools—SWOT, PESTEL, Porter's Five Forces, scenario planning—and technologies like AI and war-gaming are discussed. Emphasis is placed on ethical practices, leadership alignment, and embedding a CI-driven culture. Future trends, including predictive analytics and big data, are highlighted as essential for innovation, agility, and long-term resilience.

This paper examines how short-term technology investments support digital transformation and competitiveness in small and medium-sized enterprises (SMEs). Focusing on agile, low-capital technological solutions, it analyzes how SMEs improve operational efficiency, decision-making, and risk management under financial and resource constraints. Through a structured literature review and illustrative case studies, the study identifies key success factors, performance metrics, and limitations of short-term investments. The findings highlight how technology integration enables SMEs to achieve rapid returns while maintaining strategic flexibility and sustainable growth.

Preface

INTRODUCTION

Organizations today operate in an increasingly complex and interconnected global environment. Rapid technological advances, economic volatility, and the continuous evolution of global markets have fundamentally reshaped the way organizations grow, restructure, and compete. In this context, mergers and acquisitions (M&A) and organizational redesign have emerged as critical strategic mechanisms through which organizations pursue expansion, innovation, and resilience. Rather than relying exclusively on organic growth, many firms now pursue acquisitions, strategic partnerships, and structural transformations to accelerate strategic development and respond effectively to new competitive realities.

The book *Navigating Mergers, Acquisitions, and Organizational Redesign* explores these dynamics by presenting a multidisciplinary perspective on the challenges and opportunities associated with corporate transformation. The contributions gathered in this volume examine mergers, acquisitions, and organizational redesign from strategic, financial, technological, governance, and managerial perspectives. Together, they provide readers with a comprehensive understanding of the processes that shape organizational restructuring in the contemporary global economy.

Corporate restructuring has become a central component of strategic management. Organizations must continuously evaluate their competitive position and determine whether their existing structures, capabilities, and market strategies remain adequate in an environment characterized by rapid change. Mergers and acquisitions allow companies to enter new markets, acquire technological expertise, diversify operations, and achieve economies of scale. Organizational redesign complements these strategies by enabling firms to adapt internal structures, processes, and governance mechanisms to support evolving strategic objectives.

Despite their potential benefits, mergers and acquisitions remain complex undertakings that involve significant risks. Numerous studies have shown that many transactions fail to generate the expected value due to difficulties related to cultural integration, leadership alignment, governance structures, and operational coordination. Similarly, organizational redesign initiatives may generate uncertainty among employees and disrupt established routines if not managed effectively. The success of these initiatives therefore depends not only on financial planning or strategic intent but also on leadership capabilities, effective communication, and a deep understanding of organizational dynamics.

The importance of this topic has become even more evident in recent years as digital transformation continues to reshape industries across the world. Technologies such as artificial intelligence, big data analytics, and machine learning are transforming decision making processes and enabling organizations to analyze complex data environments with unprecedented accuracy. At the same time, global sustainability agendas and governance frameworks increasingly influence how organizations approach restructuring and strategic transformation. Companies are now expected to align their strategies with broader environmental, social, and governance considerations while maintaining competitiveness and financial performance.

In this context, understanding how organizations navigate mergers, acquisitions, and structural transformation is essential for both scholars and practitioners. Academic research provides valuable frameworks for analyzing these processes, while practical experiences offer insights into the real world challenges faced by organizations undergoing significant change. By bringing together contributions from diverse academic and professional backgrounds, this volume provides a balanced perspective that integrates theoretical analysis with practical implications.

This book is intended for a wide audience that includes academics, researchers, graduate students, and industry professionals interested in strategic management and organizational transformation. Scholars working in fields such as management, finance, innovation, and organizational behavior will find theoretical insights that contribute to the academic literature on mergers, acquisitions, and corporate restructuring. At the same time, practitioners including executives, consultants, policymakers, and business analysts will benefit from the practical perspectives presented throughout the chapters, particularly regarding strategic decision making, governance structures, and post merger integration.

The chapters included in this book address different dimensions of mergers, acquisitions, and organizational redesign, offering readers a comprehensive overview of both theoretical frameworks and practical applications.

CHAPTER OVERVIEW

Chapter 1, *Artificial Intelligence and How It Improves Results and Performance in Management in Conjunction With ESG*, examines how artificial intelligence technologies can enhance managerial performance while supporting environmental, social, and governance principles. The chapter explores the role of data driven decision making in improving organizational outcomes and aligning corporate strategies with responsible and sustainable management practices.

Chapter 2, *Cultural Synergy in Mergers and Acquisitions: Strategies for Building Unified and Resilient Organizations*, focuses on the critical role of organizational culture in the success of mergers and acquisitions. The authors analyze strategies for achieving cultural alignment between merging organizations and discuss how leadership and communication can facilitate the development of unified and resilient corporate structures.

Chapter 3, *Ethical Governance and Anti-Corruption in M&A: Building Trust for SDG 16*, highlights the importance of ethical governance and transparency in corporate restructuring processes. The chapter explores how anti corruption frameworks and responsible leadership practices contribute to building trust among stakeholders while supporting global sustainable development objectives.

Chapter 4, *Financial Resilience and Strategic Value Creation in Post-Merger Integration: A Case Study of the STC Solutions and Devoteam Middle East Acquisition in Saudi Arabia*, presents a detailed case study that examines how organizations manage financial integration and value creation following a merger. The chapter illustrates how financial resilience and strategic planning contribute to successful post merger integration.

Chapter 5, *Legal Frameworks for M&A in Emerging Markets as Catalysts for Economic Resilience*, analyzes the regulatory and legal environments that shape mergers and acquisitions in emerging economies. The authors discuss how legal frameworks influence corporate transactions and support economic resilience in rapidly developing markets.

Chapter 6, *Organizational Redesign in Indian M&A Deals: A Strategic Tool for Sustainable Integration*, examines the role of organizational restructuring in mergers and acquisitions within the Indian business context. The chapter highlights how redesigning organizational structures can facilitate sustainable integration and long term strategic alignment.

Chapter 7, *Role of Competitive Intelligence in Organizational Redesign*, explores how competitive intelligence supports strategic decision making during periods of organizational transformation. The chapter emphasizes the importance of information gathering, market analysis, and strategic foresight in guiding organizational redesign initiatives.

Chapter 8, *Short Term Investments in the Context of Technology Integration*, focuses on financial decision making in environments characterized by technological change. The chapter discusses how organizations balance short term investment strategies with long term technological integration objectives.

Chapter 9, *Strategic Realignment and Cultural Integration: Human Centric Approaches to Post-Merger Organizational Redesign*, examines the human dimension of post merger integration and organizational transformation. The authors analyze how human centered leadership and cultural integration strategies contribute to successful organizational realignment.

Chapter 10, *The Technological Transformation of Competitive Intelligence Through AI, Big Data, and ML*, investigates how emerging technologies are transforming competitive intelligence practices. The chapter highlights the role of artificial intelligence, big data, and machine learning in enhancing strategic analysis and supporting organizational decision making.

Chapter 11, *Digital Marketing and Globalization*, explores the relationship between digital marketing strategies and global business expansion. The chapter discusses how digital platforms and marketing technologies influence organizational growth and competitive positioning in international markets.

Chapter 12, *Optimizing Financial Decision Making for Strategic Planning Success*, addresses the role of financial analysis and decision making in strategic planning processes. The chapter highlights how financial frameworks support effective resource allocation and long term organizational performance.

CONCLUSION

Taken together, the chapters included in this volume provide a comprehensive exploration of the strategic, financial, technological, and human factors that influence mergers, acquisitions, and organizational redesign. The contributions illustrate how organizations can navigate complex transformation processes while maintaining strategic coherence and long term sustainability.

In an era characterized by rapid technological change and increasing global competition, the ability to manage organizational transformation effectively has become a defining capability for successful organizations. This book contributes to the advancement of knowledge in this field by presenting diverse perspectives that illuminate both the opportunities and challenges associated with corporate restructuring.

It is my hope that this volume will inspire further research and provide valuable guidance for scholars and practitioners seeking to better understand how organizations can navigate mergers, acquisitions, and organizational redesign in an increasingly dynamic global environment.

Filipa Martinho
ISLA Santarém – Polytechnic University, Portugal

Chapter 1
Artificial Intelligence and How It Improves Results and Performance in Management in Conjunction With ESG

Lucas Lacerda
http://orcid.org/0009-0008-6483-5222
ISLA Santarém, Portugal

Filipa Martinho
ISLA Santarém, Portugal

ABSTRACT

The connection between Artificial Intelligence (AI) and ESG (Environmental, Social and Governance) criteria is transforming management practices in digital and traditional organizations. This article examines, from theoretical and empirical perspectives, how Artificial Intelligence contributes to enhanced organizational performance and ESG criteria. It presents practical applications in management, the methodology of the studies, limitations, and opportunities for future research. It concludes by interconnecting all the topics covered, such as: AI capabilities, digital transformation, data-driven management practices, and improvements in ESG metrics. Finally, it demonstrates the most effective and impactful measures for the management area.

DOI: 10.4018/979-8-3373-5233-6.ch001

INTRODUCTION

The adoption of AI in companies has grown exponentially, not only for efficiency gains, but also as a means to improve sustainability and governance metrics. Recent studies indicate that corporate AI capabilities can be associated with improvements in ESG indicators, through mechanisms such as greater operational efficiency, real-time monitoring and compliance (Alqahtani et al., 2025).

The objective of this article is to synthesize existing knowledge on how AI improves management outcomes when integrated with ESG objectives, to propose a conceptual framework and methodological lines for empirical analysis, and to identify practical applications, challenges and research opportunities. The contributions aim to support both the academic community and business decision-makers seeking to operationalize ESG with digital and AI support.

1 METHODOLOGY

To structure this chapter, three methodological steps were followed:

1- Systematic literature review: research and screening of recent works (20202025) on AI, ESG, digital transformation, and business-model innovation. Examples of key works included: review on AI-driven business model innovation, empirical studies on AI and ESG, and analyses on AI and strategic decision-making (Amaral, 2022).
2- Construction of a conceptual framework: based on the literature, a proposed causal model was developed relating to AI capabilities, digital/analytical capabilities, data-driven management practices, operational improvements and ESG.
3- Methodological proposal for future empirical studies: recommendations for detailed study design in the corresponding section.

2 CONCEPTUAL BACKGROUND

AI is understood here as a set of technologies (machine learning, predictive analytics, LLMs, integrated vision/IoT systems) that increase the information processing capacity of organizations, improving forecasting, optimization, and automation of complex tasks. Strategy literature suggests that digital and AI capabilities can be sources of competitive advantage when integrated into organizational processes and routines (Csaszar et al., 2024). ESG is a set of criteria that evaluate environmental performance (resource consumption, emissions), social performance (working conditions, privacy, inclusion) and governance performance (transparency, compliance). Integrating ESG into strategy involves translating sustainability objectives into observable metrics, governance processes, and measurable operational initiatives.

Recent studies suggest that AI acts across multiple channels to influence ESG: monitoring and measurement (sensors, IoT, big data analysis), efficiency (optimization of energy consumption and logistics), governance (fraud detection, automated reporting and compliance) and product/service innovation (new sustainable business models). Empirical evidence indicates positive associations between AI adoption and improved ESG metrics in large firm-level samples, although the effects are context-dependent and may be heterogeneous (Alqahtani et al., 2025; Wang et al., 2025; Xie & Wu, 2025).

Beyond correlation, literature emphasizes the role of underlying mechanisms. AIdriven digital capabilities foster green innovation, improve resource allocation, and strengthen organizational transparency, enhancing ESG outcomes. In this sense, the concept of technological "catch-up" suggests that companies with lower initial digital maturity may disproportionately benefit from AI adoption, particularly in sustainability-oriented practices (Yu et al., 2025).

3 AI APPLICATIONS IN MANAGEMENT

One of the ways AI is used is through its integration with IoT, which allows for realtime measurement of energy consumption, detection of inefficiencies and optimization of workloads (data centers, supply chains), reducing emissions and costs. Empirical studies show a decrease in consumption and improvement in environmental metrics in companies that use predictive solutions for energy management (Alqahtani et al., 2025).

AI systems (text and NLP) automate the screening of regulatory documents, detect inconsistencies in reports, and generate draft ESG disclosures, reducing the risk of governance failures and decreasing the cost of manual auditing. Recent research demonstrates practical NLP-based approaches for automated compliance checking, showing the feasibility and benefits of such systems in large-scale document analysis and regulatory monitoring (Song et al., 2025).

AI improves the quality and speed of strategic analysis (forecasting, scenarios, simulations), allowing managers to test options based on real data and simulated scenarios, which is particularly useful for decisions with ESG trade-offs. Experimental studies show that LLM models can assist in generating and evaluating strategies comparable to human assessments (Csaszar et al., 2024).

AI facilitates data-driven models and services, which can align value creation with environmental and social gains. Systematic reviews on AI-driven BMI demonstrate that AI is a central driver of business model transformation (Amaral, 2022).

4 CHALLENGES AND LIMITATIONS

Not all uses of AI benefit ESG: for example, increased computational processing can increase energy consumption and poorly designed automated decisions can lead to discrimination or privacy violations. Studies point to heterogeneous effects and sometimes, trade-offs between objectives such as privacy and efficiency (Jorzik et al., 2024). The effectiveness of AI depends on reliable data and robust governance, companies without data infrastructures face considerable limitations and the quality of ESG indicators is also a critical factor for validating results.

Empirical evidence often faces identification challenges, as companies adopting AI may systematically differ from others, so that correlation with ESG does not imply direct causality. To address this issue, robust studies employ instrumental variables (IVs), difference-in-differences methods or quasi-experimental research designs (Alqahtani et al., 2025).

Automating reports or relying on superficial metrics without substantive structural changes may result in greenwashing, where firms project an image of sustainability without achieving real environmental or social improvements. Therefore, stakeholder trust depends on transparency regarding methodologies, performance metrics and independent audits.

5 FUTURE TRENDS AND RESEARCH OPPORTUNITIES

1- Causal identification and longitudinal studies: research using robust causal designs (IVs, natural experiments) to isolate the effect of AI on ESG metrics. (Necessary given the problem of endogeneity in current studies) (Alqahtani et al., 2025; Zhou et al., 2025).
2- Responsible AI for ESG: research on frameworks that balance efficiency and ethical integrity with accountability and explainability metrics.
3- Interactions between AI, regulation, and infrastructure: study of how public policies and access to infrastructure mediate the effects of AI on ESG.
4- Management experimentation with LLMs: experimental studies that concretely evaluate the role of AI in the quality of strategic decision-making and ESG outcomes in controlled scenarios (Csaszar et al., 2024).

5- Business-model innovation with ESG intent: applied research on how AI can enable business models whose value capture logic is aligned from the outset with environmental and social objectives (Amaral, 2022).

CONCLUSION

Recent literature and practice reports suggest that AI has significant potential to improve management outcomes and ESG performance when implemented with data governance, clear objectives, and robust measurement. However, the evidence is heterogeneous: positive effects depend on context, organizational assets, and how initiatives are designed. Moving forward requires more rigorous empirical methodologies and interdisciplinary research that unites technology, strategy, and ethics. In practical terms, managers should view AI as an enabler that, when aligned with ESG objectives, can transform operations, risk modeling, and product/service innovation, but requires safeguards to mitigate risks and avoid unintended outcomes.

ACKNOWLEDGMENT

The authors would like to express their sincere gratitude to Ricardo Marcão (ISLA Santarém, Polytechnic Institute & NECE-UBI, Portugal) and Vasco Ribeiro Santos (Polytechnic University of Tomar (IPT), Portugal) for their valuable editorial guidance, support, and contributions to the development of this chapter and the overall book project.

REFERENCES

Alqahtani, F., Alhassan, A., & Alshammari, M. (2025). The role of artificial intelligence in enhancing ESG outcomes: Insights from Saudi Arabia. *Journal of Risk and Financial Management*, *18*(10), 572.

Amaral, O. (2022). NLP-based automated compliance checking of data processing agreements. *arXiv*. https://arxiv.org/abs/2209.09722

Csaszar, F. A., Ketkar, H., & Kim, H. (2024). Artificial intelligence and strategic decision-making: Evidence from entrepreneurs and investors. *arXiv*. https://arxiv.org/abs/2408.08811

Jorzik, P., Klein, S. P., Kanbach, D. K., & Kraus, S. (2024). AI-driven business model innovation: A systematic review and research agenda. *Journal of Business Research*, *182*, 114764. DOI: 10.1016/j.jbusres.2024.114764

Song, Y., Mi, L., Bian, Z., Tu, W., & He, J. (2025). How does artificial intelligence impact corporate ESG performance? The catching-up effect of digital technological innovation. *Journal of Innovation & Knowledge*, *10*(6), 100843. DOI: 10.1016/j.jik.2025.100843

Wang, Y., Xu, Y., & Zhong, Y. (2025). Does artificial intelligence invariably enhance ESG performance? *Journal for Economic Forecasting*, *2*, 24–40.

Xie, H., & Wu, F. (2025). Artificial intelligence technology and corporate ESG performance: Empirical evidence from Chinese-listed firms. *Sustainability (Basel)*, *17*(2), 420. DOI: 10.3390/su17020420

Yu, X., Fan, L., & Yu, Y. (2025). Artificial intelligence and corporate ESG performance: A mechanism analysis based on corporate efficiency and external environment. *Sustainability (Basel)*, *17*(9), 3819. DOI: 10.3390/su17093819

Zhou, X., Li, G., Wang, Q., Li, Y., & Zhou, D. (2025). Artificial intelligence, corporate information governance and ESG performance: Quasi-experimental evidence from China. *International Review of Financial Analysis*, *102*, 104087. DOI: 10.1016/j.irfa.2025.104087

Chapter 2
Cultural Synergy in Mergers and Acquisitions:
Strategies for Building Unified and Resilient Organizations

Eshkulova Nasiba
Termez University of Economics and Service, Termez, Uzbekistan

Aarthi Selvakumar
http://orcid.org/0009-0006-9064-2091
Marwadi University, Rajkot, India

Ravikumar Natarajan
http://orcid.org/0009-0009-3705-1681
Marwadi University, Rajkot, India

Valisher Sapaeva
http://orcid.org/0000-0002-6751-5864
Mamun University, Khiva, Uzbekistan

Khayrulla Urozboev
Alfraganus University, Tashkent, Uzbekistan

Christo George
Dayananda Sagar College of Engineering, Bengaluru, India

ABSTRACT

Cultural synergy is a key success factor in a merger and acquisition that can affect the involvement of employees, the rate of integration, and the sustainability of the organization. Whereas the conventional M&A initiatives aimed at financial and operational measures, the cultural fit has come out as strategic requirement to create value. The chapter reviews discussion of cultural collisions in terms of trust, motivation, and performance, and identifies assessment tools which can be used to support cultural due diligence. Such strategies as inclusive leadership, focused HR practice, open communication, and participatory structures are discussed as ways to create shared meaning and entire identity. The examples of cross-border and

DOI: 10.4018/979-8-3373-5233-6.ch002

technology mergers demonstrate the importance of planned integration in changing cultural diversity into innovation and long-term development. The chapter concludes that cultural synergy is not by chance and it is the result of intentional planning and flexible management.

1. INTRODUCTION

The contemporary organizational strategy has made Mergers And Acquisitions (M&As) central to expansion of markets, their capacity to attain competitive positioning, and acquisition of capabilities in ever dynamic global business environments. Although they are strategic, the financial power or legal compatibility does not always define the success of M&As, on the contrary, the cultural assimilation has become one of the most important criteria of success in the post-merger performance. When organizations merge dissimilar values, work practice, leadership styles and communication standards, there is a propensity of cultural clashes which determine the level of organizational engagement and unity of workers (Denison & Ko, 2016). This chapter brings out the strategic value of cultural synergy, which is the controlled integration of various cultural aspects to yield stronger and more robust organizational identities. Through the study of the dynamics of cultural collisions, the frameworks of evaluation of cultural compatibility, and suggestions on how synergy could be developed, the chapter shows how a well-inspected cultural integration can turn the possible conflict into innovations and long-term survivability (Rodríguez-Sánchez et al., 2019). The chapter places cultural synergy as a keystone to the achievement of successful outcomes of M&A by using theoretical insights, case studies, and practical recommendations.

1.1 Overview of Mergers and Acquisitions in Contemporary Business Landscapes

Merging and acquisition in the current globalized economy is a necessary process by organizations that want to grow faster, diversify its products, technology development, and expansion into a new market. Firms are increasingly engaging in M&As in order to react to the competition, consumer expectation changes and digital cataclysms that necessitate quick adjustment of the organization. Modern M&A activity cuts across technology, healthcare, manufacturing, and retail sectors, and each industry has never seen the extent of consolidation that is currently being achieved through innovation cycles and globalization (Joseph, 2014). Although financial metrics and strategic fit tend to take the center stage in the decision-making process, the issue of integration of two separate systems in an organization is a critical issue that has always been a challenge. Effective M&As involve the maneuvering of multidimensional integration which involves operational harmonization, leadership redesigning, cultural integration, as well as talent harmonisation (Ravikumar et al., 2025). With organizations going international the cultural diversity becomes further pronounced and creates more considerations of behavior and managerial aspects. The concepts of organizational adaptation and integration in the post-merger settings can present significant information about factors that define the stability of operations and growth in value in the context of the contemporary business world (Frantz & Center, 2014). Figure 1 provides understanding of how cultural, leadership, operational, talent, and system-level integration are all factors that lead to long-term success and stability in mergers and acquisitions.

Figure 1. Multidimensional integration model for successful M&As in the global economy

1.2 The Strategic Importance of Cultural Integration in M&A Success

The issue of cultural integration has become one of the determinants of success or failure in a merger or acquisition. Although the initial process of an M&A is informed by financial forecasts, market positioning and legal due diligence, cultural expectations compatibility is what determines the change acceptance and further adjustment of employees to new structures and their ability to remain productive. The lack of alignment in values, norms of communication, leadership styles, and work practices tend to result in the lack of engagement, opposition, and disagreement negating the anticipated synergies (Miczka & Größler, 2010). On the other hand, companies that actively address cultural integration can open more trust, robust cooperation, and unity among formerly divided organizations. Cultural synergy helps firms to use the advantage of both legacy cultures to create innovation and resilience as they undergo change. Planned cultural incorporation, therefore, turns M&As into transactional integrations of deals to transformational prospects. Culture integration, when given priority, maximises the retention of important talent, provides uninterrupted continuity of operations and gives the psychological contract between leadership and employees, which forms the basis of a sustainable success after the merger.

1.3 Purpose, Scope, and Significance of the Chapter

This chapter aims to look at the aspect of cultural synergy as the key variable that determines the success of mergers and acquisitions, and how the deliberate integration of organizational values, behaviors, and practices results in sustainable integration. The chapter discusses the reasons why the cultural considerations should be entrenched in the early-stage planning, due diligence, and post-merger strategy instead of viewing them as secondary issues. Its area includes such basic premises of cultural synergy, theories of analysing cultural compatibility, as well as practical solutions which organizations can implement to ensure they reduce the levels of cultural conflicts and maximise the levels of collaboration. Through literature analysis, analysis of existing case studies and presentation of integration tools, this chapter offers an overall insight with regard to how organizations can capitalize cultural differences into a strategic resource in M&As. It can be important because it can show that cultural synergy is not only an HR concern, but a strategic necessity that has a direct impact on organizational resilience, innovation, employee loyalty, and value creation over the long term. The insights provided in this chapter enable the leaders, practitioners, and researchers to empower cultural integration practices in the complicated environments of consolidating.

2. BACKGROUND TO THE STUDY

The cultural aspect of mergers and acquisitions has historically affected the results of the merger and acquisition process, but this has been underexplored historically as compared to financial and legal. First M&As considered culture as a secondary concern and emphasized on operations consolidation and cost-efficiencies. Nevertheless, a growing body of evidence on the failed mergers indicated that cultural misfit frequently presents a greater risk than structural or strategic incompatibility (Weber et al., 2012). With the growth of global organizations and their operations being spread across the different cultures, countries, and organizations, the nature of cultural dynamics underpinning the process of successful integration has become critical. This section will discuss the cultural considerations that have developed in the M&A discussion, the reason why cultural clashes often fail when a merger occurs and how cultural synergy has become a competitive technology (Datta, 1991). By adopting the culture as one of the key elements of organizational identity and the experience of employees, companies are able to better structure integration into organizational processes as a driver of engagement, teamwork and purpose. After all, the background gives a background of why cultural synergy is a must in the contemporary M&A settings.

2.1 Evolution of Cultural Considerations in Mergers and Acquisitions

The cultural identification as an essential component of mergers and acquisitions has been developing over the last decades. To start with, the success of M&A was measured largely on financial values, cost savings, and strategic acquisition, and cultural fit was considered an abstract, nonessential part. Nevertheless, the repeats of failure in high profile mergers put emphasis on culture as a latent yet conclusive element that will affect the morale of the employees, speed of integration and stability of the organization. Around the 1990s, research started to focus more on the fact that cultural conflict (rather than the actual deficiencies in operation) was one of the most frequent reasons of post-merger failure (Chatterjee et al., 1992). The result of this was the creation of cultural assessment models, integration frameworks and diagnostic tools which focus on anticipating and controlling cultural fit. With the increased globalization, cross-border mergers increased cultural diversity, further proving the importance of systematic creation of cultural due diligence (Maulana et al., 2024). In the present days, cultural integration is viewed as a disciplined approach that needs planning and the intervention of a leader. The development shows a transformation of seeing culture as peripheral to seeing it as a central determinant of value creation in the process of M&A. Figure 2 shows that cultural integration in the context of M&A has been turning into a more strategic field rather than a financial-based area due to the impact of globalization, payments of failures, diagnostic instrumentation, and research focus.

Figure 2. Evolution of cultural integration in mergers and acquisitions

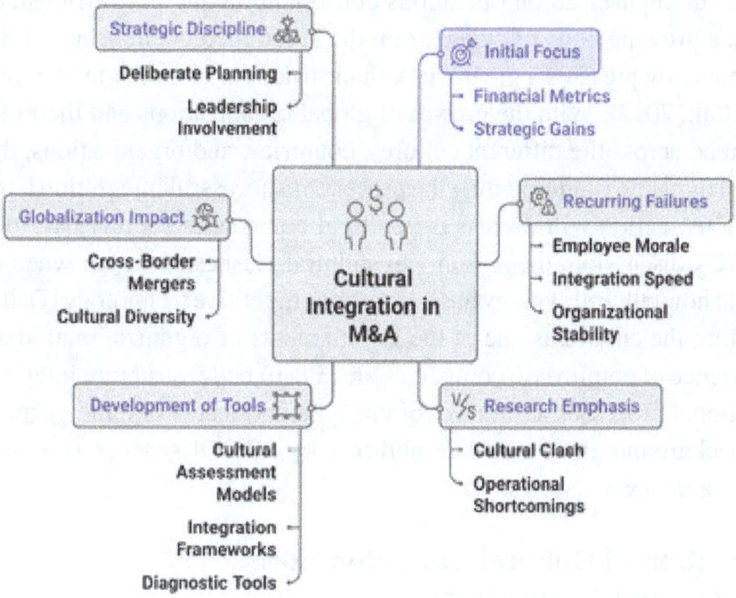

2.2 Common Causes of Post-Merger Failures Linked to Cultural Misalignment

The failures of post-mergers are very common in cases where there are huge differences in the cultures of the merging organizations that are not considered or appropriately considered. Lack of alignment of values of the organization, decision styles, and leadership philosophy may create confusion and conflict, particularly when the employees feel that the changes they are being imposed upon are a threat to their already established identity or autonomy (Department et al., 2023). Breakdown in communication frequently arises when there is a wide difference in norms regarding transparency, hierarchy or collaboration between the entities. These lack of connections build up mistrust, block the flow of knowledge, and undermine unity in the team. Also, work practices that are incompatible (e.g. differing attitudes to innovation, risk-taking, or serving the customer) may interfere with the continuity of operations. The resistance is further enhanced by power relations and the feeling of superiority of one culture over another, which puts psychological barriers to acceptance (Ang et al., 2007). Lack of certainty or disengagement leads to reduced productivity, loss of talent and expected synergies not being realized. These cultural conflicts show that effective integration of mergers and acquisitions is not just a matter of structural orientation, but a matter of sensitive, participative and active cultural coordination to help avoid the possibility of misalignment derailing strategic intentions.

2.3 The Rise of Cultural Synergy as a Competitive and Strategic Imperative

Organizations are finding cultural synergy as a strategic necessity that can change mergers and acquisitions into a structural consolidation into a possibility of innovation and renewal. Instead of coexisting or being forcibly assimilated, cultural synergy combines complementary cultural qualities to form a more powerful integrated self. This strategy helps companies to access different viewpoints, better problem-solving abilities, and gain resilience in the face of change. With the rising competition and the fast transformation of the industries, organizations are looking to integration models that are conducive to agility, teamwork, and employee empowerment which attributes are directly linked to the culturally synergistic environment (Weber & Yedidia Tarba, 2012). The sustainability focus, digitalization of work, and hybrid working have also increased the significance of the development of cultures in accordance with the current values and demands. Cultural synergy is now being considered as a source of long-term competitive advantage by boards and executives, and shapes the leadership development, communication strategies, and human resource practices. Cultural synergy emergence is an indication of paradigm shift: cultural integration is no longer an option but a necessity in achieving a successful M&A in an unstable global environment.

3. RESEARCH OBJECTIVES

The impact of culture in mergers and acquisitions demands an orderly study of the role played by organizational values, behaviors, and integration practices in determining the post-merger performance. This chapter seeks to explore the cultural synergy as a key factor that facilitates collaborations, positive organizational identity, and sustainability in the long term in M&A situations. The goals are to determine the role of cultural synergy, assessing cultural compatibility assessment models, and strategizing the way forward to support high-performing cohesive and solid post-merger organisations.

- To analyse the role of cultural synergy in improving trust, collaboration, and overall M&A performance outcomes.

- To evaluate existing frameworks and tools used during due diligence for assessing cultural compatibility between merging organizations.
- To identify the key dimensions of cultural integration that influence employee engagement and organizational resilience post-merger.
- To explore practical strategies leadership actions, HR interventions, and communication mechanisms that foster unified post-merger organizational cultures.
- To develop an integrative perspective on how cultural synergy can transform potential cultural conflicts into drivers of innovation, sustainability, and long-term value creation in M&As.

4. CONCEPTUAL MODEL

The theoretical framework used in this chapter shows how cultural synergy influences the success of mergers and acquisitions. It is based on the fact that the organizational cultures do not just amalgamate but meet, clash and stabilize, in the end, through the conscious integration that is gradually taking place. The model focuses on cultural synergy as the optimal result of the properly managed cultural integration, where the capabilities of each of the legacy organizations are used to create an integrated and strong post-merger culture (Stahl & Voigt, 2008). The drivers are important dimensions such as leadership behaviors, shared values, communication norms, and work processes that determine the integration trajectory. In plotting the process of cultural collision to alignment and eventually innovation, the model points out cultural synergy does not happen but needs to be nurtured strategically. The conceptual framework will provide a systematic perspective through which the role of organizations negotiating cultural complexity can be viewed and practitioners can predict the challenges to face, points of intervention, and integration strategies that can maximize cohesion, engagement, and organizational performance during the M&A process.

4.1 Conceptual Foundation of Cultural Synergy in M&A Contexts

The theory behind the cultural synergy is based on the idea that cultural diversity when properly utilized can contribute to the organizational capacity, as opposed to dragging it down. Cultural synergy is a phenomenon observed in mergers and acquisitions as the involved parties aim to deliberately integrate their values, behaviors, and practices in order to create a more powerful identity (Rottig et al., 2017). This premise is based on the organizational culture theory, cross-cultural management, and the theory of the psychology of integration all of which indicate that shared meaning-making is the key to effective post-merger adjustment. Cultural synergy is more than mere coexistence of culture it focuses on collaboration, mutual respect and shared problem solving (Ravikumar & Aarthi, 2025d). It also acknowledges that cultural compatibility is not a predetermined phenomenon; however, it is developed in a form of structured interactions, leadership, and unambiguity in communication (Tripathi, 2018). The framework places synergy as an evolutional process that is attained through conscious alignment processes by accepting cultural collisions as a normal occurrence that is manageable. In such a way, the conceptual background offers a theoretical framework of how the organizations can use cultural differences as sources of innovation, resilience, and long-term success of M & A. As Figure 3. demonstrates, the integration, common meaning, and cooperation are the three interconnected elements that facilitate the use of cultural diversity to create synergy and transform it into innovation when applied to M&A.

Figure 3. Cultural synergy pyramid in mergers and acquisitions

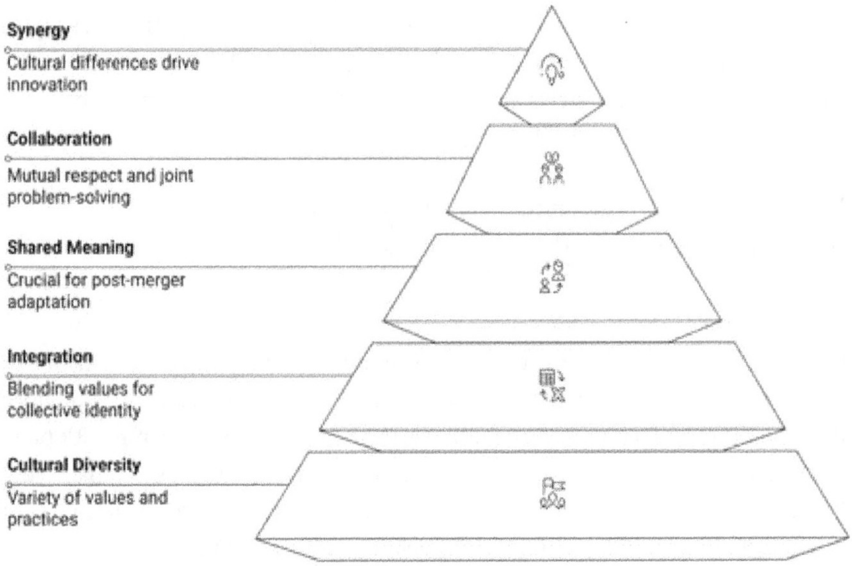

4.2 Dimensions of the Cultural Integration Model (Leadership, Values, Communication, Processes)

There are four basic dimensions that constitute the cultural integration model, which include leadership, values, communication, and processes that completely predetermine the effectiveness of the cultural synergy in mergers and acquisitions. The process of leadership influences integration through its modeling of inclusive behavior, development of expectations, and chaperoning of employees through uncertainty. Shared values, in their turn, offer moral and philosophical foundation to the new organization formed as the result of the merger, assisting the personnel to ground themselves on the same purpose (Napier, 1989). Communication is the glue of the integration effort, as it allows transparency, less ambiguity, and trust to be built between legacy teams. Processes are the working routines and processes in which the cultural expectations are applied on day-to-day basis. Any lack of alignment in these dimensions may result in friction and resistance whereas alignment results in less resistance and better engagement(Stahl et al., 2011). The model demonstrates the interaction between the dimensions, which affects the perceptions, motivation and commitment of employees (Ravikumar & Aarthi, 2025b). By working jointly on these aspects, the organizations will be able to better address cultural complexity and create an integrated environment that will facilitate performance right after merger and sustainability in the long run.

4.3 The Cultural Synergy Pathway: From Collision to Alignment and Innovation

The cultural synergy pathway is a sequence of events through which organizations can go through cultural collision to subsequent alignment and innovation in the merger process. During the initial phases, the disparity in values, norms of communication and work styles tends to generate tension and misunderstanding (Ravikumar & Aarthi, 2025c). These collisions are not in themselves bad, but these collisions would indicate the places that need to be attended to during integration. Organizations start making a transition towards cultural alignment through strategic interventions, including, but not limited to, leadership involvement, facilitated communication, and setting expectations in harmony (Bristol-Alagbariya et al., 2022). During this stage, common norms, common purposes, and common practices start to emerge and curb resistance, and create and strengthen collective identity. After achieving the alignment, the organization will be able to move to an innovation level where the unified forces of strength and different worlds of view of the legacy cultures will give rise to new ideas, better performance and better adaptability. The journey proves that cultural synergy is an active, dynamic process that needs to be carefully undertaken through deliberate effort and active observation. When well handled, it may turn sources of conflict into the drivers of creativity and sustained competitive edge.

5. RESEARCH METHODOLOGY

The research methodology used in this chapter is made in such a manner to offer a wholesome insight into the concept of cultural synergy in mergers and acquisitions it combines the qualitative insights, descriptive analysis as well as the use of cases. Since cultural integration is context-specific and multi-dimensional as a complex issue, a qualitative method allows further investigation of behavioural, psychological, and organizational issues of synergy (Čirjevskis, 2020). The descriptive elements serve to express the patterns, issues and practices that are witnessed in various M&A environments and case studies provide practical examples that illustrate how cultural integration process can be realized in the real-life scenarios. The methodology is organized into three main elements namely, research design, data sources, and analytical frameworks. These elements have combined to make the chapter an embodiment of both theoretical and practical approach to cultural synergy (Wengel, 2023). The hybrid qualitative design provides the opportunity of triangulation, which will increase the credibility and depth of insights. The systematic investigation of cultural variables and approaches to integration enables the methodology to generate evidence-based suggestions, which are likely to influence practitioners and other researchers in balancing cultural complexity in mergers and acquisitions.

5.1 Research Design and Approach (Qualitative, Descriptive, Case-Based)

This chapter has a research design that is qualitative, descriptive and case based to reflect the complex and multilayered nature of cultural integration in mergers and acquisitions. The qualitative approach is most appropriate since the cultural processes are deeply entrenched in the behavior of people, their perception, mode of communication, and organizational dynamics all of which cannot be perfectly comprehended by applying quantitative measures. The descriptive part allows to determine common themes, integration issues, and success factors that emerge in different M&A situation ("Leadership Era," 2023)s. Making use of case studies also makes the findings deeper and more applicable to practice by basing theoretical ideas with concrete organizational experiences. This triangulated design will help me belief in a bigger and more comprehensive picture of cultural synergy and enable this chapter to demonstrate not only what happens as a part of cultural integration but also why and how these processes affect results. This would make the insights more credible and would give practical relevance to leaders and practitioners engaged in M&A activities.

5.2 Data Sources, Selection Criteria, and Case Identification

The information utilized in this chapter is informed by variety of sources of secondary information such as peer-reviewed scholarly articles and reports, organizational case study, and documented assessment of mergers performed post-merger period. The variety and credibility of sources used also increases the strength of the analysis and guarantees that the results are based on academic and practical views as well as the facts in the industry. The selection strategy used in identifying cases is purposive and involves mergers and acquisitions in which cultural integration was important in shaping organizational outcomes (Hutasoit et al., 2023). The selection criteria are recency, relevancy, documentation of the practices of the cultures, and clarity in reporting the results of integration. This will make sure that the selected cases make valuable contributions to the workings of cultural synergy. Sectors like technology, health care, finance, and manufacturing are of primary concern to capture cross sector variation. Combining various data points and using demanding selection criteria, the chapter creates a well-founded perception of the way cultural synergy occurs in various organizational settings and what can be learnt to implement further M&A programs.

5.3 Analytical Framework for Interpreting Cultural Integration Practices

The analytical model as presented in this chapter offers a systematic strategy of making sense of the cultural integration practices within the chosen M&A cases. It centers on the identification of significant areas of cultural variation, mapping the areas of agreement and disagreement, and the study of leadership interventions that promoted or inhibited the synergy. The framework uses thematic analysis to classify patterns that keep on reoccurring as far as communication, trust-building, decision-making and employee engagement are concerned (Thelisson, 2023). It also studies the relationship that exists between the operations of structural integration and cultural responses, and it is known that cultural perceptions are influenced by operational decisions. Particular emphasis is laid on defining turning points upon which conflicts have either been solved or escalated, providing the indication of successful and unsuccessful practices. The framework is based on case evidence and the combination of theoretical perspectives that allow examining the processes of cultural integration holistically. This enables coming up with recommendations that can be implemented on practitioners and helps build a more insightful body of scholarly knowledge on how cultural synergy can be attained in an intricate post-merger setting.

6. LITERATURE REVIEW

The cultural dynamics of mergers and acquisitions is the most fundamental requirement in the process of analysing the merger and acquisition process in terms of how organizations change, adapt and eventually reach a stable performance after the merger. The literature proves that cultural differences can be either obstacles to integration, or the strategic resources in the case of their proper management (Rosendale et al., 2024). There are three main themes examined in this section, namely cultural collisions and the impact on trust, motivation, and engagement; the instruments utilized to evaluate cultural compatibility during due diligence; and the means through which organizations can develop cultural synergy in terms of leadership, HR practices, and communication.

6.1 Cultural Collisions: Trust, Motivation, and Organizational Engagement

Cultural collisions happen due to the fact that two merging organizations have vastly different values, beliefs, and work norms and thus they do not align their expectations and behaviors. The cultural collision is always mentioned in the literature as one of the most common factors of post-merger underperformance. The lack of trust and any resistance is evident when employees feel that the new environment threatens their well-known practices or professional identity (Ashiedu et al., 2024). Such mistrust has a negative effect on motivation because the workers find it hard to comprehend new requirements or doubt the justice of enforced modifications. The motivation is further undermined when there is lack of clear communication, the leadership is not quite on track or when the work process changes abruptly without a proper explanation.

Cultural tensions are very sensitive to organizational engagement. When workers do not feel included in the integration process or one of the legacy cultures leads in an overwhelming manner, they tend to tune out, which eventually impacts productivity and innovation. On the contrary, mergers that consider and seek a way out of cultural issues at the beginning by creating open communication, respecting and preserving past traditions, and providing collaborative opportunities were more prone to promote engagement (Sun, 2024). Cultural collisions are not to be taken merely as barriers according to the literature but as the signs of fields where a deliberate effort with regard to alignment should take place. Managing them constructively would create a chance of further organizational learning and synergy-building. Table 1 Overviews several important aspects of culture such as leadership, values, communication, HR practices, which determine the success of post-mergers.

Table 1. Cultural drivers influencing post-merger success

Cultural Driver	Simple Description	Influence on Outcomes
Leadership Alignment	Leaders share the same vision and approach.	Builds trust and helps employees accept changes faster.
Shared Values	Common beliefs that guide how people work.	Brings unity, reduces conflict, and improves teamwork.
Communication Quality	Clear, frequent, and transparent communication.	Reduces confusion, keeps employees engaged, and builds safety.
HR Integration Practices	Training, talent retention, and clear roles.	Keeps employees stable and committed during transition.
Employee Engagement Mechanisms	Ways for employees to share ideas and concerns.	Increases involvement, lowers resistance, and boosts morale.
Cultural Due Diligence	Studying cultural differences before merging.	Helps predict problems early and plan better integration.

6.2 Cultural Compatibility Assessment Tools and Due Diligence Approaches

The cultural compatibility tests have increased in value as firms understand that effective mergers should not only be driven by operational or financial harmony. Historically, due diligence activities were based on financial and legal due diligence due and strategic fit. Nonetheless, studies indicate that incorporation of cultural evaluation in the due diligence significantly increases the effectiveness of predicting the difficulties that follow the merger. Differences in communication norms, leadership style, level of risk-taking, and decision-making structures are mainly identified with the use of cultural mapping tools, value-alignment surveys, interviews, behavioral tests, and observational diagnostics (Avrillia et al., 2025). Such tools enable organizations to have a sense of the distance that is used in cultural integration, i.e. the degree of discrepancy between the merging cultures, and as a result, the organizations are able to anticipate where the friction can arise. The study of similarities and differences between cultures at the blueprint stage will allow leaders to develop informed integration strategies that consider realities of culture and not assumed principles.

The literature stresses that cultural due diligence should be systematic and objective as it provides information that would inform integration schedules, leadership placement, and transition strategy of employees (Wu et al., 2025). When done correctly, compatibility analysis will minimize ambiguity, enhance effective communication, and enhance employee acceptance. All in all, due diligence turns out to be a proactive instrument not only in the kind of risk detection, but also in the exploiting of the cultural advantages as grounds of synergy. Table 2 Compares key cultural assessment models, measurements and relevance in the M&A planning.

Table 2. Cultural compatibility assessment tools used during due diligence

Tool / Model	Simple Description	What It Measures	Why It Helps in M&A
Cultural Mapping	Shows where two cultures are similar or different.	Values, communication, decision-making, leadership style.	Helps spot potential cultural conflicts early.
OCAI (Culture Assessment Tool)	Categorizes each company's culture type.	Clan, Adhocracy, Market, Hierarchy scores.	Helps understand culture fit and plan integration.
Employee Surveys	Gathers employee opinions on culture and work environment.	Trust, engagement, satisfaction, readiness for change.	Gives real employee feedback for better cultural planning.
Leadership Style Assessments	Checks if leaders from both companies have compatible styles.	Control, autonomy, collaboration, risk tolerance.	Reduces leadership conflict and helps assign roles wisely.
Interviews & Focus Groups	Uses conversations to explore expectations and cultural norms.	Motivators, conflict points, communication habits.	Provides deeper insights for designing communication and onboarding.
Document Review	Looks at policies and processes to understand how each company works.	Governance, HR rules, ethics, communication procedures.	Identifies structural differences that may affect integration.

6.3 Strategies for Building Cultural Synergy: Leadership, HR Practices, and Communication

Cultural synergy is built by ensuring that different cultural aspects are deliberately merged into one unit of an organization that performs well. The key factor in this process is leadership since leaders influence the way employees perceive things, establish priorities of integration, as well as modeling anticipated behaviors (Ranajee et al., 2025). It has been shown in literature that empathetic leaders, those who are inclusive and communicative, will opt to provide an environment in which trust and cooperation develop. Their contribution towards the expression of common vision is paramount, and they encourage the employees to know the reason why the merger is taking place and how they fit in it.

The human resource practices also assist in building the synergy by stabilizing the workforce and learning the culture. Some of the HR strategies that are effective involve talent retention initiatives, cross-cultural trainings, team building, and participative design in which employees have a say in the culture change. Such practices lower anxiety levels, facilitate interaction among legacy groups and foster the sense of ownership of the process of integration. Communication is over and over again known to be one of the most potent tools towards bringing cultural synergy (Sales et al., 2022). Two-way communication, timely and transparent communication reduce ambiguity, strengthen the alignment, and foster the development of psychological safety in a period of transition. Companies that invest into communication systems, integration retreats, and team projects establish shared meaning-making and understanding (Liang et al., 2021). Table 3 Lists the leadership behaviors, HR intervention and communication models that enhance cultural integration.

Table 3. Strategies for building cultural synergy in M&As

Category	Simple Strategy	What It Means	Outcome
Leadership Actions	Inclusive Leadership	Leaders treat both company cultures with fairness and respect.	Builds trust and reduces resistance.
	Shared Vision	Leaders clearly explain the goals and direction of the new organization.	Helps employees stay aligned and focused.
	Role Modeling	Leaders practice the behaviors expected in the new culture.	Encourages employees to follow the same values.
HR Interventions	Talent Retention	Keeping key employees and giving clear roles during the transition.	Reduces turnover and keeps important skills.
	Cross-Cultural Training	Training to understand each other's cultural differences.	Improves teamwork and reduces misunderstandings.
	Participatory Teams	Employees join mixed teams to help make decisions.	Increases involvement and ownership of the new culture.
Communication Frameworks	Transparent Communication	Regular, clear updates about the merger and expectations.	Reduces confusion and builds psychological safety.
	Two-Way Feedback	Employees can share concerns and ideas openly.	Encourages dialogue and early problem-solving.
	Collaboration Tools	Digital platforms for teams to work together easily.	Supports strong connections, even across borders.

7. CASE STUDY

Case studies provide tangible information on the nature of how cultural integration works in a real organization environment as they offer evidence of effective practices as well as the challenges that are usually faced during the process of merging and acquiring. By analyzing the recent M&A ventures in the industry, one will be able to understand further how cultural synergy can be attained and the impact of integration strategies on long-term results. The case studies chosen show two different but complementary environments: a cross-border merger where culture diversity was naturally acute, and a merger in the technology sector where innovation and agility became the key characteristics of synergy-making. (Drori et al., 2011) These instances point to the role played by leadership, communication, talent management and well-organized integration planning in enabling the process of cultural alignment. Through the analysis of these real-life situations, this section illustrates how organisations can use cultural differences as a common source of strength that improves performance, innovation and organizational resiliency. The lessons gained in the cases can also be used in future M&A strategies, as the cultural synergy can be attained when handled in a coherent and planned way.

7.1 Case Study 1: Successful Cultural Integration in a Cross-Border M&A

In 2022, one of the major European pharmaceutical companies bought an Asian biotechnology firm to further the research and achieve faster entry into the emerging economies. The merger posed a major integration risk considering the fact that the European and Asian organizational structure has a significant difference in terms of culture. The preliminary evaluation showed differences in the hierarchy in leadership, norms of communication, and decision-making processes. Due diligence resulted in a specific cultural integration task force to review these differences and describe specific interventions (Ahammad et al., 2016). There were cross-cultural workshops, which were facilitated by leadership of both organizations on shared goals, ethical standards, and scientific collaboration. Open communication lines were also established to ensure that there was less ambiguity and mentorship programs were established between employees of both the legacy organizations to create trust and understanding. The combined company assumed hybrid cultural framework which maintained the culture of agility and innovation in the Asian firm and merged the European company with its structured research-based culture and regulatory knowledge. After a year, the unified organization said it saw greater cross-team cooperation, increased research speed, and increased employee contentment, indicating that by taking the initiative to change the culture, diversity can become strategic benefit.

Figure 4 presents the process of business integration into a cross-border M&A in the cultural dimension, demonstrating that orderly interventions can result in enhanced cooperation, faster research, and an increase in the level of employee satisfaction.

Figure 4. Cultural integration process in a cross-border merger and acquisition

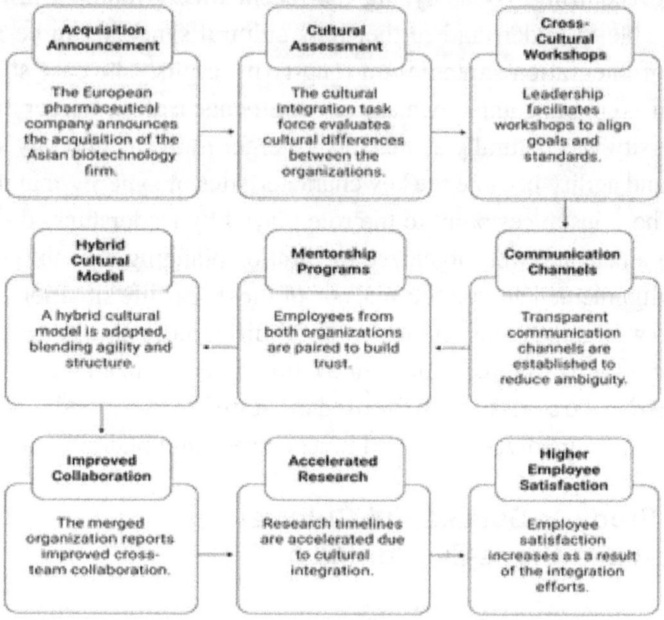

7.2 Case Study 2: Leveraging Cultural Synergy for Innovation in a Technology-Sector Merger

In 2023, one of the largest cloud computing companies acquired one of the rapidly growing artificial intelligence startups to boost its product innovation process and competitiveness. The technology-oriented nature of both companies, however, did not make much difference in their internal cultures. The bigger company used standardization and formalism in its working processes and workflows whereas the startup adopted the principle of rapid experimentation, flexibility, and high level of autonomy (Sarala & Vaara, 2010). As opposed to enforcing assimilation, leadership aimed at creating cultural synergy through integrating matching strong points in the two entities. Labs of innovation were established to facilitate cross-functional cooperation, having a creative spirit of a startup, and the technical base and global presence of the parent company. HR established agile integration principles, reformulated performance measures, and spent large sums on cultural on-loading to reduce friction. Leaders were the proponents of open communication, the focus on psychological safety, and collective ownership of innovation objectives. Consequently, the combined company created new AI-based cloud solutions within months, a feat previously unheard of by either of the companies also. This case is an indication that cultural synergy in a carefully cultivated manner can hasten the innovation process and increase flexibility in rapidly changing technology markets. Figure 5 shows the development process of a technology merger in relation to the recognition of cultural differences to the creation of synergy leading to a faster innovation process and creation of new AI solutions.

Figure 5. Cultural synergy process in a technology-sector merger

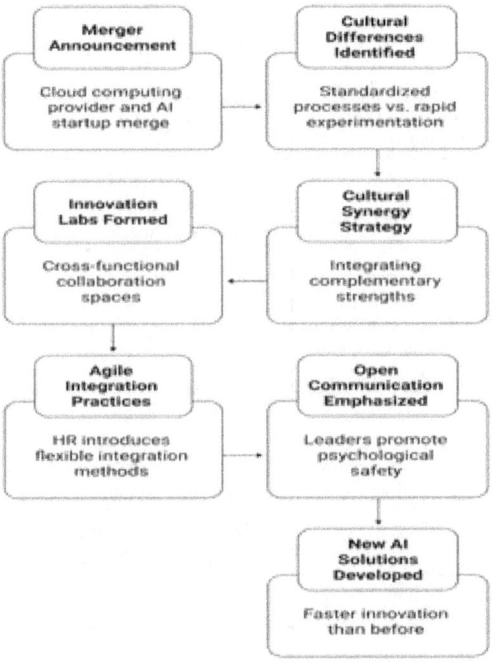

7.3 Cross-Case Comparative Insights and Lessons Learned

In both case studies, cultural synergy turned out to be a determining factor of post-mergers success though not realized in the same ways. The cross-border merger entailed more intensive intercultural comprehension and systematic alignment undertakings whereas the merger in the technology sector entailed equilibrium between resourcefulness and functional discipline. In both examples, leadership dedication, open communication, and synergistic arrangements were the focus of minimization of cultural friction. The cases demonstrate that synergy is not realized by means of imposing one predominant culture but by purposeful combination of the strengths of each organization (Jarvenpaa & Leidner, 2006). Timely cultural evaluation, specifically designed HR initiatives, and trust building exercises were very helpful sources of positive results. One of the lessons learned is that cultural integration should commence at a due diligence stage and be maintained during post-merger stages. Cultural diversity can be a resource which contributes to innovativeness, fast integration and long-term resilience of the organization when managed effectively. Table 4 Compares the two case studies according to the integration actions, challenges, results and lessons learned.

Table 4. Case study comparison: Cultural integration across two recent M&As

Comparison Dimension	Case Study 1: Cross-Border Pharma–Biotech Merger	Case Study 2: Technology-Sector Cloud–AI Merger	Key Lessons Learned
Primary Integration Focus	Harmonizing hierarchical and collaborative cultural norms across geographies.	Balancing structured processes with agile, innovation-driven work styles.	Integration must reflect contextual cultural realities of each industry.
Major Cultural Challenges	Differences in communication norms, leadership hierarchy, and work expectations.	Conflicting levels of autonomy, experimentation, and workflow formality.	Cultural friction is natural but manageable through targeted interventions.
Leadership Actions	Joint leadership workshops and paired mentoring across legacy organizations.	Leaders promoted psychological safety, experimentation, and transparent communication.	Leadership alignment significantly accelerates cultural acceptance.
HR Integration Practices	Cross-cultural training, talent retention programs, and structured onboarding.	Redefined performance metrics, agile onboarding, and integrated innovation teams.	HR plays a central role in shaping employee experience during transition.
Communication Approach	Frequent town halls, cross-regional coordination, and multilingual messaging.	Digital platforms, collaborative tools, and open innovation forums.	Transparent, two-way communication reduces ambiguity and builds trust.
Integration Outcome	Increased collaboration, improved research timelines, and high employee satisfaction.	Faster innovation cycles, quicker product development, and enhanced team agility.	Cultural synergy enhances operational efficiency and innovation capability.
Overall Impact	Strengthened global research capacity and unified identity.	Creation of a dynamic, future-oriented tech ecosystem.	Synergy transforms cultural diversity into strategic advantage.

8. RESULTS / DISCUSSION

The results of the case study and literature review indicate that the level of cultural integration is one of the core factors defining the success of the post-merger periods, as it determines the success of operations and the organizational viability. Cultural motivators like leadership compatibility, shared responsibility, open communications and inclusive human resource management processes proved to be vital issues that made transitions and working synergy smoother. Meanwhile, there remain serious problems in the context of M&A, especially the asymmetry of power, unconscious biases, and different governance systems. Such problems may hinder trust, derail engagement, as well as integration unless addressed in advance. New trends, such as the increased power of digital collaboration tools, remote work systems, and sustainability-oriented values, only serve to transform cultural expectations in terms of mergers. Organizations that can change integration strategies in response to these new dynamics will be in a better position to create cultural synergy and attain innovation-based results. In general, the discussion highlights that cultural synergy is not random but rather a part of deliberate, systematic, and adaptive integration processes that appreciates the dynamics of relating the identities of individuals with different identities.

8.1 Key Findings on Cultural Drivers of Post-Merger Success

The most valuable results are that the cultural drivers have a major role in the way employees view, respond, and contribute to the integration effort after mergers. The strongest determinant was leadership, as the leadership styles that encouraged trust and stability at transitional stages were inclusive, empathetic, and collaborative. By communicating and co-creating the organization values, it saw the establishment of a unifying identity that would make employees in the two background organizations to identify with the purpose of the new entity. Another factor that played a critical role was open communication because the flow of information constantly minimized uncertainty and led to the shared comprehension (Oh & Johnston, 2021). HR practices such as cross-cultural training, talent retention programmes and participatory decision-making processes also enhanced cohesiveness in the organization. These drivers collaborated effectively to convert the original cultural differences into learning and innovating opportunities. The mergers that took the initiative to assess cultural, engage early and have well-organized processes of integration, were found to report higher degrees of collaboration, lesser levels of resistance and better operational performance. The results support the thesis that cultural drivers need to be well-planned in order to make M&As successful in the long-term perspective.

8.2 Challenges: Power Asymmetry, Bias, Governance Differences

Although the advantages of cultural synergy are evident, the results indicate that some of the challenges that persist in undermining post-merger integration include the following. A power disparity tends to occur when a single organization takes cultural entitlements with the employees of the acquired organization believing that they are under-appreciated or sidelined. This disparity destroys the confidence and strengthens opposition, complicating the cooperation. Assumptions related to competence, disciplined work, or norms of communication are also examples of unconscious biases that make integration even more complicated, making an implicit impact on making decisions and human relations (Steigenberger, 2017). The structural barriers are also caused by the differences in governance especially with the merging entities whose approach to authority, accountability, and risk management being opposite. Such differences may drag operational alignment process and create confusion regarding functions and duties, and performance expectations. Unless these challenges are uncovered early and overcome with open practices, they may grow to greater levels along the cultural lines (Richter et al., 2021). Effective mergers hence need a conscious effort of balancing power, minimizing bias and harmonizing models of governance to facilitate equal participation and easy cultural assimilation. Table 5 Highlights such issues as power asymmetry, bias, and governance differences and the mitigation strategies.

Table 5. Challenges in cultural integration and recommended managerial responses

Challenge	Description	Impact on Integration	Recommended Managerial Response
Power Asymmetry	One legacy organization dominates decision-making, culture, and role allocation.	Creates resentment, reduces trust, and increases resistance to change.	Establish balanced leadership teams, ensure equal representation, and promote shared decision-making structures.
Unconscious Bias	Preconceived assumptions about competence, work style, or cultural superiority.	Leads to mistrust, stereotyping, and employee disengagement.	Implement bias-awareness training, promote inclusive behaviors, and encourage cross-cultural interactions.
Governance Differences	Conflicting structures regarding authority, accountability, and risk-taking.	Slows operational alignment and creates confusion about roles and priorities.	Harmonize governance systems through clear guidelines, integration workshops, and unified performance frameworks.

continued on following page

Table 5. Continued

Challenge	Description	Impact on Integration	Recommended Managerial Response
Communication Barriers	Differences in communication norms, languages, and transparency expectations.	Causes misunderstandings, ambiguity, and misalignment.	Use multilingual communication, standardize messaging, and establish two-way feedback channels.
Loss of Identity	Employees feel their legacy culture is being absorbed or undervalued.	Reduces morale and psychological commitment to the new organization.	Co-create new cultural values, celebrate legacy strengths, and involve employees in culture-building initiatives.
Talent Attrition	High-performing employees leave due to uncertainty or cultural discomfort.	Weakens organizational capability and slows integration progress.	Offer retention incentives, clarify career paths, and strengthen onboarding programs focused on cultural adaptation.

8.3 Emerging Themes: Digital Collaboration, Remote Work, and Sustainability-Oriented Values

Recent trends in modern M&As show that the process of cultural integration is being influenced more by digital transformation, models of changing work, and values of sustainability. Digital collaboration platforms, including virtual communication platforms, shared workspaces, and AI-enhanced coordination systems, are the key tools in enabling distributed teams to collaborate with each other and exchange knowledge within the context of legacy organizations. The remote and hybrid work policies present new demands in the areas of flexibility, autonomy, and work-life balance, so the integration strategies should be built on the principles of trust, empowerment, and digital readiness (Graebner et al., 2017). The cultural expectations during mergers, as well as among younger and purpose-driven workforces, are also impacted by sustainability-oriented values, such as ethical responsibility, environmental consciousness, and social impact. These themes show that cultural integration should not only be practiced in the traditional ways but also should be able to encompass the modern work values and technological strengths. Companies that align the cultural strategies with these new factors can engage better, attract new talents and develop a progressive culture that would be relevant to the evolving business worlds.

9. FUTURE RESEARCH

The future study of cultural synergy in mergers and acquisitions should go beyond conceptual debates and have empirical/data-driven models that reflect the dynamic and complex issues involving cultural integration. Although available literature points at the significance of leadership, communication, and shared values, there is still scanty quantifiable research on the impact of these cultural variables on various measurable organizational outcomes in the long run. The development of digital technologies, artificial intelligence-based analytics, tools to track cultural alignment, and sentiment-mapping can be seen as an opportunity to work out more accurate approaches to track cultural alignment during the integration process. Also, the emergence of global virtual teams and the transnational governance forms present new culture aspects yet to be exhaustively studied in M&A literature (Oberoi, 2025). These new contexts demand new theoretical perspectives and longitudinal research studies to comprehend how distributed workforces create coherent identities along geographical and cultural borders. Future studies must then concentrate on the creation of sound models, the utilization of digital means and a study of new organizational types in the effort to develop a better understanding of how cultural synergy may be achieved and maintained at a systematic level.

9.1 Need for Empirical Models for Measuring Cultural Synergy Impact

Cultural synergy has been accepted as a factor that determines success in post-merger but its effects have not been explained scientifically but rather qualitatively. The empirical models are required that would determine the cultural alignment, monitor the process of integration, and establish a correlation between cultural variables and operational performance outcomes. The existing evaluation methods are based on either perception assessment models or anecdotal data analysis and thus are constrained in their predictability (Cartwright & Schoenberg, 2006). Future studies are required to devise measures to reflect both behavioral and structural measures of cultural synergy including the levels of trust, the effectiveness of collaboration, the frequency of communication and the output of innovations. Longitudinal studies would enable the researchers to study the way cultural processes change with time and how early integration choices impact on the long-term outcomes. Data-driven empirical models might also be used in assisting organizations to carry out cultural due diligence, with more accuracy, which would facilitate risk assessment and integration planning. This kind of research would improve the strategic decision-making process and add to a more scientific perspective of cultural synergy in the context of M&A.

9.2 Role of AI, Digital Tools, and Analytics in Cultural Integration Mapping

Digital analytics and AI promise to provide an excellent mapping of the cultural integration with more accuracy and transparency. This is because machine learning tools can be used to examine patterns of communication, employee feelings, collaboration patterns, and behavioural patterns in order to determine areas of fit or strain in the process of merging. Real-time visualizations of the integration progress can be given through digital dashboards and culture-mapping software, which will allow the leaders to intervene at the earliest stages of the cultural conflict. Sentiment analysis, powered by AI can determine how much employees are morally motivated to stay in the company and mentally prepared to make the change, whereas natural language processing tools can reveal latent biases or barriers to communication within teams that existed in the past (Stahl et al., 2013). Predictive analytics further enable the organizations to test the integration scenarios and which cultural variables have the greatest impact of synergy. Remote work, as well as hybrid work settings, is more widespread, whereas digital tools allow gathering essential information on the interaction within a distributed team (Ravikumar & Aarthi, 2025a). Further studies in the future ought to investigate how AI can be used to promote evidence-based cultural integration, minimise uncertainty, and instruct leaders on making data-informed choices that would promote cultural synergy during mergers and acquisitions.

9.3 Unexplored Areas: Global Virtual Teams and Transnational Governance

The new cultural complexities brought about by the global virtual teams and transnational structures of governance have not been appropriately analyzed in current research done on M&A. With organizations becoming more Multi geographical in their operating locations, the workers communicate via digital networks and not the physical workplaces, which poses special issues with forming a common identity, trust and communication norms. The next task of the research should be to find out how the cultural synergy can be attained when the team members hardly see each other in real life and may represent different languages, nations, and companies. Transnational models of governance that decentralize power to different regions also complicate integration as it brings different regulatory expectations and leadership approaches (Presbitero, 2020). These distributed systems affect the cultural alignment, decision making and accountability during mergers and it is important to understand their effect on these practices. The discussion of these areas will offer an important insight to organizations that are going through cross-border consolidations in a globalized and digital business environment. These studies can be used to make integration efforts more accommodating, flexible, and culturally resilient.

10. MANAGERIAL IMPLICATIONS

The results of this chapter point out the importance of managers taking mergers and acquisitions as a strategic priority with a particular focus on cultural integration. Leaders should realize that cultural synergy does not come as a natural event and that one has to plan it, work on it, and be adaptive. Establishing culture-oriented playbooks might assist the organizations in predicting the issues of integration and establishing explicit rules of communication, alignment, and engagement of employees. The HR practitioners are key agents in promoting cultural synergy by practicing specific cultural oriented issues like talent retention, cross cultural training and participatory structures that enable employees of both parent organizations (Killingsworth et al., 2016). The behavior of leaders has a specific impact, as employees seek leadership guidance on how to deal with uncertainty, adapt new cultural norms, and accept the collective identity. Managers also need to acknowledge the new trends, including the value of digital collaboration and sustainability and consider them as a part of the culture. Organizations can build cohesion, mitigate resistance, and speed up post-merger success by embracing proactive and inclusive and data-driven practices.

10.1 Strategic Guidelines for Designing Culture-Focused M&A Playbooks

This can be achieved by developing M&A playbooks that are culture-oriented, and therefore, organizations can enter into integration with more clarity, predictability, and alignment with the strategy. Good playbooks provide a cultural vision, integration principles, communication protocols and expected behaviors that inform employees during the process of the merger. They also give systematic principles of how to conduct cultural assessment during due diligence, finding possible source of friction, and prioritization of integration activity according to cultural risks (Mockaitis et al., 2012). These playbooks can help managers to set cultural milestones, track progress, and change strategies (where needed). Playbooks make cultural considerations central, as opposed to peripheral because they contain mechanisms of stakeholder engagement, employee feedback, and cross-functional interaction. Also, they assist in sustaining uniformity among regions and departments especially in cross-border or large mergers. Finally, culture-centered playbooks are useful aids that help leaders to transform strategic intents to coherent and actionable integration practices that can create synergy between cultures.

10.2 HR-Driven Practices: Talent Retention, Cross-Cultural Training, Participatory Structures

The HR functions have a vital role in context of influencing cultural outcomes in case of mergers and acquisitions where they control most of the processes that determine employee experience and organizational identity. Talent retention programs help in maintaining the core competencies and institutional learning, and cross-cultural training teaches employees the competency and consciousness to work with other groups that are viewed as legacy. This kind of training contributes to the minimization of misunderstanding, the destruction of prejudices, and encouragement of mutual respect (Zakaria & Ab Rahman Muton, 2022). Engagement is further enhanced through participatory structures that include joint task forces, worker committees, and co-creation workshops since they provide the employees with a voice when it comes to defining the new organizational culture. These mechanisms to promote psychological ownership and minimize resistance since the cultural integration becomes the collective responsibility and not a top-down requirement. With a well-thought-out mix of these practices, the HR departments will be able to provide a scene in which cultural synergy may prosper, as well as how employee welfare and organizational performance can be maintained, during the entire merger process.

10.3 Leadership Actions for Fostering a Shared Vision and Unified Identity

During mergers, leadership is a characteristic in establishing conditions that help to achieve cultural synergy. The leaders should be able to express an interesting common vision that combines the capabilities and ambitions of both legacy organizations to give a sense of direction to employees in the transitioning organizations. Effective and open communication prevents uncertainty and strengthens trust in the decisions of a leader. Leaders who have exemplary behavior of collaboration, empathy, and openness to other ideas are the ones who create the context of cultural alignment among teams. When employees are engaged by means of frequent communication, attempts to appreciate them, and seen as dedicated to being fair, it serves as a powerful tool in promoting psychological safety and persuading the employees to accept the emerging cultural standards. Also, the leaders are expected to work proactively to combat power differences and create equal participation of all groups since this will create a feeling of belonging. As role models and cultural custodians, leaders can steer employees to have a single identity that will facilitate innovation, sustainability and resilience of post-merger performance. Table 6 integrates the strategic directions, human relations, and the leadership behaviours that are necessary in terms of cultural synergy.

Table 6. Managerial practices supporting unified post-merger culture

Practice Category	Managerial Practice	Description	Contribution to Cultural Synergy
Strategic Guidelines	Development of Culture-Focused Integration Playbooks	Clear frameworks outlining cultural expectations, integration steps, and communication protocols.	Provides consistency, reduces uncertainty, and aligns integration activities across units.
	Early Cultural Risk Assessment	Identification of cultural clashes, misalignments, and strengths during due diligence.	Enables proactive interventions and shapes realistic integration strategies.
	Vision and Values Co-Creation	Collaborative development of shared cultural values for the merged organization.	Promotes ownership, strengthens identity, and enhances long-term alignment.
HR Practices	Cross-Cultural Capability Building	Training programs, workshops, and mentoring to enhance cultural awareness.	Reduces bias, improves collaboration, and enhances intercultural competence.
	Talent Retention and Transition Support	Structured approaches to retain key employees and support teams through cultural change.	Maintains stability, preserves knowledge, and reduces turnover during integration.
	Participatory Decision-Making Mechanisms	Inclusion of employees in committees, integration teams, and cultural forums.	Increases engagement, builds trust, and supports shared responsibility for cultural outcomes.
Leadership Behaviors	Transparent and Frequent Communication	Leaders provide regular updates and encourage open dialogue.	Builds psychological safety, reduces ambiguity, and supports acceptance of change.
	Role Modeling Expected Cultural Norms	Leaders consistently demonstrate behaviors aligned with the desired new culture.	Reinforces culture expectations and accelerates cultural adoption across teams.
	Fairness in Power Distribution	Ensuring balanced representation and equitable participation in key decisions.	Minimizes resentment, strengthens unity, and promotes cultural harmony.

11. CONCLUSION

The issue of cultural synergy has become one of the most dramatic determinants of the success of mergers and acquisitions that affects not only the short-term integration practices but also the organizational resilience and sustainability in the long term. This chapter analysis reveals that the issue of cultural integration should be viewed as a strategic need, not as an additional activity, since the integration of different values, behaviors, work practices have a significant influence on employee engagement, trust, collaboration, as well as on general performance. Effective mergers are based on leaders willing to set good examples of inclusive behaviours, engaging openly and proactively in resolving power imbalances and biases that can lead to poor alignment. No less important are HR-led practices, e.g., the cross-cultural training, talent retention programs and participatory frameworks, which assist the employees to negotiate the change and become the participants in shaping a cohesive organizational image. Between the emerging trends of digital collaboration, remote work and sustainability-focused values, there is an additional indication that the cultural needs in contemporary organizations continue to shift, necessitating strategies of integration that are dynamic, progressive and technologically powered. By recognizing cultural diversity as a strategic resource and not a liability, the organizations will turn the merging process into a chance of renewing, innovation, and competitive advantage. By re-imagining M&As as driving forces of organizational change, leaders will be able to create the conditions in which cultural synergy will lead to the creation of long-term value, strategic agility, and sustainable growth.

REFERENCES

Ahammad, M. F., Tarba, S. Y., Liu, Y., & Glaister, K. W. (2016). Knowledge transfer and cross-border acquisition performance: The impact of cultural distance and employee retention. *International Business Review*, *25*(1), 66–75. DOI: 10.1016/j.ibusrev.2014.06.015

Ang, S., Van Dyne, L., Koh, C., Ng, K. Y., Templer, K. J., Tay, C., & Chandrasekar, N. A. (2007). Cultural intelligence: Its measurement and effects on cultural judgment and decision making, cultural adaptation and task performance. *Management and Organization Review*, *3*(3), 335–371. DOI: 10.1111/j.1740-8784.2007.00082.x

Ashiedu, B. I., Ogbuefi, E., Nwabekee, U. S., Ogeawuchi, J. C., & Abayomi, A. A. (2024). The silent dealbreaker: Why organizational culture should be a due diligence priority. *International Journal of Scientific Research in Science and Technology*, *11*(4), 565–586. DOI: 10.32628/IJSRST241151214

Avrillia, S., Hakim, L., Sulfia, S., & Anshori, M. I. (2025). Hybrid leadership and organizational performance: A literature review approach. *Implementasi Manajemen & Kewirausahaan*, *5*(1), 14–30. DOI: 10.38156/imka.v5i1.540

Bristol-Alagbariya, B., Ayanponle, L. O., & Ogedengbe, D. E. (2022). Integrative HR approaches in mergers and acquisitions ensuring seamless organizational synergies. Magna Scientia Advanced Research and Reviews, 6(1), 078–085. DOI: 10.30574/msarr.2022.6.1.0070

Cartwright, S., & Schoenberg, R. (2006). Thirty years of mergers and acquisitions research: Recent advances and future opportunities. *British Journal of Management*, *17*(S1), S1–S5. DOI: 10.1111/j.1467-8551.2006.00475.x

Chatterjee, S., Lubatkin, M. H., Schweiger, D. M., & Weber, Y. (1992). Cultural differences and shareholder value in related mergers: Linking equity and human capital. *Strategic Management Journal*, *13*(5), 319–334. DOI: 10.1002/smj.4250130502

Čirjevskis, A. (2020). Valuing reciprocal synergies in merger and acquisition deals using the real option analysis. *Administrative Sciences*, *10*(2), 27. DOI: 10.3390/admsci10020027

Datta, D. K. (1991). Organizational fit and acquisition performance: Effects of post-acquisition integration. *Strategic Management Journal*, *12*(4), 281–297. DOI: 10.1002/smj.4250120404

Denison, D. R., & Ko, I. (2016). Cultural due diligence in mergers and acquisitions. In *Advances in Mergers and Acquisitions* (pp. 53–72). Emerald Group Publishing Limited., DOI: 10.1108/S1479-361X20160000015004

Department of Information Systems and Security 6178 College Station Drive Williamsburg KY 40769 United States of America, U. of the C., Mohammed, M. H. S., Khan, M. S. A., Syed, M. M., Prosis Technologies Inc TX United States of America, D., & Cloud Resources - Irving United States of America, T. X. 75038. (2023). Remote work culture: The impact of digital transformation on workforce productivity. Journal of E-Science Letters, 4(1), 1–5. DOI: 10.51470/eSL.2023.4.1.01

Drori, I., Wrzesniewski, A., & Ellis, S. (2011). Cultural clashes in a "merger of equals": The case of high-tech start-ups. *Human Resource Management, 50*(5), 625–649. DOI: 10.1002/hrm.20446

Frantz, T. L., & Center, D. T. I. (2014). A behavioral theory of the merger: Dynamics of the post-merger integration process. DOI: 10.21236/ADA606347

Graebner, M. E., Heimeriks, K. H., Huy, Q. N., & Vaara, E. (2017). The process of postmerger integration: A review and agenda for future research. *The Academy of Management Annals, 11*(1), 1–32. DOI: 10.5465/annals.2014.0078

Hutasoit, A. W., Yusuf Sirat, M., & Erisusanto, R. (2023). Company performance and achievements post merger case study of pt Indosat Tbk (ioh). International Journal of Social Science, Educational, Economics [IJSET]. *Agricultural Research & Technology: Open Access Journal, 2*(7), 203–210. DOI: 10.54443/ijset.v2i7.174

Jarvenpaa, S. L., & Leidner, D. E. (2006). Communication and trust in global virtual teams. Journal of Computer-Mediated Communication: JCMC, 3(4), 0–0. DOI: 10.1111/j.1083-6101.1998.tb00080.x

Joseph, J. (2014). Managing change after the merger: The value of pre-merger ingroup identities. *Journal of Organizational Change Management, 27*(3), 430–448. DOI: 10.1108/JOCM-10-2013-0184

Killingsworth, B., Xue, Y., & Liu, Y. (2016). Factors influencing knowledge sharing among global virtual teams. *Team Performance Management, 22*(5/6), 284–300. DOI: 10.1108/TPM-10-2015-0042

Leadership development strategies of human resources in digital era. (2023). Journal of Human Resource Development, 5(6). DOI: 10.23977/jhrd.2023.050620

Liang, S., Ullrich, J., Dick, R., & Lupina-Wegener, A. (2021). The intergroup sensitivity effect in mergers and acquisitions: Testing the role of merger motives. *Journal of Applied Social Psychology, 51*(8), 769–778. DOI: 10.1111/jasp.12785

Maulana, S., Nurhayati, P., Sumarwan, U., & Sukmawati, A. (2024). Managing organizational culture integration post-acquisition: Lessons from PT "X" in the oil and gas sector. *Evolutionary Studies in Imaginative Culture*, •••, 1611–1620. DOI: 10.70082/esiculture.vi.1486

Miczka, S., & Größler, A. (2010). Merger dynamics. Kybernetes. The International Journal of Cybernetics. *Kybernetes*, *39*(9/10), 1491–1512. DOI: 10.1108/03684921011081132

Mockaitis, A. I., Rose, E. L., & Zettinig, P. (2012). The power of individual cultural values in global virtual teams. *International Journal of Cross Cultural Management*, *12*(2), 193–210. DOI: 10.1177/1470595812439868

Napier, N. K. (1989). Mergers and acquisitions, human resource issues and outcomes: A review and suggested typology. *Journal of Management Studies*, *26*(3), 271–290. DOI: 10.1111/j.1467-6486.1989.tb00728.x

Oberoi, J. K. (2025). Future of work: Will hybrid work culture become the norm in MNCs? *INTERNATIONAL JOURNAL OF SCIENTIFIC RESEARCH IN ENGINEERING AND MANAGEMENT*, *09*(05), 1–9. DOI: 10.55041/IJSREM48958

Oh, J.-H., & Johnston, W. J. (2021). How post-merger integration duration affects merger outcomes. *Journal of Business and Industrial Marketing*, *36*(5), 807–820. DOI: 10.1108/JBIM-11-2019-0476

Presbitero, A. (2020). Task performance in global virtual team. *Personnel Review*, *49*(5), 1091–1105. DOI: 10.1108/PR-10-2018-0415

Ranajee, R., Naik, K. R., & Iyengar, S. R. (2025). Unlocking long-term value in M&A: The role of HR strategies. *The International Journal of Organizational Analysis*, *33*(11), 4117–4135. DOI: 10.1108/IJOA-05-2024-4492

Ravikumar, A. Olimbaevich, I. R., Mashkhura, S., & Musayeva, S. (2025). Transforming Healthcare with Large Language Models and AI agents. In Advances in Computational Intelligence and Robotics (pp. 51–82). IGI Global Scientific Publishing. DOI: 10.4018/979-8-3373-2008-3.ch003

Ravikumar, R. N., & Aarthi, S. (2025b). Climate data without borders. In *Cross-Border Cooperation in the Age of Climate Change* (pp. 61–90). IGI Global Scientific Publishing., DOI: 10.4018/979-8-3373-3972-6.ch003

Ravikumar, R. N., & Aarthi, S. (2025c). Federated Learning for cross-enterprise supply chain collaboration. In *Advances in Computational Intelligence and Robotics* (pp. 47–84). IGI Global Scientific Publishing., DOI: 10.4018/979-8-3373-2833-1.ch002

Ravikumar, R. N., & Aarthi, S. (2025d). Integrated cross-border renewable energy infrastructure for a green transition. In *Cross-Border Cooperation in the Age of Climate Change* (pp. 301–332). IGI Global Scientific Publishing., DOI: 10.4018/979-8-3373-3972-6.ch011

Ravikumar, & Aarthi, S. (2025a). Natural Language Processing in conversational AI tutors. In Advances in Computational Intelligence and Robotics (pp. 275–306). IGI Global Scientific Publishing. DOI: 10.4018/979-8-3373-4217-7.ch011

Richter, N. F., Martin, J., Hansen, S. V., Taras, V., & Alon, I. (2021). Motivational configurations of cultural intelligence, social integration, and performance in global virtual teams. *Journal of Business Research, 129*, 351–367. DOI: 10.1016/j.jbusres.2021.03.012

Rodríguez-Sánchez, J.-L., Ortiz-de-Urbina-Criado, M., & Mora-Valentín, E.-M. (2019). Thinking about people in mergers and acquisitions processes. *International Journal of Manpower*, *40*(4), 643–657. DOI: 10.1108/IJM-05-2018-0143

Rosendale, J., Wilkie, L., & Lowry, W. (2024). On strategic communication during mergers & acquisitions: A pragmatic perspective to improve outcomes. *Development and Learning in Organizations*, *38*(5), 1–4. DOI: 10.1108/DLO-10-2023-0226

Rottig, D., Schappert, J., & Starkman, E. (2017). Successfully managing the sociocultural integration process in international acquisitions: A qualitative analysis of canon's acquisition of océ. *Thunderbird International Business Review*, *59*(2), 187–208. DOI: 10.1002/tie.21831

Sales, A., Roth, S., Grothe-Hammer, M., & Azambuja, R. (2022). From play to pay: A multifunctional approach to the role of culture in post-merger integration. *Management Decision*, *60*(7), 1922–1946. DOI: 10.1108/MD-01-2021-0136

Sarala, R. M., & Vaara, E. (2010). Cultural differences, convergence, and crossvergence as explanations of knowledge transfer in international acquisitions. *Journal of International Business Studies*, *41*(8), 1365–1390. DOI: 10.1057/jibs.2009.89

Stahl, G. K., Angwin, D. N., Very, P., Gomes, E., Weber, Y., Tarba, S. Y., Noorderhaven, N., Benyamini, H., Bouckenooghe, D., Chreim, S., Durand, M., Hassett, M. E., Kokk, G., Mendenhall, M. E., Mirc, N., Miska, C., Park, K. M., Reynolds, N.-S., Rouzies, A., & Yildiz, H. E. (2013). Sociocultural integration in mergers and acquisitions: Unresolved paradoxes and directions for future research. *Thunderbird International Business Review*, *55*(4), 333–356. DOI: 10.1002/tie.21549

Stahl, G. K., Larsson, R., Kremershof, I., & Sitkin, S. B. (2011). Trust dynamics in acquisitions: A case survey. *Human Resource Management, 50*(5), 575–603. DOI: 10.1002/hrm.20448

Stahl, G. K., & Voigt, A. (2008). Do cultural differences matter in mergers and acquisitions? A tentative model and examination. *Organization Science, 19*(1), 160–176. DOI: 10.1287/orsc.1070.0270

Steigenberger, N. (2017). The challenge of integration: A review of the M&A integration literature. *International Journal of Management Reviews, 19*(4), 408–431. DOI: 10.1111/ijmr.12099

Sun, A. (2024). Talent management and organizational change in corporate mergers and acquisitions. *Frontiers in Business, Economics and Management, 12*(3), 99–102. DOI: 10.54097/dcjd4ghk

Thelisson, A.-S. (2023). Coopetition in a failed merger project: Why two French companies called it quits. *The Journal of Business Strategy, 44*(1), 44–49. DOI: 10.1108/JBS-06-2021-0102

Tripathi, A. A. (2018). Factors affecting effective mergers and acquisition: An empirical investigation. *INFORMATION TECHNOLOGY IN INDUSTRY, 6*(3). Advance online publication. DOI: 10.17762/itii.v6i3.823

Weber, Y., Rachman-Moore, D., & Tarba, S. Y. (2012). HR practices during post-merger conflict and merger performance. *International Journal of Cross Cultural Management, 12*(1), 73–99. DOI: 10.1177/1470595811413111

Weber, Y., & Yedidia Tarba, S. (2012). Mergers and acquisitions process: The use of corporate culture analysis. *Cross Cultural Management, 19*(3), 288–303. DOI: 10.1108/13527601211247053

Wengel, J. (2023). Cultural intelligence and trust in global virtual teams. *Business and Professional Communication Quarterly*. Advance online publication. DOI: 10.1177/23294906231179915

Wu, C.-C., Liu, T.-Y., & Yang, T.-H. (2025). Unraveling the dynamics of cross-border mergers and acquisitions: Motivations and performance implications. *SAGE Open, 15*(2), 21582440251338684. Advance online publication. DOI: 10.1177/21582440251338684

Zakaria, N., & Ab Rahman Muton, N. (2022). Cultural code-switching in high context global virtual team members: A qualitative study. *International Journal of Cross Cultural Management, 22*(3), 487–515. DOI: 10.1177/14705958221137256

KEY TERMS AND DEFINITIONS

Cross-Cultural Training: Programs designed to help employees understand and work effectively across different cultural backgrounds.

Cultural Collision: The clash that occurs when two organizational cultures differ significantly, leading to misunderstandings, resistance, or conflict.

Cultural Compatibility: The degree to which two organizations share similar values, leadership styles, and work norms before a merger.

Cultural Integration: The deliberate effort to align values, behaviours, communication styles, and work practices between merging organizations.

Cultural Synergy: The process of blending different organizational cultures to create a stronger, unified culture that enhances collaboration and performance.

Digital Collaboration: Use of online tools and virtual platforms to support teamwork and communication during and after a merger.

Due Diligence (Cultural): The assessment of cultural strengths, weaknesses, and differences between merging firms during the planning stage.

Governance Differences: Variations in decision-making structures, accountability systems, and managerial control between merging organizations.

Leadership Alignment: Agreement among leaders on shared goals, communication approaches, and cultural expectations during integration.

Organizational Identity: The shared values, beliefs, and characteristics that define how employees perceive their organization.

Post-Merger Integration (PMI): The phase after a merger where organizations combine operations, systems, and cultures to function as a single entity.

Power Asymmetry: An imbalance in influence or authority between merging organizations that may hinder fair integration.

Sustainability-Oriented Values: Cultural expectations focused on ethical responsibility, environmental stewardship, and long-term social impact.

Talent Retention: Strategies aimed at keeping key employees from leaving during the uncertainty of a merger.

Chapter 3
Ethical Governance and Anti-Corruption in M&A:
Building Trust for SDG 16

Pranjal Khare
http://orcid.org/0000-0002-9937-9588
Jindal Global Law School, O.P Jindal Global University, India

ABSTRACT

This chapter examines the critical role of ethical governance and anti-corruption within the mergers and acquisitions (M&A) lifecycle, aligning corporate conduct with United Nations Sustainable Development Goal 16. While M&A frameworks traditionally prioritize financial and operational performance, it argues proactive, value-based decision-making to mitigate systemic risks such as insider trading and successor liability. The chapter reviews international regulatory landscapes, including the FCPA, UK Bribery Act, and India's Companies Act 2013, alongside high-profile cases like Siemens and Enron. It proposes a three-pillar framework consisting of Integrity Assurance Systems, Institutional Accountability Structures, and Stakeholder Inclusivity to operationalize integrity. By integrating ethical due diligence from deal origination through post-merger integration, organizations can transform M&A into a strategic mechanism for building institutional trust and advancing global justice.

INTRODUCTION

The need for ethical governance has become increasingly important as the world becomes more globalized, and businesses operate across borders. As a result of this increased complexity in capitalistic systems resulting from the flow of capital across

DOI: 10.4018/979-8-3373-5233-6.ch003

borders and the rapid evolution of the digital economy, as well as the increase in public awareness regarding corporate responsibility, companies must go beyond merely maximizing profits through operational strategies. Ethical governance is the application of moral principles in the daily operations of a company, including ethical and socially responsible practices, as well as accountability to all stakeholders involved in the company. Therefore, ethical governance is not simply an opportunity to comply with regulatory requirements. It is a proactive approach to decision-making based on values (Crane & Matten, 2021).

For many years, sustainability was viewed only from the environmental and economic position; however, sustainability is beginning to incorporate an ethical dimension regarding the conduct of business practices. By establishing sustainable approaches to governance, organizations establish their legitimacy and, consequently, create an environment conducive to maintaining investor confidence and market stability. With the increased emphasis on Environmental, Social, and Governance (ESG) metrics in global capital markets today, ethical governance protects organizations from opportunistic behavior and ensures that when making decisions, organizations take into account the interests of multiple stakeholders, including employees, customers, and communities, and do not just focus solely on the interests of shareholders. The United Nations Sustainable Development Goal 16 (SDG 16) includes this idea as part of the global development agenda, highlighting the importance of peace, justice and strong institutions (United Nations, 2015).

The transactions involved in M&A change control, ownership and organizational structure, thereby creating repercussions for governance, market integrity, and stakeholder welfare. M&A transactions are governed by intricate legal frameworks that deal with securities law, competition regulation and fiduciary duties. In addition to financial due diligence, ethical due diligence has become a critical component of M&A transactions.

The M&A process can reveal weaknesses in governance. Valuation methods that are unclear can conceal liabilities, and incomplete disclosures can mislead investors. The collapse of the Enron-Dynegy merger in 2001 is an example of how the lack of internal controls and limited transparency created instability in entire market verticals. The acquisition of Flipkart by Walmart in 2018 demonstrates the complexities associated with cross-border compliance in jurisdictions that have mixed governance standards, such as India. When there is no transparency about a transaction, it creates information asymmetry, which leads to situations where one party has more information than others. This creates an environment that allows for insider trading or selective leakage of material facts. These activities are illegal in both India, where Section 24 of the SEBI (Prohibition of Insider Trading) Regulations, 2015 prohibits insider trading, and in the United States, where Rule 10b-5 prohibits all forms of insider trading. If there is no sufficient ethical oversight now, it could create an environment that allows corrupt conduct to occur.

SDG 16 and Its Relevance to Global M&A Practices

SDG 16 is an important landmark in the context of ethical governance, not only in the domestic context but in the global environment. The framework envisaged in SDG 16 contributes to the promotion of responsible and ethical governance. The objectives of SDG 16 include curbing corruption (Target 16.5) and building strong and ethical institutions (Target 16.6). These goals are in line with the requirements of corporate governance and anti-corruption in the case of international mergers and acquisitions. SDG 16 is the first attempt to develop a broader framework for corporate responsibility, establishing the benchmark for how corporations should be accountable to the state, as well as to society. In the context of international mergers and acquisitions, the conformity with SDG 16 is particularly important. Mergers and acquisitions now take place between entities rooted in regions with vastly different governance standards. International companies must deal with a wide range of anti-corruption laws and reporting requirements, from the US Foreign Corrupt Practices Act (FCPA), through the UK Bribery Act to EU Corporate Sustainability Due Diligence Directive, requiring proper strategies to meet these obligations in practice.

Corporate mergers and acquisitions that do not follow an ethical practice can erode the trust people and institutions place in governments and create a culture of impunity, which ultimately undermines the UNSDGs. Conversely, when a company engages in an ethical manner throughout the entire process of acquiring another entity. For example, conducting thorough and transparent due diligence, demonstrating compliance with all laws regarding corruption both throughout the due diligence process and in the future. The result is a stronger governance ecosystem within which businesses operate. Thus, the act of engaging in ethical diligence and diligence that supports the goals of SDG 16 expands the due diligence process beyond legal requirements to encompass things such as supply-chain integrity, risk related to the political affiliations of counterparties, and beneficial ownership of assets. An example of ethical M&A is the Siemens bribery case; Siemens' use of acquisitions to shield itself from paying bribes caused the company to lose considerable amounts of reputational capital as well as irreparably harm its brand. In total, the fines imposed against Siemens for its FCPA and German Criminal Code violations were over $1.6 billion (U.S. Department of Justice, 2008). Aligning M&A governance with the goals of the SDGs 16 thus converts the M&A process from market consolidation to the empowerment of society. Additionally, the symbiotic relationship between ethical M&A governance and SDG 16 represents a new model for corporate advancement in which businesses will measure success based on equitable and inclusive practices, rather than solely profitability.

Rationale for Ethical Governance in M&A

The central focus of ethical governance when doing M&A is based upon two interconnected essentials. First is legitimizing corporate conduct and secondly creating long-term value. Corporate conduct can have a significant impact upon the organization's legitimacy if its internal processes are aligned or have conformed to the social, political, and legal norms of society. Trust among all stakeholders provides an intangible asset to an organization which is vital for its survival within an uncertain and rapidly changing global marketplace (Donaldson & Walsh, 2015). Several studies have shown that companies with good ethical governance have greater success in implementing their M&A strategies after the M&A has been completed, while those companies also have less exposure to compliance violations because of their M&A transactions.

In addition, ethical governance serves as a constraint on what is referred to as governance arbitrage, a strategic opportunity to take advantage of the differences in regulatory frameworks and governance practices within different jurisdictions (Bozos et al., 2025). As an example, if a publicly traded corporation that is headquartered in a country with strict governance standards decides to acquire a target company that is located in a jurisdiction that has weak enforcement of governance rules, then there will be temptation for the acquiring corporation to reduce their Ethical Standards in order to gain a competitive advantage. Therefore, embedding ethical governance throughout all aspects of the M&A process will provide a neutralization of these temptations and create consistency in global business ethics.

Regulations like the Companies Act of 2013 in India, along with various other regulations such as Schedule VII for Corporate Social Responsibility and Section 177 for Audit Committees, are designed for the purpose of enhancing accountability within organizations. Another example is SEBI's recently introduced Business Responsibility and Sustainability Reporting (BRSR) Regulation which requires companies to report against a new Sustainability Framework concerning ethics, bribery and corruption, as well as integrity systems (SEBI, 2021). Through the application of these regulations in M&A transactions, businesses will not only maintain compliance but also promote the SDG 16 Vision of Integrity and Justice within their organizations.

LITERATURE SYNTHESIS AND RESEARCH GAP

The literature concerning ethical governance in M&As, which is available at present, can be divided into three strands. The first strand addresses M&As from the point of view of corporate governance, fiduciary responsibility, valuation, disclosure, and transaction performance. Although important elements such as boards, internal control systems, and responsible decision making are discussed, ethics are viewed only as a part of strong governance rather than the fourth component of the M&A process. This strand features the issues of anti-bribery and anti-corruption compliance such as integrity due diligence, third-party risk, successor liability, and post-acquisition remediation. Although the literature elaborates on the ways in which corruption compromises transaction value and exposes acquirers to legal implications, the emphasis is placed on preventive measures and compliance. The third strand of literature related to governance can be called ESG and sustainable corporate governance literature; it expands the idea of corporate responsibility by introducing transparency and accountability to the issue of the requirements of stakeholders and institutional legitimacy.

When viewed together, these strands of research highlight a key shortcoming in each of these areas. Corporate governance literature deals with questions on how transaction activities should be governed. Anti-corruption research deals with issues of how the risks of corruption and successor liability should be monitored and managed. And sustainability literature indicates our need to think about corporation's functions beyond strict financial goals. Yet the methods and insights proposed by different bodies of literature are not sufficiently integrated. In particular, none of these strands is able to explain how ethical governance throughout all stages of the M&A process, start with choosing a target for acquisition and finish with deal closing and post-merger integrations, can work both as a tool for preventing corruption and as a means of businesses' contribution to institutional integrity. Therefore, the connection between transaction-level governance and institution-building goals resulting from SDG 16 is still underexplored.

This chapter's particular research gap is thus located at the intersection of governance in M&As, anti-corruption compliance, and sustainable-development governance. Though previous methodologies include ample information on legal compliance and managing corruption risks, they fail to understand M&A as an institutional governance process that could either perpetuate governance weaknesses or enhance the principles of integrity, accountability, transparency, and trust. Furthermore, previous approaches do not provide any integrated framework connecting pre-transaction ethical screening with board-level accountability, contractual safeguards, post-transaction cultural integration, stakeholder reporting, and institutional trust to SDG 16 Targets 16.5 and 16.6. SDG 16 is crucial since it offers a normative criterion based on which the effects of governance in M&As can be monitored after the completion of a transaction and particularly from the perspective of whether a corporate merger prevents corruption and assures proper governance institutions.

The chapter is contributing by helping in conceptualizing the ethical governance of M&A that is in sync with SDG 16 as well as has a connection between the integrity mechanisms and institutional outcomes. As a theory, it integrates together business ethics, stakeholder-oriented corporate governance, anti-corruption compliance and institutional legitimacy to explain the actual role of integrity in the M&A process. In practical terms, it provides a theoretical basis for the formation of three separate governing pillars for facilitating ethical decisional processes in the context of mergers and acquisitions. With respect to politics, it indicates the possibility and ways in which corporate processes may foster anti-corruption efforts by adding practices of transparency, oversight, whistleblower protection, remediation and accountability to the existing anti-corruption policies. Finally, this approach lays the grounds for future empirical analysis targeting the impact of SDG-oriented governance mechanisms on such parameters as post-merger integrity, trustworthiness, regulatory effect and long-term stability of transactions in different jurisdictions.

Research Methodology

The above synthesis of existing literature reveals that the problem lies not in the unavailability of rules related to fighting against corruption or the existence of rules of corporate governance but their disintegration throughout stages of the life cycle of M&A processes and their lack of relationship with ethical controls at the transaction level and the resulting institutional outcomes. Existing corporate governance systems often focus more on examining financial and legal risks than on ethical control and the ethics itself (Khare, 2025). This chapter will try to fill that existing gap.

The increasing awareness of the need to introduce good governance into M&A Governance Frameworks, however, has not resulted in consistent implementation of this concept across all M&A transactions. According to most of the literature and regulatory practices, the M&A governance frameworks focus on financial and operational performance instead of value-based governance mechanisms. This is illustrated by the fact that the global M&A volume was estimated at $3.6 trillion in 2023 (Levy, 2024). Both compliance mechanisms and ethical oversight mechanisms currently exist. However, ethical oversight mechanisms tend to be reactive to events such as Corporate Scandals rather than integrated into creditor due diligence processes.

To fill this gap in literature, this research will investigate how organizations can introduce ethical governance mechanisms into their M&A processes to support the objectives of SDG. This research adopts a combination of normative and doctrinal methodologies enriched through a multi-faceted approach utilizing comparative analysis and case study analysis. At its core, the doctrinal analysis is focused on a detailed analysis of the core legal foundations for ethical governance (i.e., The FCPA, The UK Bribery Act 2010, The UNCAC and The Indian Prevention of Corruption Act 1988). This ethical governance foundation will then be supplemented with a framework for the comparison of governance practices and a corporate reporting requirement assessment for OECD, EU and India. This research uses empirical mapping to link theory to real-world practice, with a specific focus on M&A from an ethical standpoint. It reviews numerous global M&A cases, including those with high-profile governance failures (e.g., the Petrobras-Lava Jato case), as well as leading companies that have implemented best practices for M&A (e.g., Unilever's sustainable acquisitions).

The outcome of this research is to design value-based frameworks that will help support SDG 16 (Peace, Justice and Strong Institutions) through a normative inquiry based on business ethics, corporate jurisprudence, and mixed methodology. As a result of combining the two methodologies, academia is ensured that this research has academic rigor, while at the same time, the resulting findings will be of practical use to policymakers and corporate executives. Initial analyses indicate that ethical M&A governance should consist of three interrelated, interdependent pillars to support corporate integrity. The first pillar, Integrity Assurance Systems, provides comprehensive pre-transaction ethics vetting through robust third-party integrity due diligence, transparent disclosure mechanisms, and full corruption risk mapping. Additionally, the second pillar, Institutional Accountability Structures, allows independent boards, audit committees and whistleblower systems to serve as an ongoing source of structural oversight during the negotiation and integration phases. The final pillar, Stakeholder Inclusivity and Reporting, enhances transparency of M&A communications and Sustainability Reports by introducing SDG-aligned disclosure metrics to quantify the ethical impacts from a stakeholder perspective. Together, these pillars operationalize the institutional goals of SDG 16 within private-sector governance frameworks, providing a replicable model applicable across diverse jurisdictions.

CORRUPTION RISKS AND ETHICAL CHALLENGES IN M&A TRANSACTIONS

To avoid potential corruption-related losses due diligence reviews are essential in M&A transactions. Since M&A transactions include many stages from initial research, negotiations, through to post-acquisition integration, the need for thorough assessments cannot be overstated (Handley, 2012). Most acquirers focus on fast-growing sectors and markets where the likelihood of experiencing bribery or facilitating payments is high. This tends to exacerbate the potential for conflicts between an acquirer's drive to achieve superior return on investment in high-growth industries and a desire to adhere to ethical standards, especially in developing regions of Asia, Africa and Latin America where regulatory enforcement is often less robust and where non-corrupt practices may be the norm (Williams et al., 2022).

In addition to the problem of a lack of reliable data concerning a target's potential illegal activity, asymmetric positions during negotiations and valuations create an environment conducive to inappropriate behavior. Many M&A transactions, particularly high-risk deals, have indicated through forensic analysis evidence of questionable disbursements, suspicious consulting agreements, and politically exposed intermediaries that a high-level analysis of the transaction alone was unable to capture. As M&A transaction timelines typically are short in an auction-like manner and senior management evaluations and recommendations may be based on closing timeframes, there exists considerable pressure to reduce time spent conducting integrity checks, thereby increasing the possibility that corruption will go undetected until after the closing of the transaction. (Agence Française Anticorruption, 2021).

Anti-Bribery Due Diligence and its Limits

The evolving view on anti-bribery and anti-corruption (ABC) due diligence has established ABC due diligence as an integral aspect of responsible mergers and acquisition instead of something relegated as an ancillary service in the pursuit of legal compliance (Transparency International UK, 2012). Organizations such as Transparency International and national regulators provide guidance to conduct risk-based ABC due diligence that examines a company's books and records, third-party relationships, prior dealings with public officials, and internal controls (Arnold & Porter, 2011). For example, in India, legal and advisory firms have begun to highlight that due diligence for ABC issues must include how to assess risk for bribery, fraud or white-collar crime in both domestic transactions and transactions involving cross-border elements of the Prevention of Corruption Act and other industry-specific regulations (Ahlawat & Associates, 2024).

While this guidance has been provided, ABC due diligence continues to be inconsistent and/or only moderately effective. Acquirers frequently rely on submissions of questionnaires and document reviews to fulfil their ABC due diligence obligations without conducting thorough forensic investigations such as transaction testing, focused email reviews or targeted interviews of workers who are deemed high risk. In addition to a lack of resources available in high-risk jurisdictions, many companies that are being acquired often face challenges in accessing adequate and reliable public documentation to support their ABC due diligence efforts. In addition, where the target company does have sensitive information about the workings of its ABC compliance program, the company may be hesitant to share that information until a signed agreement is in place. A recurring weakness is the failure to translate due diligence findings into binding legal protections, such as specific indemnities, escrow arrangements, price adjustments, or post-closing remediation covenants, which leaves acquirers exposed to successor liability when issues later surface.

Successor Liability and Enforcement Dynamics

In M&A, one of the largest legal and ethical challenges faced by acquiring companies is their potential liability for the pre-acquisition of misconduct of the acquired target. The U.S. Foreign Corrupt Practices Act has established a long record of following the principle that corporate acquirers may be subject to enforcement actions for bribes made prior to the acquisition closing, when the acquirer becomes an issuer or a domestic concern and where the corrupt conduct is ongoing or left unresolved post-acquisition by the acquirer (Debevoise & Plimpton, 2018). According to Financier Worldwide, FCPA successor liability can wipe out the value of an acquisition and can lead to the cancellation of contracts, fines, and reputational harm to the acquirer, particularly where the acquirer is entering high-risk jurisdictions such as China or portions of Latin America.

Over the past few years, some policy changes have aimed to create a better balance between the need to deter unethical practices from occurring and the desire to encourage a broader acceptance of mergers and acquisitions with less ethically compliant businesses. The updated FCPA Resource Guide indicates that a more pragmatic approach to the concept of successor liability will allow acquirers to move forward with mergers and acquisitions with companies that may have weak compliance cultures as long as they make a commitment to conducting thorough post-acquisition investigations and making timely improvements to their compliance programs (Stephenson, 2021). U.S. enforcement action and the scholarship suggest that under traditional state law doctrines in asset transactions, the civil successor liability may be limited for some types of transactions, which could result in regulatory gaps in the accountability of corporate entities unless wider theories of corporate responsibility are asserted by regulatory authorities (Phillips, 2015).

Another critical pathway of risk for acquisitions comes from the use of third-party relationships, including agents, distributors, lobbyists, consultants, and joint-venture partners. For the acquirer to make an informed and proper due diligence effort, the acquirer must identify and thoroughly scrutinize its third-party intermediaries. Global enforcement actions in connection with the FCPA and other anti-corruption laws reveal that many of the corrupt schemes facilitated through intermediaries were perpetrated by an acquirer who ultimately failed to identify and sufficiently scrutinize the intermediary as part of its due diligence process (OCEG, 2020). Thus, as part of their due diligence process, practical guidance recommends that acquirers map and assign a risk rate to all of their intermediaries and access and evaluate the commercial rationale for each and evaluate the presence of potential 'Red Flags' such as disproportionate compensation for services, vagueness in the scope of services provided and connections to politically exposed persons.

Ethical Tensions in Valuation, Negotiation and Disclosure

In addition, it presents additional ethical tensions beyond just the legal risks and exposures associated with mergers and acquisitions related to the valuation, negotiation, and disclosure of the transaction terms. For instance, the discovery of corrupt action by a company, or the risk thereof, can be manipulated by parties in the negotiation process for the purpose of reducing the purchase price or otherwise increasing the level of protection in favor of the buyer or stockholder while further creating disincentives to resolve the integrity issues that created the risk of corruption in the first place. Proper ethical governance would require that discovering corrupt action or discovering a risk of corrupt action be viewed as triggers for serious remediation, potential withdrawal from the transaction, and/or notification of law enforcement authorities (Transparency International UK, 2012).

The incentives related to the fees paid to the transaction team members for successful completion of the deal, or internal pressure to successfully complete the transaction, could lead them to downplay or selectively disclose any adverse results of the anti-bribery and corruption due diligence process to the board of directors or any special committee responsible for providing oversight to the transaction. This practice will compromise a director's fiduciary duty and decrease the integrity of the corporation's decision-making and therefore increase the disparity between the formal structures of compliance and the actual governance actions taken (Arnold & Porter, 2011). In response to this situation, emerging best practices include, for serious integrity-related concerns, providing a well-defined escalation process, mandatory involvement of the compliance and internal audit departments in all high-risk transactions, and document board of director's discussions when significant concerns about corruption arise from the anti-bribery and corruption due diligence process (DLA Piper, 2022).

Post-Merger Integration, Culture Clash and Remediation

Once the M&A transaction is completed, the focus of the transaction's due diligence and compliance process moves from identifying problems to creating a plan to fix these problems and successfully integrating culture. The Organization for Economic Co-operation and Development (OECD) recommended in its 2021 Recommendation that organizations assess the risk of mergers and acquisitions based on a risk-based approach and that organizations promptly integrate the new entity into their existing internal controls and compliance programs and conduct a post-acquisition audit of the newly acquired entity. The US approach appears to mirror this view, where the new owners of the entity are expected to implement their codes of conduct, update their gift and hospitality policies, and provide training to directors, employees, and relevant third parties of the newly acquired entity.

In real-world situations, the integration of an acquired company is often inconsistent, particularly when the targets operate with informal networks or lack transparency in their local business practices (Norton Rose Fulbright, 2020). Local management may resist adoption of stricter ethical standards for fear of losing contracts that rely on 'relationship-based' decision-making, and/or may not have the resources to adopt new ethical standards (Financier Worldwide, 2022). If former corrupt activities are allowed to continue for any length of time, the new owner will be liable for the actions of the previous owner (the principle of successor liability) and the reputational harm that results from this liability will be very acute, damaging the potential of M&A to positively contribute to the strengthening of institutions and to the United Nations Sustainable Development Goal 16 (Debevoise & Plimpton, 2018).

Systemic Implications for SDG 16

From the lens of SDG 16, the issue of corruption in mergers and acquisitions transcends being an internal issue within a company's corporate governance and acts as a systemic threat to public institutions and development outcomes. M&A deals that continue to perpetuate the acts of bribery in public procurement or licensing are effectively taking money from the general public and allocating it to the private sector, thereby limiting resources available to provide for public health care, public education, and the establishment of public infrastructure (DLA Piper, 2022). Further, they create networks of favoritism and protect individuals engaged in corrupt behavior, making it difficult for companies acting in good faith to be competitive, eroding trust in both government entities and free market systems, and undermining the law and the rule of law.

On the other hand, strong anti-bribery compliance due diligence conducted by acquirers as well as effective post-acquisition remediation will create various positive spillover effects on governance systems. Where the acquirer insists upon using clean contracts, transparency throughout the M&A process, as well as internal controls that are effective and credible, then the acquirer is creating a new floor and increasing expectations for corporate conduct, even in high-risk jurisdictions. Therefore, the acquisition of a company at the M&A stage creates an opportunity to either further strengthen the corrupt equilibrium or provide a means for incremental changes to be made in creating stronger institutional integrity that is in alignment with SDG 16's targets on reducing corruption (Target 16.5) and creating effective, accountable institutions (Target 16.6).

Towards Risk-Responsive Ethical Governance in M&A

To address corruption risk and ethical issues when acquiring companies, we need to shift from reactive compliance to proactive risk management throughout the entire M&A process. An approach like this that incorporates ABC factors from the start of the deal through to successful integration will treat material red flags as strategic priorities requiring Board involvement and incorporate SDG 16 transparency, accountability, and justice principles into corporate M&A policies. Additionally, this approach will require close coordination of legal, finance, compliance, and sustainability teams to ensure that the governance of ethics is pursued as a value-creating service rather than an obstacle to completing transactions.

International developments such as updates to the OECD Anti-Bribery Recommendations and changes to the way the US Foreign Corrupt Practices Act places successor liability on companies are raising expectations via increased clarity around risk-based due diligence, third-party monitoring and post-acquisition integration. This creates opportunities for academics, regulators and practitioners to create an incentive structure and system of accountability so that ethical M&A are not only viewed as a legal responsibility, but also as a source of competitive advantage and institutional resilience, thus creating alignment between private consolidations with public aspirations found in SDG 16.

REGULATORY AND GOVERNANCE FRAMEWORKS FOR ANTI-CORRUPTION COMPLIANCE IN M&A

Mergers and acquisitions have traditionally been governed by corporate law, securities regulations, and competition policy. All issues of corruption and ethics have historically taken a secondary role in the requirements of disclosure and fiduciary obligations. However, as domestic firms increasingly engage in cross-border M&A, there has been a growing emphasis on anti-corruption law and corporate governance elements of M&A. This is due, in part, to both the rapid rise in cross-border M&A over the last 20 years, and the increasing focus on the role of M&A as vehicles for continuing corruption and fraud, as seen in recent high-profile enforcement actions. In addition, the emergence of SDG 16 has created a framework for economic activity that includes the creation of an effective, accountable and transparent institution, and the expectation of significant reductions in corruption and bribery (as outlined in Targets 16.5 and 16.6).

This shift in perspective towards M&A regulation through the lens of SDG 16 creates a broader understanding of the impact of corporate consolidations on the rule of law and public confidence in corporations. M&A laws, regulations and codes of governance collectively establish the expected ranges of acceptable behavior of companies seeking regulatory approvals, companies that engage with government officials, and companies that acquire opaque business models through acquisitions. At the same time, these laws, regulations and codes of governance provide a more robust definition of the expectations for transparency, whistleblower protections and board oversight, and in this way support the overall normative project of building institutions with integrity and justice.

International Anti-Corruption Instruments and Their Relevance for M&A

Three important global frameworks provide insights into the backdrop of the anti-corruption landscape surrounding M&A's: 1) The United Nations Convention Against Corruption (UNCAC), 2) The Organization for Economic Co-operation and Development Anti-Bribery Convention and its re-endorsement in 2021, and 3) The United Nations Guiding Principles on Business and Human Rights (UNGP). The United Nations Convention Against Corruption was established in 2003 with near-universal adherence among all nations. It establishes a variety of obligations that state parties must fulfill, including passing laws to criminalize the bribery of foreign and domestic officials, taking preventive actions to limit corruption, and improving integrity within both public and private sectors. Specifically, Article 12 requires state parties to establish measures to prevent private sector corruption, such as through promoting internal audit processes, requiring due diligence, and implementing transparency of the ownership of natural and legal persons for all public entities. These developments in article 12 directly reflect many of the governments' expectations for proper corporate governance standards and appropriate financial reporting for the purposes of mergers and acquisitions.

While the OECD's Convention on Combating Bribery of Foreign Public Officials and the OECD's 2021 recommendations for combating foreign corrupt practices will be limited to members of OECD, or certain countries who have signed on to the treaty, the Convention continues to have significant implications due to its focus on the supply-side of international bribery and its extensive mechanism of monitoring. With the publication of the 2021 recommendations for further combating bribery, the OECD has updated its previous recommendations with an emphasis placed on: 1) The importance of risk-based due diligence; 2) Corporate liability; and 3) That corporations cannot escape accountability for engaging in corrupt practices by using mergers or acquisitions or any other methods to change their corporate identity. It also highlights mergers and acquisitions as specific contexts in which states should encourage comprehensive due diligence and robust compliance integration.

The UNGPs are related to mergers and acquisitions in that they require businesses or companies to perform human-rights due diligence on all aspects of the business and any relationships it has with third parties, including in the context of corporate mergers and acquisitions. Some governments have started to propose legislation making it mandatory for companies to undertake human-rights due diligence as well as environmental due diligence in their business operations, based on the UNGPs, and include consideration of corruption-related risks as part of the overall integration with other issues which negatively impact people and the planet through the process of M&A.

National Anti-Corruption Regimes and Extraterritorial Effects

Anti-corruption laws are necessary for compliance with international norms and are enforced at the national level in terms of M&A. U.S. FCPA and U.K. Bribery Act 2010 are considered standards as both regimes establish broad jurisdictional reach as well as standards for corporate liability. Under the FCPA, the issuers and domestic concerns can be held liable for bribery relating to takeover entities when there is continued misconduct after closing and/or when the acquiring party has not complied with timely remediation. Enforcement actions of guidance issued by the U.S. Government places emphasis on both thorough due diligences performed pre-acquisition and continued integration post-acquisition as mitigating factors. As for the U.K. Bribery Act, its corporate offence of failure to prevent bribery exposes commercial organizations to liability for bribery by individuals associated with them including subsidiaries and joint ventures.

In India, the anti-corruption environment affecting M&A activity is established by the Prevention of Corruption Act 1988, specific regulations and the corporate governance reform of the Companies Act 2013. Under Section 177 of the Companies Act, certain companies are required to have an audit committee, as well as a documented procedure for establishing vigilance mechanisms for directors and employees to make complaints, with protections from victimization and direct access to the audit committee chair. The Securities and Exchange Board of India (SEBI) Listing Obligations and the regulations surrounding Corporate Governance also serve to underscore the accountability of a company's Board to supervise, maintain Internal Controls, investigate allegations of fraud, and safeguard Whistleblowers as they relate to the major acquisition of another company. This trend is amplified by similar activity occurring in other countries through legislative changes associated with corporate criminal liability as dictated by the OECD Anti-Bribery Convention. The result is a tendency toward a converging approach. Corporate growth through the mechanism of mergers and acquisitions will be accompanied by the adoption of strong anti-corruption policies and by the establishment of effective supervisory structures within the Companies themselves. (Karavadi, 2014)

Corporate Governance Codes, ESG Standards and Soft-law Expectations

In addition to statutory obligations, corporate governance codes, regulatory frameworks, including stock-exchange rules, and environmentally focused (ESG)-driven standards have a considerable influence on the way businesses govern their approach to M&A compliance with respect to anti-corruption legislation. Examples of this would be the OECD Principles on Corporate Governance; the stewardship codes for institutional investors; and the guidance provided by national governance codes all emphasize the role of boards of directors in managing operational and financial risks, implementing a robust internal control system, and creating an ethos of ethical business conduct and compliance. In India, for example, SEBI's Listing Obligations and Disclosure Requirements (LODR) Governance Norms place particular emphasis on the role of independent directors, audit committees, and the use of vigil mechanisms to oversee acquisition-target due diligence and monitor management misconduct with respect to acquisition risks. (Singhal & Sharma, 2024)

The ESG reporting framework and sustainability indices further strengthen the ESG expectations placed upon companies regarding their anti-corruption programs, their record of anti-corruption program failures, and their management of non-compliance risk. Likewise, the United Nations Office on Drugs and Crime (UNODC) and the UN Global Compact, through initiatives like Principle 10 of the Global Compact and joint programs promoting business integrity, encourage companies to develop codes of conduct, compliance programs, and collective-action initiatives against corruption. This scrutiny by responsible investing funds and rating agencies will give rise to other pressure points and therefore create additional incentives for acquirers to diligently perform the requisite anti-bribery due diligence and respond to red flags when integrating newly acquired entities into their compliance systems and processes, thus creating market-driven incentives for achieving ethical M&A.

Internal Compliance Systems, Controls and Oversight Actors

The methods in which regulatory and soft law expectations affect how companies develop systems for complying with these laws and internal controls on how companies evaluate acquisitions and sales by looking at the number of acquisitions and sales to date. With international guidelines such as the OECD's 2021 anti-bribery recommendations, companies are encouraged to create accessible anti-corruption policies, conduct risk-based due diligence using M&A, establish the ability to make confidential and anonymous reports, and to protect whistleblowers from retaliation. To ensure that corporate compliance with M&A laws, A company's M&A compliance framework must include formal company policies, ABC procedures specific to the target company screening & due diligence process, company policies governing every phase of the M&A process including contractual protections, and formalized training for all deal team members and protocol protocols for post-closing audits and remediation. (Basel Institute on Governance, 2021)

Oversight actors like audit committees, general counsels, chief compliance officers and internal auditors, are critical to carry out and implement the M&A compliance frameworks that guide the decision of whether to move ahead with an M&A transaction. For example, Section 177 of the Companies Act, 2013 requires auditors to provide oversight in relation to enterprises involving all vigil mechanisms and empower whistleblower protection. Additionally, international practice around corporate governance specifies that boards of directors should receive regular updates regarding material ABC found in M&A transactions. Challenge management with respect to their risk appetite. And condition approval for transactions based on the promised implementation of corrective action plans.

Furthermore, UNCAC and OECD instruments set forth the international norms to comply with the prevention and tasks of corporate accountability and integrity. FCPA and UK Bribery Act transform the concerns into realizable corporate risks with extensive cross-border implications. Indian framework consists of the mix of anti-corruption laws, supervisory and audit structure, disclosure, and monitoring tools. ESG and soft-laws mark yet another layer of compliance making sure the value of corporate integrity is stressed for investors and stakeholders even when there is no direct liability. Hence, the literature should not be seen as indicating the presence of specific regulatory instruments, rather it demonstrates steps toward lifecycle governance, meaning that the goals of prevention, monitoring, reporting, and accountability are not isolated. However, there are still differences in the intensity of enforcement, rules of successor liability, protection of whistleblowers, and institutional effectiveness, thus regulatory arbitrage is possible.

Governance Gaps and Emerging Reform Directions

Even though there are numerous legal and soft law systems governing M&A, there are still significant gaps in how these systems approach M&A from an anti-corruption perspective. Not only has enforcement experience and investigative reporting shown that many acquirers still view the completion of anti-bribery due diligence as a mere formality, but many do not take the appropriate remedial actions with respect to serious red flags discovered during that due diligence process, and in many cases allow preexisting corrupt practices to flourish during the lengthy integration process between the acquirer and the acquired. There are numerous jurisdictional variances among countries in terms of their corporate liability standards, resource allocation for enforcement, and protection of whistleblowers, which provides a platform for the governance arbitrage by which acquirers shift their higher-risk activities from jurisdictions with enhanced regulation to those with lesser regulatory environments or attempt to conceal those activities within complex corporate structures that lack transparency. (Screpante, 2021)

Emerging reform efforts seek to fill these gaps by clarifying the legal frameworks that govern successor liability for multi-national corporations, embedding risk-based integrity due diligence into an acquirer's statutory duty of care obligations, and increasing the expectation for post-acquisition remediation of violations and reporting of violations to the government. The OECD's 2021 Anti-Bribery Recommendations request that all states adopt laws that require corporations to conduct risk-based due diligence as part of the M&A process, prevent corporations from evading liability their pre-merger activity by (a) merging with another corporation, or (b) changing the corporate identity of the corporation, and (c) improve the protections provided to individuals who report violations. In addition, there are legislative initiatives in some parts of the world to mandate the conduct by corporations of human rights and environmental due diligence, which suggests a growing desire to adopt more holistic models of responsible corporate conduct that address corruption as a risk factor in addition to ESG risks. Properly implemented, these developments can reinforce SDG 16 by making integrity a non-negotiable component of corporate consolidation and by aligning private-sector growth strategies with the public interest in just, accountable, and transparent institutions.

INTEGRATING ETHICAL GOVERNANCE INTO M&A STRATEGYINTEGRATING ETHICAL GOVERNANCE INTO M&A STRATEGY

When mergers and acquisitions have ethical governance integrated into the process it begins by re-defining what integrity means; it should no longer just be considered a compliance cost, but rather an essential component of establishing long term value and legitimacy for the company (Crane & Matten, 2021). The boards of organizations that view anti-corruption and governance risks as part of the business case for M&A transactions, are much more likely to develop their transaction diligence processes from target screening through to post-integration with the objective of protecting or enhancing trust and institutional resilience (OECD, 2021). This is very much aligned with the objectives of SDG 16, which holds that peace, justice and strong institutions are prerequisites for, not mere by-products of, sustainable development (United Nations, 2015).

In terms of the strategic implications of ethical governance in M&A, ethical governance impacts at least three areas: risk, reputation, and relational capital. First, through the application of rigorous screening for integrity issues, organizations minimize their exposure to enforcement, debarments and significant remediation expenses, which can totally erode deal value. Second, organizations that have well established and visible ethical standards tend to have enhanced reputations with regulators, investors, and civil society. This is especially relevant given the recent rise in ESG Investors, who have adopted a rigorous stance on anti-corruption performance. Third, consistent, responsible acquisition practices enhance relationships between organizations and the public authorities and communities. Partnerships between organizations and governments, and between organizations and communities create a more predictable environment for future M&A transactions and indirectly contribute to the institutional aspects of SDG 16.

Embedding Ethics in Deal Origination and Target Selection

The integration of ethical considerations into the development of an acquisition strategy should be made as early as possible in the company's lifecycle (Norton Rose Fulbright, 2020). The company's ethical integration governance strategy should place potential integrity criteria as part of the assessment of potential targets based on risk appetite. For example, companies may apply additional due diligence when assessing targets for acquisitions within jurisdictions affected by state capture or exclude counterparties who work primarily through dirty agents or politically tied intermediaries (Norton Rose Fulbright, 2020). Transparency International UK (2012) notes that there are now recommended anti-bribery guides that include high-level country and sector corruption scores along with an organization's internal risk matrix as an ethical filter on top of a commercial or financial filter when completing an acquisition assessment.

Ethical Governance must also include an examination of how new acquisition opportunities originate during the origination phase of a potential acquisition. For example, an acquisition opportunity could be identified via close relationships with government officials, exclusive license access, or an urgent request that required a timely response indicating involvement in a long-term corrupt network (Agence Française Anticorruption, 2021). Deal authors should be trained to view these scenarios as red flags and escalate them to the compliance/risk committee for review, rather than viewing them as a competitive advantage. In these situations, extending awareness of red flags to the origination workflow of the company can help an organization avoid opportunistically entering a high-risk acquisition, thereby reducing the likelihood of establishing a corrupt equilibrium when acquiring in sensitive markets.

Designing Robust Ethical Due Diligence and Decision-making

Ethical governance is established with the identification of a potential transaction and the execution of a due diligence process by the board or committee that reviews the findings (Arnold and Porter, 2011). A strong ethical due diligence structure should include a risk-based and multi-disciplinary approach, which incorporates legal and financial analysis, forensic accounting, compliance assessment, and, in appropriate cases, discreet reputational inquiries (Handley, 2012). The structure of ethical due diligence determines where the target has potential exposure to corruption through its business model, including public-sector contacts, high-risk third parties, cash-intensive operations, and prior investigations, sanctions, or credible media allegations.

The ethical governance of a company also requires that the outputs of a due diligence assessment be presented to decisionmakers in such a way that integrity risks are highlighted, rather than being buried in technical appendices. Ethical governance requires that board or deal of committee summaries highlight serious corruption findings, describe likely enforcement and successor liability scenarios, and specify reasonable remediation plans, timelines, and costs (OECD, 2021).

The post-merger integration period is usually seen as one of the most important times for ethical governance, as this stage determines the degree to which the acquirer's standards will filter through to the combined company compared to how much the weaker ethical practices of the acquired company will lower the integrity of the entire organization. In the OECD's 2021 Anti-Bribery Recommendation, companies are encouraged to perform a post-acquisition review of the acquired entity about their internal controls and to quickly integrate the acquired entity into their ethics and compliance program. For an integration plan to be successful, it needs to be developed alongside the financial and operational plans, and it needs to have adequate resources to be implemented. Over time, consistent ethics-driven integration can contribute to SDG 16 by strengthening internal institutions, compliance, audit, oversight, and by raising expectations for business conduct in markets where the combined entity operates.

If an M&A transaction is to incorporate ethical governance into the deal-making process, organizations must consider organizational culture, the incentives that incentivize unethical behavior, and how leaders behave. Deal team members may be driven by bonuses for completing a transaction; by the status that comes from closing a deal; or by the opportunity to advance their careers; all of which can create unintentional pressure for team members to ignore or justify their integrity concerns about a merger or acquisition. For incentives to align with ethical outcomes, organizations could explore creating incentives based on variable pay that considers both quantitative measures as well as qualitative measures, such as maintaining adherence to all of the due-diligence procedures and protocols, demonstrating a willingness to work to fix any concerns raised, and not having integrity crises immediately following the closing of a deal.

The leadership of an organization plays a critical role in creating an environment where ethical governance is encouraged. Senior management and board members who continuously communicate to their companies that they can stop a merger or acquisition transaction that fails an ethical test and who visibly support compliance officers and internal audit personnel when they raise ethical and governance-related concerns create an environment for ethical behavior. Conversely, if management communicates ethical behaviors only through policy supplements, while incentivizing executives for taking risks and obscuring what is truly happening in a transaction, then the formal governance process will likely not make an impact. Embedding ethical governance into M&A strategy thus requires a sustained commitment to integrity as part of the organization's identity, linking day-to-day decisions in specific deals to the broader normative horizon of SDG 16, a world in which corporate power reinforces, rather than undermines, peaceful, just and accountable institutions.

POLICY AND PRACTICE PATHWAYS IN M&A

Both markets and institutions utilize trust as the leading form of currency. In addition, M&A transactions offer a very public avenue for either reinforcing or eroding trust. Acquisitions with opaque processes, advantages for insiders, or corrupt practices limit public trust in regulators, the courts, and the overall economic structure, thus undermining SDG 16's goals of promoting justice and strong institutions. Trust exists on multiple levels with respect to M&A: among the merging companies, between companies and regulators, between companies and investors, and between companies and affected communities. Each of these levels is mediated through the decision maker's perception of the company's integrity, whether the decision maker is acting in accordance with law and ethics, whether the company has provided accurate information, and whether the company has lived up to its commitments to mitigate harm to the impacted communities. Therefore, when establishing SDG 16 as an umbrella for direction of activity in this area, it is important to consider each major acquisition as an opportunity to build the institutional trust in which corporate power can create and maintain benefits rather than destroy institutional trust.

Corporate Practice Pathways: Strengthening Internal Institutions

The internal structure of corporations is one way to help develop trust as corporations grow larger and have more complex internal structures. The various levels of governance within the corporation test and monitor the processes associated with M&A. Each level of governance has independent authority, as well as ample resources and support, to challenge executive decisions. At each of these levels of governance, ethical governance should be an integral part of M&A, to reduce the potential for unacceptable corruption, including bribery (Singhal & Sharma 2024).

Concretely, firms seeking to align M&A with SDG 16 can:

- Formalize board-approved M&A ethics policies that articulate risk appetite, escalation triggers and non-negotiable integrity standards.
- Require that high-risk transactions receive explicit sign-off from audit or risk committees, based on comprehensive anti-bribery and corruption due-diligence reports and remediation plans (Lakshmikumaran & Sridharan, 2014).
- Integrate ethics and compliance performance into senior-management and deal-team incentives, so that walking away from tainted deals is professionally rewarded rather than penalized (Crane & Matten, 2021).
- Strengthen vigil mechanisms and internal reporting systems so that employees in both acquirer and target entities can safely disclose concerns about deal-related misconduct, with credible follow-up (Kurthalanathan, 2016).

Additionally, beyond minimizing legal liability, these levels of governance demonstrate to employees, regulators, and investors that they are operating within the constraints of a principled approach to growth and can be trusted, enhancing the trustworthiness of these organizations in connection with the expectations placed on organizations under SDG 16 to have accountable institutions.

Regulatory and Policy Pathways

The second approach is the regulatory and policy mechanisms used to create the environment for M&A transactions. As mentioned in earlier sections, there is a strong framework of expectations in relation to anti-corruption conventions, national legislation, and soft-law standards. However, through the experience of enforcing these standards, there continues to be a lack of clarity in the areas of successor liability, post-acquisition remediation, and integrity due diligence. Closing these gaps will help ensure that M&A does not serve to launder corrupt business models or provide a method of avoiding responsibility through corporate reorganization.

Policy-makers seeking to align M&A regulation with SDG 16 might consider:

- Clarifying, through statute or guidance, how and when acquirers will be held liable for pre-acquisition corruption and which steps, such as robust pre-closing due diligence and timely post-closing integration, will be treated as mitigating factors.
- Encouraging or requiring risk-based integrity due diligence in significant transactions, potentially as part of broader mandatory due-diligence regimes covering human-rights, environmental and governance risks.
- Strengthening whistleblower protection and reporting channels, including safe options for employees in target companies to alert authorities or the acquirer about corruption risks without fear of retaliation.
- Enhancing coordination between competition, securities and anti-corruption authorities so that high-risk M&A deals receive integrated scrutiny rather than fragmented review.

Such reforms can reduce uncertainty for responsible acquirers while increasing the costs and unpredictability of attempts to use M&A to shield or perpetuate corrupt practices, thus contributing directly to SDG 16's goals of reducing corruption and building effective institutions

Multi-Stakeholder Collaboration and Collective Action

The third path to creating trust around SDG 16, in the M&A context, maintains that neither corporations nor regulators are responsible for developing an ecosystem of trust by themselves. To build that ecosystem of trust, many diverse stakeholders must be involved in monitoring M&A activities, establishing the standards around what constitutes good business practices and supporting the creation of new M&A practices that increase integrity. There are numerous multi-stakeholder initiatives active in building an ecosystem of trust in the M&A arena. These multi-stakeholder initiatives may focus on business integrity, responsible investment, and/or transparency/reliability across a specific sector. The collaborative nature of these multi-stakeholder initiatives may create a shared set of business integrity standards to help alleviate the competitive disadvantage faced by companies that wish to adhere to a higher ethical standard in their M&A practices.

Increasingly, investors have signaled a strong preference for those acquirers that have strong processes and procedures in place to conduct robust due diligence and integrate acquired companies. Investors may engage or divest from an acquirer that participates in a continued pattern of high-risk M&A transactions without having adequate safeguards in place for protecting their investment. Civil society organizations and investigative journalists can investigate high-profile M&A transactions, highlighting governance issues raised and advocating for increased disclosure of beneficial ownership interests, political connections and potential public interests stemming from these transactions. International organizations such as the OECD, UNODC and United Nations Global Compact hold conferences and provide guidance on lessons learned from M&A enforcement actions as well as best practices. Together, these various stakeholders are creating an environment in which integrity-based M&A activities will become increasingly observable and ultimately rewarded, consistent with the SDG 16 emphasis on transparency and participatory governance.

Towards a Normative Framework of SDG-Aligned M&A

Drawing on the analysis in previous chapters, a normative framework for SDG-aligned M&A would position ethical governance and anti-corruption commitments as constitutive features of legitimate transactions rather than optional add-ons. At a minimum, such a framework would require that the strategic rationale for major acquisitions can be assessed not only in financial terms but also for compatibility with the company's human-rights, environmental and governance commitments, including SDG 16. Integrity due diligence be conducted on a risk-based bases for all significant deals, with transparent reporting to boards and, where material, appropriate external disclosure of identified risks and mitigation steps.

The crucial point is to view ethical governance and anti-corruption in M&A as more than simply a risk management practice. They help to create new institutions that align with the Sustainable Development Goals target for SDG. Ethical governance and anti-corruption provide a way for companies to implement Integrity within their growth and development strategies, processes, contractual agreements, and corporate culture. Connecting active corporate practice with the changing legal and soft-law standards associated with ethical governance and anti-corruption allows for collaboration among companies, governments, and civil society to further professionalized and responsible deal making. These collaborative efforts will provide further building institutional trust through the way M&As are conducted.

In addition to establishing trust with respect to SDG 16 as an outcome of specific transactions conducted according to law, ethics, and stakeholders' interests, the concept of building integrity through ethical governance and anti-corruption continues with each instance of ethical governance reinforcing the norms and expectations that create institutional capacity for future misconduct reduction. The way in which ethical governance and anti-corruption fit into the broader framework of corporate governance allows researchers and practitioners working in the field of corporate law and corporate governance to pursue research and public policy agendas based on the new area of focus provided by M&A. The ability to connect researchers and practitioners working on business strategy and sustainable, equitable, and well-governed societies will provide a platform for productive collaboration between the two separate fields.

CONTRIBUTION TO THEORY, PRACTICE AND FUTURE RESEARCH

This chapter offers three interrelated contributions. In theoretical terms, it enhances the knowledge about ethical M&A by presenting corporate activities within a wider institutional-governance context. This shifts the meaning of transparency, anti-corruption measures, and accountability of stakeholders from being only the means of affecting the conduct of corporations toward being the means of influencing the reputation of institutions and trust. In practical terms, the framework of three pillars allows corporate boards, compliance officers, and government representatives to take the principles of integrity into consideration during target picking, due diligence, approval, contracting, integration and reporting. Thus, it transfers ethical governance from a reactive measure to its agenda in M&A.

Future studies based on the model created in this research can generate necessary hypotheses exceeding doctrinal and normative inquiry conducted in this chapter. Empirical research can figure out whether firms using increased integrity due diligence have lesser number of failures in terms of post-acquisition compliance, whether independent board oversight alters judgments regarding high-risk acquisitions, whether SDG-compliant disclosures lead to improved confidence of stakeholders and investors, and whether speedy compliance integration after a merger reduces the risks of successor liability.

REFERENCES

Agence Francaise Anticorruption. (2021). Anti-corruption due diligence for mergers and acquisitions: Practical guide. https://www.agence-francaise-anticorruption.gouv.fr/files/files/Practical%20Guide%202021%20FUSACQ.pdf

Ahlawat., & Associates. (2024). Anti-corruption due diligence in India transactions. https://www.ahlawatassociates.com/blog/anti-corruption-due-diligence-in-india-transactions

Arnold & Porter. (2011). Anti-corruption due diligence in mergers and acquisitions. https://www.arnoldporter.com/-/media/files/perspectives/publications/2011/07/anticorruption-due-diligence-in-mergers-and-acqu__/files/newsletter-item/fileattachment/advisory_anticorruption_due_diligence_in_mergers__.pdf?rev=7c55fc285ac941848313327d92b8df42&sc_lang=en&hash=6EC5DB12BD540827ABEF32AA6D932F54

Basel Institute on Governance. (2021). Recommendation of the Council for OECD Further Combating Bribery of Foreign Public Officials in International Business Transactions (2021 Anti-Bribery Recommendation). *OECD*. https://baselgovernance.org/publications/recommendation-council-oecd-further-combating-bribery-foreign-public-officials

Bozos, K., Filatotchev, I., & Goergen, M. (2025). Corporate governance, finance, and global strategy. *International Business Review*, *34*(6), 102499. DOI: 10.1016/j.ibusrev.2025.102499

Crane, A., & Matten, D. (2021). *Business ethics: Managing corporate citizenship and sustainability in the age of globalization*. Oxford University Press., https://global.oup.com/academic/product/business-ethics-9780198810070?cc=in&lang=

Debevoise & Plimpton. (2018). FCPA update: Successor liability and post-acquisition risk. https://www.debevoise.com/~/media/files/insights/publications/2018/12/201812_fcpa_update_december_2018.pdf

Donaldson, T., & Walsh, J. P. (2015). Toward a theory of business ethics and governance. *Academy of Management Review*, *40*(3), 436–457. https://repository.upenn.edu/handle/20.500.14332/38342

Handley, M. (2012). Anti-corruption due diligence in M&A. *Gibson Dunn*. https://www.gibsondunn.com/wp-content/uploads/documents/publications/Handley-AntiCorruptionDueDiligenceInMA.pdf

Karavadi, A. K. (2014). Committees under the Companies Act, 2013. *Lakshmikumaran Sridharan Attorneys*. https://www.lakshmisri.com/insights/articles/committees-under-the-companies-act-2013/#

Khare, P. (2025). Integrating the SDGs Into Corporate Governance: A Legal Imperative for Global Sustainability. *IGI Global*, 391-416. https://doi.org/DOI: 10.4018/979-8-3373-4192-7.ch015

Kurthalanathan, C. S. M. (2016). Whistle-Blowing/ Vigil Mechanism Under Companies Act, 2013. *Taxguru*. https://taxguru.in/company-law/whistleblowing-vigil-mechanism-companies-act-2013.html

Levy, B. (2024). Global M&A Industry Trends. *PWC*. https://www.pwc.com/gx/en/services/deals/trends/2024.html

Norton Rose Fulbright. (2020). Divergent diligence? Uncovering M&A anti-corruption risks. https://www.nortonrosefulbright.com/en-in/knowledge/publications/9b8dfb45/divergent-diligence-uncovering-ma-anticorruption-risks-in-asia-pacific

OECD. (2017). OECD guidelines for multinational enterprises. *OECD Publishing*. https://www.oecd.org/en/publications/2017/07/oecd-transfer-pricing-guidelines-for-multinational-enterprises-and-tax-administrations-2017_g1g71100.html

Phillips, T. (2015). The federal common law of successor liability and the FCPA. *William & Mary Business Law Review, 6*(1). https://scholarship.law.wm.edu/wmblr/vol6/iss1/4/

Piper, D. L. A. (2022). The new OECD Anti-Bribery Recommendation. https://www.dlapiper.com/en/insights/publications/global-anti-corruption-perspective/global-anticorruption-perspective-q1-2022/the-new-oecd-anti-bribery-recommendation

Screpante, M. S. (2021). OECD anti-bribery convention. Implications on corporate criminal liability in Latin America. *Business Law Review*, *42*(1), 26–38. DOI: 10.54648/BULA2021003

SEBI. (2021). Business responsibility and sustainability reporting guidelines. Securities and Exchange Board of India. https://www.sebi.gov.in/legal/circulars/may-2021/business-responsibility-and-sustainability-reporting-by-listed-entities_50096.html

Singhal, A., & Sharma, K. (2024). Companies Act 2013, Procedures for constitution of audit committee and vigil mechanism policy. *Lawrbit*. https://www.lawrbit.com/companies-act-procedures/constitution-of-audit-committee-and-vigil-mechanism-policy/

Stephenson, M. (2021). The new FCPA Resource Guide wisely suggests a more flexible approach to successor liability. *Global Anticorruption Blog*. https://globalanticorruptionblog.com/2021/02/15/the-new-fcpa-resource-guide-wisely-suggests-a-more-flexible-approach-to-successor-liability/

Transparency International UK. (2012). Anti-bribery due diligence for transactions. https://archive.transparency.org.uk/sites/default/files/pdf/publications/Anti-Bribery_Due_Diligence_for_Transactions_1.pdf

United Nations. (2015). Transforming our world: The 2030 Agenda for Sustainable Development. https://sdgs.un.org/2030agenda

U.S. Department of Justice. (2008). Siemens AG and Three Subsidiaries Plead Guilty to Foreign Corrupt Practices Act Violations and Agree to Pay $450 Million in Combined Criminal Fines. https://www.justice.gov/archive/opa/pr/2008/December/08-crm-1105.html

Williams, N., Ved, K., & Lim, N. (2022). Anti-bribery, corruption and risk diligence recommendations for M&A activity in Asia. *Financier Worldwide*. https://www.financierworldwide.com/anti-bribery-corruption-and-risk-diligence-recommendations-for-ma-activity-in-asia

Chapter 4
Strategic Value Creation in Digital Post-Merger Integration: The STC Solutions-Devoteam Middle East Acquisition

Afef Amdouni
http://orcid.org/0000-0001-9625-300X
Taibah University, Saudi Arabia

ABSTRACT

Digital transformation has increased the strategic importance of technological capabilities and knowledge-intensive services, leading firms to use mergers and acquisitions to accelerate digital capability development. This chapter examines how strategic value may emerge during digital post-merger integration through the acquisition of Devoteam Middle East by solutions by stc. Using a qualitative case-based analytical approach drawing on publicly available corporate and industry sources, the analysis identifies the mechanisms through which acquired digital capabilities are integrated and expanded. The findings suggest that value creation depends on stabilizing specialized human capital, aligning technological and organizational structures, and scaling capabilities through hybrid organizational arrangements.

1. INTRODUCTION

Over the past decade, digital transformation has moved from being a peripheral organizational initiative to becoming a central strategic imperative. Across industries, firms are under increasing pressure to build digital capabilities, redesign service

DOI: 10.4018/979-8-3373-5233-6.ch004

architectures, and respond to technological discontinuities that reshape both competition and value creation. Recent research shows that digital transformation influences firms' innovation performance, internal control systems, resource allocation, and strategic repositioning, making it a critical driver of organizational adaptation in turbulent environments (Fang & Liu, 2024; Tangwaragorn et al., 2024; Li & Li, 2026; Wang et al., 2024). At the same time, the growing complexity of digital technologies has made internal capability development slower and more uncertain, encouraging firms to seek external routes to transformation.

Within this context, mergers and acquisitions have become an increasingly important strategic mechanism for obtaining advanced technological capabilities, specialized talent, and access to new knowledge domains. In particular, digital mergers and acquisitions have attracted growing scholarly attention because they differ in important ways from traditional transactions focused primarily on market share, scale, or cost synergies. Digital acquisitions are often motivated by the need to access intangible assets such as analytics capabilities, cloud expertise, cybersecurity knowledge, software architectures, and digitally enabled service models (Maisenhelder et al., 2025; Chen & Liu, 2025; Firk et al., 2025). Research further suggests that digitalization can shape acquisition behavior itself by facilitating international expansion, improving innovation capabilities, and reducing managerial constraints associated with complex strategic moves (Wang et al., 2024; Tao et al., 2026).

While digital acquisitions provide access to valuable technological capabilities, their strategic outcomes remain uncertain. Yet the acquisition of digital assets does not automatically generate value. Indeed, one of the central tensions in the mergers and acquisitions literature is that firms frequently acquire strategically attractive targets but struggle to realize the value anticipated at the time of the deal. This tension becomes even more pronounced in digital acquisitions, where the acquired value often resides not in easily transferable physical assets but in embedded knowledge, professional expertise, organizational routines, and relational networks. Recent work has shown that the outcomes of digital M&A can vary considerably. Under some conditions, digital acquisitions enhance innovation and create positive market signals; under others, they may produce overvaluation, integration friction, or disappointing post-acquisition performance (Firk et al., 2025; Maisenhelder et al., 2025; Chen & Liu, 2025). The strategic problem, therefore, is not simply whether digital acquisitions occur, but how value is created—or eroded—during the post-merger integration phase.

Post-merger integration (PMI) has long been recognized as a decisive stage in determining acquisition outcomes (Haspeslagh & Jemison, 1991; Birkinshaw et al., 2000; Safavi, 2021). It is during PMI that firms attempt to coordinate structures, combine systems, align routines, and preserve or recombine critical capabilities. Prior studies have shown that integration processes can influence innovation upgrading, organizational adaptation, and the longer-term developmental trajectory of the combined firm (Safavi, 2021; Chen et al., 2022; Meglio et al., 2025). More specifically, PMI in knowledge-intensive settings involves a delicate balance between integration and preservation: too much absorption may damage the very capabilities that motivated the acquisition, while too little integration may prevent the acquiring firm from scaling and leveraging those capabilities strategically.

This challenge is especially salient in digital capability acquisitions. Digital transformation initiatives often fail not because firms lack technology investments, but because they struggle to align technologies with organizational processes, human capabilities, and broader strategic priorities (Oludapo et al., 2024; Tangwaragorn et al., 2024). In knowledge-intensive acquisitions, the central issue is therefore not only resource possession, but also the capacity to integrate, coordinate, and redeploy newly acquired capabilities without destroying their underlying value. This requires attention to multiple interdependent dimensions, including human capital retention, technological compatibility, governance structures, and cross-unit coordination.

Several theoretical perspectives are useful for analyzing this problem. The Resource-Based View (RBV) suggests that firms can gain advantage when they access valuable, rare, and difficult-to-imitate resources, including expertise and organizational know-how. From this perspective, acquisitions can function as vehicles for securing strategic assets that would be difficult to build internally within a comparable timeframe. However, RBV alone offers only a partial explanation, because value does not arise from resource ownership in isolation. It also depends on the firm's capacity to mobilize and deploy those resources in productive ways.

This is where the dynamic capabilities perspective becomes particularly relevant. Dynamic capabilities emphasize the ability of firms to sense opportunities, seize them, and reconfigure organizational resources under changing conditions. In digital environments characterized by rapid technological shifts, capability reconfiguration becomes central to organizational survival and growth. Recent studies link digital transformation to improved innovation, adaptive performance, and knowledge transfer by showing how digitization enables firms to reorganize internal processes and strengthen strategic responsiveness (Feng & Liu, 2024; Liu et al., 2026; Fang & Liu, 2024). When viewed through this lens, PMI is not merely an integration task; it is a capability reconfiguration process through which acquired assets are selectively preserved, recombined, and scaled.

A third useful lens is strategic alignment, which draws attention to the fit between organizational structures, technological systems, operational routines, and strategic intent. This perspective is especially important in digital settings because value creation increasingly depends on how well firms synchronize platforms, processes, and knowledge flows across units and partners. Studies in adjacent digital domains have shown that platform alignment, process synchronization, and governance arrangements can have a direct effect on relational value creation and inter-organizational performance (Wu et al., 2026). Similarly, research on digital HR strategy and digital leadership indicates that performance gains emerge when technological change is aligned with organizational design and human capability systems rather than pursued as a stand-alone technical initiative (Ruiz et al., 2024; Bellis et al., 2024). Applied to acquisitions, this suggests that integration success depends on more than strategic intent; it requires the alignment of acquired capabilities with the acquiring firm's broader organizational architecture.

Although these perspectives have each contributed important insights, the literature remains fragmented in at least two respects. First, much of the research on digital transformation focuses on innovation outcomes, strategic repositioning, or digital readiness at the firm level, rather than on the organizational mechanics of integrating acquired digital capabilities after a transaction has occurred (Fang & Liu, 2024; Tangwaragorn et al., 2024). Second, the mergers and acquisitions literature has only recently begun to address digital M&A as a distinct category of transaction with its own valuation challenges, knowledge dynamics, and integration risks (Firk et al., 2025; Maisenhelder et al., 2025). As a result, we still know relatively little about how strategic value is actually generated during the integration of acquired digital capabilities, particularly in emerging-market contexts where institutional priorities, digital policy agendas, and organizational ecosystems may shape integration conditions differently from those in Western settings.

This gap is important for both theoretical and practical reasons. Theoretically, it points to the need for a more integrated explanation of how resource acquisition, organizational reconfiguration, and alignment processes interact during digital PMI. Practically, it matters because firms in emerging digital economies increasingly pursue acquisition-led strategies to accelerate their positioning in cloud services, cybersecurity, data-driven operations, and digital consulting. Such strategies are particularly visible in regions where state-backed digital agendas and market modernization efforts create strong incentives for firms to expand beyond traditional business models.

The acquisition of a stake in Devoteam Middle East by solutions by stc offers a useful context through which to examine these issues. Announced as part of the company's strategic expansion into digital consulting and transformation services, the case provides an illustrative example of digital capability acquisition in an emerging market setting. The transaction reflects a broader strategic shift in which large regional players seek to strengthen their digital consulting and transformation capabilities by acquiring specialized firms with strong expertise in cloud, cybersecurity, and digital advisory services. As such, the case is analytically valuable not because it "proves" a theory, but because it illustrates how the integration of digital capabilities may unfold within an emerging technology ecosystem.

Accordingly, this chapter addresses the following research question:

How can strategic value emerge during the post-merger integration of digital capability acquisitions?

To answer this question, the chapter adopts a qualitative case-based analytical approach. It uses publicly available corporate and industry materials to examine how the STC Solutions–Devoteam Middle East transaction can be interpreted through the combined lenses of RBV, dynamic capabilities, and strategic alignment. The aim is not to test causal claims statistically, but to identify the mechanisms through which value creation may occur during digital post-merger integration.

The chapter makes three contributions. First, it offers a conceptually integrated reading of digital PMI by linking resource acquisition, capability reconfiguration, and organizational alignment within a single analytical frame. Second, it extends discussion of digital acquisitions into an underexamined regional context by focusing on a Middle Eastern technology market characterized by rapid digital expansion and capability-seeking growth strategies. Third, it provides practical insight into the organizational conditions that may support value creation after acquisition, particularly with respect to human capital stabilization, capability preservation, and cross-structural coordination.

The remainder of the chapter is organized as follows. The next section reviews the relevant literature on digital capability acquisitions, post-merger integration, and the theoretical perspectives that inform the analysis. The chapter then presents the analytical framework and research design, followed by a case-based examination of the STC Solutions–Devoteam Middle East acquisition. The final sections discuss the broader implications of the case for theory and practice and conclude by outlining limitations and directions for future research.

2. LITERATURE REVIEW AND THEORETICAL FOUNDATIONS

2.1 Digital Transformation and Capability Development

Digital transformation has fundamentally reshaped how firms create, deliver, and capture value. Organizations increasingly rely on digital technologies to enhance innovation capabilities, optimize operational efficiency, and develop new business models that integrate data, platforms, and network-based services. Empirical research shows that digital transformation can significantly enhance firms' innovation capacity by improving resource allocation, strengthening internal control mechanisms, and enabling collaborative knowledge creation (Fang & Liu, 2024; Li & Li, 2026; Tangwaragorn et al., 2024). Similarly, the digital economy has been shown to promote high-quality firm development by facilitating technological breakthroughs, industrial upgrading, and improved productivity (Li & Li, 2026).

Beyond operational improvements, digital transformation also influences firms' strategic decision-making processes. In particular, the adoption of digital technologies has been associated with changes in corporate diversification strategies, international expansion, and innovation investment patterns (Tao et al., 2026). These transformations reflect the increasing importance of knowledge-intensive capabilities in modern competition. Firms must integrate technological expertise, organizational learning, and strategic coordination to remain competitive in digital ecosystems characterized by rapid technological change.

However, the development of digital capabilities internally can be both costly and time-consuming. As technological complexity increases, many firms choose to acquire external capabilities through strategic partnerships, alliances, or mergers and acquisitions. Digital mergers and acquisitions have therefore emerged as a prominent strategy for firms seeking to accelerate technological upgrading and gain access to specialized expertise (Maisenhelder et al., 2025). In such transactions, the primary motivation is often the acquisition of intangible assets such as knowledge, digital infrastructure, analytics capabilities, and specialized human capital rather than traditional physical assets.

Research has further shown that digitalization itself can facilitate acquisition strategies. Firms with higher levels of digital maturity are more likely to engage in cross-border mergers and acquisitions because digital technologies enhance innovation capabilities and reduce managerial uncertainty in strategic decision-making (Wang et al., 2024). Similarly, digital transformation can increase firms' ability to integrate new knowledge and technological resources, making acquisitions more effective tools for strategic renewal (Chen & Liu, 2025).

Despite these advantages, digital acquisitions also introduce significant risks. The valuation of digital firms is often uncertain because technological capabilities are difficult to measure and future technological trajectories remain unpredictable. As a result, managerial decision-making may be influenced by cognitive biases or technological hype, leading firms to overestimate the value of potential targets and pay excessive acquisition premiums (Firk et al., 2025). These challenges highlight the importance of examining not only the motivations behind digital acquisitions but also the mechanisms through which value is realized after the transaction.

2.2 Digital Mergers and Acquisitions and Strategic Value Creation

The relationship between mergers and acquisitions and value creation has long been debated in the strategic management literature. While acquisitions can provide firms with access to new markets, resources, and capabilities, empirical evidence suggests that many transactions fail to generate the expected performance improvements. This paradox has led scholars to focus increasingly on the processes through which acquisitions create—or destroy—value.

In the context of digital industries, acquisitions often serve as vehicles for technological upgrading and innovation expansion. Recent research indicates that digital M&A activity can stimulate innovation investment within firms and across supply chains, particularly when knowledge transfer mechanisms are effectively implemented (Chen & Liu, 2025). Such acquisitions may strengthen innovation ecosystems by facilitating the diffusion of technological knowledge and enabling firms to leverage complementary capabilities.

Nevertheless, digital acquisitions can produce heterogeneous outcomes. Some transactions generate positive market reactions and long-term innovation benefits, while others lead to integration difficulties and disappointing financial performance (Maisenhelder et al., 2025). The variability of these outcomes suggests that value creation in digital M&A depends on contextual and organizational factors beyond the transaction itself.

Recent conceptual work has proposed that mergers and acquisitions should be understood not merely as bilateral transactions between two firms but as processes embedded within broader service and innovation ecosystems. From this perspective, value is co-created through interactions among multiple actors—including organizations, institutions, and technological platforms—rather than generated solely within the boundaries of the acquiring firm (Meglio et al., 2025). This ecosystem perspective highlights the importance of understanding how acquisitions reshape networks of knowledge exchange, technological collaboration, and resource integration.

In digital contexts, these dynamics become particularly important because technological capabilities often depend on platform infrastructures, innovation networks, and collaborative ecosystems. Consequently, the strategic value of digital acquisitions may emerge not only from the resources directly acquired but also from the acquiring firm's ability to position itself within evolving digital ecosystems.

2.3 Post-Merger Integration in Knowledge-Intensive Contexts

While acquisitions may provide access to valuable capabilities, the realization of strategic value depends largely on the effectiveness of post-merger integration processes. PMI involves coordinating organizational structures, aligning technological systems, integrating teams, and harmonizing operational processes between the acquiring and acquired organizations.

Research on PMI has increasingly emphasized the importance of organizational routines, knowledge integration, and social dynamics in shaping integration outcomes.

For example, Safavi (2021) demonstrates that the compatibility of organizational routines can significantly influence the success of integration processes. When routines embedded in the acquired organization conflict with those of the acquiring firm, integration may generate resistance or coordination difficulties.

Similarly, research on innovation-oriented acquisitions suggests that post-merger integration can reshape firms' innovation capabilities by facilitating knowledge recombination and network restructuring (Chen et al., 2022). In these contexts, integration is not merely an administrative process but a dynamic organizational transformation through which capabilities are reconfigured.

The challenge becomes even more complex in digital capability acquisitions. Digital expertise is often deeply embedded in teams, professional communities, and technological architectures. As a result, integration efforts must balance two competing objectives: preserving the specialized capabilities of the acquired firm while simultaneously integrating those capabilities into the broader strategic architecture of the acquiring organization.

Scholars frequently describe this tension as the integration–preservation dilemma. Excessive integration may undermine the innovative capacity of the acquired organization by disrupting its knowledge networks or organizational culture. Conversely, insufficient integration may prevent the acquiring firm from leveraging the acquired capabilities at scale.

Understanding how firms navigate this dilemma requires theoretical perspectives capable of explaining both resource acquisition and organizational transformation. Three perspectives are particularly useful in this regard: the Resource-Based View, dynamic capabilities theory, and strategic alignment.

2.4 Resource-Based View

The Resource-Based View (RBV) provides one of the foundational frameworks for analyzing strategic value creation in mergers and acquisitions (Wernerfelt, 1984; Barney, 1991; Peteraf, 1993). According to RBV, firms achieve sustained competitive advantage when they possess resources that are valuable, rare, difficult to imitate, and organizationally embedded.

From this perspective, acquisitions represent a strategic mechanism through which firms can obtain such resources more quickly than through internal development. In digital capability acquisitions, these resources often include technological expertise, data assets, digital platforms, and highly specialized human capital.

However, RBV also emphasizes that resource ownership alone is insufficient to generate value. Firms must possess the organizational capabilities necessary to deploy those resources effectively. In digital acquisitions, this means that the acquiring organization must be able to integrate technological capabilities into existing processes, coordinate teams with different expertise, and translate technological assets into marketable services.

2.5 Dynamic Capabilities

While RBV focuses on resource possession, the dynamic capabilities perspective emphasizes the processes through which firms adapt and reconfigure resources in changing environments. Dynamic capabilities refer to the ability of organizations to sense opportunities, seize them, and transform their resource base accordingly. (Teece et al., 1997; Eisenhardt & Martin, 2000; Teece, 2007).

Digital environments are characterized by rapid technological change, evolving customer expectations, and shifting competitive landscapes. In such contexts, firms must continually reconfigure capabilities in order to remain competitive. Research indicates that digital transformation enhances firms' adaptive performance by strengthening strategic learning processes and facilitating knowledge integration (Feng & Liu, 2024).

Within post-merger integration processes, dynamic capabilities play a critical role. The integration of newly acquired technological resources requires firms to redesign organizational processes, develop new governance structures, and coordinate knowledge flows across organizational boundaries. Firms that possess strong dynamic capabilities are better positioned to recombine acquired and existing resources in ways that generate new forms of competitive advantage.

2.6 Strategic Alignment

Strategic alignment represents a third important perspective for understanding digital capability integration (Henderson & Venkatraman, 1993; Chan & Reich, 2007). Alignment refers to the degree of consistency between an organization's strategy, technological infrastructure, business processes, and governance mechanisms.

In digital contexts, value creation increasingly depends on how effectively firms align digital platforms, organizational routines, and collaborative processes. Studies on digital supply chains show that alignment between technological platforms, governance systems, and knowledge-sharing processes can significantly enhance interorganizational value creation (Wu et al., 2026).

Similarly, research on digital human resource strategies suggests that integrating digital technologies with HR practices can improve organizational performance by aligning technological capabilities with human expertise (Ruiz et al., 2024). These findings highlight the importance of organizational coherence in digital transformation initiatives.

When applied to mergers and acquisitions, the alignment perspective suggests that successful integration requires more than structural consolidation. Firms must also align technological architectures, governance systems, and organizational routines in ways that enable the effective deployment of acquired capabilities.

2.7 Toward an Integrated Analytical Framework

Taken together, the Resource-Based View, dynamic capabilities theory, and strategic alignment provide complementary perspectives for analyzing digital post-merger integration. RBV explains why firms pursue acquisitions in order to obtain valuable resources. Dynamic capabilities explain how organizations reconfigure those resources in response to changing environments. Strategic alignment explains how technological and organizational systems must be coordinated in order for those capabilities to generate value.

Building on these perspectives, this chapter adopts an integrated analytical framework in which strategic value creation in digital acquisitions is understood as the outcome of three interrelated processes:

- Capability acquisition – the acquisition of technological and knowledge-based resources.
- Capability integration – the alignment of acquired capabilities with organizational structures and processes.
- Capability scaling – the deployment and expansion of integrated capabilities within the broader organizational ecosystem.

This framework provides the conceptual basis for examining the STC Solutions–Devoteam acquisition. By analyzing the integration process through these dimensions, the chapter seeks to identify the mechanisms through which digital acquisitions may contribute to long-term strategic value creation.

3. RESEARCH DESIGN AND METHODOLOGY

3.1 Research Design

This chapter adopts a qualitative case-based analytical approach to examine how strategic value may emerge during the post-merger integration of digital capability acquisitions. Case-based research is particularly appropriate for studying complex organizational processes that involve multiple interacting factors such as knowledge transfer, capability recombination, and organizational restructuring. These processes are often difficult to capture through purely quantitative methods because they unfold over time and involve organizational dynamics that cannot easily be reduced to numerical indicators.

In strategic management and innovation research, qualitative case studies have frequently been used to investigate organizational transformation, post-merger integration processes, and digital innovation dynamics. Such approaches allow researchers to analyze how organizational actors interpret and implement strategic decisions and how capabilities evolve during integration processes (Chen et al., 2022; Safavi, 2021).

The use of a case-based analytical approach is particularly relevant in the context of digital capability acquisitions, where much of the strategic value resides in intangible assets such as knowledge, technological expertise, and collaborative routines. These forms of value are embedded within organizational processes and professional networks, making them difficult to analyze using traditional quantitative indicators alone. As a result, qualitative approaches can provide deeper insights into the mechanisms through which acquired capabilities are integrated and scaled within the acquiring organization.

The present chapter therefore adopts an illustrative case design, in which a single case is analyzed in depth to explore the strategic dynamics of digital post-merger integration. Rather than seeking statistical generalization, the analysis aims to provide analytical insights into how value creation mechanisms may operate in capability-driven acquisitions.

3.2 Case Selection

The case examined in this chapter is the acquisition of Devoteam Middle East by STC Solutions, a major digital services and technology provider in Saudi Arabia. This acquisition, announced in 2023, represents a strategic move to strengthen digital consulting capabilities. The case was selected for several reasons that make it analytically relevant for examining digital post-merger integration.

First, the transaction represents a capability-driven acquisition. Unlike acquisitions primarily motivated by cost synergies or market consolidation, this transaction was strategically oriented toward expanding digital consulting capabilities, cloud expertise, and cybersecurity services. Such capability-oriented acquisitions are increasingly common in digital transformation strategies, as firms seek to strengthen their technological portfolios and accelerate innovation through external knowledge acquisition.

Second, the case occurs within an emerging digital ecosystem, where firms are rapidly expanding digital capabilities in response to technological change and policy-driven digital transformation initiatives. Emerging digital ecosystems often create strong incentives for firms to pursue capability-building strategies through acquisitions and strategic partnerships. In such contexts, firms must integrate newly acquired capabilities while simultaneously adapting to evolving market structures and institutional priorities.

Third, the case provides an opportunity to examine how large regional organizations attempt to reposition themselves within global digital services markets. Telecommunications and technology firms are increasingly expanding beyond infrastructure-based services toward higher-value digital consulting and transformation services. Acquisitions of specialized digital consulting firms therefore represent an important mechanism for accelerating this strategic shift.

These characteristics make the STC Solutions–Devoteam acquisition a suitable context for exploring how digital capabilities can be integrated and leveraged within an evolving organizational and technological environment.

3.3 Data Sources

The analysis presented in this chapter is based on secondary data collected from publicly available sources. Secondary data sources are widely used in strategic management research when examining corporate transactions, industry developments, and organizational strategies, particularly when access to internal corporate data is limited.

The case analysis relies on publicly available sources, including corporate press releases issued by solutions by stc and Devoteam, company communications, and industry news reports covering the transaction and its strategic context. These materials provide insight into the strategic motivations behind the acquisition, the organizational characteristics of the firms involved, and the integration initiatives undertaken after the transaction. Although secondary data sources do not provide the same level of internal detail as interviews or internal documents, they allow researchers to construct a coherent narrative of the strategic and organizational dynamics associated with the acquisition.

The use of secondary sources is common in studies of digital transformation and mergers and acquisitions, particularly when the objective is to analyze strategic positioning and integration processes at the organizational level rather than individual managerial decision-making.

3.4 Analytical Strategy

The analytical approach adopted in this chapter is theory-informed interpretive analysis. Rather than applying statistical models, the analysis interprets the case through the theoretical lenses developed in the previous section: the Resource-Based View, dynamic capabilities, and strategic alignment.

The analysis focuses on identifying mechanisms through which value creation may occur during post-merger integration. Specifically, the case is examined across three analytical dimensions:

- Capability acquisition – the types of technological and knowledge-based capabilities obtained through the acquisition.
- Capability integration – the processes through which these capabilities are incorporated into the acquiring organization.
- Capability scaling – the ways in which integrated capabilities contribute to strategic value creation and organizational development.

These dimensions reflect the broader insight that digital transformation and innovation often emerge from the recombination of technological capabilities, organizational processes, and knowledge resources. Research on digital transformation suggests that firms achieve innovation and competitive advantage when they successfully align technological capabilities with organizational structures and strategic priorities (Tangwaragorn et al., 2024; Fang & Liu, 2024).

Similarly, studies of digital innovation ecosystems emphasize that value creation increasingly depends on how organizations coordinate technological resources, collaborative networks, and governance structures (Wang et al., 2025; Wu et al., 2026). By applying these perspectives to the case under investigation, the analysis seeks to identify the organizational conditions under which digital acquisitions may contribute to strategic value creation.

3.5 Research Limitations

As with any qualitative case-based analysis, this study has several limitations that should be acknowledged. First, the analysis relies primarily on publicly available data sources. While these sources provide valuable insights into strategic positioning and integration initiatives, they do not offer detailed access to internal organizational processes or managerial decision-making dynamics.

Second, the chapter focuses on a single illustrative case, which limits the ability to generalize findings across all digital acquisitions. However, the purpose of the analysis is not statistical generalization but conceptual exploration. By examining the mechanisms through which digital capability integration may occur, the chapter aims to contribute to theoretical understanding rather than provide universally applicable empirical conclusions.

Finally, digital transformation processes often unfold over extended time horizons. As a result, the long-term outcomes of the acquisition may continue to evolve beyond the period covered by available public information.

Future research could build on this work by conducting comparative case studies across multiple digital acquisitions or by incorporating interview-based data to examine managerial perspectives on integration processes.

4. CASE ANALYSIS: THE STC SOLUTIONS–DEVOTEAM ACQUISITION

4.1 Strategic Context of the Acquisition

Over the past decade, the Middle East has witnessed rapid growth in digital transformation initiatives driven by both governmental strategies and private-sector investment. National digital agendas, large-scale infrastructure development, and increasing demand for cloud, cybersecurity, and data-driven services have created strong incentives for organizations to expand their digital capabilities. Within this environment, firms increasingly pursue acquisitions as a mechanism to accelerate technological capability development and strengthen their position within evolving digital ecosystems.

The case is used as an illustrative analytical example intended to explore the mechanisms through which digital capability acquisitions may contribute to strategic value creation, based on publicly available corporate and industry sources.

Research indicates that digital transformation reshapes firms' competitive strategies by encouraging them to integrate advanced technological capabilities and develop new service architectures built around data, platforms, and knowledge-intensive services (Fang & Liu, 2024; Tangwaragorn et al., 2024). In many industries, digital capabilities have become critical sources of competitive advantage, enabling firms to enhance innovation performance, strengthen operational efficiency, and improve their ability to respond to rapidly changing market conditions.

Against this background, telecommunications and technology firms are increasingly expanding beyond traditional infrastructure-based business models toward digital consulting, cloud services, cybersecurity solutions, and digital transformation advisory services. Such strategic shifts often require capabilities that cannot be developed quickly through internal training or incremental technological investment. Consequently, acquisitions have become an important strategic tool for firms seeking to accelerate capability development.

The acquisition of a 40% stake in Devoteam Middle East by solutions by stc, announced in 2023 and completed in 2024, represents a strategic move intended to strengthen the company's digital consulting, cloud, and cybersecurity capabilities in the region.(solutions by stc, 2024; Devoteam, 2023). Rather than a full acquisition of the parent company, the transaction concerns Devoteam Middle East and is therefore best understood as a targeted digital capability acquisition within an emerging technology market. Devoteam is known internationally for its expertise in digital transformation consulting, cloud services, and cybersecurity solutions. By acquiring Devoteam's regional operations, STC Solutions aimed to strengthen its digital consulting portfolio and enhance its ability to deliver end-to-end digital transformation services.

From a strategic management perspective, the acquisition can be interpreted as a capability-driven transaction rather than a purely financial or market-expansion strategy. The value of the acquisition lies primarily in intangible assets such as technological expertise, consulting methodologies, professional networks, and specialized human capital. Such assets are typical targets in digital mergers and acquisitions, where firms seek to obtain knowledge-based resources that support innovation and strategic repositioning (Maisenhelder et al., 2025).

However, acquiring these capabilities does not automatically generate strategic value. The integration of digital consulting capabilities into an existing technology organization requires careful coordination between technological infrastructures, organizational processes, and professional expertise. As the literature on digital M&A suggests, the success of such acquisitions depends heavily on how effectively acquired capabilities are integrated and scaled during the post-merger phase (Chen & Liu, 2025).

4.2 Acquisition Rationale and Capability Acquisition

The strategic rationale behind the STC Solutions–Devoteam transaction can be understood through the lens of capability acquisition. In digital industries, firms increasingly pursue acquisitions to obtain advanced technological capabilities that support innovation, service development, and digital transformation initiatives.

The Resource-Based View suggests that firms seek to acquire resources that are valuable, rare, and difficult for competitors to replicate. In the case of digital consulting firms, such resources often include specialized expertise in cloud architecture, cybersecurity frameworks, digital transformation strategy, and enterprise platform integration. These capabilities are typically embedded within professional teams and organizational routines, making them difficult to imitate through internal development alone.

Devoteam Middle East possessed a strong reputation in digital consulting and technology services, particularly in areas related to cloud computing and cybersecurity. These competencies complemented STC Solutions' existing technological infrastructure and enterprise service capabilities. By combining infrastructure-based digital services with consulting expertise, the acquiring firm could potentially offer a more comprehensive digital transformation portfolio.

Recent research on digital M&A suggests that acquisitions of technology-driven firms can stimulate innovation and knowledge transfer across organizational boundaries. For example, digital acquisitions have been shown to enhance innovation investment and knowledge diffusion within supply chains when organizations effectively integrate newly acquired capabilities (Chen & Liu, 2025). In this sense, The acquisition of a 40% stake in Devoteam Middle East by solutions by stc represents a strategic move intended to strengthen the company's digital consulting, cloud, and cybersecurity capabilities in the region.

At the same time, capability acquisition introduces integration challenges. Digital expertise often resides in teams of highly specialized professionals whose knowledge is embedded in collaborative routines and project-based work environments. The departure of key employees or the disruption of established working practices can therefore undermine the strategic value of the acquisition. As a result, organizations must carefully manage the integration process in order to preserve the knowledge assets that motivated the transaction in the first place.

4.3 Post-Merger Integration Mechanisms

Following the acquisition, the integration process required STC Solutions to incorporate Devoteam's capabilities into its broader organizational structure while maintaining the professional expertise and innovative capacity of the acquired firm. The integration process can be analyzed across three interrelated dimensions: human capital stabilization, technological alignment, and organizational coordination.

Human Capital Stabilization

One of the most critical challenges in capability-driven acquisitions is the retention of specialized human capital. In digital consulting organizations, the value of the firm often resides in the expertise of its consultants, engineers, and technology specialists. These professionals possess tacit knowledge that cannot easily be transferred through formal documentation or technological systems.

Research on digital organizations highlights the importance of human expertise in driving technological innovation and organizational performance. For example, studies on digital human resource strategies show that firms achieve better performance outcomes when technological capabilities are aligned with human expertise and organizational learning systems (Ruiz et al., 2024). Similarly, research on digital leadership emphasizes the role of managerial agility in coordinating multidisciplinary teams operating across digital and physical environments (Bellis et al., 2024).

In the case of the STC–Devoteam integration, preserving the expertise of consulting teams was essential for maintaining the value of the acquisition. This required creating organizational conditions that encouraged collaboration between newly integrated teams while allowing sufficient autonomy for professional experts to continue delivering specialized consulting services.

Technological Alignment

A second dimension of integration involved aligning technological infrastructures and service architectures. Digital consulting firms typically operate with flexible project-based systems designed to support consulting engagements and innovation activities. In contrast, telecommunications organizations often rely on large-scale infrastructure platforms designed for operational stability and service delivery.

The integration of these two technological environments required careful coordination. Strategic alignment theory suggests that organizations create value when technological systems, organizational structures, and strategic objectives are mutually reinforcing. When alignment is weak, technological capabilities may remain isolated within specific units and fail to contribute to broader organizational performance.

Research on digital supply chains shows that alignment between technological platforms, governance mechanisms, and knowledge-sharing processes can significantly enhance value creation in collaborative environments (Wu et al., 2026). Applying this perspective to the STC–Devoteam case suggests that technological integration was necessary to ensure that consulting capabilities could be effectively combined with STC's existing digital infrastructure and service platforms.

Organizational Coordination

The third dimension of integration concerns the coordination of organizational structures and processes. Digital consulting firms often operate with relatively flexible organizational structures that emphasize creativity, innovation, and project-based collaboration. Telecommunications organizations, by contrast, frequently rely on more formalized structures designed to support operational efficiency and large-scale service delivery.

Balancing these organizational logics required the development of hybrid structures that allowed consulting teams to maintain their innovative capabilities while still integrating their expertise into the broader organizational strategy. Such hybrid arrangements are increasingly common in digital transformation initiatives, where firms must combine stable operational systems with agile innovation capabilities.

Research on digital innovation ecosystems highlights the importance of coordination mechanisms that enable organizations to integrate technological capabilities, collaborative networks, and governance structures (Wang et al., 2025). In the context of post-merger integration, such coordination mechanisms can facilitate the recombination of acquired capabilities with existing organizational resources.

4.4 Capability Scaling and Strategic Outcomes

Beyond the initial integration phase, the long-term strategic value of the acquisition depends on the acquiring firm's ability to scale and deploy newly acquired capabilities across the organization. Capability scaling involves extending the reach of acquired expertise beyond the boundaries of the acquired unit and embedding it within broader organizational operations.

In digital transformation contexts, capability scaling often occurs through the integration of consulting expertise with technological platforms and service offerings. This allows organizations to develop new digital solutions, expand their service portfolios, and strengthen their position within digital ecosystems.

Research suggests that digital transformation initiatives create value when organizations successfully combine technological capabilities with organizational learning processes and innovation strategies (Fang & Liu, 2024). Similarly, digital innovation studies emphasize the importance of recombining technological resources with complementary assets such as organizational knowledge, partnerships, and market access.

In the STC–Devoteam case, the acquisition potentially allowed STC Solutions to expand its digital service portfolio by integrating consulting capabilities into its broader digital infrastructure and enterprise services. By combining consulting expertise with existing technological platforms, the firm could potentially offer integrated digital transformation services to clients across multiple sectors.

However, the long-term success of such strategies depends on continuous organizational adaptation. Digital transformation initiatives require organizations to continually update technological infrastructures, develop new skills, and adjust governance structures in response to changing technological and market conditions. As research on digital transformation suggests, firms that develop strong adaptive capabilities are better positioned to sustain innovation and strategic competitiveness over time (Feng & Liu, 2024).

These observations should therefore be interpreted as analytical insights derived from publicly available information rather than as definitive evidence of post-merger integration outcomes.

5. DISCUSSION

The analysis of the STC–Devoteam Middle East acquisition provides insights into the organizational mechanisms through which digital capability acquisitions may contribute to strategic value creation during post-merger integration. Rather than assuming that value automatically arises from acquiring digital assets, the case highlights the organizational mechanisms through which such value may gradually emerge. In particular, the findings suggest that the integration of specialized expertise, the alignment of technological and organizational structures, and the ability to scale acquired capabilities represent key processes shaping the strategic outcomes of digital acquisitions.

From a Resource-Based View perspective, the acquisition can be interpreted as an attempt to access valuable and specialized knowledge resources that are difficult to develop internally. Digital consulting capabilities, cloud expertise, and cybersecurity knowledge represent intangible assets that may enhance a firm's strategic resource base. However, the case also illustrates that the acquisition of such resources does not in itself guarantee competitive advantage. Consistent with RBV arguments, the potential value of acquired capabilities depends on how effectively these resources are integrated with existing organizational processes and strategic priorities.

The case also highlights the relevance of dynamic capabilities in explaining the integration process. Digital acquisitions often involve combining different organizational routines, knowledge bases, and technological infrastructures. In this context, firms must develop the ability to reconfigure resources, coordinate expertise, and adapt organizational structures in order to translate newly acquired capabilities into strategic outcomes. The integration of Devoteam Middle East within the broader strategic activities of solutions by stc can therefore be interpreted as an example of how firms may attempt to develop or strengthen dynamic capabilities in response to technological change.

Strategic alignment represents a third important dimension of the integration process. Digital acquisitions frequently involve firms with different organizational cultures, technological architectures, and operational models. Achieving alignment between these elements is therefore essential for realizing potential synergies. In the present case, the acquisition appears to reflect an effort to align consulting expertise with the broader digital infrastructure and service ecosystem developed by solutions by stc. Such alignment may enable the organization to combine advisory services, technological solutions, and implementation capabilities within an integrated digital transformation offering.

The analysis also suggests that the broader institutional and market context may influence the trajectory of post-merger integration in digital sectors. Emerging digital ecosystems often present both opportunities and constraints for firms seeking to expand their technological capabilities. On one hand, growing demand for digital transformation services creates incentives for firms to acquire specialized expertise. On the other hand, differences in organizational practices, talent retention challenges, and evolving technological standards may complicate integration processes. The case therefore illustrates how digital capability acquisitions may unfold differently in emerging markets compared to more mature technology ecosystems.

Finally, the findings highlight the importance of human capital in digital post-merger integration. Unlike acquisitions focused primarily on physical assets, digital capability acquisitions often center on highly specialized expertise embedded in professional teams. As a result, the retention and effective integration of human capital becomes a central factor influencing the success of the integration process. The case suggests that maintaining the autonomy of specialized teams while gradually aligning them with broader strategic objectives may represent a viable integration approach in knowledge-intensive acquisitions.

Overall, the case illustrates that strategic value in digital acquisitions is less likely to emerge from the transaction itself than from the subsequent processes through which acquired capabilities are integrated, aligned, and scaled. The interaction between resource acquisition, organizational adaptation, and strategic alignment therefore represents a critical area of analysis for understanding value creation in digital post-merger integration.

6. CONCLUSION

This chapter explored the organizational mechanisms through which strategic value may emerge during digital post-merger integration. In the context of accelerating digital transformation across industries, firms increasingly rely on mergers and acquisitions to access specialized technological capabilities, knowledge resources, and digital consulting expertise. However, the analysis presented in this chapter suggests that the creation of strategic value in such transactions depends less on the acquisition itself and more on the organizational processes through which acquired capabilities are integrated, aligned, and scaled.

Drawing on the Resource-Based View, dynamic capabilities, and strategic alignment perspectives, the chapter proposed an analytical framework for understanding value creation in digital acquisitions. The case analysis suggests that three interrelated mechanisms may shape post-merger integration outcomes. First, the stabilization and retention of specialized human capital play a central role in preserving the knowledge resources embedded within acquired organizations. Second, the alignment of technological capabilities with existing organizational structures and strategic priorities may influence the effectiveness of capability integration. Third, the ability to scale acquired capabilities through hybrid organizational arrangements may enable firms to expand digital service offerings and strengthen their position within evolving technology ecosystems.

The chapter contributes to the growing literature on digital mergers and acquisitions by highlighting the organizational mechanisms that may underpin strategic value creation in knowledge-intensive acquisitions. While much of the existing research focuses on financial performance outcomes, the analysis emphasizes the importance of integration processes and capability alignment in shaping long-term strategic outcomes. In addition, the chapter extends the literature by examining digital capability acquisition within the context of an emerging digital ecosystem in the Middle East.

From a managerial perspective, the findings suggest that firms pursuing digital acquisitions should place particular emphasis on capability integration rather than viewing acquisitions solely as transactions for acquiring technological assets. Retaining specialized expertise, ensuring alignment between consulting capabilities and digital infrastructure, and developing organizational mechanisms for scaling newly acquired capabilities may represent critical factors influencing integration success.

Several limitations should be acknowledged. The analysis relies primarily on publicly available information, including corporate announcements and industry reports. As a result, the chapter focuses on strategic interpretation rather than detailed examination of internal organizational processes. Future research could build on these insights by conducting in-depth qualitative studies, interviews with managers involved in integration processes, or comparative analyses of multiple digital acquisitions across different industry contexts.

Overall, the chapter highlights that digital post-merger integration represents a complex organizational process in which strategic value emerges through the interaction of resource acquisition, capability integration, and organizational alignment. Understanding these mechanisms remains an important area for future research as firms continue to rely on digital acquisitions to navigate rapidly evolving technological environments.

REFERENCES

Barney, J. (1991). Firm resources and sustained competitive advantage. *Journal of Management, 17*(1), 99–120. DOI: 10.1177/014920639101700108

Bellis, A., De Stefano, V., & Zaninotto, E. (2024). Digital leadership and hybrid work: Organizational agility in the digital era. *Journal of Business Research, 172*, 114412. DOI: 10.1016/j.jbusres.2023.114412

Birkinshaw, J., Bresman, H., & Håkanson, L. (2000). Managing the post-acquisition integration process: How the human integration and task integration processes interact to foster value creation. *Journal of Management Studies, 37*(3), 395–425. DOI: 10.1111/1467-6486.00186

Chan, Y. E., & Reich, B. H. (2007). IT alignment: What have we learned? *Journal of Information Technology, 22*(4), 297–315. DOI: 10.1057/palgrave.jit.2000109

Chen, W., & Liu, W. (2025). Digital M&A triggers innovation: When the going gets tough, the tough get going. *Research in International Business and Finance, 78*, 102957. DOI: 10.1016/j.ribaf.2025.102957

Chen, Y., Liu, H., & Tang, J. (2022). Post-merger integration and innovation upgrading: Evidence from knowledge-intensive acquisitions. *Technovation, 113*, 102450. DOI: 10.1016/j.technovation.2021.102450

Devoteam. (2023). Devoteam announces strategic partnership with solutions by stc in the Middle East. https://www.devoteam.com

Eisenhardt, K. M., & Martin, J. A. (2000). Dynamic capabilities: What are they? *Strategic Management Journal, 21*(10–11), 1105–1121. DOI: 10.1002/1097-0266(200010/11)21:10/11<1105::AID-SMJ133>3.0.CO;2-E

Fang, X., & Liu, M. (2024). How does digital transformation drive digital technology innovation of enterprises? Evidence from Chinese listed firms. *Technological Forecasting and Social Change, 204*, 123428. DOI: 10.1016/j.techfore.2024.123428

Feng, Y., & Liu, Z. (2024). Digital transformation and firm adaptive performance: Evidence from emerging markets. *Journal of Business Research, 169*, 114215. DOI: 10.1016/j.jbusres.2023.114215

Firk, S., Gehrke, Y., Meier, J., & Wolff, M. (2025). Fooled by the hype? The influence of technology hype on acquisition premiums in digital M&As. *Long Range Planning, 58*(6), 102589. DOI: 10.1016/j.lrp.2025.102589

Haspeslagh, P., & Jemison, D. (1991). *Managing acquisitions: Creating value through corporate renewal.* Free Press.

Henderson, J. C., & Venkatraman, N. (1993). Strategic alignment: Leveraging information technology for transforming organizations. *IBM Systems Journal, 32*(1), 4–16. DOI: 10.1147/sj.382.0472

Li, Y., & Li, X. (2026). Digital economy and high-quality enterprise development: Evidence from emerging markets. *Technological Forecasting and Social Change, 210*, 124501. DOI: 10.1016/j.techfore.2025.124501

Maisenhelder, F., Rapp, M. S., & Wolff, M. (2025). Digital acquisitions and corporate innovation: Evidence from global technology markets. *Research Policy, 54*(3), 104873. DOI: 10.1016/j.respol.2024.104873

Meglio, O., King, D. R., & Risberg, A. (2025). Mergers and acquisitions as service ecosystems: Toward a value co-creation perspective. *Journal of Management Studies, 62*(1), 98–125. DOI: 10.1111/joms.12910

Oludapo, S., Carroll, N., & Helfert, M. (2024). Why do so many digital transformations fail? A bibliometric analysis and future research agenda. *Journal of Business Research, 174*, 114528. DOI: 10.1016/j.jbusres.2024.114528

Peteraf, M. (1993). The cornerstones of competitive advantage: A resource-based view. *Strategic Management Journal, 14*(3), 179–191. DOI: 10.1002/smj.4250140303

Ruiz, J., López-Cabrales, Á., & Valle-Cabrera, R. (2024). Digital human resource strategies and firm performance in the digital era. *Human Resource Management Journal, 34*(2), 451–468. DOI: 10.1111/1748-8583.12480

Safavi, M. (2021). Organizational routines and post-merger integration: A dynamic capabilities perspective. *Journal of Management & Organization, 27*(5), 982–1002. DOI: 10.1017/jmo.2019.73

solutions by stc. (2024). solutions by stc completes acquisition of Devoteam Middle East. https://solutions.com.sa

Tangwaragorn, P., Dhir, A., & Kaur, P. (2024). Digital transformation and corporate strategy: A systematic review and research agenda. *Technological Forecasting and Social Change, 199*, 122995. DOI: 10.1016/j.techfore.2023.122995

Tao, Q., Li, S., & Liu, Y. (2026). Digital transformation and corporate diversification: Evidence from emerging markets. *Journal of Business Research, 175*, 114526. DOI: 10.1016/j.jbusres.2024.114526

Teece, D. J. (2007). Explicating dynamic capabilities: The nature and microfoundations of sustainable enterprise performance. *Strategic Management Journal*, *28*(13), 1319–1350. DOI: 10.1002/smj.640

Teece, D. J., Pisano, G., & Shuen, A. (1997). Dynamic capabilities and strategic management. *Strategic Management Journal*, *18*(7), 509–533. DOI: 10.1002/(SICI)1097-0266(199708)18:7<509::AID-SMJ882>3.0.CO;2-Z

Wang, Y., Chen, X., & Zhang, L. (2024). Digital transformation and cross-border mergers and acquisitions: Evidence from emerging economies. *International Business Review*, *33*(5), 102123. DOI: 10.1016/j.ibusrev.2023.102123

Wang, Z., Luo, X., & Li, J. (2025). Digital innovation ecosystems and strategic collaboration: A network perspective. *Technovation*, *128*, 102741. DOI: 10.1016/j.technovation.2024.102741

Wernerfelt, B. (1984). A resource-based view of the firm. *Strategic Management Journal*, *5*(2), 171–180. DOI: 10.1002/smj.4250050207

Wu, J., Li, H., & Zhao, X. (2026). Platform alignment and value co-creation in digital supply chains. *Industrial Marketing Management*, *118*, 213–225. DOI: 10.1016/j.indmarman.2025.09.004

Chapter 5

Legal Frameworks for M&A in Emerging Markets as Catalysts for Economic Resilience

Shashank Solanki
http://orcid.org/0009-0002-5923-0516
Christ University, India

Sheetal Singh
http://orcid.org/0000-0002-7266-8910
Christ University, India

Vijeta Verma
http://orcid.org/0000-0001-9255-9132
Christ University, India

Vijaishree Dubey Pandey
http://orcid.org/0000-0003-3207-7814
Christ University, India

Rituraj Sinha
http://orcid.org/0000-0001-5790-9571
Christ University, India

ABSTRACT

This chapter explores how legal and regulatory frameworks for mergers and acquisitions (M&A) act as critical enablers of economic resilience in emerging markets. It analyzes the interplay between competition law, corporate governance,

DOI: 10.4018/979-8-3373-5233-6.ch005

and foreign direct investment (FDI) controls, highlighting their role in fostering investor confidence, regulatory transparency, and sustainable growth. Through comparative analysis of key jurisdictions—such as the U.S., EU, India, Brazil, and ASEAN—and landmark case studies like Microsoft–Activision and Grab–Uber, the chapter demonstrates how legal clarity and institutional maturity shape M&A outcomes. It further emphasizes the importance of integrating ESG standards and enhancing cross-border legal coordination. The study positions legal infrastructure not just as a compliance mechanism but as a strategic foundation for inclusive and resilient economic development.

1. INTRODUCTION

The process of creating a merger and acquisition (M&A) no longer remains part of the conventional business restructuring, but instead it has an established role of market realignment, corporate agility and industrial renewal in the world market. M&A transactions are strategic devices in the developed and emerging economies to realise other objectives such as penetration, technological gain of the business, integrated supply, and competitive advantage in the world market (Kayser & Zülch, 2024). Such transactions have developed to be the main events capable of radically changing the market's landscape through the figure of fragmentation, creation of operational synergy, and rational distribution of resources.

M&A often has been historically enacted by firm-level hope of development and incomes. But within the last several decades, the concept of M&A transactions has emerged to not only be regarded as a corporate strategy issue but also as a macroeconomic phenomenon with larger policy aspects. M&A transactions have the potential to affect national employment rates, tax bases, innovation systems and consumer welfare when a transaction is conducted either at large scale or across borders; in emerging markets, M&A takes on a whole new meaning, being even more convoluted and far-reaching. Some of the factors that define the emerging economies include the volatility of the institutional framework, infrastructural weaknesses, dynamic policy environments and legal uncertainty (Babu & Jagadish, 2022). In these circumstances, such success of an M&A transaction usually depends not only on financial or operational numbers but also on its capability to operate in complex legal and regulatory environments. Such frameworks as the competition law, the corporate governance regulations, the foreign direct investment (FDI) regulations, and the national security screening mechanisms are all put in place to determine whether an M&A can be made, when the process should be undertaken, and whether it is legal. Legal infrastructure is, in this meaning, an economic catalyst or, on the other hand, a shackle, in that regard to the level of consolidation of organisations and economic modernization (Itan, Sylvia, & Septiany, 2025).

1.1 Role of Legal and Regulatory Structures in Emerging Economies

The regulatory and legal environment in which it is best to frame M&A transactions is paramount in deciding to what degree M&A pursuits form part and parcel of the larger picture of economic resilience. Legal institutions also reduce risks and provide protection to the stakeholders in well-managed markets but, more importantly, provide a predictable environment and confidence to the business environment. This predictability is necessary in order to attract foreign stakeholders, safeguard minority stakeholders, safeguard labour rights and ensure smooth technological spillovers, which are all very central to sustainable economic development (Han & Lee, 2023).

Nevertheless, a number of states emphasis on new economies cannot overcome the challenge of regulatory asymmetries, enforcement inconsistencies, and political influences, which consequently destabilise the transformational possibilities of M&A activity. Insufficient regulations can encourage the so-called regulatory arbitrage that involves the effect of strategic benefit by firms operating in weak jurisdictions, which can eventually harm the possibility of monopoly practices and lowered testability or contestability of a market. Also, the lack of specific legal and administrative frameworks in the process of transaction review and settlement could delay the transaction process, discourage foreign investments and threaten the confidence of multinational players (Sherwood & Pollard, 2018). Furthermore, this legal weakness could also compound the injustices in domestic capital markets where the larger players could dominate without any checks, and the other categories, such as the small and medium enterprises and domestic investors, could not afford the required legal input to participate actively in the transformations of corporate entities. Thus, in the example of the emerging markets, not only should the enforcement of law and regulations be aimed at preventing the anti-competitive action, but it should also be proactive in effecting an inclusive, transparent and responsible corporate ambiance (Dissanaike, Liu, & Sturm, 2021).

1.2 Objectives of the Chapter

The following chapter attempts to offer a broad-based and interdisciplinary discussion of interaction amid law systems, regulatory systems and economic resilience, with an overview of mergers and acquisitions in emerging economies (Kim & Park, 2020). There are threefold goals of this chapter:

1. In order to analyse the legal principles that are used to regulate M&A transactions in the chosen jurisdictions, paying attention to the convergence and divergence of national and international standards of competition law, corporate governance, and investment regulation.
2. To examine the empirical case report of major M&A deals, including the Microsoft-Activision deal, the Vodafone-Hutchison transaction and the Grab-Uber consolidation, to show the physical outcomes of regulatory certainty, legal uncertainty and institutional robustness/weakness.
3. To provide policy and legal suggestions to achieve the purpose of making regulations more predictable, advancing institutional abilities and cross-border legal relations in the presence of better results and financial defences in new economies to M&A proceedings.

The chapter is made to be diagnostic and prescriptive. It also unites comparative legal research with the practical assessment of a case study in order to offer practical recommendations to legal theorists, regulatory experts, in-house legal counsel and policymakers interested in enhancing the economic usefulness of M&A systems in the Global South and other jurisdictions (Claessens & Yafeh, 2019).

1.3 Methodology: Comparative Legal Research and Case-Based Approach

The chapter has a comparative legal research methodology in which there is an attempted verification with doctrinal, institutional or normative research. This approach makes it possible to do the subtle investigation of the effects in which legal systems affect the process of M&A activities across various geopolitical and economic frames of reference (Gao & Johnston, 2021). The methodology will unite major sources of law: laws, court cases, policymaker announcements, and legal instructions, and secondary materials: scholarly articles, policy studies, and expert opinions.

Key methodological pillars include:

- **Doctrinal Legal Analysis**: An approach based on reading the text and its interpretation by the courts regarding M&A-related laws in various jurisdictions (e.g., antitrust laws, corporate governance structure, FDI screening regulation).
- **Comparative Institutional Study**: Assessment of how various regulatory bodies – the U.S. Federal Trade Commission (FTC), European Commission DG COMP, Competition Commission of India (CCI) and Brazil

Administrative Council for Economic Defence (CADE) – do merger reviews and provide enforcement in their jurisdiction.

- **Empirical Case Studies**: Intensive examination of the chosen cross-border M&A deals, focusing on such aspects as legal obstacles, procedural bottlenecks, regulatory inventions, and strategic compliance patterns.
- **Normative and Policy Analysis**: The investigation of the correspondences and mismatches of legal frameworks to a larger development agenda that includes such imperatives as transparency, labour rights, corporate responsibility and sustainable growth.

The above combination of approaches enables depth and breadth in an analysis of the legal and regulatory complexities bound up in M&A activity in emerging markets (Liu, Fang, Hu, & Lv, 2024).

2. THEORETICAL AND LEGAL FOUNDATIONS OF M&A REGULATION

2.1 Conceptual Architecture: Corporate Law, Antitrust, and FDI Control

Mergers and acquisitions (M&A) are vibrant tools of firm policy, and they are also rooted firmly in the structure of law. In the emerging economies, any transaction to become sustainable and economically viable has to be supported by stable legal principles, including corporate governance, antitrust controls, and foreign investment (Huang, Yang, & Yang, 2024). All these three spheres being different in their functionality create an entire regulatory staging within which strategies of players on the market are shaped and the general environment of the economic growth is built.The legal framework of any M&A transaction is formed by the corporate law. It regulates the inner dynamics of business practices like board consent, shareholder elections, fiduciary duty, reporting requirements and defence of minority interest. Transaction costs incurred to achieve the desired outcome may be elevated due to lack of calculability and certainty on how the law will be applied in emerging economies where the norms of corporate governance are still dynamic. This factor will repel the investor from investing in the market. Incoherent, ambiguous laws; unfavorable ownership; or a lack of effective enforcement laws may mean hostility towards shareholders and problems with merger integration, as well as destruction of value (Bekaert, Harvey, Lundblad, & Siegel, 2021).

Simultaneously, through antitrust or competition law, M&A activity is not excessively causing markets to be concentrated or causing the markets to develop dominance. Mergers which pose to reduce competition significantly can prompt regulatory enquiries and solutions, such as dividing up or outright rejection. Major gatekeepers are regulatory bodies like the United States Federal Trade Commission (FTC), the European Commission Directorate-General for Competition (DG COMP), the Competition Commission of India (CCI), etc. Nonetheless, it is seen that a number of emerging markets have poor institutional capacity, deficiencies in economic analysis tools and limited legal training of regulators, which causes erratic or slow decision-making which influences transaction certainty.

The third regulatory pillar is foreign direct investment (FDI), which requires a vetting of alien investments to ensure that they do not cause insecurity or financial sovereignty for the nation or even for the general population. Equity limits, compulsory local ownership or technology transfers can be included in the policy of FDI, which can be very sector-specific (Umashankar, Bahadir, & Bharadwaj, 2022). The emergence of national security reviews, notably in the United States via the Committee on Foreign Investment in the United States (CFIUS) or in India with the introduction of Press Note 3 amendments, has created a new line of review, especially in the telecommunication, energy, and digital infrastructural sectors. They can be fuelled by both protectionist ideology in economics and geopolitical manoeuvres and make it harder to legalise cross-border mergers (Knittel & Stango, 2021). The three spheres determine the legal possibility of a merger or acquisition, its structure and the strategy of implementation. The relationship between FDI regulation, corporate law and competition governance in emerging economies touches upon the character of the legal maturity as well as the generality of the political economy and the credibility of the state.

2.2 Legal Infrastructure as a Mechanism for Economic Resilience

The most visible comprehension that legal structures are just compliance measures is false because an adequately operating regulation structure potentially can manipulate an economic sense of resiliency (Teece, 2022). Economic resilience in this context is a capability of a nation to endure economic shocks and changing structural developments and achieve durable and inclusive growth. The legal framework that supports M&A also helps to make it resilient through strengthening the transparency, investor protection, competition, and accountability. A straightforward and predictable merger review procedure limits uncertainty, develops investor certainty and eases the movement of domestic and foreign capital (Godwin & Osei, 2022). This especially plays a crucial role in the banking, insurance, and telecommunication industries, where this category of investment is mostly privileged in the case of an economic change or crisis. In addition, the practice of the antitrust law avoids monopolistic forms that inhibit innovation and price controls and place tiny companies at a disadvantage. In this regard, the competition law does not only safeguard the forces of the market but also helps to build a more inclusive and sustainable front on the economy. Effective regulations on markets tend to encourage long-term investment and make markets less susceptible to external shocks, including shocks on the supply chain or the instability of the world financial situation (Sherwood & Pollard, 2018).

Importantly, the legal framework also gives an opportunity to consider Environmental, Social, and Governance (ESG) factors in the M&A due diligence and transactional designs (Lestari, 2022). Through ESG integration, it is guaranteed that M&A activity does not contribute to failing to win sustainable development, labour standards, ecological safety, and social well-being. Legal systems that compel or promote disclosures on ESG in mergers improve the character of strategic planning between companies and national development outcomes that strengthen the economy through responsible capitalism (Siri & Zhu, 2024). Overall, the legal systems are not mere libraries of rules but agents in defining the profile of economic change. Properly designed and executed, they become a solid foundation on which the private sector can invest, institutional trust will be built and the economy will gain longer-term competitiveness (La Porta, Lopez-de-Silanes, & Shleifer, 2021).

2.3 Transnational Legal Influence and the Role of Institutional Theory

Globalisation of capital markets and the existence of transnational corporate transactions have led to the unification of legal norms and approaches to regulatory philosophy. No jurisdiction in the current world exists with a bubble. In the emerging markets there is an increased use of the transnational norms and best practices globally, along with multilateral governance further influencing the legal frameworks governing M&A (Gallagher & Pisani, 2019). The organisations like the Organisation for Economic Co-operation and Development (OECD) (OECD, 2022), the United Nations Conference on Trade and Development (UNCTAD, 2023) and the World Trade Organisation (WTO) have been of paramount value in the creation of M&A regulatory regimes. These institutions have promoted the adoption of harmonised standards in merger notification, antitrust review and protection of investors through the issuance of model laws and policy recommendations as well as peer review mechanisms. The laws that are used in countries that desire foreign investments usually match the international systems to ease the credibility and access of the market (Brouthers & Brouthers, 2020).

According to the institutional theory perspective, the success of such transnational pressures is mediated by the institutional capabilities that happen to be found in domestic areas. They can simply transplant legal doctrines, and they may be successful, as they are dependent on the autonomy, professionalism, and enforcement capacity of local regulatory institutions (Allee & Yohn, 2018). To give an example, whereas numerous nations have incorporated merger thresholds and competition review processes based on the U.S. or EU model, their implication in the local setting is hugely diverse because of discrepancies in the training of judges, liberty of the bureaucracy, and determination. Also, there could be selective assimilation or homogenisation of worldwide legal frameworks in emerging economies. That leads to a different kind of regulatory mosaic where the procedural standards can be aligned, but the substantive interpretation and method of enforcement can be within diverse frameworks. An example of such a phenomenon is a review of the GrabUber deal in Asia and the VodafoneHutchison transaction in India, where international structures of transactions face local legal issues and policy solutions (Botta & Kozul-Wright, 2021). It leads to modernisation of the law and integration in the international context, but it emphasises separately the distance between de jure convergence and de facto execution. This gap has to be bridged not only through legal reforms but also through regulatory institutions and capacity building as well as cross-border cooperation.

Figure 1. Interdisciplinary foundations of M&A legal governance

The integrative framework explains how law, regulation, and economic resilience are mutually reinforcing links in situations involving mergers and acquisitions (M & A) deals, particularly in emerging markets.

3. COMPARATIVE LEGAL FRAMEWORKS IN KEY JURISDICTIONS

In a setting in which there has been an increased level of cross-border capital movement, the normative frameworks determining mergers and acquisitions (M&A) display a notable cross-jurisdictional variability, thus impacting the structure of the transaction itself as well as the post-deal business combination. On the one hand, a comparative analysis of the two frameworks demonstrates that regulatory oversight plays an essential role in the design of market behaviour, defending the competitive forces, securing the national security interests, and maintaining economic strength, especially in the developing economies still trying to stabilise their institutions. The given analysis shall perform comparative analysis among the M&A legal framework in the United States, European Union, India, Brazil, and the member states of the Association of Southeast Asian Nations (ASEAN). Each of the jurisdictions offers a different high ground to look over the interaction between corporate law, competition policy, and foreign direct investment (FDI) controls. Through the review of their merger control tools, institutional setup, and transforming jurisprudence, this evaluation aims at shedding light on both the most successful examples and the constant problems that influence the domestic and international deal flow and create regulatory disparity (Musandu & Schoombee, 2019).

3.1 United States: Dual Agency Oversight under the FTC and DOJ

In the past, the United States has been a model that has been used all over the world in their antitrust and merger control regimes. Its system of regulations passed in clear codes and developed by court precedent has been highly institutionalised and has become divided between the Federal Trade Commission (FTC) and the Antitrust Division of the Department of Justice (DOJ), both of which have concurrent jurisdiction under the Clayton Antitrust Act of 1914 to review mergers and acquisitions. The Hart-Scott-Rodino (HSR) Antitrust Improvements Act of 1976 requires parties to qualifying transactions to involve pre-merger notifications when the price of the transaction is beyond a published annual value threshold by the FTC. After being filed, a preliminary review is performed by the agencies (usually within 30 days), and they may give a so-called Second Request, a request for more information to further the investigation (Kotsantonis, et al., 2020). The U.S. scenario involves aggressive economic scrutiny, transparency in the process and strong enforcement means involving the potential of litigation against blocking of anticompetitive mergers.

A more recent turn of events has slightly changed this paradigm to adjust to new challenges surrounding digital consolidation, market power through data, and geopolitics. The Committee on Foreign Investment in the United States (CFIUS) has ever been a highly prominent body that has been looking into transactions that involve sensitive industries or foreign buyers, especially those that originate in adversarial countries (Lins et al., 2017). At the same time, the agencies have started to look at the environmental, social, and governance (ESG) factors as well as labour-market impacts on merger evaluations. These evolutions signify an argument moving away from the market-share-only-based ratings in favour of a more comprehensive, resilience-driven regulatory system.

3.2 European Union: Centralised Control via DG COMP and the Digital Markets Act (DMA)

The merger and acquisitions (M&A) regulatory regime in the European Union is underpinned by the European Community Merger Regulation (ECMR) that identifies one mechanism of reviewing mergers and acquisitions with a so-called community dimension where aggregate turnover is reached between the EU member countries. Directorate-General for Competition (DG COMP), which acts in the power of the European Commission, serves as the administrative central authority in regard to merger control. Importantly, it is divided into a two-stage model: Phase I is an initial examination (25 working days) of rather non-complex concentrations, and Phase II offers a more comprehensive analysis of the transactions that are characterised by a high level of strain or represent an increased risk of substantive competition (Broome & Quigley, 2021).

Compared to the U.S. regime, adoption of M&A regulation by the EU lays more stress on market dominance and structural barriers to competition, which tend to resort to both structural and behavioural solutions. A conceptual shift is also reinforced by the recent adoption of the Digital Markets Act (DMA). The DMA includes increased oversight and a requirement on so-called gatekeeper platforms, which are usually large technology companies with a strong market presence; all mergers must be notified, even where the targets fall below the usual thresholds. This is to express Eurowide alert to data ghettoes, algorithmic cartels and closed-shop business practices that can lead to the destruction of digital competition and a plural economy. Notably, the DMA, which introduces a crossroad between classical competition and digital market regulation, also shows how new modes of regulation are able to balance economic stability and technological dynamism (Gallagher & Pisani, 2019).

3.3 India: Hybrid Framework through the Competition Commission and FDI Controls

India has a mixed regulatory framework, which combines the traditional forms of competition regulation that include the Competition Commission of India (CCI), established under the Competition Act, 2002, with a progressive cycle of planning tools and interventions directed towards the advancement of the national causes. The main merger control body is the CCI, and the transacting parties have to notify the authority in all those cases when the value of assets and the turnover within the group reach the statutory limits (Koopman & van Tongeren, 2021). These notifications either activate the Form I process in the case of combinations that are uncomplicated or the Form II process in cases when the transactions are considered complex or may have heavy ramifications. With the maximum legal limit of 210 days, most of the cases are settled within 30 to 60 working days.

The features of the framework lie in the dual control of foreign direct investment (FDI) that the Department for Promotion of Industry and Internal Trade (DPIIT) and Reserve Bank of India (RBI) have (Haunschild & Beckman, 2020). These agencies run regimes with different types of approaches to approval hierarchy, sector caps, and automatic as opposed to administrative approaches to approval. One relatively new trend in the legal environment, Press Note 3 (2020), requires the pre-review of FDI to be conducted by the government where the source country is located along the land border with India, which is generally understood as the reaction to Chinese investment in strategic areas under a pretext of security concerns. At the same time, the regime is turning towards including environmental, social, and governance (ESG) standards, data governance standards, and labour compliance aspects in due diligence related to mergers, which highlights the fact that the country simultaneously pursues liberalisation and the retention of sovereign control over key sectors of its economy, which locates India as a jurisdiction that is simultaneously responsible and market-orientated (Xu & Bradley, 2022).

3.4 Brazil: CADE's Emerging Influence in Global Merger Oversight

The Administrative Council for Economic Defence (CADE), the Brazilian competition authority, enjoys international fame because of its technical quality and autonomy of decisions. Brazil requires pre-merger notification of transactions that do not meet the turnover thresholds in Law No. 12,529/2011 but have a nexus with Brazil that meet the domestic market impact qualifications. CADE is a two-tier review system and provides channels for fast-tracking simple deals and thorough analysis of more complicated or sensitive deals (Huang et al., 2024).

Notable among the Brazilian regime is that it is becoming more affirmed to unilateral effects theories, especially in situations whereby the market has high entry barriers, no substitutes or asymmetric information. CADE has shown its readiness to block or make conditional mergers that may be worldwide in terms of operation but have a local competitive effect, like in the case of Bayer-Monsanto and AT&T-Time Warner deals. The agency has also embarked on the consideration of the aspect of public interest, such as ESG principles and labour rights, in aid of its analytical structures, which has been a wider trend in Latin America of socially responsible enforcement of regulations (Teece, 2022). Despite this success, Brazil has institutional shortcomings that include judicial inefficiency, poor coordination between federal and state entities, and a lack of a specific mechanism to screen foreign direct investments. Regulatory predictability is also an issue because there are very few formal mandates around ESG, and political interventions at times muddy the waters. Nonetheless, Brazil has demonstrated an exemplary way of developing technically and internationally harmonised competition authorities among emergent economies.

3.5 ASEAN: Fragmented Regulatory Landscape with Aspirations for Integration

The legal and regulatory system that surrounds the M&A practice in the ASEAN region is significantly fragmented, with the intense differences of lawful maturity and strength of enforcement and the independence of agencies to comply with laws and governmental regulations between the ten member countries of ASEAN. Formal merger-control competition laws and implementing national competition laws are in place already in some jurisdictions, such as Singapore, Malaysia and the Philippines, whilst Cambodia, Laos and Myanmar remain in the process of implementing their frameworks. This non-homogeneity subjects cross-border firms, even in the regional firms that venture into cross-border business, to a considerable amount of challenge, especially in the digital areas where borders to markets are becoming more transnational (Reddy, 2016). Lack of a common merger-review procedure introduces arbitrage and uncertainty; as an example, the GrabUber merger can be provided: the merger was fined in certain jurisdictions (e.g., Singapore and the Philippines) and was not scrutinised by regulation in others. Despite the ASEAN Competition Action Plan (2021–2025) aiming at the harmonisation and capacity building, lack of enforceable regional prescriptions and agreements on mutual recognition restricts successful coordination. Moreover, ESG principles, digital-market regulations, and data-privacy factors are applied unevenly across the world, which exposes investors and acquirers to an unevenly peppered regulatory liability.

The implementation of these issues requires the creation of a regional platform/ system of M&A publicity, the strengthening of institutional links (including that of the ASEAN Expert Group on Competition), and the facilitation of convergence via model laws, technical assistance, and online integration (Khan & Khan, 2024). Those reforms would increase the predictability of the law and the appeal of the region as a single investment point.

Table 1. Comparative overview of M&A regulatory frameworks

Jurisdiction	Merger Control Authority	Review Thresholds	Review Timelines	FDI Screening	Digital/ESG Integration
United States	FTC & DOJ	HSR Act thresholds	30 days (extendable)	CFIUS reviews	Emerging focus on data and ESG
European Union	DG COMP	EU-wide turnover	Phase I (25 days), Phase II (90+ days)	Limited centralized FDI	Strong on DMA & digital platforms
India	CCI & DPIIT	Asset/Turnover-based	Up to 210 days	Yes (sector- and origin-based)	Policy shift towards ESG
Brazil	CADE	Turnover thresholds	240 days max	No formal process	ESG and public interest integration growing
ASEAN	Multiple National Bodies	Varies by country	Varies	Varies	Fragmented, minimal digital/ESG focus

This discussion gives a comparative analysis of the five jurisdiction rule regimes, which are crucial. In the United States, the Federal Trade Commission and the Department of Justice are authorised by the Hart-Scott-Rodino (HSR) Act to impose a 30-day review period. As a supplement to this, the Committee on Foreign Investment in the United States (CFIUS) regulates foreign direct investment (FDI) and pursues a data-driven approach, which is very sensitive to data stewardship and ESG considerations. The selection of a turnover threshold is done EU-wide by the Directorate General for Competition (DG COMP) in the European Union, and the review process is held in two phases. Noting that on the one hand, national regulators are still screening FDI, the EU can be seen as the leader in digital regulation, as the Digital Markets Act (DMA) proves, and does consider ESG factors. Assets-based/ turnover-based thresholds are used by India, and the maximum time the asset/turnover can be reviewed is 210 days; in this country, both origin-based and sector-based reviews of FDI exist, and this is gradually progressing in ESG policy alignment.

Brazil is based on turnover caverns and a provision of 240 days of review, and even though there is no formal FDI screening procedure, ESG sensibility is on the rise. On the contrary, the constituent nations within the ASEAN exhibit a massive heterogeneity: the elements of the M&A regime in the country are heterogeneous as well, and ESG and digital regulation are unfinished and disorganised.

4. CASE STUDIES: LEGAL OUTCOMES AND STRATEGIC IMPACT

This section will focus on critically analysing three key M&A deals in order to identify the real-life effects of the framework of laws and regulations on strategic business performance and economic durability. Through observation of real-life transactions, such as the Microsoft-Activision merger, the Vodafone-Grade-Hutch merger, and the Grab and Uber merger, this section brings out the role that legal clarity, institutional maturity, and economic competitiveness play in both the developed and emerging economies (Pantazi, 2012). These case studies highlight the fact that the power and form of the regulatory institutions can advance or restrain economic change with mergers and acquisitions.

4.1 Microsoft–Activision Merger: Convergence of Antitrust and National Security Regulation

The merger between Microsoft and Activision Blizzard, in which Microsoft got it for an estimated USD 68.7 billion, is an incident that is a landmark in terms of competition law and national security in the digital world. The agreement, which had been announced in January 2022, was met immediately with increased interest worldwide, especially given the size of the acquisition and the rise of Microsoft in the field of cloud computing and gaming.

United States: Aggressive Antitrust Oversight

In the United States, the Federal Trade Commission (FTC) was a vocal opponent of the merger based on the concerns of antitrust fairness founded on the prospects of Microsoft limiting the use of Activision's popular gaming material, including the Call of Duty franchise, by its competitors (Han & Lee, 2023). The FTC commission's administrative complaint and the legal challenge that followed highlighted the new and energised strategy of reviewing Big Tech transactions by the federal agency under the Biden Administration. Even though the federal court finally permitted the transaction to go through, the proceeding was a sign of a larger movement to increase the application of Section 7 of the Clayton Act.

European Union: Conditional Approval and Remedies

Conversely, the European Commission conditionally approved the decision after behaviour remedies were accepted, such as (among other things) Microsoft committing not to do anything to undermine rival cloud game services by setting out ten-year licensing agreements (Itan, Sylvia, & Septiany, 2025). This policy revealed the tendency of the EU towards ex-ante regulation, including market access provisions rather than structural relief. The subtlety of the Commission showed its concern to preserve competition in the dynamically developing tech markets.

United Kingdom: The National Security Layer

The deal had earlier been ruled out in April 2023 by the Competition and Markets Authority (CMA) of the United Kingdom because of the dominance of cloud gaming by Microsoft. But an updated format involving the transfer of cloud streaming rights to a third party eventually persuaded the CMA to clear the acquisition later in the year (Knittel & Stango, 2021). The regulating feature demonstrated a new propensity of the UK to exercise its sovereign economic authority after Brexit, bringing an element of national security into the process of merger scrutiny.

Strategic Impact

It is through this case that we see how difficult it is to provide multi-jurisdictional review coordination, particularly when the rationales of the regulation, antitrust, data protection, and national security vary depending on regions. In the case of emerging market economies, it also points to the need to develop technologically competent regulatory agencies that shall be able to evaluate new market forms in the digital economy.

4.2 Vodafone–Hutchison Deal: The Taxation Paradox in FDI Law

The VodafoneHutchison deal of 2007 has become the landmark in the legal and regulatory framework of the country, especially in the aspect of foreign direct investment (FDI), indirect transfer, and retroactive taxation. Vodafone bought out Hutchison's 67 per cent share in Hutchison Essar, which was an offshore deal, planned through a Coop broker or operator under the Cayman Islands. Although technically, the deal was signed not in India, it implied a direct effect on dominance over Indian telecom resources (Gallagher & Pisani, 2019).

Supreme Court Ruling and Retrospective Tax Law

The Indian tax authorities wanted to tax the transaction on capital gains grounds, based on the fact that the transaction amounted to a transfer of Indian assets. The tax demand was opposed by Vodafone and was ruled by the Supreme Court in 2012 against the taxation department in a landmark judgement in favour of the company Vodafone. The court ruled that the Indian tax department had no jurisdiction to tax indirect transfers made offshore, stating that there was a legal certainty in tax law, but the Indian government reverted with amendments to the Income Tax Act, 1961, with a retrospective effect of 1962 to tax such deals. This action attracted immense reaction among the global business community, and it had an adverse impact on the FDI environment of India (Reddy, 2016).

International Arbitration and Legal Reform

Vodafone engaged in arbitration during the India and the Netherlands Bilateral Investment Treaty. In 2020, the Permanent Court of Arbitration at The Hague concluded that the retrospective tax demand by India contravened the principle of fair and equitable treatment under international law. The decision compelled India to revalue its taxation plan and triggered the repealing of the retrospective taxation measure in 2021.

Strategic Impact

The case is an example of the harm regulatory uncertainty and legal intervention cause in developing markets. It makes notable the fact that legal certainties and institutional confidence are essential to economic buoyancy. The Vodafone case further led to the faster liberalisation of FDIs in India, and it underlined the importance of transparent regulation and the rule of law in the dynamics of complicated cross-border dealings (Haunschild & Beckman, 2020).

4.3 Grab–Uber Consolidation: Regional Enforcement in Digital Market M&A

One of the most influential mergers in the ASEAN digital economy was the acquisition of Uber in Southeast Asia by Grab in 2018. The deal saw Uber paving the way to the Southeast Asian market in exchange for a share in Grab, where the company's business operation was basically sold across eight jurisdictions, such as Singapore, Malaysia, Indonesia, Thailand, and the Philippines.

Fragmented Enforcement across ASEAN

Competition issues were of immediate concern to the merger since Grab and Uber were the two competitive firms in the ride-hailing market. The Competition and Consumer Commission of Singapore (CCCS) in Singapore concluded that the merger had reduced the competition significantly. It charges a monetary fine and requires a solution, such as monitoring of prices and restriction of driver exclusivity (Koopman & van Tongeren, 2021).

In Malaysia, the Malaysia Competition Commission (MyCC) made its investigations and made an offer for the fine. Yet, the absence of enforcement in continuity of other countries of ASEAN showed a serious gap in regulation.

Lack of Regional Regulatory Harmonisation

The GrabUber acquisition revealed the regulatory fragmentation in the ASEAN. The enforcement of laws, the enforcement abilities, and the review procedures differ extremely among the member countries, even though the plan of action on competition exists in the form of an ASEAN Competition Action Plan. Consequently, the transaction moved on with minimal or no interference at all in certain jurisdictions, which may give the impression that future companies may strategise to abuse jurisdictions in the under-regulated markets (Gallagher & Pisani, 2019).

Strategic Impact

This case indicates that it is high time that laws surrounding competition in digital markets converge regionally (Allee & Yohn, 2018). ASEAN emerging economy By having a supranational system of merger reviews or a unified system of cross-border digital deal checks that can avoid the monopolisation of a market and bring benefits to consumers, emerging economies can take advantage by securing a similar system.

Figure 2. Regulatory timeline of major M&A transactions

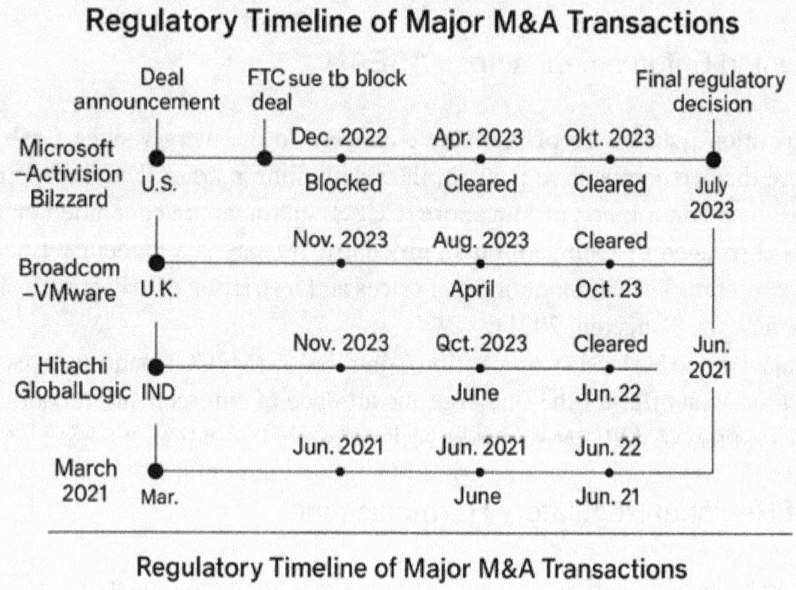

The present comparative schematic shows the regulatory chronology of three high-profile mergers, such as Microsoft-Activision Blizzard, Broadcom-VMware, and Hitachi-GlobalLogic, across key jurisdictions (U.S., U.K., and India). The visual focuses on the most important milestones, such as deal announcements, regulatory investigations (e.g., FTC intervention), and clearance results. It highlights the difference in the regulatory timetables, disparities in how the process is handled in different jurisdictions and a rising trend of coordinated antitrust reviews in complicated international transactions.

Figure 3. Comparative regulatory timelines for microsoft–activision, vodafone–hutchison, and grab–uber transactions

The figure provides a comparative analysis of regulatory milestones of three major transactions, i.e., Microsoft-Activision, Vodafone-Hutchison and Grab-Uber. The timelines record developments such as the date of announcement, court decision, enforcement of remedy, and final approval of the U.S., U.K., Singapore and the Philippines.

- The announced Microsoft Activision merger in January 2022 went to court in the U.S. in December 2022, and remedies were imposed in February 2024, and it has been approved in Singapore as of January 2019.
- Vodafone Hutchison deal started in September 2023, and regulatory notices/remedies followed in February 2024, and finalised Singapore was noted in January 2019.
- The GrabUber merger commenced with ASEAN regulatory notices in April 2018, with the Philippines and Singapore granting approvals between October 2023 and February 2019.

This process of comparisons reveals even greater differences between the amounts and sequences of review time and approvals in various jurisdictions and the complexity and multi-jurisdictional aspect of international mergers and acquisitions.

4.5 Legal Clarity vs. Institutional Maturity: Comparative Lessons

With rence to the three case studies, it can be explained that both the legal clarity and institutional maturity are the important characteristics to determine successful M&A governance (Allee & Yohn, 2018). These lessons are of special concern to new markets, which want to achieve economic resilience and at the same time attract foreign investment.

Key Insights:

1. Known legal regimes (e.g.,, EU merger process) are likely to lower transaction risks and promote capital movements across borders.
2. Inconsistency in the institutional setting (viz..: retrospective tax case of Vodafone) makes trust meaningless and can cause long court battles and distress to the investors.
3. In most of the emerging jurisdictions, the capability to regulate digital markets is insufficient, and thus major platforms are free to develop uncontrolled (as in the casecase of Grab-Uber).
4. Some form of remedial flexibility, perhaps behavioural remedies or planned divestitures, can strike a balance between innovation and competition, as in the case of Microsoft and Activisionision.
5. Effective mechanisms in the coordination of regions are vital to effective management of cross-border M&A, particularly within trade blocks such as ASEAN where regulatory capacities are different (Bekaert, Harvey, Lundblad, & Siegel, 2021).

5. THE INTERNATIONAL INSTITUTION'SS ROLE IN M&A HARMONISATION AND POLICY

5.1 Introduction: Cross-Border Legal Coherence in the Regulation of M&A Need

With the mergers and acquisitions (M&A) making cross-institutional boundaries out to a bigger level, the probability of harmonising the laws of different countries becomes a major issue,, especially forr the emerging economies. Such jurisdictions are not necessarily mature in terms of their institutionalisation, lack strength in regulatory action and have fragmented legal traditions. This intricacy may make handling massive and international business mergers quite tasking. In this regard,, international institutions are important in creating global standards, cooperation among regulatory bodies, and the developmentment of capacities of countries thatt are still in the processcess of forming competition and investment regulatory systems (Lins et al., 2017). Even soft institutional power like that exerted by the Organisationtion for Economic Co-operation and Development (OECD), the United Nations Conference on Trade and Development (UNCTAD), and the World Trade Organisation (WTO) exceeds the capacity to influence policy; they are building the legal infrastructure through which M&A governance in the developing world becomes resilient and transparent. These organisations have their own instruments, mandates and areas of interest,, and all these enhance harmonised, rule-based market systems.

5 2 OECD: Creating Norms and Best Practices in Merger Control

The OECD is one of the most authoritative arenas in terms of the policy debate and the harmonisation of law in the area ofcompetition law,, such as merger control. Although the instruments of the OECD are non-binding, it has strong influence as a norm-setter since it can command a consensus among not only developed ut also developing economies. The body has made some important guidelines,, especially the Recommendation of the Council on Merger Review (2005, revised),, containing guidelines relating to pre-merger notification processes, reviewing the competition impact of mergers and applying structural and behavioural remedies. The guidelines also promote a convergence of standards in key aspects of procedural aspects such as jurisdictional limits, openness in enforcement, and deadlines which is missing in emerging economies (Huang et al., 2024).

Additionally, the OECDOECD organises a peerer review process, which becomes a diagnostic and benchmarking instrument of the national legal frameworks. These are reviews discussing the extent to which national competition agencies meet the principles of good practices internationally, finding the sources of legal ambiguity or inefficiency of the processes. The emerging economies can learn new models of laws, as well as experience in enforcement,, by engaging in the OECD Global Forum on Competition. Such sharing of regulatory intelligence aids capacity-building without significant risk of regulatory arbitrage in sectors where digitalisation is increasing at a rapid rate. The OECD therefore serves as the important fulcrum between local development of law and international harmonisation in terms of having blueprintsin the legal architecture that can be scaled down by developing countries coming up with a modern M&A system (Kim & Park, 2020).

5.3 UNCTAD: Strength of Legal Means and Development-Based Regulation

Whereas the OECDOECD appeals more to harmonisation of policy within more or less developed legal systems, the United Nations Conference on Trade and Development (UNCTAD) has a developmental orientation, which focuses on the needs of low— and middle-income economies (Liu, Fang, Hu, & Lv, 2024). The involvement of UNCTAD in the policylicy of M&A is rooted in its general mission of promoting itable trade, investment and development. Its main instrument, the United Nations Set of Principles and Rules on Competition, acts as a multilateral treatise promoting the use of fair and transparent laws on competition. Contrary to the nature of soft law mechanisms of the OECD,ECD, the UN Set actively encourages the development of of friendly competition policy by taking into account the market'ss vulnerabilities and asymmetries in the economy that are frequently observed in the Global South (UNCTAD, 2023).

UNCTAD provides a completete package of technical assistance – draughting ofof antitrust and merger law, setting up regulatory authorities and dispute resolution organs. It has made voluntary peer reviews in many jurisdictions,, such as the case of Zambia, Kenya or Indonesia,, and it has offered policy roadmaps specific to national jurisdictions. These reviews not merely detect the legality gaps ut also suggest the specific reforms with reference to the merger thresholds, public interest issues, and the structure of remedies. Moreover, UNCTAD hosts regional training forums, including the African Competition Forum and the Latin American Competition Forum, which convenes legislators, regulators and legal academicians to concentrate on comparative cross-border legal homogenisation. Most importantly, UNCTAD stresses need forr legal capacity building that is inclusive (Siri & Zhu, 2024). It enables the developing nations to engage innovatively in international M&A activity by strengthening their legal sovereignty and allowing the fashioning of control systems on mergers that consider the domestic economy traditions without breaking any global trade or investment regulations (Xu & Bradley, 2022). In other words, the role played by UNCTAD is transformational; it does not just play the role of a legal adviser but a development partner that assists in building resilient legal institutions on a bottom-up basis.

5.4 WTO: Legal commitments in order to safeguard market access and rights to investments

The World Trade Organisation (WTO) is not involved in the regulation of the M&A transactions; however, its legal frameworks play a major role in determining the circumstances under which the transactions occur, particularly in those areas where they have committed to the liberalisation of natural relations. The WTO is facilitating market access, investor protection and non-discrimination through its agreements, including the Generaleral Agreement on Trade in Services (GATS) and the Agreementment on Trade-Related Investment Measures (TRIMs). These legal obligations limit the regulatory discretion of the domestic authorities and facilitate the making of a predictable legal environment of foreign acquisition and corporate restructuring (WTO, 2021).

With M&A deals with foreign investors, the WTO disciplines are especially delicate because the merger control processes at the national level, including the decisions made, are likely to nullify the concept of Most-Favouredd Nation (MFN) or National Treatment (NT). As an example, it can be when a country prevents a merger on a nationalal interest basis without fairly definable legal-like standards, which can be treated as an indirect hurdle to trade/investment,which is subject to legal challenge/redress under the WTO dispute settlement mechanism. More so, the WTO trade transparency rules urge governments to publish their merger review laws,, which createclarity in the law and lowerinformation asymmetries. Another significant contribution of the WTO WTO is that it offers a dispute settlement system, which is neutral in the sense that it gives the governments peace to address the issue of regulatory protectionism (Claessens & Yafeh, 2019). Although there are only a few WTO disputes to date that have related to M&A specifically, its jurisprudence regarding the trade-relatedinvestment measures nevertheless limits states in their use of arbitrary or discriminatory merger policies indirectly. In the casecase of the emerging economies, this this architecture of the WTO WTO is adequate in terms that they still have the sovereign discretion to operate markets by regulating themem; however, such regulation should be on the lines of adhering to rule-of-law practices in the international trading regime.

5.5 Synthesis of Comparative Institutional Contributions: A Synthesis

All these three institutions, including the OECD, the UNCTAD and the WTO, play progressively unique but complementary roles to ensure that the legal environment facing mergers and acquisitions at the international level is well established. The OECD is very advanced in the merging of policies and the simplification of the process, providing the soft law instruments and the concept of peer learning that enable the collaboration across borders. In its developmental role, UNCTAD concentrates on enhancing capacity-building and the strength of the legal system of under-resourced jurisdictions, conforming merger control policies to the domestic economic realities. In the meantime, the WTO offers a rule-based system of trade and investment which poses legal restraint and limits discretionary regulation (Umashankar, Bahadir, & Bharadwaj, 2022).

Table 2. To contextualize their respective contributions

Institution	Primary Legal Function	Core Instruments	Key Benefits to Emerging Markets
OECD	Legal and procedural convergence	Recommendations, Peer Reviews, Policy Dialogues	Exposure to global best practices, legal benchmarking, procedural consistency
UNCTAD	Legal capacity-building and reform	UN Set on Competition, Peer Reviews, Training Programs	Tailored legislative drafting, institutional development, regulatory empowerment
WTO	Trade-related investment discipline	GATS, TRIMs, Dispute Settlement Body	Non-discrimination, market access guarantees, legal predictability

The table gives some outline of the roles that major international institutions play in influencing the answers to legal and regulatory frameworks in emerging markets. The OECD provides and encourages legal and procedural convergence with recommendations, peer reviews and policy discussions, providing exposure to the global best practice and increasing the legal consistency of countries. With instruments such as the UN Set on Competition, UNCTAD is able to strengthen institutional and regulatory frameworks by boosting legal capacity-building through custom legislative assistance, peer-to-peer reviews, and training initiatives. The WTO additionally plays its role that includes enforcement of trade-related investment disciplines like GATS, TRIMs, and the dispute settlement body, which offers non-discrimination, market access, and other legal predictability disciplines of international trade and investment.

With the invaluable support of international institutions, legal harmonisation is fostered both vertically (domestic-to-international) and horizontally (across different countries). This robust foundation empowers emerging markets to establish resilient, sustainable, and inclusive M&A regulatory policies, instilling a sense of stability and confidence.

5.6 Toward a Multilateral Legal Framework for M&A

The participation of international organisations in establishing merger control and corporate governance policies implies great consequences for the growing economies. Although legal harmonisation does not mean legal uniformity, the normative, technical and dispute-settlement arrangements offered by institutions such as the OECD, UNCTAD and WTO are aids to creating foreseeable, transparent and investment-friendly environments. Their endeavours assist in calming down the threats of regulatory multiplicity, political appendage and legal uncertainty which are still languishing in many emerging market territories. In the end, through the incorporation of international legal principles into the national system of M&A, states will more easily trade off one of the two driving forces of the globalised economy: the need to protect competition and the need to enable a strong economy (Sherwood & Pollard, 2018).

6. LEGAL SYSTEMS AS ECONOMICAL BALANCERS

Legal systems in the context of merger and acquisition (M&A) activities in the emerging markets one surpasses the traditional role of legal regulation, which is primarily regulatory in nature. Well-designed and well-intentionally implemented infrastructural legal systems form the basis of maintaining a conservative status of the national economies and are most effective in the cases where the maturity of the institutions is still young. The legal system is a bulwark in such markets where volatility in governance, judiciary and policymaking may discourage investments; a framework that economic participants can use to interpret, anticipate and react to structural and transactional risks to minimise them. Through these means of predictability, sustenance of corporate governance, inculcation of gradual standards such as ESG compliance, and compulsion of socially responsible behaviour by creating corporate social responsibility (CSR), the law systems play not only the role of enforcement but also enable the wider economy to be resilient. Specifically, this is the part where we discuss five greater legal means through which certain legal processes enhance economic stability: increasing the predictability of foreign investment, preserving the rights of minority shareholders and employment, encouraging the incorporation of ESG principles in due diligence procedures, restructuring the transactions or deals around CSR requirements and, last but not least, developing long-term models of economic governance (Kayser & Zülch, 2024).

6.1 Predictability, Law and Foreign Investor Confidence

Legal predictability is an important determiner of investor confidence in emerging markets where legal uncertainty in many cases is aggravated by poor institutions, inconsistent regulation and political interference. The determination of foreign direct investment (FDI) transactions, albeit M&A, is based on the premise that the application of legal rules is subject to application based on equity, transparency and consistency. Investors in such cases will view the market as high-risk when regulatory organisations are not clear on the thresholds regarding merger review, instances where the court makes judgements on antitrust or competition laws which contradict prior conclusions and cases where the deal approvals are excessively politicised, and they thus fly their capitals or attach risk premiums to them (Broome

& Quigley, 2021). Legal predictability thus is not only a technical issue, but it is also a macroeconomic requirement. The predictability and the clarity of the legal regime facilitate the ability of international or local companies to carry out due diligence, which is more precise; the ability to deploy resources more efficiently; and the ability to design deals with sound underlying strategy.

The United States and the European Union serve as excellent examples of how a combination of codification (e.g., the Hart-Scott-Rodino Act in the United States) and administrative uniformity (e.g., the merger procedure of the European Commission within DG COMP) can create a strong investment environment. These regions have established a rule-based atmosphere through well-defined deadlines in merger notification, clear jurisdictional review thresholds, and established procedures on how to behave competitively with prohibited practices. To build credibility, emerging markets should consider adopting similar legal engineering practices. The lack of such predictability can lead to overregulation, delays, or unexpected legal conflicts, ultimately hindering the overall economic vitality.

6.2 Corporate Governance: Workers Rights and Minority Protection

Another critical stabilising role of legal regimes is in the sphere of corporate governance. The M&A transactions are often concerned with the changes in the control, ownership, and operational combination, the latter providing notable implications to the minority shareholders and the workforce. When in the process of merging, minority shareholders are more often than not subjected to the risk of marginalisation or expropriation, especially in emerging markets where family-owned and promoter-led firms reign (Khan & Khan, 2024). The greatest remedy to this effect is legal standards, including public compulsory disclosures, approval of shareholders, exit terms and self-certification of valuation. In other countries such as India, legal frameworks to protect the minority shareholders exist in the Companies Act, 2013, along with SEBI provisions. However, in reality, weak implementation of these laws and slow or expensive legal recourse have neutralised such legal protections.

Besides the protection of shareholders, there has to be protection of labour rights in the course of the M&A transitions to avoid the socio-economic disruption. When regulatory measures lack strength, job losses, reduction in benefits, and the worsening workplace environment may be the most frequent result. In this respect, the ARD of the European Union provides a universal standard, as it requires the transit of the contracts of the employees within the change of ownership of the business to ensure continuation of the job. The analogous policies are available to be integrated by the emergent economies so that the labour would no longer become a victim bull on the altar of corporate efficiencies. Addressing the question of worker consultation requirements, enforceable severance promises and recognising trade unions even after the merger are thus issues that must be included in the jurisdiction of such legal systems. Such provisions are not only safeguarding the vulnerable populations but also serving long-term industrial peace and productivity, which are two of the essential elements of economic stability (Musandu & Schoombee, 2019).

6.3 Incorporating ESG Criteria into M& Compliance

Environmental, Social, and Governance (ESG) standards have now evolved not only into mandatory principles but also into significant measures during regulatory reviews (that are above-average or high-impact M&A deals). In the legal system of the emerging markets, there is a need to acknowledge how structural the risk compliances to ESG integrators can be in securing the consolidation of corporates to avoid any risk of environmental degradation, social displacement, or failure of governance. This is especially true of those jurisdictions that are at risk of exposure to climatic vulnerability, resource inadequacy, and socio-political instability. In an ESG-orientated due diligence, not just financial and operational risk areas are assessed, but also the legal risks such as carbon footprints, safe waste disposal, and even violations of human rights and lack of diversity on the board. Therefore, laws should require that the ESG parameters be included in disclosures before transactions and reporting requirements after mergers.

A number of mature economies already started efforts to institutionalise ESG within the corporate governance and M&A laws. To give an example, the Supply Chain Due Diligence Act of Germany or Directives on Corporate Sustainability Due Diligence of the European Union reveal the growing demands on legally binding compliance with ESG. In India, there is another programme launched by the Securities and Exchange Board of India (SEBI), called the Business Responsibility and Sustainability Report (BRSR), which would help standardise ESG disclosures of the top 1000 listed companies. However, the developing economies are quite behind in the application of these requirements in M&A reviews (Brouthers & Brouthers, 2020). The legal systems should develop so that the compliance with ESG becomes a core aspect of the merger approval process, not a secondary objective under soft law. This transformation would not only bring the emerging markets closer to the international standards of investments but also support wider climate resiliency, inclusive growth, and stakeholder capitalism.

6.4 Regulatory Techniques to CSR in Deal Making

Corporate Social Responsibility (CSR) is a concept which has gained popularity in the legal framework of the emerging economies, especially countries with stakeholder-based forms of governance. Although CSR had always been considered as a voluntary or philanthropic initiative, the rise of legal norms has aimed at making CSR an obligation to be secured by legal means, particularly in areas where corporate activities touch on broader social aspects (Dissanaike, Liu, & Sturm, 2021). In India, the legality of the qualified companies obliged to part with some of their profits to provide socially beneficial schemes as dictated by Section 135 of the Companies Act, 2013, has established a precedent as to how CSR can be embedded in statutes and laws that govern such companies. When M&A deals are being processed, these mandates may affect the way deals are structured, assessed and implemented. As an example, acquirers might require the determination of whether their set-after-merger body will breach the CSR limit, which requires new legal requirements. Moreover, regulators in emerging economies can tactically employ CSR commitments in the condition of mergers, particularly in events that involve public concerns. Conditional approvals can be used to include behavioural remedies related to CSR, i.e., requiring a company to invest in local infrastructure, education, or public health, thus relating the actions of firms to achieving positive outcomes in the public realm. This kind of CSR adoption in the laws and regulations will focus the M&A transactions on the long-term objectives of the society and not on short-term profitability. In addition, it enhances the political and social legitimacy of massive corporate mergers, which will minimise opposition by civil society, labour unions and local governments (Babu & Jagadish, 2022).

6.5 ESG Legal Screening Process in M&A Due Diligence (Visual Representation)

In order to provide the examples of how legal systems may organise the ESG review mechanisms in the context of M&A transactions, the following model may be taken – ESG Legal Screening Workflow (Kotsantonis et al., 2020). This figure is shown to specify different points during which ESG factors come into contact with legal review, including the initial due diligence, during or after the merger. The model entails:

1. Pre-Transaction Screening: Pending litigations regarding social/labour or governance red flags, identification of environmental liabilities, and the use of legal guidance and ESG consultants to complete risk assessment. This stage entails examination of pollution control records, opposition of the community and board structure.
2. Regulatory Filing and Disclosure: The party must also disclose ESG-related information in filings with competition authorities and regulators in the party

sectors when seeking approval of a merger. Consultations with stakeholders can also be required at this point.

3. This review and clearance: Regulatory Authorities review ESG data as an input in their general risk and interest analysis. The acceptance can be limited to ESG commitments like emission cut initiatives, gender equality policies, or hiring local workers.
4. Hen post-merger monitoring and enforcement: When the merger has been accepted, it should be monitored and even enforced through the legal systems to ensure the ESG obligations signed are met. This can consist of regular compliance reports, third-party audits and non-compliance penalties.

This framework stresses that ESG goes beyond the periphery of legality evaluation; it is central to the long-term effectiveness, legality, and acceptability of M&A transactions. Conclusively, the legal framework of any given economy, and more so in the emerging markets, is a determinative factor towards stabilising the economic effects of mergers and acquisitions (Allee & Yohn, 2018). The law can be used as both a moderator and as a proactive framework of economic resilience through making the law more predictable, improving corporate governance, enforcing ESG compliance, institutionalising CSR and instituting enforceable accountability tools. It is along this line of stabilisation interventions that international legal norms and local socio-economic realities are being made to collide, turning M&A into an engine of broad-based growth, rather than a market-distorting force. Making such a shift lies in the reforming and strengthening of the legal systems in developing regions of the world, which is not only a technical prerequisite but a strategic one as well that will ensure that the transformative potential of the M&A can be used towards achieving more inclusive, transparent, and sustainable growth.

7. SYSTEMIC LEGAL CHALLENGES IN EMERGING MARKETS

The effectiveness of a merger and acquisition (M&A) transaction in emerging markets critically depends on the nature and strength of the legal infrastructure on which it rests. Although such economies usually pursue goals of foreign investment attraction and market competitiveness in relation to M&A accomplishment, a great number of legal issues at the systems level undermine achievement of these purposes. These obstacles are not only technical and administrative but, rather, institutional and political and socio-economic limitations (Pantazi, 2012). It is in this section that the existence of these challenges is systematically reviewed so as to show how legal loopholes not only weaken the stability of the M&A events in developing countries but also weaken their strategic performance.

7.1 Regulatory Arbitrage and Forum Shopping

Regulatory arbitrage, in which companies use differences in national regulation to design transactions in friendlier jurisdictions, is one of the key demands that firms face in emerging economies. In cross-border M&As, firms might deliberately choose nations that have laxer competition regulation or have little FDI investigation, which entails the weakening of material merger control. Such a type of forum shopping makes the playing field uneven and fragmented, undermining the capacity of the national regulators. As an example, companies operating in the ASEAN can exploit the regulatory gaps present in those countries that do not have the merger notification regime in place and therefore avoid the stricter jurisdiction, such as Singapore or the Philippines (Babu & Jagadish, 2022). This movement creates unfairness in the market, promotes anti-competitive behaviour, and deteriorates the investor trust in the predictability of the law.

Policy Implication: Regional legal convergence, especially in a bloc, such as ASEAN, BRICS, and MERCOSUR, is necessary to limit regulatory arbitration and increase harmonious enforcement.

7.2 Institutional Gaps and Unequal Enforcement

In emerging markets, the problem of institutional fragility is common, in which the regulatory authorities, like competition commissions, securities regulators or the national investment regulators, are unable to impose the legal provisions in a uniform manner by virtue of their authority, resources or independence. It leads to the unequal application of M&A regulations, particularly where a politically connected or state-affiliated enterprise is concerned. In some cases the competition laws may even appear on paper, yet selective enforcement practices on the ground take priority. Courts and administrative organs may lack the technical capacity to interpret difficult economic evidence, and on certain occasions, legal decisions may even differ according to regional or political interests (Sherwood & Pollard, 2018). This erodes the credibility of the law, discourages quality investment and may also be a source of corruption.

Policy Implication: Decisions on capacity-building programmes should focus on strengthening legal institutions and be assisted by international institutions such as UNCTAD and the OECD, which should focus on providing technical assistance, judicial training and procedural changes.

7.3 Political Interference and Regulatory Capture

The constraints of political economy also take the form of regulatory capture whereby the decision-making of the public is swayed by the interests of the private sector without fairness. In several emerging markets, the M&A decision-making is not isolated from political influence, often when they involve strategic or sensitive industries like telecommunications, defence or natural resources. Interference may lead to a lack of openness in the approval procedure, selective release of acquirers (especially foreigners) or even retrogressive changes in the law to suit powerful interests. Regulatory capture is a serious threat to the independence of merger control bodies and is a threat to the legitimacy of the rule of law. As an illustration, there have been instances of political influencing of the review process of high-profile deals, particularly those involving politically prominent parties or sovereign investors in India or Brazil (Gallagher & Pisani, 2019).

Policy Implication: To depoliticise M&A regulation, it is important to have the independent competition bodies that have statutory protection and transparent decision-making patterns.

7.4 Shortage of Antitrust Legal Expertise and Professional Capacity

Institutional deficiency in terms of specialised human capital in terms of competition law, corporate restructuring, and antitrust economics is a frequent bottleneck in most developing jurisdictions. The lawyers, judges, and regulatory staff do not receive the necessary training to manage the standards and complexity of merger review, such as economic modelling or digital platforms or ESG due diligence. This gap in skills makes the consistent and uniform application of merger regulations difficult, delays the decision-making cycle, and introduces procedural uncertainty into the business environment. In addition, in many instances, access to academic and practice-orientated research on issues related to domestic competition is scarce, an aspect that hampers the spread of knowledge and development of policies.

Policy Implication: Collaboration with educational organisations, BAR councils, and international research centres ought to be sought to set up specialised teaching curriculums and generate a wisdom interchange environment of the M&A regulation.

Figure 4. Challenges to M&A regulatory effectiveness in developing economies

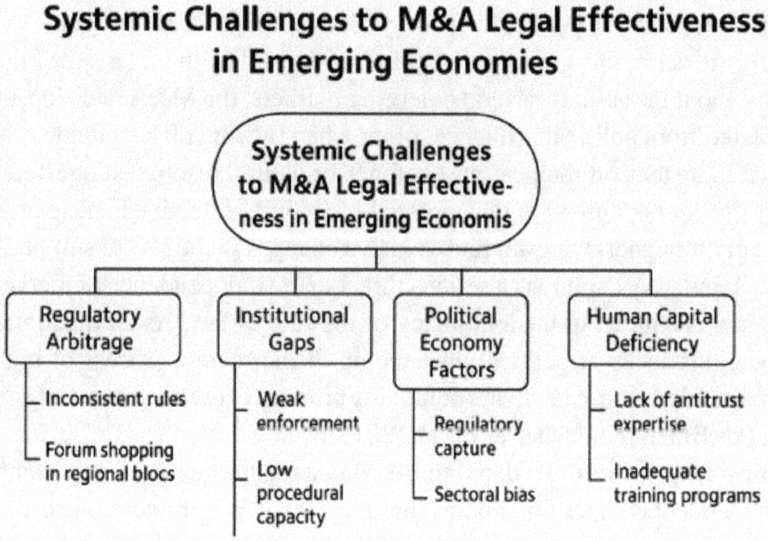

This mind map elaborates on the four important dimensions that limit effective regulation of M&A in the developing economies; they are regulatory arbitrage, institutional gaps political economy factors and human capital deficiency The presence of each of the branches exemplifies the root causes they describe, such as the existence of varied legal thresholds, restrictions in enforcement, regulatory capture and skills gaps as some of the underlying factors playing a crucial role in influencing the procedural fairness and antitrust control in cross-border transactions.

8. STRATEGIC LEGAL AND POLICY RECOMMENDATIONS

This chapter has so far shown that legal and regulatory frameworks are neither merely the procedural requirements of a merger and acquisition (M&A) process nor, literally, strategic means that can shape national economic resilience, investor confidence, and corporate sustainability. In the case of developing economies specifically, the quality, effectiveness in their clarity, and efficacy of such frameworks directly affect the outcome of the complicated merger and acquisition events. Nevertheless, the issues presented, such as regulatory unpredictability and institutional inefficiency, cross-border systems being fragmented, and strategic and multidimensional reformation agendas. In this part, the authors suggest a five-point legal-policy agenda to strengthen the M&A regulation architecture in emerging recommendations on the comparative legal research, expert interviews and global trends and governance trends, which should guide policy makers, legal practitioners and regulators on how to improve on the legal ecologies that form the backbone of sustainable M&A transactions (Botta & Kozul-Wright, 2021).

8.1 Enhancing Legal Certainty and Transparency in Merger Review Processes

Legal uncertainty and lack of transparency in the merger reviews may be one of the most conspicuous and harmful flaws of the majority of the emerging jurisdictions. One of the main pillars supporting economic agents interacting with each other in high-stakes corporate mergers entails certainty being measured as the predictability of its legal outcome, its accessibility and its reliability. Where there is ambiguity, inconsistency, or discretion in merger regulation, including discretion based on politics or bureaucracy, there is increased risk on the part of investors, and transaction costs are higher. Jurisdictions need to start by entering into the statutes limiting merger review, procedural timelines, etc. Lots of countries in development are guided by executive discretion or non-binding recommendations, thus causing inconsistencies in interpretation and indiscriminate application. This could be done by setting legal levels (e.g., size of assets, turnover) and by defining time limits to review and should help to normalise the procedure. In addition, pre-merger consultation mechanisms should be introduced, such as the step of informal guidance that is in European Union (EU) regulation or the early consultation that is taken under the Hart-Scott-Rodino Act in the United States, which would offer clarity on regulatory issues at the very beginning of planning a deal (Babu & Jagadish, 2022).

Transparency should also be provided by making decisions on mergers, reasonable regulations, and economics used by competition authorities. This furthers the responsibility, informs the market, and leads to the creation of antitrust jurisprudence in the home country. Moreover, it is possible to make the process of filing and tracking the approvals of mergers more efficient by digitising the system. Collectively, the reforms can minimise uncertainty, develop social confidence in the institutions, and increase longer-term investment in emerging economies.

8.2 Developing Cross-Border Legal Cooperation Platforms for Merger Control

Since temporary M&A has become inevitably cross-jurisdictional, especially when applied in the technology, telecommunications, and pharmaceutical industries, the legal system of any one nation can no longer exist in isolation. Regulatory inconsistency among countries brings about duplication of procedures, incompatibility of solutions, and immense delays in the duration of getting approvals, which compromises the viability and efficiency of cross-border transactions. This is particularly outrageous in the developing world, where the economies are integrated, yet the law systems are not.

New markets should focus on establishing frameworks of cross-border cooperation on merger control. Such platforms can be in the shape of bilateral memoranda of understanding (MoUs) on competition authorities or multilateral by regional economic communities (Dissanaike, Liu, & Sturm, 2021). As an illustration, ASEAN has embarked on a regional competition framework, which is, however, non-binding and rarely enforced. Better collaboration, including regular investigation procedures, notification, and mutual decision-making, has enormous potential to make cross-border transactions much more efficient. Formalising their inclusion on such platforms, not only do we improve on the home country's expertise, but it also promotes convergence in regulation, making it much easier to address multi-jurisdictional transactions in a similar and impartial way.

8.3 Building Institutional and Judicial Capacity in Competition Law Enforcement

The foundational issue of successful regulation of mergers is institutional capacity, not only at the administrative but also at the judicial level. Many of the emerging jurisdictions find their competition authorities plagued by low budgets, lack of independence, and lack of technical know-how on how to audit difficult mergers. Similarly, the judiciary seldom has expert knowledge of antitrust economics and thus renders untenable or unwarranted decisions over merger-related cases. The governments distribute resources to the capacity-building measures, particularly for regulatory agencies as well as the judicial institutions, in order to prevent such inadequacies. This also involves continuous upskilling in market analysis, economic modelling, forensic accounting and digital market investigations (Broome & Quigley, 2021). Such a learning process can be fast-tracked by technical collaboration with other regulators who can offer added experience, including the U.S. Federal Trade Commission, DG COMP on the European Commission and CADE in Brazil. A large response of this type has been realized on capacity-building missions with multilateral organisations like WTO and UNCTAD (Allee & Yohn, 2018).

At the justice level, the introduction of a dedicated bench or tribunal in competition law, such as the Indian competition law National Company Law Appellate Tribunal (NCLAT), would foster better outcome adjudication. Also, building up central databases of merger decisions, economic analyses, and legal precedents can help regulators and the courts to make consistent and high-quality judgements.

Finally, no legal regime can be effective, however well written it is, where there is no institutional capacity to make it work. This capacity building at institutional and judicial levels is thus imperative for the sustainability and credibility of M&A regulation.

8.4 Mainstreaming ESG and Digital Economy Standards in Merger Law Reforms

In the modern process of incorporating the aspect of Environmental, Social, and Governance (ESG) into the regulatory measures and other characteristics taken into account by digital markets, it stopped being an obligation. Since long-term investors are becoming more inclined to initiatives and policies that are sustainable and ethically governed, the regulations present in the emerging economies need to be upgraded to consider such factors as the aspects of merger approval (Lestari, 2022). Meanwhile, the emergence of digital monopolies and platform dominance necessitates the need for new regulatory instruments, which are not limited to the market share analysis. In this regard, ESG due diligence must be incorporated into the regime of merger notification and evaluation. Regulatory agencies shall have the authority to examine whether the proposed huge transactions are likely to cause environmental degradation, labour or right erosions, governance risk or cause a concentration of unsustainable applications. Such considerations are already becoming popular in the EU Sustainable Finance Disclosure Regulation and may be implemented as a role model.

At the same time, specific policies governing the digital era should be developed to evaluate mergers within the field in the data-driven Based on the Digital Markets Act (DMA) of the EU, new regulators might formulate regulatory principles for assessing data concentration, access on platforms, and platform-level algorithmic bias. This would involve establishing new regulatory departments inside competition authorities dealing with digital markets and the use of sophisticated technological devices in the monitoring of the markets. The merger law mainstreaming of ESG and digital considerations will not only make the regulation consistent with international norms but will also position emerging markets as progressive jurisdictions in the eyes of international investors (Reddy, 2016).

8.5 Promoting Regionally Aligned Merger Control Frameworks

Lastly, it is important to harmonise merger control regionally to save transaction costs, to eliminate match-fixing by regulatory arbitrage and to add legal coherence to economic blocs. Whereas international economic integration is taking deeper roots, there still exist serious impediments to successful, effective, and equitable

M&A activities, especially in developing global blocs like the ASEAN, BRICS, and the African Union. To eliminate this, regional blocks are supposed to work on the creation of harmonised protocols of merger review, including formulating common notification formats, unified thresholds, and timelines. Cooperation agreements, including binding agreements, or even regional competition authorities, can complement the use of soft-law forms of instruments (i.e., regional guidelines, model laws, etc.) (Gao & Johnston, 2021). A good example of such integration is the European Union, whereby the European Commission has exclusive powers to review largecross--border mergers under the European Union Merger Regulation.

In cases in which complete legal integration is impossible, mutual recognition methods can be used or synchronisation mechanisms, even though the benefits originating therefrom are significantly abundant. Such reforms will not only support cross-border transacting but also regional economic stability, mutual enforcement capability, and mutual validity of the law (Godwin & Osei, 2022).

9. CONCLUSION AND FINAL RECOMMENDATIONS

9.1 Legal Frameworks as Strategic Tools for Economic Resilience

This chapter has demonstrated that legal and regulatory regimes are not marginal tools of compliance but are critical in the formulation of successful, stable and competitive mergers and acquisitions (M. & A.), especially in emerging markets. Through poor institutional frameworks, uneven compliance, and regulatory incompleteness, the complete potential of M&A as an instrument of economic development is not realised in such jurisdictions. Using the comparative examples, as seen in the United States, European Union, India, Brazil, and ASEAN states, the chapter showcased how in countries with predictable laws that are applied with the accuracy of a technical measure, M&As are used in enhancing the stability of the nation financially, consolidation in the market, and innovation (Babu & Jagadish, 2022).

Additionally, when in the dynamics of M&As, legal frameworks should take into consideration broader issues such as national security, ESG criteria and international data transfers. The reactions of institutions to these issues — by the U.S. FTC, European Commission and CCI in India — demonstrate that well-draughted, strong legislation can reconcile the goals of private investors with the interests of the public (Godwin & Osei, 2022). Notably, the introduction of the ESG standards into merger due diligence is one transition toward the more responsible and sustainable transactional approach, a phenomenon that the legal system must enable. Legal regulation of M&As, therefore, is not just a matter of pure compliance with a technical set of rules but an economic and policy issue of equitableness in an increasingly rapidly globalising world.

9.2 Strategic Recommendations and Future Outlook

In an attempt to enhance the governance and economic resilience of M&A in emerging markets, this chapter presents 5 recommendations that can be adopted to fully strengthen what is proposed (Teece, 2022).

To begin with, the appointment of independent merger review bodies is to be done to make sure that the review has to be conducted in a manner that is professional, depoliticised and expert-led.

Second, legal integration must be achieved at the regional level to lessen the level of fragmentation and provide a predictable way of cross-border transactions, particularly within multi-jurisdictional economic blocs such as ASEAN and the African Continental Free Trade Area.

Third, the issue of ESG compliance should be integrated into merger determinations where regulatory expectations are clear and the action of the abiding regulations to facilitate a sustainable business environment are apparent.

Fourth, there must be more capacity partnerships with international institutions, e.g., OECD and UNCTAD, to build antitrust proficiency and institutional frameworks for emerging economies.

Last but not least, digitalisation of merger review is the area of priority that needs to be implemented to ensure further transparency, minimised delays, and the possibility to adjust the regulatory framework towards the modern business world.

Such transformations have implications for academicians who study the legal harmonisation; for practitioners faced with the challenges of making complex transactions; and for policy-makers trying to establish investment-friendly and yet socially responsible regulatory regimes. Well thought-out and correctly implemented, their role is not to prevent anything but rather to support economic recovery, become just and grant the necessary competitiveness in the long term.

REFERENCES

Allee, T., & Yohn, T. L. (2018). A yardstick approach to merger retrospectives. *The Journal of Finance*, *73*(2), 887–914. DOI: 10.1111/jofi.12589

Babu, S. R., & Jagadish, A. (2022). ESG compliance and firm value: Evidence from emerging markets. *Journal of International Financial Management & Accounting*, *33*(3), 345–372. DOI: 10.1111/jifm.12123

Bekaert, G., Harvey, C. R., Lundblad, C. T., & Siegel, S. (2021). Global growth opportunities and market integration. *Journal of International Economics*, *132*, 103533. DOI: 10.1016/j.jinteco.2021.103533

Botta, E., & Kozul-Wright, R. (2021). Industrial policy and institutional capacity in the global South. *Development Policy Review*, *39*(S1), O7–O27. DOI: 10.1111/dpr.12560

Broome, A., & Quigley, F. (2021). Harmonizing merger control: A global comparative analysis. *The Journal of Law & Economics*, *64*(3), 387–420. DOI: 10.1086/714431

Brouthers, K. D., & Brouthers, L. E. (2020). Acquisition or greenfield investment: An institutional perspective. *Strategic Management Journal*, *41*(9), 1679–1697. DOI: 10.1002/smj.3139

Claessens, S., & Yafeh, Y. (2019). How does corporate governance affect emerging market M&As? *Corporate Governance*, *27*(5), 343–364. DOI: 10.1111/corg.12266

Dissanaike, G., Liu, Y., & Sturm, A. (2021). The dynamic effects of antitrust policy on growth and welfare. *Journal of Development Economics*, *157*, 102719. DOI: 10.1016/j.jdeveco.2021.102719

Gallagher, K. P., & Pisani, N. (2019). State as global capitalist: FDI screening and national security. *International Affairs*, *95*(3), 685–707. DOI: 10.1093/ia/iiz095

Gao, X., & Johnston, D. (2021). Legal infrastructure and cross-border deal success. *International Business Review*, *30*(1), 101751. DOI: 10.1016/j.ibusrev.2020.101751

Godwin, A., & Osei, K. A. (2022). Investment treaty obligations and national security reviews in M&As. *Journal of International Economic Law*, *25*(4), 983–1006. DOI: 10.1093/jiel/jgac047

Han, J., & Lee, W. (2023). ESG disclosure and acquisition premiums in Asia. *Sustainability Accounting. Management and Policy Journal*, *14*(1), 34–51. DOI: 10.1108/SAMPJ-04-2021-0121

Haunschild, P. R., & Beckman, C. M. (2020). Vertical integration and market power in emerging economies. *Strategic Management Journal, 41*(12), 2360–2388. DOI: 10.1002/smj.3120

Huang, X., Yang, H., & Yang, P. (2024). The impact of cross-border mergers and acquisitions on organisational resilience. *Sustainability, 16*(6), 2242. DOI: 10.3390/su16062242

Itan, I., Sylvia, S., Septiany, S., & Chen, R. (2025). The influence of environmental, social, and governance disclosure on market reaction: Evidence from emerging markets. *Discover Sustainability, 6*(1), 347. Advance online publication. DOI: 10.1007/s43621-025-01085-0

Kayser, C., & Zülch, H. (2024). Understanding the relevance of sustainability in mergers and acquisitions: A systematic literature review on sustainability and its implications throughout deal stages. *Sustainability (Basel), 16*(2), 613. DOI: 10.3390/su16020613

Khan, R., & Khan, M. (2024, March 30). Legal challenges of mergers and acquisitions in global markets. https://lawresearchreview.com/index.php/Journal/article/view/52

Kim, S., & Park, T. (2020). Hart–Scott–Rodino notification compliance and fill delays. *Journal of Competition Law & Economics, 16*(2), 255–277. DOI: 10.1093/joclec/nhaa004

Knittel, C. R., & Stango, V. (2021). Industrial organization and competition in digital M&As. *The Journal of Industrial Economics, 69*(2), 229–260. DOI: 10.1111/joie.12210

Koopman, A., & van Tongeren, F. (2021). FDI screening & competition law interplay in the EU. *International Review of Law and Economics, 65*, 105952. DOI: 10.1016/j.irle.2020.105952

Kotsantonis, S., Pinney, C., & Serafeim, G. (2020). ESG integration in M&A deal-making: Global evidence. *Journal of Corporate Finance, 65*, 101760. DOI: 10.1016/j.jcorpfin.2020.101760

La Porta, R., Lopez-de-Silanes, F., & Shleifer, A. (2021). Corporate ownership around the world. *Review of Financial Studies, 34*(3), 107–161. DOI: 10.1093/rfs/hhaa130

Lestari, H. D. (2022). Cross-border platform mergers in ASEAN's digital market. *Singapore Academy of Law Journal, 34*, 768–794.

Lins, K. V., Servaes, H., & Tamayo, A. (2017). Social capital, trust, and firm performance: The value of CSR. *The Journal of Finance, 72*(4), 1785–1824. DOI: 10.1111/jofi.12505

Liu, X., Fang, J., Hu, X., & Lv, Y. (2024). Cross-border M&As and productivity: Technology absorption. *Systems, 12*(5), 161. DOI: 10.3390/systems12050161

Musandu, G., & Schoombee, A. (2019). Building antitrust capacity in Africa: Challenges and opportunities. *Journal of Competition Law & Economics, 15*(3), 433–462. DOI: 10.1093/joclec/nhz007

OECD. (2022). *OECD Merger Control Guidelines*. OECD Publishing.

OECD. (2023). *Competition policy in Latin America and the Caribbean*. OECD Publishing.

Pantazi, T. (2012). The legal framework for mergers and acquisitions in the European Union and the United States. In *Palgrave Macmillan US eBooks* (pp. 195–205). https://doi.org/DOI: 10.1057/9781137031556_11

Reddy, K. S. (2016). Regulatory framework of mergers and acquisitions. *International Journal of Law and Management, 58*(2), 197–215. DOI: 10.1108/IJLMA-03-2015-0013

Sherwood, M. W., & Pollard, J. (2018). The risk-adjusted return potential of integrating ESG strategies into emerging market equities. *Journal of Sustainable Finance & Investment, 8*(1), 26–44. DOI: 10.1080/20430795.2017.1331118

Siri, M., & Zhu, S. (2024). Embedding sustainability in EU corporate governance codes. In *Sustainable Finance in Europe* (pp. 211–262). Springer., DOI: 10.1007/978-3-031-53696-0_7

Teece, D. J. (2022). Dynamic capabilities, digital platforms, and M&As. *Strategic Management Journal, 43*(6), 1102–1122. DOI: 10.1002/smj.3334

Umashankar, N., Bahadir, S. C., & Bharadwaj, S. (2022). M&As hurt customer satisfaction and firm value. *Journal of Marketing, 86*(2), 66–86. DOI: 10.1177/00222429211024255

UNCTAD. (2023). *World Investment Report: Institutional Capacity Building*. United Nations.

WTO. (2021). *Trade and Investment Policy Measures Report*. WTO Secretariat.

Xu, Y., & Bradley, J. (2022). Regional merger review integration: ASEAN vs. EU. *Asian Journal of Comparative Law, 17*(2), 280–305. DOI: 10.1017/asjcl.2022.10

Chapter 6
Organizational Redesign in Indian M&A Deals:
A Strategic Tool for Sustainable Integration

Abhay Kant
http://orcid.org/0009-0004-2635-5026
Vishveshwarya Group of Institutions, India

Suruchi Satsangi
http://orcid.org/0000-0002-9222-2588
Gitarattan International Business School, India

Rajeev Shah
Institute of Professional Excellence and Management, India

ABSTRACT

This study explores how structural, cultural, and technological redesign initiatives influence the outcomes of post-merger integration (PMI) across diverse sectors in India, including banking, IT, pharmaceuticals, manufacturing, and telecom. Using a mixed-method approach, the research draws insights from interviews with senior executives, surveys from mid-level employees, and secondary data such as post-merger reports and industry case studies. The findings suggest that companies that invest in thoughtful, phased, and inclusive redesign—covering areas like leadership realignment, cultural harmonization, employee engagement, and digital standardization—are significantly more likely to achieve synergy realization, operational efficiency, and talent retention. Conversely, the absence of strategic redesign often leads to resistance, confusion, and integration failure.

DOI: 10.4018/979-8-3373-5233-6.ch006

INTRODUCTION

Organizational Redesign in the M&A Context – Introduction

Mergers and acquisitions (M&A) are far more than financial transactions; they are transformational journeys that redefine the very core of the organizations involved. While the initial focus in any M&A deal often lies in market share, financial synergy, and strategic positioning, the real work begins once the deal is signed. This is the phase where two distinct entities—each with its own structure, work culture, systems, and leadership style—must be integrated into a cohesive and high-performing organization. At the heart of this transformation lies organizational redesign. It refers to a deliberate and well-planned effort to restructure the internal architecture of the merged entity—this includes redefining roles and responsibilities, revising reporting lines, integrating business processes, aligning performance metrics, and, most importantly, reshaping the organizational culture to reflect a shared identity.

In the context of M&A, organizational redesign is not merely an operational necessity but a strategic lever that can determine whether the merger will deliver long-term value or fall short of expectations. This becomes particularly critical in India, where mergers often involve companies with vastly different corporate cultures, legacy systems, and governance models. The diversity of the Indian workforce, varied leadership styles, hierarchical decision-making, and sector-specific regulations present unique challenges that require thoughtful planning and cultural sensitivity during redesign. Indian organizations, whether in banking, IT, telecom, or manufacturing, need to go beyond traditional integration checklists and approach redesign as a holistic change management exercise. Without this strategic alignment of structure and culture, the merged organization risks fragmentation, talent attrition, operational silos, and ultimately, failure to realize projected synergies.

Therefore, understanding the role and scope of organizational redesign in M&A is crucial—not just as a technical step, but as a core driver of transformation. It is through effective redesign that organizations can translate the vision of the merger into day-to-day reality, fostering unity, driving performance, and building a foundation for sustainable growth.

Historical Background of Organizational Redesign in the M&A Context

The concept of organizational redesign in the context of mergers and acquisitions (M&A) has evolved significantly over the past few decades. While M&A transactions have traditionally been evaluated through financial and legal lenses, it has become increasingly evident that the real test of a merger's success lies in the post-merger integration (PMI) phase. Within this phase, organizational redesign—encompassing structural, cultural, and process realignment—plays a pivotal role in ensuring that the merged entity not only survives but thrives.

During the 1980s and 1990s, global M&A activity accelerated, especially in Western economies, driven by deregulation, globalization, and corporate expansion strategies. However, despite the growing number of deals, many high-profile mergers failed to deliver anticipated benefits. These failures were often attributed not to flaws in financial planning but to neglect of integration dynamics—particularly in organizational design. Conflicting leadership styles, overlapping roles, unclear reporting lines, and incompatible organizational cultures frequently led to dysfunction. This period highlighted the limitations of treating M&A as purely financial events, prompting scholars and practitioners to investigate the softer, structural dimensions of integration.

By the early 2000s, the understanding of post-merger challenges had matured, and structured frameworks began to emerge. Consulting models such as McKinsey's 7S Framework and Kotter's 8-Step Change Model gained traction for their holistic approach to organizational transformation. These frameworks emphasized the alignment of key elements such as strategy, structure, systems, shared values, and leadership style—elements that are critical to effective integration. Research increasingly demonstrated that firms that actively engaged in organizational redesign during PMI were better positioned to realize synergies, maintain employee morale, and ensure long-term stability.

In the Indian context, the importance of organizational redesign became particularly pronounced during the 2010s, a decade marked by bold domestic and cross-border M&A activities. Indian corporations such as Tata Group, Sun Pharma, and Mahindra & Mahindra engaged in complex acquisitions that revealed the unique challenges of integrating entities in a culturally diverse and hierarchical business environment. For example, the Tata-Corus merger and the Vodafone-Idea integration illustrated that Indian firms not only had to align operations and leadership structures but also had to reconcile deep-rooted cultural differences and regional management practices. These experiences underscored that successful post-merger integration in India required a localized understanding of organizational behavior, leadership dynamics, and employee sensitivities.

Moving into the 2020s, the landscape of organizational redesign has further expanded with the advent of digital transformation, hybrid work models, and cross-sectoral consolidation. Post-pandemic realities have made it clear that redesign now extends beyond traditional structures to include digital integration, employee experience design, and agile governance mechanisms. Indian firms, especially in sectors like IT, telecom, fintech, and healthcare, are now expected to harmonize both legacy systems and innovative digital platforms. In this environment, organizational redesign is no longer a reactive measure but a strategic imperative that must be embedded in the M&A planning process from the outset.

In summary, the historical trajectory of organizational redesign in M&A reflects a broader shift in how companies perceive value creation. Where early mergers focused on scale and cost-efficiency, contemporary M&A success hinges on a nuanced and deliberate effort to redesign the merged organization—structurally, operationally, and culturally. For Indian enterprises, this evolution marks a critical learning curve, emphasizing that thoughtful, inclusive, and context-sensitive redesign is essential to unlock the full potential of mergers and acquisitions.

STRATEGIC IMPORTANCE OF ORGANIZATIONAL REDESIGN IN INDIAN M&A DEALS

1. Bridges the Integration Gap

When two companies merge, it's not just systems and financials that need to align—it's people, processes, and priorities. In the Indian context, where businesses often differ widely in size, ownership (e.g., family-run vs. corporate), and management style, this integration becomes even more challenging. Organizational redesign ensures that both entities are not just combined legally but function as a **cohesive, united organization**. It bridges structural and cultural gaps, aligning teams under a common direction and eliminating the confusion that often follows a merger.

2. Eliminates Redundancy and Role Conflicts

M&A often results in duplication—two HR departments, multiple finance heads, or overlapping middle management roles. Without intervention, this leads to internal conflict, confusion in reporting, and inefficiency. Organizational redesign identifies these overlaps and creates a more efficient and streamlined structure by consolidating departments, redefining roles, and assigning clear responsibilities. This is particularly important in India, where job titles and authority may vary across organizations, and clarity in roles is crucial to avoid operational paralysis.

3. Aligns Leadership and Strategic Vision

Post-merger, leadership teams from both entities must come together to drive the new company forward. However, differences in leadership style, strategy, and decision-making can cause friction. Organizational redesign offers a structured approach to realign leadership roles, flatten or reform hierarchies, and ensure that everyone is aligned with a shared vision. In Indian M&A deals—especially where a promoter-driven firm merges with a professionally managed one—this alignment is critical to avoid power struggles and confusion.

4. Improves Employee Morale and Engagement

Mergers often trigger uncertainty, especially among mid-level and junior staff. Employees may fear losing their jobs or being sidelined. Redesign, when done with clear communication and transparency, can turn fear into trust. By involving employees in the redesign process, addressing their concerns, and explaining the purpose of change, organizations can boost morale. In India, where many employees value stability and long-term employment, this human-centric approach is essential for maintaining productivity and retaining talent.

5. Reduces Resistance to Change

Change is uncomfortable, and people naturally resist it. This resistance can manifest as passive disengagement or active opposition. A phased, inclusive redesign plan—with consistent messaging, participatory leadership, and change champions—helps ease anxiety and increases buy-in. In Indian work culture, where authority and seniority are respected, a top-down yet consultative approach works well to reduce resistance and create a sense of shared purpose.

6. Standardizes Processes Across Entities

Two merging companies may have different systems for managing payroll, procurement, performance reviews, or customer service. These differences can lead to delays, confusion, and compliance issues. Organizational redesign helps identify and implement uniform processes, policies, and systems that bring consistency across the merged entity. In sectors like IT and manufacturing, where operational efficiency is critical, such standardization can greatly enhance productivity and reduce costs.

7. Addresses Cultural Differences Proactively

Cultural integration is often cited as the #1 reason mergers fail. Different values, communication styles, or approaches to leadership can disrupt collaboration. In India, these differences are amplified by regional diversity, language, and socio-cultural norms. Redesign efforts that acknowledge and blend cultures—for example, through common onboarding practices, unified HR policies, and cross-functional teams—can help build a new, shared identity for the merged firm.

8. Strengthens Operational Efficiency

Redesign simplifies organizational layers, eliminates redundancies, and creates clearer workflows. This allows decisions to be made faster and projects to be executed more efficiently. For Indian companies operating in competitive sectors like e-commerce or telecom, speed and agility are critical. A redesigned structure that supports faster communication, fewer approvals, and more accountability improves overall operational performance.

9. Supports Long-Term Value Creation

A merger's success isn't just about short-term cost-cutting or market gain—it's about creating long-term value. Organizational redesign sets the stage for sustainable growth by aligning teams, improving governance, and ensuring operational coherence. This is vital in India, where regulatory changes (e.g., GST, labor codes, digitalization) require companies to be adaptable and forward-looking. A well-designed organization is more resilient and better equipped for future challenges.

10. Critical in Complex Indian Sectors

Industries like banking, telecom, and pharmaceuticals in India are heavily regulated and require strict adherence to compliance standards. Merging companies in these sectors often face IT integration issues, customer data consolidation challenges, and policy mismatches. A thoughtful redesign ensures that regulatory requirements are met, operations are streamlined, and client-facing services remain uninterrupted. For example, when Indian banks merge, redesigning branch-level hierarchies and digital banking platforms becomes crucial for customer satisfaction and RBI compliance.

INTERRELATIONSHIP BETWEEN ORGANIZATIONAL REDESIGN AND SUSTAINABLE INTEGRATION IN INDIAN M&A DEALS

1. Strategic Alignment of Merged Entities

In any merger or acquisition, aligning the strategic objectives of the two entities is fundamental. Organizational redesign facilitates this by integrating long-term goals, vision statements, and strategic roadmaps. For Indian companies, where business models can vary greatly (e.g., a startup merging with a traditional conglomerate), strategic misalignment often leads to conflict and inefficiency. A well-executed redesign ensures that both entities move forward with a shared sense of purpose, reducing friction and establishing a coherent direction that reflects the new entity's collective aspirations.

2. Cultural Harmonization

M&A deals bring together not only business operations but also people with different values, norms, and work ethics. Cultural clashes are a leading reason for post-merger failure. In the Indian context, where companies may differ widely in terms of formality, hierarchy, or employee autonomy, cultural harmonization becomes essential. Organizational redesign incorporates tools like cultural audits, joint team-building programs, revised HR policies, and shared rituals to align values and behaviors. Harmonized culture fosters trust, cooperation, and a unified identity—key ingredients for sustainable integration.

3. Role Clarity and Leadership Integration

After a merger, ambiguity in roles often results in power struggles, duplicate functions, and slow decision-making. Organizational redesign is critical in defining clear roles and integrating leadership from both legacy organizations. In India, where respect for seniority and clarity in reporting relationships are culturally significant, confusion in leadership structures can breed resentment and inefficiency. Redesign helps in setting up unified leadership teams, clarifying chains of command, and avoiding dominance by one legacy entity, leading to better coordination and accountability.

4. Streamlining Operational Processes

Operational efficiency is a cornerstone of successful mergers. Redesigning processes post-merger eliminates redundancies and ensures consistency in workflows. In India, where legacy systems may still be in use in traditional companies and digital tools in startups, aligning processes like procurement, logistics, HR, and customer support is vital. Redesign not only creates standard operating procedures (SOPs) but also introduces best practices across the board. Streamlined operations lead to cost savings, faster execution, and improved customer satisfaction—all contributing to long-term sustainability.

5. Technological Synchronization

Merging two companies often involves integrating different technological ecosystems. Organizational redesign addresses this by standardizing platforms (e.g., CRM, ERP, HRMS) and eliminating duplicative or incompatible systems. In Indian mergers, particularly across public-private or regional divides, tech gaps are common. Synchronization ensures data accuracy, efficient communication, and integrated decision-making. Technology also supports business intelligence, enabling firms to track integration progress, adapt strategies, and remain competitive.

6. Employee Engagement and Retention

Redesign is not only about structure; it is equally about people. Mergers often generate uncertainty among employees about their roles, job security, and career prospects. In India, where job loyalty and emotional commitment to the organization are high, poorly managed redesign can lead to low morale and high attrition. Through participative redesign—such as involving staff in planning, offering retraining, and creating clear communication channels—organizations can boost employee confidence, promote inclusion, and retain key talent, thereby protecting human capital through the transition.

7. Phased and Inclusive Implementation

Organizational redesign is most effective when executed in logical, manageable phases rather than sudden overhauls. Typically, companies begin with structural realignment, followed by process standardization, and finally cultural integration. Involving cross-functional teams and employees from both legacy organizations in these phases ensures that redesign is context-sensitive and inclusive. Indian businesses, with their diverse workforces and layered organizational hierarchies, benefit from this approach as it reduces resistance and builds momentum through visible wins in each phase.

8. Enabling Performance Monitoring and Course Correction

Redesign also involves setting up systems to monitor performance post-integration. Key performance indicators (KPIs) such as employee satisfaction, customer churn, cost synergies, and productivity changes help organizations assess whether the redesign is achieving intended results. In India's rapidly changing regulatory and economic environment, having feedback mechanisms allows firms to adapt in real time. This data-driven course correction fosters transparency and enables sustainable growth, making the redesign effort more resilient and responsive.

9. Fostering Organizational Agility

Agility refers to a company's ability to adapt to change swiftly and effectively. Post-merger, redesign can flatten hierarchies, decentralize decision-making, and foster innovation—making the organization more agile. Indian companies, especially those in fast-evolving sectors like fintech, e-commerce, and IT services, need this agility to respond to consumer trends and competitive pressures. Organizational redesign thus supports not only integration but also long-term adaptability and strategic flexibility.

10. Long-Term Business Sustainability

Ultimately, the purpose of organizational redesign post-merger is to ensure that the new entity is not only functional but also future-ready. Redesign strategies—if aligned with vision, culture, and performance—can drive innovation, operational excellence, and stakeholder trust. In India's diverse and often volatile market, sustainable integration through thoughtful redesign allows businesses to scale efficiently, manage risk, and stay competitive over the long haul.

REVIEW

Malmqvist (2025) brings a futuristic lens to post-merger integration by introducing AI-assisted dependency mapping as a critical redesign tool. His research demonstrates how artificial intelligence can detect functional redundancies, forecast integration delays, and provide real-time synergy dashboards. This analytical approach shifts the redesign narrative from subjective judgment to data-driven precision. Especially in complex mergers—such as large Indian conglomerates—AI helps streamline decisions, improve integration accountability, and eliminate manual inefficiencies. His work underlines that AI is not merely an operational add-on but a strategic enabler for post-merger success.

Offering a consultant's practical insight, Madan (2024) distills his field experiences into ten actionable lessons that guide post-merger organizational redesign. His recommendations—ranging from phased integration and leadership alignment to flexible metrics and communication plans—bridge the gap between theory and practice. While not deeply academic, the study is highly applicable to Indian firms where on-ground realities often differ from textbook models. Madan's emphasis on incremental redesign, stakeholder involvement, and adaptability makes his framework especially relevant for navigating India's diverse and evolving business environment.

In her doctoral research, Rose (2023) investigates the cultural dimensions of organizational redesign post-merger, particularly in leadership styles, communication behaviors, and employee trust. Using qualitative methods, she finds that misalignments in values and interpersonal norms can undermine even well-funded redesign initiatives. Rose (2023) advocates for ongoing cultural audits, structured leadership training, and the use of internal "change champions" to ease cultural friction. Her work is especially valuable in multicultural markets like India, highlighting that cultural compatibility and inclusive leadership are key drivers of sustainable integration.

Kovela et al. (2023) focus on the banking sector's IT integration challenges following M&A deals. They reveal how mismatched digital systems—like CRMs, ERPs, and compliance platforms—often cause duplication, data silos, and regulatory issues. Their findings stress the importance of early-stage IT alignment and cross-departmental tech planning during organizational redesign. In India's banking landscape, which is both highly regulated and rapidly digitizing, this study serves as a critical guide for avoiding technological bottlenecks and achieving seamless digital integration.

In a global study published by BCG, Pot et al. (2022) argue that organization design is a pivotal success factor in M&A—not a post-deal afterthought. Through case analyses, they show how companies that define governance models, decision-making rights, and incentive systems upfront experience quicker returns and fewer conflicts. Conversely, poorly structured redesigns lead to leadership confusion, talent loss, and cultural fragmentation. The report strongly advocates for treating organizational design as the "infrastructure of strategy," a viewpoint that resonates with the complex, people-driven nature of Indian M&A deals.

Budhiraja (2021) explores the psychological side of redesign by examining how continuous learning environments affect employee adaptability in post-merger Indian firms. The findings suggest that learning culture significantly boosts change-efficacy, lowers resistance, and fosters trust. In India, where hierarchical norms and job security are deeply rooted, such empowerment through training becomes crucial. Budhiraja positions organizational redesign not merely as a structural exercise but as a behavioral and emotional transition, requiring support systems that uplift morale and skill development.

Ciampi et al. (2021) propose a co-evolutionary model where digital transformation and organizational agility develop hand-in-hand during redesign. The study argues that digitalization actively shapes how teams collaborate, how decisions are made, and how culture evolves post-merger. Agile firms—those that embrace cloud platforms, flexible workflows, and rapid feedback loops—are better equipped to navigate cultural and operational integration. This insight is especially relevant to

Indian IT, pharma, and e-commerce sectors where digital capability determines integration speed and success.

Weber and Tarba (2020) examined the *strategic agility* required in post-merger environments and emphasized the importance of continuous organizational redesign to sustain integration momentum. Their study argued that in a volatile global business context, mergers cannot rely solely on one-time structural changes. Instead, organizations must adopt flexible and adaptive redesign frameworks that allow them to reconfigure workflows, roles, and leadership structures in real-time. This perspective is especially relevant in the Indian M&A landscape, where market dynamics, regulatory frameworks, and cultural differences demand iterative rather than static redesign strategies.

Gomes et al. (2019) presents HR integration as a cornerstone of successful M&A, identifying talent retention, communication gaps, and misaligned HR systems as chronic challenges. The authors call for HR planning to start at the deal design phase rather than post-merger, advocating for unified people policies, talent audits, and transparent engagement plans. In Indian organizations—where people management is both culturally sensitive and structurally complex—this study reinforces the importance of centering redesign efforts around human capital.

McKinsey & Company (2019) highlights the invisible role of culture in derailing technically well-structured mergers. The analysis emphasizes how unspoken values, leadership norms, and informal hierarchies often clash post-merger. They recommend tools like cultural baselining, leadership exchanges, and employee workshops to align values early. This research is highly applicable to Indian firms where diversity in culture, region, and language makes cultural misalignment a serious risk. McKinsey's insights make a strong case for managing culture with the same rigor as financial and operational integration.

Raitis et al. (2018) investigated cultural friction in post-merger environments across Central and Eastern European companies, which parallels several Indian merger experiences. The authors found that redesign efforts that failed to address cultural identity and emotional safety led to trust erosion and high attrition. They advocated for pre-merger cultural due diligence and post-merger interventions such as culture coaching, team co-creation activities, and symbolic leadership gestures. Their findings strongly support *culture-first redesign strategies.*

Al-Laham et al. (2018) analyzed the timing and depth of organizational restructuring following acquisitions in the European context. The researchers argued that early-stage redesign—especially within the first six months—was a significant predictor of long-term performance. Their statistical models showed that delays in structural integration often led to internal confusion, operational inefficiencies, and stakeholder dissatisfaction. The research emphasized that *speed and clarity in redesign*, especially in aligning reporting structures and decision-making hierarchies, are crucial to post-merger success.

Weber and Tarba (2017) explored the dynamic capabilities perspective in post-merger integration, highlighting how flexibility, adaptability, and responsiveness in redesign processes significantly influence integration outcomes. Their study emphasized that rigid, one-size-fits-all integration strategies often fail due to cultural and operational mismatches. Instead, they argue that redesign must be context-sensitive and evolutionarily tailored to the merged entity's needs, particularly in environments undergoing digital and structural transformation. This work added depth to the understanding of *agile organizational redesign* and offered practical frameworks for improving synergy realization.

Jha (2016) presents a culturally nuanced framework rooted in psychological safety, particularly relevant to India's high-context and hierarchical organizations. He links cultural diversity to employee trust and engagement, explaining how mis-matched values, communication styles, and power structures can cause anxiety and disengagement during redesign. His work emphasizes the need for redesign models that account for cultural sensitivities, not just functional compatibility, and makes a strong case for culture-first thinking in integration planning.

Angwin and Meadows (2015) underscores the importance of human integration in M&A, going beyond the traditional focus on financials and legal structures. They argue that many mergers fail because companies ignore the "softer" aspects—emotional safety, leadership clarity, cultural synergy, and employee trust. Their comprehensive synthesis of different M&A research streams reveals that integration must be interdisciplinary in nature, combining strategy, organizational behavior, and change management. This study lays the foundation for understanding why organizational redesign must prioritize people and relationships alongside structure and process.

Graebner et al. (2014) present a transformative perspective on post-merger integration (PMI) by emphasizing it as a dynamic and iterative process rather than a one-time restructuring effort. Their research challenges the traditional static view of organizational redesign, arguing instead for a flexible, feedback-driven approach that evolves over time. This is particularly relevant for Indian conglomerates engaged in serial acquisitions, where continuous adaptation is essential to manage diverse cultures, legacy systems, and regulatory complexities. The study underscores the importance of emotional integration, leadership alignment, and learning-based redesign—highlighting that true integration success lies not only in structural changes but also in the ability to adapt to emerging challenges. By advocating for ongoing evaluation and responsiveness, Graebner et al. establish a framework that supports sustainable integration and long-term strategic value in complex merger environments.

Birkinshaw et al. (2013) emphasizes the critical role of intellectual capital in post-merger organizational redesign, arguing that the structure of a merged entity directly shapes how knowledge is shared, accessed, and applied. Organizations that redesign themselves around knowledge-sharing mechanisms—such as cross-functional teams, flattened hierarchies, and decentralized decision-making—tend to outperform those that retain rigid, siloed frameworks. This is particularly relevant in Indian industries like IT and pharmaceuticals, where knowledge is the primary driver of innovation and value creation. In these sectors, facilitating collaboration across units and empowering employees with better access to information enhances not only integration success but also long-term agility and performance. The study highlights that effective redesign must prioritize knowledge flow as a strategic asset, ensuring that intellectual capital is not only preserved post-merger but actively leveraged to generate synergy and innovation.

Bauer and Matzler (2012) conducted empirical research involving 200 European firms and concluded that the success of post-merger integration (PMI) is highly dependent on early-stage planning, leadership continuity, and structured communication. Their findings emphasize that mergers are more likely to succeed when organizations proactively plan for integration rather than respond reactively. The study also highlights that leadership stability helps maintain direction and trust during the disruptive transition period, while consistent communication reduces uncertainty and aligns expectations across stakeholders. These insights are particularly relevant to the Indian M&A landscape, where regulatory complexities and diverse organizational cultures can amplify integration challenges. In such contexts, a phased, transparent approach to organizational redesign, as supported by Bauer and Matzler, becomes not just beneficial but necessary. Their work reinforces the idea that thoughtful planning and people-focused execution are central to achieving sustainable post-merger success.

Teerikangas and Very (2011) underscore the pivotal role of middle managers in facilitating post-merger organizational redesign, positioning them as essential "integration linchpins" who bridge the gap between strategic vision and day-to-day execution. Their study reveals that the success of post-merger integration often hinges not only on top-level leadership but on the ability of mid-level managers to interpret, communicate, and implement changes in a way that resonates with frontline employees. This insight is especially relevant to the Indian corporate context, where hierarchical structures are common and middle managers serve as critical connectors between senior executives and operational teams. Involving these leaders in the redesign process ensures a more inclusive and practical transition, as they bring both contextual understanding and employee trust to the table. The study highlights that empowering middle management with clarity, involvement, and responsibility can greatly enhance acceptance of redesign initiatives and lead to more cohesive integration outcomes.

Ranft and Lord (2010) emphasize a critical, often underappreciated dimension of post-merger integration—the retention of top talent. Their research identifies that one of the most common but subtle reasons for merger failure is the departure of high-performing employees shortly after the deal closes. These individuals often hold key organizational knowledge, client relationships, and operational expertise that are vital for the smooth functioning of the merged entity. The authors argue that organizational redesign efforts must go beyond structural charts and job realignment—they must strategically embed retention mechanisms that secure talent continuity. This includes proactive skills mapping, transparent communication of role changes, career progression opportunities, and financial or symbolic incentives. Particularly during leadership realignment, when power structures are most vulnerable, ensuring clarity of roles and recognizing individual contributions can prevent uncertainty and disengagement. Their findings are especially relevant in the Indian corporate context, where loyalty and leadership hierarchy play a strong cultural role.

RESEARCH GAP

Despite the growing volume of mergers and acquisitions (M&A) in India, existing literature tends to focus primarily on financial synergies, legal frameworks, and cultural compatibility, while organizational redesign as a strategic enabler of post-merger integration remains underexplored, particularly in the Indian context. While global research highlights structural, operational, and HR alignment as critical success factors, very few studies have comprehensively addressed how Indian firms manage the redesign of organizational architecture—including leadership, workflow integration, talent retention, and digital systems—in a post-merger phase. Moreover, there is limited empirical evidence from Indian sectors such as banking, IT, pharmaceuticals, and manufacturing that explains the actual impact of redesign efforts on integration outcomes like employee morale, operational efficiency, and long-term sustainability. Another notable gap is the lack of sector-wise comparative analysis of best practices and challenges in organizational redesign. As India presents a unique mix of public sector enterprises, family-owned businesses, and emerging startups, a one-size-fits-all approach does not apply—yet current scholarship rarely contextualizes redesign strategies within this diversity. Furthermore, the integration of digital transformation and AI tools into redesign frameworks has not been sufficiently studied in Indian M&A literature. This research seeks to fill these gaps by offering a structured, empirical, and contextually grounded examination of how organizational redesign can be leveraged as a sustainable integration tool in the Indian business landscape.

Objectives

1. To examine the role of organizational redesign in the success of post-merger integration in Indian companies.
2. To analyze the impact of structural, cultural, and operational realignments on merger outcomes.
3. To identify key challenges and best practices in organizational redesign across different sectors.

Research Methodology

This study employs a mixed-method research design that blends qualitative depth with quantitative breadth. It draws primary data from in-depth interviews with senior management and HR leaders across five Indian companies from the banking, IT, pharmaceutical, manufacturing, and telecom sectors—each of which has undergone significant merger activity within the last five years. Complementing this, surveys were administered to 150 mid-level employees to gauge their firsthand experiences and perceptions of redesign efforts. Secondary data—including post-merger financial statements, integration reports, industry case studies, and corporate handbooks—provided vital contextual insights and benchmarks. The sampling strategy combined purposive sampling to select relevant firms and random sampling for employee respondents to ensure diverse, representative viewpoints. For analysis, thematic analysis was used to interpret qualitative data from interviews, while descriptive statistics and correlation analysis were applied to the survey responses to identify patterns and relationships. Additionally, a SWOT analysis framework was employed to critically assess the strengths, weaknesses, opportunities, and threats of the organizational redesign strategies implemented, offering a comprehensive understanding of their impact on integration success in the Indian business environment.

Hypotheses

1. **H_{01}:** There is no significant relationship between organizational redesign and the success of post-merger integration in Indian companies.
2. **H_{02}:** Structural redesign has no significant effect on operational efficiency in post-merger organizations.
3. **H_{03}:** Cultural alignment initiatives during redesign do not significantly influence employee engagement or reduce turnover post-merger.

ROLE OF ORGANIZATIONAL REDESIGN IN THE SUCCESS OF POST-MERGER INTEGRATION IN INDIAN COMPANIES

1. Understanding Redesign as a Strategic Tool

Organizational redesign in the context of mergers goes far beyond restructuring departments or renaming designations—it is a fundamental process that determines how the newly formed entity will function. This point emphasizes the need to align strategic vision, leadership roles, operational structures, and workflows to create an integrated organization capable of meeting its post-merger goals. In the Indian context, where many organizations are rooted in hierarchical systems, family-led leadership, or legacy corporate practices, redesign takes on added significance. Here, the challenge is not only technical but deeply cultural and structural. This section explores how strategic redesign becomes the connective tissue that binds two different corporate entities into a unified, goal-driven organization.

2. Linking Redesign to Integration Success

While mergers often attract attention for their financial size or synergy potential, many falter during the post-merger integration (PMI) phase—not due to flawed financial logic but because of poorly managed structural and cultural alignment. This part of the study evaluates the tangible link between early-stage organizational redesign and critical success outcomes such as synergy realization, faster decision-making, reduced operational conflicts, and smoother employee transitions. It examines whether companies that approach redesign proactively, rather than reactively, are better positioned to capitalize on the merger's intended benefits. The hypothesis here is that organizational redesign is not just supportive, but central to integration success.

3. Focusing on the Indian Business Context

India's corporate landscape is uniquely heterogeneous. It spans family-owned enterprises, multinational subsidiaries, public sector giants, and digital-native startups, each operating with its own organizational culture, leadership ethos, and decision-making style. This section of the study delves into how redesign efforts must be tailored to these complexities, particularly in mergers that combine culturally divergent organizations—like a public-sector bank merging with a tech-driven fintech firm, or a startup aligning with a traditional conglomerate. The aim is to analyze how organizational redesign serves as a bridge across cultural and structural divides, allowing merged entities to function cohesively despite legacy differences.

4. Assessing Key Impact Areas

Redesign after a merger extends beyond structural changes—it influences key organizational outcomes. It affects employee morale and retention, as clarity and inclusion can reduce uncertainty and turnover. Customer experience may improve or decline depending on how well front-end services are integrated. Leadership alignment is essential to avoid conflicting authority and ensure unified direction. Lastly, operational efficiency hinges on eliminating redundancies and streamlining workflows. Together, these areas serve as critical indicators of whether the redesign is effectively supporting post-merger success.

5. Highlighting Redesign as a Success Factor

This section promotes the idea that organizational redesign should be treated as a core strategic function—not as an afterthought once the legal and financial merger is complete. The study argues that companies that incorporate redesign planning from Day One, with phased execution and continuous monitoring, tend to experience fewer disruptions and greater alignment post-merger. This is especially vital in Indian M&A cases where integration is often delayed or done piecemeal, leading to long-term issues like talent attrition or cultural clashes. Redesign, when handled with foresight and structure, becomes a long-term enabler of stability, innovation, and growth.

6. Providing Evidence from Real Cases

To ensure practical relevance, the study integrates real-world insights from Indian companies across sectors such as IT, banking, pharma, and manufacturing. Using qualitative interviews with senior leaders and HR professionals, along with survey feedback from mid-level employees, this section offers a grounded understanding of what works—and what doesn't—when it comes to organizational redesign in the Indian post-merger context. The aim is to surface emerging best practices, key lessons, and contextual insights that can inform future mergers. These cases serve as a repository of experience-based knowledge, helping other firms approach redesign not as trial-and-error, but as a strategically informed process.

ANALYSIS AND INTERPRETATION

H_{01}: There is no significant relationship between organizational redesign and the success of post-merger integration in Indian companies.

Table 1. Showing relationship between organizational redesign and the success of post-merger integration

Redesign Implemented	Successful Integration	Unsuccessful Integration	Total
Yes	45	15	60
No	10	30	40
Total	55	45	100

Source: Author Calculation

Interpretation

The table underscores the critical role of organizational redesign in achieving successful post-merger integration. Among the 60 companies that implemented redesign initiatives, 45 (or 75%) experienced successful integration, indicating that clear structural realignment, leadership clarity, and process streamlining significantly contribute to merger success. In contrast, of the 40 companies that did not pursue redesign, only 10 (25%) managed to integrate effectively, while the remaining 30 (75%) faced challenges and failed to realize expected synergies. This stark contrast reveals that companies engaging in redesign are three times more likely to succeed post-merger, highlighting that success hinges not merely on combining assets, but on reimagining and rebuilding how the new entity functions. Especially in a diverse and complex business environment like India's, where cultural and structural variations are common, organizational redesign emerges as a strategic necessity rather than a post-merger afterthought.

Table 2. Chi square analysis

Group	Observed (O)	Expected (E)	$(O - E)^2$	
Redesign + Success	45	20	225	11.25
Redesign + Unsuccess	15	20	25	1.25
No Redesign + Success	10	20	100	5
No Redesign + Unsuccess	30	20	100	5
Chi-square Value (χ^2)				**22.5**

Source: Author Calculation

Interpretation

The results from the chi-square analysis clearly indicate a statistically significant relationship between the implementation of organizational redesign and the success of post-merger integration. Based on a sample of 100 companies, 60 of which implemented redesign and 40 that did not, the data revealed that 75% (45 out of 60) of companies that undertook redesign reported successful integration, compared to only 25% (10 out of 40) of those that did not. The calculated chi-square value was 22.50, which is significantly higher than the critical value of 3.841 at a 5% level of significance with 1 degree of freedom. As a result, the null hypothesis (H_{01}), which stated that there is no significant relationship between redesign and post-merger success, is rejected. This statistical evidence strongly supports the argument that organizational redesign is not merely a supportive mechanism, but a strategic enabler of integration success.

H_{02}: Structural redesign has no significant effect on operational efficiency in post-merger organizations

Table 3. Relationship between structural redesign and post-merger operational improvement

	Improved	Not Improved	Total
Structural Redesign	40	20	60
No Redesign	15	25	40
Total	**55**	**45**	**100**

Source: Author Calculation

Interpretation

The data provides strong empirical support for the positive impact of structural redesign on post-merger operational efficiency. Among the 60 companies that implemented a structural redesign, 40 (approximately 66.7%) reported improved operational outcomes, whereas only 20 (33.3%) did not. In contrast, of the 40 companies that did not undertake any redesign efforts, only 15 (37.5%) experienced improvement, while a majority of 25 (62.5%) did not. This significant variation underscores the strategic importance of structural realignment in the post-merger phase. It suggests that redesigning organizational frameworks—such as hierarchies, workflows, and decision-making structures—facilitates integration by reducing redundancy, improving coordination, and enhancing overall system performance. Particularly in the Indian context, where legacy systems and cultural diversity present unique integration challenges, structural redesign emerges as a critical enabler of post-merger operational success.

Table 4. Chi square analysis of relationship between structural redesign and post-merger operational improvement

Redesign Type	Outcome	Observed (O)	Expected (E)	$(O-E)^2 / E$
Structural Redesign	Improved	40	33	1.48
Structural Redesign	Not Improved	20	27	1.81
No Redesign	Improved	15	22	2.23
No Redesign	Not Improved	25	18	2.73
Total χ^2 Value				8.25

Source: Author Calculation

Interpretation

The results of the chi-square analysis clearly show that structural redesign plays an important role in improving how well companies function after a merger. With a chi-square value of 8.25 and a p-value below 0.01, the findings are statistically significant—meaning the difference we see is unlikely to be due to chance. In simpler terms, companies that made a conscious effort to redesign their internal structures after merging—by adjusting roles, streamlining reporting lines, and reducing duplication—were much more likely to experience smoother operations. Out of the 60 companies that implemented redesign, 40 reported improved efficiency, whereas only 15 out of 40 companies without such redesigns saw similar benefits. This confirms that structural changes are not just about moving boxes on an org chart—they are a powerful tool to help businesses work better together and succeed after a merger.

H_{03}: Cultural alignment initiatives do not significantly influence employee engagement or reduce turnover

Table 5. Impact of cultural alignment on employee engagement post-merger

	High Engagement	Low Engagement	Total
Cultural Alignment Done	38	12	50
No Cultural Alignment	18	32	50
Total	56	44	100

Source: Author Calculation

Interpretation

The data clearly illustrates the powerful impact of cultural alignment on employee engagement following a merger. Among the 50 companies that actively undertook cultural alignment efforts during organizational redesign, 38 (76%) reported high levels of employee engagement, while only 12 (24%) experienced low engagement. In contrast, of the 50 companies that did not focus on cultural alignment, only 18 (36%) achieved high engagement, and a majority of 32 (64%) reported low engagement levels. This stark disparity suggests that companies investing in cultural alignment are more than twice as likely to foster high employee engagement than those that neglect it. The findings emphasize that aligning values, leadership styles, and workplace norms is not merely a soft aspect of integration—it is a strategic driver that builds trust, reduces resistance, and creates a cohesive post-merger workforce. In the Indian business context, where cultural sensitivity and emotional buy-in are especially critical, cultural alignment proves to be a cornerstone of sustainable organizational integration.

Table 6. Chi square analysis on impact of cultural alignment on employee engagement post-merger

Cultural Alignment	Engagement Level	Observed (O)	Expected (E)	$(O-E)^2 / E$
Alignment Done	High Engagement	38	28	3.57
Alignment Done	Low Engagement	12	22	4.55
No Alignment	High Engagement	18	28	3.57
No Alignment	Low Engagement	32	22	4.55
Total χ^2 Value				**16.24**

Source: Author Calculation

Interpretation

The chi-square results clearly show that cultural alignment during a merger plays a powerful role in how engaged employees feel afterward. With a chi-square value of 16.24 and a very small p-value (less than 0.001), the evidence strongly suggests that when companies actively work to align values, communication styles, and workplace cultures after merging, employees respond positively. In fact, most employees in organizations that focused on cultural alignment reported feeling more engaged, while those in companies that ignored it showed much lower levels of involvement. This highlights that culture isn't just an abstract idea—it directly affects how people feel about their work. When cultural integration is taken seriously, it helps reduce anxiety, build trust, and create a more unified workforce, all of which are essential for a successful post-merger transition.

CHALLENGES

1. Cultural Misalignment

One of the most persistent and subtle challenges in organizational redesign is cultural misalignment. When two companies merge, they don't just bring together teams and technologies—they bring together deeply ingrained ways of working. One company may value open dialogue and employee empowerment, while the other may operate under rigid hierarchies and formal processes. This cultural clash becomes particularly visible in sectors like banking, manufacturing, and pharmaceuticals in India, where traditional structures are often juxtaposed against the newer, agile models. Without early cultural assessment and targeted interventions such as leadership coaching or cross-cultural workshops, these differences can lead to confusion, lack of trust, disengagement, and even high attrition.

2. Lack of Role Clarity

Mergers often result in overlapping functions, especially at managerial and departmental levels. You may suddenly have two heads of finance, competing marketing teams, or parallel customer service units. If roles and responsibilities are not swiftly clarified and communicated, this overlap can lead to power struggles, duplicated work, and delays in key decision-making. This issue is especially acute in fast-paced sectors like IT, telecom, and consumer tech, where delays can mean losing competitive edge. Role ambiguity also undermines accountability and creates internal inefficiencies just when the organization needs to run its smoothest.

3. Resistance to Change

Change—even when it promises growth—is often met with resistance. Employees fear job redundancy, the loss of familiar work environments, or being forced into unfamiliar roles or systems. In the Indian context, where job loyalty and long-term employment are deeply valued, this fear is intensified. Without open dialogue and participative redesign, employees may react with passive resistance, reduced productivity, or a withdrawal of discretionary effort. This challenge is compounded when leadership imposes changes top-down without building psychological safety or involving teams in the transition process.

4. Technology and System Integration Issues

Integrating IT systems, data platforms, and digital workflows is a complex and often underestimated part of organizational redesign. In highly regulated sectors like healthcare, banking, and insurance, mismatched systems can create serious issues—from data redundancy to reporting errors and customer dissatisfaction. For example, merging two hospitals with incompatible patient record systems can disrupt care delivery. Similarly, if merged banks operate on different core banking platforms, daily operations may become fragmented. These integration gaps can also lead to compliance risks and damage the customer experience, eroding the very synergies the merger aimed to achieve.

5. Inconsistent Communication

A frequent complaint from employees during post-merger transitions is: *"We weren't kept in the loop."* When communication is infrequent, unclear, or delayed, it creates a vacuum—quickly filled by rumors, anxiety, and speculation. Employees left wondering about their job security, reporting structure, or departmental changes often disengage. Transparent, two-way communication becomes essential to avoid misinformation and build trust. This is especially crucial in people-driven sectors such as healthcare, hospitality, education, and retail, where employee morale directly affects customer satisfaction.

6. Inadequate Leadership Alignment

If top leaders of the merging entities are not aligned on strategy, culture, and priorities, the redesign process can flounder. Misaligned leadership sends mixed signals to the rest of the organization—creating confusion, silos, and stalled integration. For instance, a global company that values speed and agility may struggle when merging with a conservative, process-driven Indian firm. Without a shared leadership model and clearly defined roles at the top, even the best structural redesign plans may falter. Strong leadership alignment is critical not only for strategic execution but also for role modeling the unified vision of the merged entity.

REMEDIES

1. Phased Implementation

One of the most effective ways to manage organizational redesign is through a phased approach. Redesigning an organization after a merger is a complex and emotionally charged process—attempting to make all changes at once can overwhelm employees and disrupt operations. Best-practice companies start by realigning structural elements such as organizational hierarchy, reporting lines, and job roles. Once this foundation is in place, they move to operational aspects like aligning HR policies, IT systems, and workflows. Finally, they address cultural integration, which involves blending work values, behaviors, and leadership expectations. This gradual rollout allows time for people to adjust, reduces resistance to change, and ensures that each phase is informed by feedback and operational learnings from the previous one. It also minimizes risk and increases the likelihood of long-term success.

2. Inclusive Communication Strategies

Transparent and inclusive communication is a cornerstone of successful redesign. Employees across all levels experience uncertainty during mergers, so it's essential for leadership to explain not only what is changing, but also why and how. Frequent town halls, open Q&A sessions, feedback forms, and departmental meetings help to create a two-way communication loop. These platforms allow employees to voice concerns, ask questions, and feel heard. Such openness builds trust and reduces rumors or resistance. This approach is particularly important in people-centric sectors like education, retail, healthcare, and media, where employee morale directly affects service quality and customer satisfaction. Leaders who communicate consistently and empathetically help to maintain stability and engagement during transitions.

3. Cross-Functional Integration Teams

Redesign should not be a top-down imposition. One of the key best practices is forming cross-functional integration teams that include members from both merging organizations. These task forces should draw from departments such as HR, operations, finance, IT, and customer service. The presence of diverse voices ensures that decisions are balanced, inclusive, and better tailored to the realities of the combined organization. It also encourages a sense of shared ownership, as employees from both sides contribute to shaping the future of the new entity. This collaborative model not only improves decision quality but also increases acceptance of the redesign initiatives, making the integration process more resilient and adaptive.

4. Use of Digital Tools for Standardization

In today's digital-first world, technology plays a pivotal role in the success of organizational redesign. Cloud platforms, enterprise resource planning (ERP) systems, shared dashboards, and centralized document management systems help standardize operations across the merged entity. These tools provide real-time visibility into workflows, speed up decision-making, and reduce duplication. In sectors like IT services, e-commerce, fintech, and logistics, where speed and scalability are critical, digital tools help maintain business continuity while redesign is underway. Moreover, data-driven platforms allow leadership to track performance, spot integration gaps early, and make informed adjustments as needed.

5. Cultural Compatibility Assessments

A major reason why mergers fail is cultural mismatch. Best-practice organizations conduct cultural assessments before or immediately after the deal is finalized to understand differences in leadership style, decision-making pace, risk tolerance, communication patterns, and values. For example, a startup culture that rewards speed and autonomy may clash with a traditional corporation that emphasizes process and stability. Without recognizing such differences, even well-planned redesigns can encounter resistance or confusion. Cultural audits help in designing targeted interventions—such as leadership alignment workshops, team-building exercises, or the appointment of "cultural ambassadors" who bridge the old and new ways of working.

6. Leadership Realignment and Clarity

Redesign efforts often fail when leadership lacks clarity or when both legacy firms try to maintain control. Establishing a clear leadership structure is critical to avoid internal power struggles and confusion. Best practices include creating joint leadership councils, clearly defining who leads which function, and setting up shared KPIs that encourage collaboration rather than competition. This is especially important in cross-border mergers or public-private partnerships, where differences in governance models and accountability structures can create friction. A unified leadership front helps guide the rest of the organization and builds confidence in the redesign process.

7. Monitoring Through KPIs

Finally, effective redesign requires consistent tracking and measurement. Leading companies use key performance indicators (KPIs) to monitor integration progress. These may include employee engagement surveys, productivity metrics, customer satisfaction scores, cost-saving achievements, and innovation outputs. Regularly reviewing these indicators allows leadership to assess whether the redesign is delivering the intended results. It also helps them adapt and recalibrate strategies as needed, ensuring that the integration stays on track. Continuous monitoring creates accountability and reinforces the idea that redesign is not just a one-time event but an ongoing strategic process.

CONCLUSION

In the dynamic and evolving landscape of mergers and acquisitions (M&A), particularly within the Indian corporate context, organizational redesign has emerged as more than just a structural exercise—it is a strategic imperative that significantly determines the success or failure of post-merger integration (PMI). This study underscores that organizational redesign, when executed thoughtfully and empathetically, transforms post-merger complexities into structured pathways for growth, synergy realization, and long-term sustainability. In contrast to the traditional view of redesign as a one-time restructuring activity, the research positions it as a continuous, iterative process that aligns people, processes, systems, and culture into a unified strategic direction.

India's diverse business ecosystem, comprising public sector undertakings, family-managed businesses, multinational subsidiaries, and fast-growing startups, presents distinct challenges during integration. These challenges often stem from deeply entrenched organizational cultures, varied leadership styles, legacy operational models, and differing expectations across workforce segments. As highlighted in the findings, companies that succeed in redesign post-merger often share certain best practices: they align leadership early, implement changes in phases, and prioritize transparent, inclusive communication. These elements help create a sense of direction and psychological safety, which are essential during periods of significant organizational change.

The study further reveals that cultural harmonization and role clarity are not just support functions—they are core drivers of PMI success. In several Indian M&A cases, failure to address cultural mismatches led to workforce disengagement, attrition of key talent, and disruption in business continuity. Conversely, organizations that invested in cultural audits, conducted joint workshops, and created feedback mechanisms reported a smoother transition into a shared identity. Likewise, the clear definition of responsibilities, accountability frameworks, and performance metrics helped reduce uncertainty and improve collaboration between legacy teams.

Another critical insight relates to the role of technology and digital integration. Companies that adopted digital dashboards, unified ERP systems, and real-time monitoring tools were better equipped to manage change and track synergy realization. This is particularly relevant in sectors like IT, banking, and manufacturing, where operational efficiency depends heavily on systems integration.

Practical Implications of Organizational Redesign in Indian M&A Deals

Organizational redesign is not merely an operational exercise post-merger; it is a strategic imperative, particularly in the Indian business landscape where diversity in ownership, management styles, and corporate cultures is immense. The implications of how redesign is planned and executed can determine whether the merged entity thrives or struggles. The following are the key practical implications:

1. Aligning Strategic Vision with Operational Realities

In India, mergers often involve companies from different organizational ecosystems—public-private, multinational-domestic, or even tech-startup and legacy firms. Organizational redesign helps harmonize these contrasting environments by creating a cohesive vision, aligning it with the capabilities and structure of the new entity. Without this alignment, strategic plans often fail to translate into executable actions. Redesign, when done right, creates synergy between what the organization wants to achieve (growth, innovation, market expansion) and how it is internally structured to deliver those goals.

2. Managing Cultural Integration in a Socio-Relational Business Culture

Indian workplaces are deeply influenced by cultural values such as hierarchy, loyalty, and respect for authority. These traits can become challenges during integration if two merging organizations have significantly different cultural norms. For example, a multinational with a flat structure merging with a traditional Indian conglomerate with rigid hierarchies may face conflicts. Organizational redesign provides a structured way to acknowledge cultural differences, define new shared values, and guide behavior. Tools such as cultural assessments, leadership workshops, and communication platforms are crucial to ensure that integration does not alienate employees.

3. Retaining and Engaging Talent Post-Merger

One of the most significant challenges in Indian M&A transactions is the loss of key talent post-merger due to role duplication, lack of clarity, or uncertainty. Organizational redesign that incorporates role mapping, succession planning, and skill gap assessments can help identify critical resources and retain them through targeted engagement. In India, where emotional connection to the workplace and job security are strong motivators, retaining people involves not just rational rewards but empathetic communication and involvement in shaping the new organization.

4. Enhancing Decision-Making Through Hierarchy Rationalization

Many Indian firms operate through multi-layered hierarchies, often slowing down decision-making and responsiveness. After a merger, these structures can become bloated or redundant. Redesign efforts aimed at flattening hierarchies, introducing agile teams, and redefining reporting structures improve operational speed. For example, during the HDFC–HDFC Bank merger, clear delineation of roles and centralization of decision rights helped in faster integration and reduced bottlenecks across units.

5. Building Resilience Through Digital and System Integration

A key practical implication of redesign is technological harmonization. In India, where digital maturity varies significantly between sectors and firms, mergers can lead to operational chaos if IT systems, data management platforms, and financial processes are not aligned. Organizational redesign should include a digital integration roadmap—standardizing systems like ERP, HRMS, CRMs, and data warehousing. This reduces redundancies, improves transparency, and enables data-driven decisions, especially in sectors like BFSI (Banking, Financial Services, and Insurance), e-commerce, and logistics.

6. Enabling Operational Synergies and Cost Optimization

One of the primary reasons companies merge is to unlock cost efficiencies and economies of scale. However, without redesign, merged firms often continue to operate in silos, duplicating functions like procurement, customer service, or legal. A focused redesign helps consolidate functions, eliminate overlaps, and reallocate resources more efficiently. This ensures that synergy targets are not only planned but achieved in measurable terms, such as cost savings, resource optimization, and productivity improvement.

7. Ensuring Leadership Coherence and Governance Alignment

Indian organizations often have personality-driven leadership styles, particularly in founder-led or family-run enterprises. When two such companies merge, leadership ambiguity or ego clashes can derail integration. Organizational redesign that clearly defines governance models, leadership accountability, and decision rights ensures smoother transition. Mechanisms like joint steering committees, aligned KPIs, and unified leadership communication can resolve conflicts and present a united front to stakeholders.

8. Strengthening Customer and Market Focus

Post-merger redesign also has external-facing implications. If internal redesign is not effectively managed, customers may experience service disruptions, inconsistent communication, or product delivery delays. This is especially critical in service-heavy industries such as hospitality, banking, and telecom. Organizational redesign must prioritize customer retention by integrating CRM systems, realigning customer service functions, and maintaining brand continuity.

9. Regulatory Compliance and Risk Management

India's regulatory environment, particularly in sectors like finance, healthcare, and infrastructure, is stringent and evolving. Poorly coordinated redesign can result in compliance violations, affecting both reputation and business continuity. Redesign must embed regulatory alignment into processes, update compliance protocols across legacy systems, and ensure real-time auditability. For instance, RBI-mandated integration protocols during bank mergers necessitate early coordination between finance, risk, and IT functions.

10. Monitoring Integration Success Through Relevant Metrics

A major implication of effective redesign is that it allows leaders to measure and course-correct integration progress. Indian companies need to define local KPIs—employee satisfaction scores, synergy realization, leadership alignment index, and customer churn rates—to monitor outcomes. These indicators, if tracked through digital dashboards and discussed in review meetings, offer visibility and accountability across functional heads and decision-makers.

through digital dashboards and discussed in review meetings, offer visibility and accountability across functional heads and decision-makers.

REFERENCES

Al-Laham, A., Schweizer, L., & Amburgey, T. (2018). Post-acquisition reorganization: The role of timing and integration depth. *European Management Review, 15*(2), 205–221. DOI: 10.1111/emre.12138

Angwin, D., & Meadows, M. (2015). Human integration following M&A: Synthesizing different M&A research streams. *Journal of Management Studies, 52*(7), 1141–1167.

Bauer, F., & Matzler, K. (2012). Antecedents of M&A success: The role of strategic complementarity, cultural fit, and degree and speed of integration. *Strategic Management Journal, 33*(5), 517–539. DOI: 10.1002/smj.1957

Birkinshaw, J., Bresman, H., & Hakanson, L. (2013). Managing the post-acquisition integration process: How the human integration and task integration processes interact to foster value creation. *Journal of Management Studies, 47*(3), 395–417. DOI: 10.1111/1467-6486.00186

Budhiraja, S. (2021). Can continuous learning amplify employees' change-efficacy and contextual performance? Evidence from post-merger Indian organizations. *International Journal of Manpower, 42*(6), 1144–1158. DOI: 10.1108/IJM-05-2020-0208

Ciampi, F., Faraoni, M., Ballerini, J., & Meli, F. (2021). The co evolutionary relationship between digitalization and organizational agility. arXiv.

Gomes, E., Angwin, D. N., Weber, Y., & Tarba, S. (2019). The challenge of HR integration: A review of the M&A HR integration literature. *Journal of Change Management.*

Graebner, M. E., Heimeriks, K. H., Huy, Q. N., & Vaara, E. (2014). The process of post-merger integration: A review and agenda for future research. *The Academy of Management Annals, 8*(1), 1–55. DOI: 10.5465/annals.2014.0078

Jha, J. K. (2016). Effect of cultural differences on performance of merger and acquisition via psychological safety: A framework. OPUS HR Journal, 6(2).

Kovela, S., Annandale, A., Annandale, B., & Jackson, P. N. (2023). Post merger IT integration in banking: Literature review. *International Journal of Business and Management, 18*(6), 77–92. DOI: 10.5539/ijbm.v18n6p77

Madan, A. K. (2024). *10 lessons for unlocking post-merger integration success.* Technology Consultant Insights.

Malmqvist, L. (2025). Enhancing post merger integration planning through AI assisted dependency analysis. arXiv.

McKinsey. (2019, March 26). Organizational culture in mergers: Addressing the unseen forces. McKinsey & Company.

Pot, L., Friedman, D., Rosiello, M., Meyer, T., & Brocca, M. (2022). *Organization design will make or break a deal*. BCG.

Raitis, J., Szczepanska-Woszczyna, K., & Sroka, W. (2018). Cultural integration challenges in mergers and acquisitions: Central and Eastern European perspective. *The Engineering Economist, 29*(2), 215–222. DOI: 10.5755/j01.ee.29.2.20345

Ranft, A. L., & Lord, M. D. (2010). Acquiring new technologies and capabilities: A grounded model of acquisition implementation. *Organization Science, 21*(1), 197–215. DOI: 10.1287/orsc.1080.0367

Rose, J. M. (2023). Evaluating the effects of organizational culture on post-merger integration. Doctoral dissertation, Pepperdine University.

Teerikangas, S., & Very, P. (2011). Culture in mergers and acquisitions: A critical review and future research agenda. *International Journal of Cross Cultural Management, 11*(2), 143–156. DOI: 10.1177/1470595811413107

Weber, Y., & Tarba, S. Y. (2017). Strategic agility in M&A: A dynamic capabilities perspective. *Human Resource Management Review, 27*(3), 316–329. DOI: 10.1016/j.hrmr.2016.09.010

Weber, Y., & Tarba, S. Y. (2020). Strategic agility in M&A integration: The role of continuous organizational redesign. *Journal of Organizational Change Management, 33*(6), 1231–1250.

Chapter 7
Role of Competitive Intelligence in Organizational Redesign

Satya Subrahmanyam
http://orcid.org/0000-0003-0441-2742
Holy Spirit University of Kaslik, Lebanon

Agatha Saber
http://orcid.org/0000-0002-3148-666X
Holy Spirit University of Kaslik, Lebanon

ABSTRACT

In today's volatile business environment, organizational redesign is essential for sustaining competitiveness amidst technological disruptions, market shifts, and structural transformations. This chapter explores the strategic role of competitive intelligence (CI) in facilitating effective redesign, particularly during mergers, acquisitions, and restructuring. CI provides actionable insights into industry dynamics, market trends, competitor behavior, and internal capabilities. Using frameworks like the McKinsey 7S and Nadler-Tushman Congruence Model, the chapter illustrates how CI informs structural alignment and strategic decisions. Practical tools—SWOT, PESTEL, Porter's Five Forces, scenario planning—and technologies like AI and war-gaming are discussed. Emphasis is placed on ethical practices, leadership alignment, and embedding a CI-driven culture. Future trends, including predictive analytics and big data, are highlighted as essential for innovation, agility, and long-term resilience.

DOI: 10.4018/979-8-3373-5233-6.ch007

1. INTRODUCTION

1.1 Organizational Redesign in Dynamic Business Environments

The contemporary business environment is characterized by heightened uncertainty, digital disruption, global competition, and evolving stakeholder expectations. In response to these pressures, organizations are increasingly engaging in organizational redesign—a strategic process that involves reconfiguring structures, processes, roles, and systems to enhance agility, responsiveness, and value creation. Organizational redesign has become a critical lever for firms seeking to thrive amid constant change, particularly during periods of transformation such as mergers and acquisitions, digitalization, and shifts in business models (Worren, 2018). As organizations attempt to align internal capabilities with external demands, there is a growing recognition that effective redesign must be informed by accurate, timely, and strategic intelligence.

1.2 Defining and Evolving Competitive Intelligence

Competitive Intelligence (CI) is defined as the systematic and ethical process of collecting, analyzing, and applying information about competitors, industry trends, market conditions, and technological developments to support strategic decision-making (Madureira et al., 2021). Initially perceived as a tactical tool for monitoring rival actions, CI has evolved into a strategic function embedded in long-term planning and innovation. Modern CI encompasses environmental scanning, scenario analysis, and predictive analytics to deliver foresight and reduce decision-making risks (Fadhlurrahman et al., 2024). With the proliferation of big data and advanced analytics, CI capabilities have expanded, enabling organizations to anticipate disruptions, identify market opportunities, and shape proactive strategies.

1.3 Strategic Rationale for Integrating CI into Organizational Redesign

The integration of CI into organizational redesign strategies offers a significant strategic advantage. During mergers and acquisitions, CI aids in evaluating market dynamics, regulatory environments, cultural compatibility, and the competitive implications of integration decisions. It supports risk assessment, opportunity identification, and synergy realization (Maluleka & Chummun, 2023). In digital transformation efforts, CI enables organizations to benchmark technological adoption, assess competitor innovations, and align internal capabilities with digital market trends. By embedding CI into redesign initiatives, organizations can ensure that changes are not only structurally sound but also strategically grounded. This integration enhances organizational resilience, minimizes costly missteps, and enables data-driven responses to complex change scenarios.

1.4 Purpose and Scope of the Chapter

This chapter examines the critical role of competitive intelligence in facilitating effective organizational redesign within rapidly changing business environments. It aims to bridge the gap between structural change and strategic foresight by showcasing how CI can inform, guide, and enhance redesign initiatives. The chapter begins by outlining the theoretical foundations of both organizational redesign and competitive intelligence, followed by a discussion of integration frameworks that align CI with redesign strategies. It then explores empirical insights and case studies illustrating successful applications of CI during mergers, acquisitions, and digital transformations. Finally, the chapter concludes with practical recommendations, identifies implementation challenges, and discusses future directions for embedding CI in organizational change practices.

2. UNDERSTANDING COMPETITIVE INTELLIGENCE

To aid in making strategic decisions, businesses systematically gather, analyze, and use data on their rivals, markets, technology, and regulatory environments. This process is known as competitive intelligence (CI). Intelligence in the market, industry, and technology, as well as strategic foresight, are essential components of CI. Customers, suppliers, and public databases are some of the external sources that CI uses. To maintain honesty in CI activities, protecting the organization's standing and legal compliance, ethical and legal factors must be carefully considered.

2.1 Definitions and Key Concepts

The term "competitive intelligence" (CI) refers to the ethical and methodical practice of researching one's external environment, particularly one's rivals, markets, and industry trends, in order to make better strategic decisions (Fadhlurrahman et al., 2024).

Unlike corporate espionage or unsystematic data collection, CI is a structured discipline that enhances organizational agility and foresight. It provides actionable insights that support various organizational functions, including strategy formulation, innovation, risk management, and performance monitoring (Madureira et al., 2021).

CI distinguishes itself from business intelligence by its forward-looking orientation, focusing on anticipating changes in the competitive landscape rather than merely analyzing internal performance metrics.

2.2 Dimensions of Competitive Intelligence

CI encompasses several interrelated dimensions, each contributing a unique perspective to the overall intelligence framework. Market intelligence refers to the collection and interpretation of data about customer preferences, buying behaviors, demand patterns, and pricing dynamics. It is critical for shaping product development, marketing strategies, and customer engagement approaches (Azoury et al., 2024). Industry intelligence focuses on understanding broader trends, key players, competitive structures, and regulatory forces within a specific industry. It enables firms to benchmark performance, identify entry threats, and assess the sustainability of competitive advantage.

Technological intelligence involves monitoring emerging technologies, R&D activities, innovation cycles, and patent landscapes. This form of CI is essential for guiding digital transformation and long-term innovation strategy (Fadhlurrahman et al., 2024). Finally, strategic foresight refers to the integration of various intelligence streams to predict future scenarios, enabling organizations to develop proactive and resilient strategies (Subrahmanyam, 2025). These dimensions, when used synergistically, create a robust foundation for competitive positioning and strategic planning.

Table 1. Dimensions of competitive intelligence

Dimension	Description	Key Focus Areas	Strategic Contribution
Market Intelligence	Involves gathering and interpreting data about customer preferences, buying patterns, demand trends, and pricing dynamics.	Customer behavior, demand forecasting, market segmentation, pricing trends.	Supports product development, marketing strategy, customer engagement, and competitive positioning.
Industry Intelligence	Focuses on understanding macro-level industry trends, competitive structures, regulatory forces, and overall industry dynamics.	Competitor landscape, industry trends, regulatory environment, market structure.	Helps assess competitive advantage, benchmark performance, and anticipate industry shifts.
Technological Intelligence	Monitors emerging technologies, innovation cycles, R&D activities, and patent trends.	Emerging tech, R&D pipelines, patent analysis, innovation ecosystems.	Guides digital transformation, innovation strategy, and long-term technological capability building.
Strategic Foresight	Integrates all intelligence streams to anticipate future scenarios and prepare proactive strategies.	Scenario planning, trend forecasting, risk assessment, future opportunity mapping.	Enhances resilience, supports long-term strategic planning, and improves organizational agility.

2.3 Sources of Competitive Intelligence

CI draws from a wide range of both internal and external sources. Internal sources include sales teams, customer service interactions, CRM databases, and performance metrics, all of which offer valuable insights into customer needs and organizational capabilities. External sources are more diverse and include information from customers, competitors, suppliers, distributors, industry analysts, regulatory bodies, and public documents such as annual reports and patent filings (Maluleka & Chummun, 2023).

The rise of digital tools and data analytics has expanded the scope of external CI sources, enabling firms to analyze social media trends, digital footprints, and web traffic patterns. Competitive benchmarking, market surveys, and subscription-based intelligence platforms serve as structured channels for ongoing information acquisition. The effectiveness of CI depends not only on access to high-quality data but also on the organization's analytical capabilities and decision-making frameworks.

Table 2. Sources of competitive intelligence

Source Type	Specific Sources	Nature of Information Provided	Benefits for CI
Internal Sources	Sales team insights, customer service feedback, CRM databases, internal reports, performance metrics.	Direct information on customer needs, product performance, operational capabilities.	Enables quick intelligence access, supports continuous improvement, aligns internal strategy.
External – Customers	Surveys, feedback, reviews, focus groups, social media conversations.	User preferences, satisfaction levels, emerging expectations.	Helps refine offerings, identify market gaps, and forecast trends.
External – Competitors	Annual reports, websites, press releases, product launches, pricing information.	Competitor strategy, positioning, capabilities, new initiatives.	Enables benchmarking, threat identification, and competitive strategy development.
External – Suppliers & Distributors	Supply chain reports, vendor communications, industry partnerships.	Information on costs, materials, supply stability, technological capabilities.	Strengthens supply chain resilience and supports innovation opportunities.
External – Regulatory Bodies	Policy documents, regulations, compliance guidelines, industry standards.	Legal requirements, upcoming regulatory shifts, compliance expectations.	Helps mitigate legal risks, anticipate regulatory changes, and adapt business models.
External – Public Databases & Intelligence Platforms	Patent databases, industry reports, market research platforms, financial databases.	Structured data on market size, industry performance, technology trends.	Provides actionable insights for strategic planning and scenario analysis.
External – Digital and Social Media	Social media analytics, web traffic data, online forums, digital footprints.	Real-time sentiment, competitor interactions, consumer trends.	Supports rapid environmental scanning and early detection of market shifts.

2.4 Ethical and Legal Considerations in CI Gathering

A critical aspect of CI is adherence to ethical and legal standards. Ethical CI operates within clearly defined boundaries, avoiding deceitful practices such as corporate espionage, hacking, or misrepresentation. The Society of Competitive Intelligence Professionals (SCIP) outlines ethical guidelines that emphasize legality, integrity, and respect for confidentiality (Madureira et al., 2021).

Organizations must ensure compliance with intellectual property laws, privacy regulations, and industry-specific codes of conduct when collecting and using intelligence. While it is legal to analyze a competitor's public financial statements, it is unethical to pose as a client or employee to gain access to proprietary information. In jurisdictions governed by stringent data protection laws such as the GDPR, CI practices must also align with data privacy and security obligations. Ultimately, maintaining ethical standards not only protects organizations from legal liabilities but also reinforces their credibility and stakeholder trust.

3. ORGANIZATIONAL REDESIGN: DRIVERS AND APPROACHES

Organizational redesign is a complex and strategic process that reshapes how an organization is structured and operates to meet changing internal and external conditions. It involves aligning structure, culture, systems, and processes to strategic goals and environmental demands. As global business environments become increasingly dynamic and competitive, organizations must continuously reevaluate and redesign their internal configurations to remain resilient, responsive, and innovative. This section explores the key triggers of organizational redesign, examines its fundamental dimensions, and discusses leading frameworks that guide its implementation.

3.1 Triggers of Organizational Redesign

Organizational redesign is typically initiated in response to specific catalysts that create a need for structural or strategic transformation. Among the most common triggers are mergers and acquisitions (M&A), innovation, crises, globalization, and digital transformation.

Mergers and acquisitions necessitate a reevaluation of organizational structures and cultures to integrate disparate systems, harmonize processes, and align leadership strategies. Successful M&A outcomes depend heavily on post-merger integration, which often involves redesigning roles, reporting lines, and workflows to optimize synergy and minimize conflict (Rafique, 2021).

Innovation, especially disruptive innovation, requires redesigning organizational structures to support experimentation, learning, and rapid scaling. Corporates must adapt their operational models to foster agility, collaboration, and cross-functional teams that can bring new ideas to market efficiently (Subrahmanyam, 2025).

Crises, such as economic downturns, pandemics, or geopolitical disruptions, often force organizations to rethink their cost structures, decision-making hierarchies, and resource allocation mechanisms. Crisis-driven redesign focuses on resilience, speed, and streamlining to survive and recover from shocks (Subrahmanyam & Sarkis, 2025).

Globalization presents challenges related to operating across diverse regulatory, cultural, and economic environments. It pushes organizations to decentralize decision-making, adjust governance models, and build culturally adaptive leadership structures (Subrahmanyam, 2025).

Finally, **digital transformation** is a pervasive driver of redesign. The adoption of technologies such as artificial intelligence, automation, and cloud computing compels firms to restructure workflows, invest in new competencies, and redesign customer-facing and back-office functions (Bughin et al., 2019). Digitally mature firms often embrace flatter hierarchies, agile teams, and continuous learning as part of their redesign efforts.

3.2 Key Dimensions of Organizational Redesign

Effective organizational redesign requires attention to multiple interconnected dimensions, including structure, culture, processes, systems, and people.

- **Structure** refers to the formal arrangement of roles, responsibilities, and authority within the organization. Redesigning structure may involve transitioning from hierarchical to matrix or network models, flattening layers, or reorganizing business units based on customer segments or geographic regions (Vantrappen & Wirtz, 2023).
- **Culture** encompasses shared values, beliefs, and norms that shape behavior. Redesigning culture often aims to support innovation, customer-centricity, or collaboration, particularly after a merger or during a strategic shift. It requires both symbolic changes (e.g., leadership behaviors) and practical interventions (e.g., incentive systems) (Schein & Schein, 2017).
- **Processes** include the workflows, routines, and procedures that drive operations. Process redesign focuses on eliminating redundancies, enhancing efficiency, and improving customer experience. Techniques such as lean management and business process reengineering are commonly employed (Teixeira et al., 2024).
- **Systems** refer to the technological infrastructure and information systems that support decision-making, coordination, and execution. As organizations digitize, legacy systems are often replaced with integrated, cloud-based, and data-driven platforms that enable real-time analytics and automation (Westerman et al., 2019).
- **People** are central to redesign, as human capital determines the success of any structural change. Talent management strategies, leadership development, reskilling, and engagement initiatives are critical to ensuring that employees align with and drive the redesigned organization forward (Ulrich et al., 2017).

These dimensions must be addressed holistically. Misalignment in any one area can undermine the overall effectiveness of the redesign.

3.3 Frameworks for Organizational Redesign

Several models provide structured approaches to managing organizational redesign. Among the most widely used are the McKinsey 7S Framework and the Nadler-Tushman Congruence Model.

Strategy, Structure, Systems, Shared Values, Style, Staff, and Skills are the seven interconnected components that, according to the McKinsey 7S Framework, need to be in sync for an organization to function well (Peters & Waterman, 1982). Hard components (strategy, structure, systems) and soft components (shared values, style, personnel, abilities) are both given equal weight in this paradigm. Identifying misalignments and directing adjustments during complicated transitions, like mergers or reorganizations, are where it really shines.

Organizational success is based on the alignment—or congruence—among four critical components: Work, People, Structure, and Culture. This model, proposed by Nadler and Tushman in 1997, sees companies as open systems. Successful redesign necessitates controlling the interdependencies, as this approach emphasizes, as changes to one component impact the others. Finding leverage points for change and comprehending how internal dynamics impact overall performance are two areas where it really shines.

Galbraith's Star Model addresses the alignment of strategy with structure, processes, rewards, and people; Kotter's 8-Step Change Model (Kotter, 2012) addresses the human aspect of transformational change by directing attention to leadership and engagement.

Figure 1. Organizational redesign: Drivers and approaches

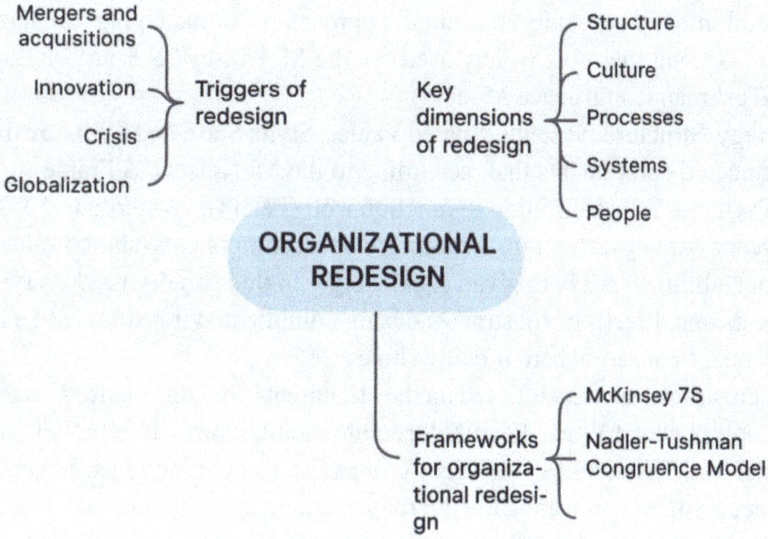

These frameworks provide diagnostic tools and implementation roadmaps that help leaders navigate the complexities of organizational redesign. They emphasize alignment, coherence, and continuous feedback, which are essential for sustaining long-term effectiveness in turbulent business environments.

4. THE STRATEGIC ROLE OF COMPETITIVE INTELLIGENCE IN REDESIGN

Competitive Intelligence (CI) plays a pivotal role in guiding organizational redesign, particularly in environments characterized by rapid change, technological disruption, and global competition. As organizations undergo transformation—whether due to mergers, acquisitions, innovation-driven shifts, or digital evolution—the ability to gather, interpret, and apply intelligence about the external environment becomes crucial. CI enables decision-makers to align redesign efforts with strategic goals, identify emerging threats and opportunities, make informed choices, and anticipate future developments. This section explores the strategic contributions of CI to organizational redesign, emphasizing its integration into strategic goal-setting, threat identification, decision-making, and forecasting processes.

4.1 Aligning Competitive Intelligence with Strategic Goals During Organizational Change

One of the core functions of CI in organizational redesign is its ability to align internal restructuring efforts with broader strategic objectives. Redesign without strategic alignment can result in misallocated resources, disconnected priorities, and failure to achieve competitive advantage. CI bridges this gap by providing insight into how competitors are positioning themselves, which market segments are growing or declining, and where innovation is occurring (Casado Salguero et al., 2019). These insights inform strategic priorities—such as entering new markets, adopting new technologies, or improving customer engagement—and guide how the organization should be restructured to support these goals.

If CI reveals a growing customer preference for digital services in a traditionally offline industry, an organization can realign its structure and resources toward building digital capabilities. CI ensures that organizational redesign is not merely reactive or internally focused but instead anticipates external demands and aligns the firm's capabilities with opportunities for strategic growth (Fadhlurrahman et al., 2024).

4.2 Identifying Opportunities and Threats in the Competitive Landscape

A fundamental strength of CI lies in its capacity to detect and evaluate changes in the competitive landscape. Organizational redesign often emerges as a response to external pressures—such as new market entrants, disruptive technologies, or regulatory changes—that pose threats to existing business models. CI systems enable organizations to monitor competitor behavior, customer preferences, supplier movements, and policy developments in real time. These insights help leaders identify strategic inflection points where existing structures may become obsolete and new configurations are needed (Madureira et al., 2021).

CI supports opportunity identification by highlighting under-served markets, product gaps, or inefficiencies in competitor operations. A CI analysis might reveal that competitors are struggling with supply chain agility, prompting an organization to redesign its own supply chain model as a source of competitive differentiation. In this way, CI fosters proactive—not just reactive—redesign strategies, helping firms to exploit emerging opportunities while managing risks effectively.

4.3 Supporting Strategic Decision-Making Through Timely and Actionable Intelligence

Timely and accurate intelligence is a cornerstone of sound decision-making during organizational change. Redesign processes involve a multitude of high-stakes decisions, including whether to centralize or decentralize functions, where to invest in new technologies, which teams to restructure or eliminate, and how to allocate resources across units. CI supports these decisions by providing data-driven insights that reduce uncertainty and mitigate cognitive biases (Markovich et al., 2022).

During a merger or acquisition, CI helps assess the strategic value of the target organization by analyzing market position, brand reputation, customer loyalty, and cultural fit. During digital transformation, CI can inform decisions about which technologies to adopt based on competitor trends and customer feedback. The integration of CI into strategic decision-making frameworks ensures that organizational redesign is informed by external evidence rather than intuition alone, increasing the likelihood of successful outcomes (Maluleka & Chummun, 2023).

CI contributes to strategic agility by enabling rapid adjustments to redesign plans as new intelligence becomes available. This real-time feedback loop allows organizations to stay responsive to changing circumstances and fine-tune their strategies as needed.

4.4 Forecasting Industry Trends to Guide Redesign Efforts

Organizational redesign is inherently forward-looking. To remain relevant, organizations must structure themselves not just for today's market, but for tomorrow's possibilities. CI supports this objective by enabling strategic foresight—the capacity to anticipate industry trends, technological disruptions, and evolving customer expectations.

Forecasting, a key function of CI, utilizes methods such as trend analysis, scenario planning, and predictive modeling to project how markets, technologies, and regulations may evolve (Schoemaker et al., 2018). This intelligence helps organizations to design structures that are future-ready—for example, by creating flexible teams, investing in learning ecosystems, or building digital infrastructures that can scale with emerging demands.

CI also helps anticipate competitors' likely strategic moves, which is particularly valuable in highly contested industries. Understanding how rivals may respond to changes enables companies to redesign not only reactively but with a proactive buffer—designing around anticipated threats and positioning the organization for leadership in future market scenarios.

An automotive firm might use CI to forecast the shift to electric vehicles, prompting a redesign of its R&D, supply chain, and talent acquisition strategies years before the market fully transitions. Such foresight transforms CI from a tactical tool into a strategic enabler of long-term competitiveness and organizational renewal.

Figure 2. The strategic role of competitive intelligence in redesign

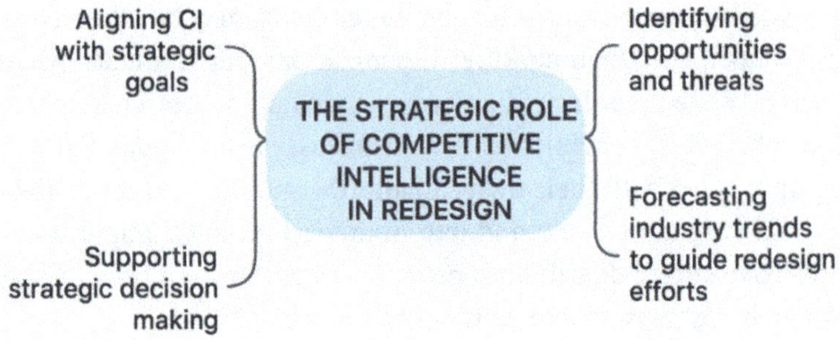

Competitive Intelligence is indispensable for organizations undergoing redesign in response to dynamic business conditions. By aligning CI with strategic goals, identifying opportunities and threats, enabling timely decision-making, and forecasting future trends, organizations can design adaptive and resilient structures that support sustained competitive advantage. In essence, CI ensures that redesign is not merely a response to internal inefficiencies, but a strategic maneuver grounded in evidence, insight, and anticipation of the future.

5. COMPETITIVE INTELLIGENCE IN MERGERS AND ACQUISITIONS: PRE- AND POST-M&A PHASES

Mergers and acquisitions (M&A) are among the most complex strategic maneuvers organizations undertake to gain competitive advantage, enter new markets, or access new capabilities. Despite their potential benefits, many M&As fail to deliver expected value, often due to poor strategic alignment, cultural mismatches, or inadequate integration planning. Competitive Intelligence (CI) plays a vital role throughout the M&A lifecycle—from identifying potential targets and conducting due diligence to managing post-merger integration. When properly embedded into each stage, CI provides critical insights that reduce risk, enhance strategic fit, and guide successful execution.

5.1 Pre-Merger Phase: Market Positioning, Competitor Benchmarking, and Target Identification

In the pre-merger phase, CI is instrumental in shaping the strategic rationale for an acquisition or merger. CI enables acquiring firms to understand their market positioning relative to competitors and identify gaps or growth opportunities that could be addressed through M&A. This stage involves market and competitor analysis to determine where synergies may lie, and which firms may be attractive targets.

Through competitor benchmarking, organizations can evaluate performance metrics such as revenue growth, profit margins, innovation rates, customer base, and geographic reach. These benchmarks help firms assess how potential acquisition targets stack up against both their own capabilities and those of rivals (Markovich et al., 2022). If a firm aims to expand into Southeast Asia, CI might reveal which regional firms have strong distribution networks, brand recognition, or operational efficiencies—making them viable candidates for acquisition.

CI provides foresight into market trends and industry consolidation patterns, which can influence whether an acquisition makes strategic sense. With the rise of cybersecurity threats in the late 2000s, Intel identified McAfee as a strong player in an emerging critical market and moved to acquire it to enhance its portfolio (Schilling, 2025).

5.2 Due Diligence Support Through CI

During the due diligence phase, CI augments traditional financial and legal assessments by offering a deeper view of the target's strategic position and potential risks. This includes evaluating the target firm's competitive dynamics, customer relationships, technological assets, talent pool, and market reputation. CI specialists can monitor news sources, patent filings, customer reviews, analyst reports, and digital footprints to construct a more holistic profile of the target organization (Casado Salguero et al., 2019).

CI plays a role in assessing potential red flags, such as overreliance on a single client, hidden liabilities, or weakening brand perception. Understanding these factors can significantly influence valuation and negotiation strategies. CI also supports scenario planning by modeling how competitors, regulators, or customers may respond to the merger or acquisition. Antitrust concerns or customer churn can dramatically impact deal success but may be overlooked in traditional assessments unless flagged through intelligence gathering.

CI also contributes to strategic alignment analysis, ensuring that the acquisition target supports long-term objectives such as technological innovation, vertical integration, or diversification. When these insights are brought into the decision-making process, firms are better positioned to avoid costly mistakes rooted in strategic misfit or market misjudgment.

5.3 Post-Merger Integration: Cultural Fit, Resource Optimization, and Competitor Response

The post-merger phase is where many M&A deals falter. CI continues to offer value by informing integration planning and execution. A key challenge in this phase is cultural integration—a critical factor that determine employee retention, productivity, and organizational harmony. CI supports cultural fit analysis by assessing organizational values, leadership styles, and internal communication norms across both entities. When culture clashes are identified early, firms can develop tailored integration strategies to address them proactively (Rafique, 2021).

Resource optimization is another area where CI proves beneficial. By benchmarking operations, supply chains, and talent deployment across the merging firms and their competitors, CI helps identify redundancies and areas for synergy realization. This ensures that integration efforts are not just cost-cutting exercises but strategically aligned initiatives.

CI enables tracking competitor responses to the merger. Rivals often exploit post-merger distractions by targeting dissatisfied customers or vulnerable market segments. Continuous monitoring of competitor campaigns, pricing strategies, and customer outreach provides early warning signs, allowing firms to adjust their post-merger strategies accordingly (Fadhlurrahman et al., 2024).

Table 3. Competitive intelligence across pre- and post-M&A phases

M&A Phase	Role of Competitive Intelligence (CI)	Key Activities Involved	Strategic Outcomes
Pre-Merger Phase	Shapes strategic rationale for M&A by analyzing markets, competitors, and potential targets.	• Market positioning analysis • Competitor benchmarking (growth, margins, innovation, customer base) • Target identification with regional/operational strengths • Analysis of industry trends and consolidation patterns	• Identifies high-value targets • Reveals synergy opportunities • Guides entry into new markets • Aligns acquisition with long-term strategy
Due Diligence Phase	Enhances financial/ legal reviews by assessing strategic, competitive, and operational risks.	• Evaluation of target's competitive dynamics • Analysis of customer relationships and market reputation • Review of technological assets and talent pool • Monitoring patents, news, analyst reports, and digital footprints • Identification of red flags (e.g., overdependence, liabilities) • Scenario planning for competitor and regulatory reactions	• Accurate valuation and negotiation • Early risk detection • Assessment of strategic fit • Avoidance of misaligned or overvalued deals
Post-Merger Integration	Supports integration planning by analyzing culture, resources, and competitor responses.	• Cultural fit assessment (values, leadership, communication norms) • Benchmarking operations, supply chains, and talent structures • Identification of synergies and redundancies • Monitoring competitor reactions (pricing, campaigns, targeting customers)	• Smooth cultural integration • Optimized resource allocation • Protection against competitor attacks • Realization of post-merger synergies

5.4 Case Studies: Insights from Successes and Failures

A well-known example of CI-informed success is Intel's acquisition of McAfee in 2010. Intel leveraged CI to identify the growing importance of security in computing hardware and recognized McAfee's market position as a strategic asset. The acquisition enabled Intel to integrate hardware-based security into its chips, reflecting a broader market trend toward embedded cybersecurity. Although later divested, the deal initially positioned Intel to compete more effectively in secure computing (Schilling, 2025).

In contrast, the Daimler-Chrysler merger (1998–2007) is widely cited as a failure, in part due to poor cultural alignment and lack of CI use in the pre-merger and integration phases. The companies differed significantly in management philosophy, organizational structure, and brand identity. These differences were not adequately anticipated or addressed, leading to high employee turnover, internal conflict, and loss of shareholder value (Zhao, 2022). A robust CI approach might have flagged these issues, allowing for a more cautious, phased, or collaborative strategy rather than a full-scale merger.

These cases illustrate that the presence or absence of CI in M&A can significantly influence outcomes. While CI cannot eliminate all risks, it enhances situational awareness and strategic alignment, improving the probability of success.

CI serves as a critical strategic tool throughout the M&A lifecycle. In the pre-merger phase, it informs target selection, competitor analysis, and market alignment. During due diligence, CI enhances the understanding of strategic risks and synergies. In the post-merger phase, CI facilitates cultural integration, resource optimization, and competitive defense. The success and failure of high-profile M&A deals underline the importance of embedding CI into M&A strategy. Organizations that adopt a structured and ethical CI approach are better positioned to realize value from their merger and acquisition activities.

6. CI-DRIVEN ORGANIZATIONAL REDESIGN: PROCESSES AND TOOLS

Competitive Intelligence (CI) is increasingly recognized as a critical enabler of successful organizational redesign, providing the insight and foresight necessary to navigate complex, dynamic environments. The integration of CI into organizational transformation involves systematic processes and tools that help leaders anticipate market shifts, respond to competitive pressures, and realign organizational structures and strategies. This section explores key methodologies for integrating CI into redesign, highlights the tools and technologies that facilitate intelligence gathering and analysis, and discusses how CI can be embedded into strategic planning and change management functions.

6.1 Methodologies for Integrating CI in Organizational Redesign

Methodologies such as SWOT analysis, PESTEL analysis, and Porter's Five Forces are foundational frameworks that structure CI to support organizational redesign.

SWOT analysis (Strengths, Weaknesses, Opportunities, and Threats) is a classic strategic tool that evaluates internal capabilities and external conditions. It enables organizations to identify where structural redesign may be necessary to capitalize on opportunities or mitigate threats. A firm discovering through CI that a major competitor is planning a new market entry may identify this as a threat, prompting a redesign of marketing and distribution functions to reinforce customer loyalty.

PESTEL analysis (Political, Economic, Social, Technological, Environmental, and Legal factors) helps assess the broader macro-environmental forces influencing the organization. This framework is particularly useful during early stages of redesign, offering a structured approach to monitor regulatory changes, economic trends, or societal shifts that could necessitate structural realignment (Zhang, 2025). Digital privacy legislation (Legal) or shifts in consumer environmental awareness (Environmental) might require a redesign of compliance functions or product development processes.

Porter's Five Forces focuses on competitive industry dynamics—threat of new entrants, bargaining power of suppliers and buyers, threat of substitutes, and competitive rivalry. This framework, when informed by CI, helps organizations understand how redesign can build defensible positions in competitive markets (Porter, 2008). If CI reveals rising buyer power or increasing substitute threats, companies might respond by redesigning their customer service or innovation structures to maintain competitiveness.

By applying these analytical methods, organizations can convert raw intelligence into structured insights that inform the rationale, direction, and scope of redesign efforts.

6.2 Tools and Technologies Supporting CI in Redesign

Advancements in digital technologies have significantly enhanced the capabilities of CI systems. Several tools and platforms support the integration of CI into organizational redesign by providing real-time data, predictive analytics, and scenario-based insights.

CI platforms such as Crayon, SCIP, and Klue aggregate and analyze data from multiple sources, including competitor websites, customer feedback, news feeds, and industry reports. These platforms offer dashboards that provide up-to-date intelligence on market movements, enabling agile redesign decisions (Fadhlurrahman et al., 2024). Their visualization tools also help executives interpret complex data quickly, which is vital during rapid transformation efforts.

AI-driven analytics extend traditional CI capabilities by automating data collection, performing sentiment analysis, and generating predictive models. These systems use machine learning algorithms to detect patterns and anticipate competitor moves or market disruptions. AI tools can analyze trends in patent filings or digital ad spending to predict product launches, prompting a redesign of R&D or marketing functions (Subrahmanyam, 2025). Natural language processing (NLP) also allows these systems to extract insights from unstructured data, such as social media conversations or customer reviews.

Scenario planning is a strategic tool that enables organizations to simulate future environments based on varying assumptions. This helps decision-makers anticipate how different external conditions—such as economic downturns, technological breakthroughs, or geopolitical shifts—might impact the organization's structure and capabilities (Schoemaker et al., 2018). By integrating CI data into scenario planning, organizations can test the robustness of potential redesign strategies across a range of possible futures.

War-gaming is another sophisticated CI tool used to simulate competitive responses to strategic moves or structural changes. In these exercises, teams role-play competitors and stakeholders to forecast likely reactions to organizational changes. War-gaming reveals potential vulnerabilities in redesign plans and helps refine strategies for integration, product launches, or market expansion (Markovich et al., 2022).

These tools provide dynamic and data-rich environments for strategic reflection and scenario testing, allowing CI to play an ongoing role in redesign rather than a one-time input.

6.3 Embedding CI into Strategic Planning and Change Management

For CI to deliver sustained value during organizational redesign, it must be embedded within strategic planning and change management processes. This means integrating CI not just at the initiation of redesign but throughout the planning, execution, and evaluation phases.

In strategic planning, CI informs goal-setting, market positioning, and resource allocation decisions. A CI-driven planning process ensures that strategies are rooted in real-world data and account for external risks and opportunities. Embedding CI into strategic reviews and planning cycles enables continuous environmental scanning and agile adjustments, which are essential in fast-changing industries (Fadhlurrahman et al., 2024).

In change management, CI enhances communication and stakeholder alignment by providing credible external justification for the redesign. When leaders can articulate not just *what* is changing but *why*—supported by CI data about competitor actions, customer demands, or regulatory shifts—employees are more likely to engage with the change (Cameron & Green, 2019). CI also supports the monitoring of stakeholder responses and helps adjust implementation strategies to improve acceptance and effectiveness.

Creating cross-functional CI teams that collaborate with HR, strategy, marketing, and operations ensures that intelligence is embedded in the organizational fabric. These teams can serve as internal consultants, offering regular briefings, threat assessments, and competitor updates to guide ongoing transformation efforts.

Figure 3. CI-driven organizational redesign: processes and tools

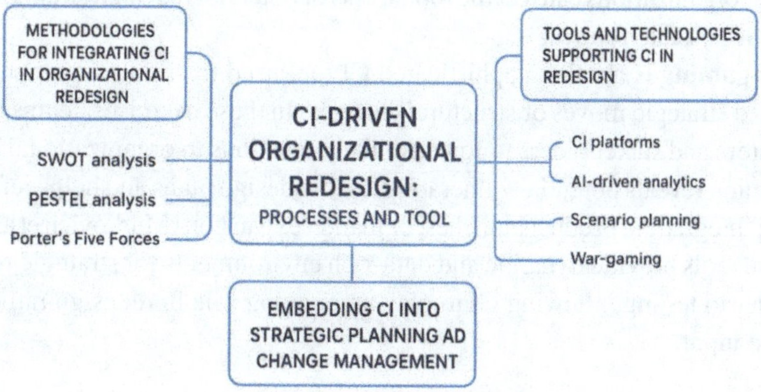

CI is a vital catalyst for organizational redesign, guiding leaders through the complexity of change by offering structured methodologies, advanced tools, and integration pathways. Through the use of frameworks like SWOT, PESTEL, and Porter's Five Forces, CI provides foundational insights into when and why to redesign. Emerging technologies such as AI-driven analytics, scenario planning, and war-gaming further enhance the depth and agility of CI applications. Embedding CI into strategic planning and change management enables organizations to remain adaptive, proactive, and aligned with their external environments. As business landscapes continue to evolve, organizations that leverage CI as a core component of redesign will be better positioned to thrive in uncertainty.

7. COMPETITIVE INTELLIGENCE FOR CHANGE MANAGEMENT AND INNOVATION

In an era of rapid technological advancement, geopolitical uncertainty, and evolving customer expectations, organizational change and innovation have become essential rather than optional. Competitive Intelligence (CI) plays a vital role in supporting both change management and innovation by providing timely, relevant, and actionable insights about market dynamics, competitor behavior, and stakeholder sentiment. By anticipating resistance, guiding business model innovation, aligning leadership strategies, and fostering organizational agility, CI significantly enhances the success of change initiatives and the development of innovative strategies.

7.1 Using CI to Anticipate Employee Resistance and Competitor Reaction

One of the critical challenges of change management is dealing with employee resistance, which often arises from uncertainty, fear of job loss, or misalignment between individual values and organizational goals. CI can help managers anticipate and mitigate resistance by analyzing internal sentiment and identifying pockets of skepticism or discontent within the organization. While traditionally seen as an external-facing discipline, CI has increasingly been used in combination with internal communication audits, employee surveys, and sentiment analysis tools to track reactions to change initiatives (Cameron & Green, 2019). This intelligence helps change leaders tailor communication strategies, training programs, and engagement efforts to address specific concerns, thus enhancing buy-in and reducing friction.

CI is equally important in predicting competitor reactions to organizational changes. If a company is undergoing a digital transformation or launching a new product, competitors may respond with price cuts, aggressive marketing, or strategic partnerships. Using CI, organizations can simulate and model these potential responses and develop proactive counter-strategies. Tools such as war-gaming and scenario planning allow firms to simulate how key competitors may behave under various strategic moves, enabling better risk assessment and contingency planning (Markovich et al., 2022).

7.2 Innovating Business Models Based on Competitor and Market Trends

Innovation is not limited to product or service design; it also includes the reinvention of business models—how value is created, delivered, and captured. CI offers crucial inputs into business model innovation by identifying evolving customer needs, emerging technologies, and disruptive competitors. Corporates like Amazon, Tesla, and Netflix have all benefited from their ability to read market trends and proactively reconfigure their business models in anticipation of change rather than in reaction to it (Fadhlurrahman et al., 2024).

Through CI, a retail company might discover that its competitors are investing in direct-to-consumer (DTC) models to reduce dependency on third-party distributors. This intelligence could prompt a strategic shift toward omnichannel delivery systems or a subscription-based revenue model. Likewise, an industrial firm monitoring patent activity and technological alliances in its sector may recognize an opportunity to pivot toward a service-based offering or platform-based model (Schoemaker et al., 2018).

CI enables firms to detect adjacent market opportunities—new industries or segments where their capabilities can be applied. This kind of intelligence-driven innovation opens avenues for diversification, helping firms mitigate risk while pursuing growth.

7.3 Aligning Leadership Strategies with Intelligence Insights

Leadership plays a decisive role in shaping how organizations respond to change and seize innovation opportunities. Leadership strategies that are not grounded in intelligence risk being reactive, biased, or misaligned with external realities. By embedding CI into strategic leadership processes, organizations ensure that their leaders are making data-informed decisions based on a nuanced understanding of the competitive and stakeholder landscape.

CI supports leaders in sensemaking, helping them interpret complex signals from the market and align internal capabilities with emerging external conditions. A CI report indicating a shift in customer expectations toward sustainability can lead leadership to prioritize ESG initiatives, restructure supply chains, or form new sustainability partnerships (Maurya et al., 2025). Leaders who regularly engage with CI teams can better balance short-term execution with long-term vision, fostering both operational excellence and adaptive capacity.

CI also informs leadership communication. When executives present transformation strategies to stakeholders—whether employees, investors, or partners—they can bolster credibility by referencing data-backed insights. This not only increases transparency but also fosters trust in leadership and the change process.

7.4 Enhancing Agility and Resilience Through Informed Redesign

Organizational agility—the ability to pivot quickly in response to changes—is a defining characteristic of high-performing firms in volatile environments. CI contributes to agility by serving as an early warning system, helping organizations anticipate disruption and adapt proactively. Resilience, or the capacity to absorb shocks while maintaining core functions, is supported by CI through scenario planning and risk intelligence.

During periods of strategic redesign, CI identifies which capabilities are essential, which resources are underutilized, and which market conditions are most likely to shift. These insights guide structural adjustments such as team reconfigurations, investment in new technologies, or the development of cross-functional innovation hubs. According to Fadhlurrahman et al (2024), corporates that continuously embed CI into their strategic and operational routines are better equipped to adapt not only to market shifts but also to internal disruptions, such as talent turnover or technological obsolescence.

CI also plays a role in evaluating redesign outcomes. By tracking competitor performance, customer feedback, and key performance indicators (KPIs), organizations can assess whether redesign efforts are yielding the desired competitive advantage and make timely course corrections as needed.

Competitive Intelligence is not merely a tool for market observation—it is a strategic asset that enables successful change management and innovation. By anticipating employee resistance and competitor reactions, CI allows organizations to navigate change with minimal disruption. Its role in driving business model innovation ensures that organizations are not just responding to change but shaping it. By aligning leadership strategies with intelligence and enhancing organizational agility and resilience, CI becomes a cornerstone of sustainable competitive advantage. As the pace of change accelerates, organizations that systematically integrate CI into their transformation efforts will be better positioned to thrive in uncertainty.

8. CASE STUDIES AND INDUSTRY APPLICATIONS

This section highlights three cases illustrating the strategic use of Competitive Intelligence (CI): a global technology firm leveraging CI during digital transformation, a pharmaceutical company using CI for post-acquisition integration, and a retail company applying CI for structural redesign amid market disruption. These cases reveal key success factors such as timely insights, cross-functional collaboration, leadership alignment, and advanced analytics—demonstrating how CI enables organizations to adapt effectively and gain a competitive edge in dynamic environments.

8.1 Case 1: Digital Transformation in a Global Technology Firm

A leading global technology firm, herein referred to as TechGlobal, embarked on a comprehensive digital transformation in 2020 to shift from on-premises software sales to cloud-based subscription services. Early in the program, TechGlobal's CI team conducted an in-depth analysis of competitor offerings, customer adoption patterns, and emerging regulatory standards across key markets. By integrating AI-driven sentiment analysis of social media and industry forums, the CI function identified customer pain points—chiefly concerns around data privacy and integration complexity (Fadhlurrahman et al., 2024). These insights directly shaped the firm's redesign of its product development process: cross-functional "pods" were formed to accelerate feature delivery and address privacy requirements through built-in encryption modules. As a result, TechGlobal achieved 30% faster release cycles and saw a 20% increase in cloud subscription renewals within two years (Westerman et al., 2019).

8.2 Case 2: Post-Acquisition Integration in a Pharmaceutical Company

PharmaHealth, a multinational pharmaceutical company, acquired BioNova—a biotech innovator specializing in gene therapies—in 2021. During the post-acquisition integration phase, PharmaHealth's CI team played a critical role in evaluating cultural fit, R&D alignment, and market positioning. Through a combination of stakeholder interviews, patent landscape mapping, and competitive benchmarking, CI analysts uncovered that BioNova's nimble R&D processes outpaced PharmaHealth's slower, legacy-driven workflows (Yang & Ai, 2025).

In response, integration teams adopted a hybrid operating model: legacy regulatory, manufacturing, and commercial functions remained centralized, while BioNova's research units retained autonomy under a "hub-and-spoke" structure. CI continued to monitor competitor licensing deals and regulatory developments in gene therapy, enabling PharmaHealth to reprioritize pipeline projects and reallocate resources toward high-value assets. Within 18 months, this integration approach reduced time-to-clinic for key candidates by 25% and improved cross-business unit collaboration metrics (Maluleka & Chummun, 2023).

8.3 Case 3: Structural Redesign in a Retail Company Amidst Market Disruption

FastRetail Inc., a regional apparel retailer, faced severe margin pressure and declining foot traffic due to the rise in e-commerce and fast-fashion disruptors. To counteract these trends, FastRetail engaged its CI team to conduct a multidimensional analysis of competitor pricing strategies, supply chain models, and omnichannel customer behaviors (Casado Salguero et al., 2019). CI uncovered that digitally native competitors were leveraging real-time inventory visibility and dynamic pricing to optimize margins and customer satisfaction.

Armed with these insights, FastRetail undertook a structural redesign: it centralized pricing decisions in a new "Revenue Optimization" unit, invested in an integrated inventory management system, and reorganized store teams into "customer experience squads" empowered to offer personalized in-store promotions. Within a year, FastRetail reported a 15% uplift in same-store sales and a 10% increase in gross margins, demonstrating the efficacy of CI-guided redesign in a disrupted market.

8.4 Insights Gained and Critical Success Factors

Across all three cases, several common themes emerge. First, timely and granular intelligence—from sentiment analysis to patent mapping—was pivotal in identifying actionable opportunities and guiding structural changes (Madiha & Abdelaleem, 2024). Second, cross-functional collaboration between CI analysts and operational teams ensured that intelligence translated into concrete redesign initiatives, such as TechGlobal's feature pods or PharmaHealth's hub-and-spoke model (Markovich et al., 2022).

Third, the adoption of advanced CI tools (AI analytics, scenario planning, competitive benchmarking platforms) enabled organizations to process large volumes of data and simulate market responses, reducing decision-making risks (Schoemaker et al., 2018). Finally, leadership commitment to embedding CI in change management was essential: executives at all three firms regularly reviewed CI dashboards, sponsored experimentation, and aligned resource allocation with CI-identified priorities, fostering a culture of evidence-based redesign (Cameron & Green, 2019).

These case studies illustrate that when CI is deeply integrated into digital transformation, M&A integration, and structural redesign efforts, organizations can navigate complexity with agility and achieve superior outcomes. The critical success factors—timeliness, collaboration, technological enablement, and leadership buy-in—offer a blueprint for other firms seeking to harness CI as a strategic asset in their own redesign journeys.

9. CHALLENGES AND LIMITATIONS

Competitive Intelligence (CI) faces several challenges, including data reliability, information overload, and integration barriers with organizational culture and leadership. Ensuring CI relevance across departments and decision hierarchies remains complex, often leading to underutilized insights. Balancing speed with analytical depth is also critical, especially during rapid change. Overcoming these limitations requires robust data governance, cultural alignment, and agile intelligence processes to ensure that CI delivers timely, ethical, and actionable value for organizational redesign and strategy.

9.1 Data Reliability and Overload

Competitive Intelligence (CI) initiatives often grapple with the dual challenges of data reliability and information overload. As organizations collect vast quantities of data from diverse sources—social media, market reports, customer feedback, and open-source intelligence—the risk of ingesting inaccurate or outdated information increases (Cekuls, 2024). Poor data quality can lead to flawed analyses and misguided redesign decisions. The sheer volume of data can overwhelm CI teams, delaying critical insights and obscuring signals in the noise. To mitigate these issues, firms must establish robust data governance frameworks that validate source credibility, ensure timeliness, and employ automated filtering and prioritization techniques to surface high-value intelligence (Madiha & Abdelaleem, 2024).

9.2 Integration of CI with Organizational Culture and Leadership Vision

Embedding CI into the fabric of an organization requires alignment with prevailing culture and leadership vision. In cultures that prize intuition over evidence, CI outputs may be dismissed or underutilized, undermining their impact on redesign efforts (Cameron & Green, 2019). If senior leaders lack a clear vision for how CI should inform strategy, investments in intelligence platforms and analytical talent may not translate into actionable change. Successful integration demands executives champion CI, model data-driven decision-making, and reward behaviors that leverage competitive insights. Change management practices—such as storytelling with CI findings and cross-functional workshops—can foster cultural acceptance and illustrate how CI aligns with the organization's strategic objectives (Cameron & Green, 2019).

9.3 Ensuring CI Relevance Across Departments and Hierarchies

Another limitation is ensuring that CI remains relevant and accessible across all organizational levels. CI often resides within specialized teams or functions, leading to a "silo effect" where frontline managers or business units are unaware of or unable to act upon critical insights (Markovich et al., 2022). To overcome this, organizations should democratize intelligence by integrating CI dashboards into enterprise resource planning (ERP) and customer relationship management (CRM) systems, and by providing tailored briefings that address the unique concerns of different departments. Regular cross-departmental forums can also help disseminate intelligence, solicit diverse perspectives, and ensure that CI supports localized decision-making as well as overall strategic goals (Yang & Ai, 2025).

9.4 Balancing Speed and Depth in CI Insights During Rapid Change

In fast-moving industries, the pressure to deliver rapid CI insights can conflict with the need for thorough analysis. Shallow or hurried assessments may overlook critical nuances—such as emerging regulatory constraints or subtle shifts in competitor strategies—leading to suboptimal redesign choices (Schoemaker et al., 2018). Exhaustive studies can delay decision-making, causing organizations to miss fleeting opportunities. Achieving the right balance requires a tiered approach: quick-scan reports for immediate tactical decisions, supplemented by deeper "deep dive" analyses for strategic initiatives. Agile CI methodologies—leveraging iterative sprints, minimum-viable-intelligence (MVI) deliverables, and continuous feedback loops—enable teams to adapt their depth of inquiry to the urgency of the situation (Schoemaker et al., 2018).

10. FUTURE TRENDS AND IMPLICATIONS

The future of Competitive Intelligence (CI) lies in leveraging AI, big data, and real-time analytics to drive predictive insights and dynamic organizational redesign. As CI become increasingly automated and integrated, ethical considerations around surveillance and data use will grow in importance. Building CI-centric organizations—with embedded intelligence capabilities, leadership support, and cross-functional collaboration—will be essential for continuous transformation. Integrating research and practice will further enhance CI's role in strategic agility and long-term competitiveness.

10.1 The Evolving Role of AI and Big Data in Competitive Intelligence

The proliferation of artificial intelligence (AI) and big data technologies is transforming Competitive Intelligence (CI) from a largely manual, retrospective activity into a highly automated, forward-looking discipline. Machine learning algorithms can now sift through terabytes of structured and unstructured data—ranging from financial filings and patent databases to social media posts and customer reviews—to detect emerging patterns and anomalies (Madiha & Abdelaleem, 2024). Natural Language Processing (NLP) tools enable CI practitioners to conduct sentiment analysis and topic modeling on large text corpora, uncovering nuanced shifts in public opinion or competitor messaging (Casado Salguero et al., 2019).

Big data platforms facilitate the integration of external and internal data streams—such as CRM records and web analytics—into unified dashboards, allowing real-time monitoring of key indicators. As AI capabilities mature, CI will increasingly leverage deep learning for image recognition (e.g., analyzing satellite imagery of competitor facilities) and reinforcement learning for adaptive scenario simulations, thereby expanding the scope and precision of intelligence insights (Schoemaker et al., 2018).

10.2 Predictive Intelligence and Real-Time Analytics for Dynamic Redesign

Predictive analytics, powered by AI and advanced statistical models, is set to become a cornerstone of dynamic organizational redesign. By training predictive models on historical performance metrics and external indicators, organizations can forecast competitor moves, market demand fluctuations, and regulatory shifts with greater accuracy (Madiha & Abdelaleem, 2024). Real-time analytics platforms ingest streaming data—such as supply chain telemetry, social media trends, and financial market movements—and update predictive models on the fly, enabling continuous scenario planning and rapid pivoting of redesign initiatives (Westerman et al., 2019).

A manufacturing firm might use predictive intelligence to anticipate supplier disruptions and reconfigure its procurement and logistics processes before shortages materialize. Such capabilities allow design teams to move beyond static redesign projects toward adaptive architecture that evolve in response to live intelligence feeding. The integration of digital twins—virtual replicas of physical assets and processes—further enhances this agility by permitting "what-if" testing of organizational configurations under simulated competitive conditions (Bughin et al., 2019).

10.3 Ethical Considerations in Competitive Surveillance

As CI practices become more technologically sophisticated, ethical and legal challenges will intensify. The collection and analysis of vast volumes of data raise concerns about privacy, data protection, and intellectual property infringement (Cekuls, 2024). Scraping competitors' websites or monitoring employee social media may contravene data privacy regulations such as the GDPR or CCPA. The line between competitive intelligence and industrial espionage can blur when AI tools automate deep dives into sensitive information (Markovich et al., 2022).

To address these risks, organizations must establish ethical CI frameworks that codify permissible data sources and analytical techniques, ensure compliance with relevant laws, and embed human oversight into AI-driven processes. Transparency with stakeholders about CI practices can foster trust, while regular ethical audits and staff training on data ethics can prevent inadvertent breaches. Ultimately, the legitimacy and sustainability of CI initiatives will depend on balancing competitive advantage with respect for legal norms and societal expectations.

10.4 Building a CI-Centric Organization for Continuous Transformation

To harness the full potential of emerging CI technologies and methodologies, organizations must evolve into CI-centric enterprises, embedding intelligence into their culture, governance, and operational rhythms. This transformation involves establishing cross-functional CI cells that work closely with strategy, R&D, marketing, and operations teams, ensuring that insights flow seamlessly to decision-makers at all levels (Markovich et al., 2022). Leadership commitment is critical: executives should sponsor CI investments, participate in intelligence briefings, and model data-driven decision-making behaviors.

Organizational processes—such as strategic planning, budget allocation, and performance management—must be redesigned to incorporate CI inputs as standard practice. Quarterly strategy reviews can include competitive heat maps generated by CI platforms, and innovation pipelines can be prioritized based on predictive intelligence signals (Madiha & Abdelaleem, 2024). Continuous upskilling programs will be necessary to equip employees with data literacy and AI-savvy competencies. By institutionalizing CI as a dynamic capability, organizations can transition from episodic redesign projects to ongoing transformation, staying ahead of competitors and adapting proactively to market disruptions (Schoemaker et al., 2018).

Table 4. Future trends and implications of Competitive Intelligence (CI)

Theme	Core Focus	Key Insights	Implications for Organizations
Future of CI	CI becoming AI-driven, automated, and embedded in strategy	• Shift toward predictive, real-time intelligence • Integration of research and practice • Growing importance of data ethics	• Need for CI-centric cultures • Continuous transformation supported by intelligence • Ethical governance becomes essential
AI & Big Data in CI	Automation and advanced analytics transforming intelligence work	• Machine learning analyzes massive structured/unstructured data • NLP drives sentiment and text analysis • Big data platforms unify internal + external intelligence • Deep learning supports image analysis and advanced simulations	• Faster, richer competitor insights • Real-time dashboards enable agile decisions • Expanded intelligence scope (e.g., satellite images, adaptive AI simulations)
Predictive Intelligence & Real-Time Analytics	Using predictive models to inform dynamic redesign	• Models forecast competitor moves, market shifts, regulatory changes • Streaming data updates dashboards in real time • Digital twins enable simulation-based redesign decisions	• Organizations redesign adaptively, not episodically • Faster response to disruptions (e.g., supply chain, consumer trends) • Increased resilience through continuous scenario planning
Ethical Considerations	Managing risks from advanced surveillance and data collection	• Risks: privacy breaches, IP violations, regulatory non-compliance • Some CI practices may overlap with espionage if misused • Automated tools increase ethical sensitivity	• Need for robust ethical CI frameworks • Legal compliance (e.g., GDPR, CCPA) • Training, oversight, and audits required to maintain trust & legitimacy
Building a CI-Centric Organization	Embedding intelligence into culture, governance, and processes	• CI teams collaborate with strategy, R&D, HR, operations • Leaders champion CI investment and data-driven culture • CI integrated into planning, budgeting, and performance reviews • Upskilling for analytics & AI capabilities	• Intelligence-driven decision-making becomes organizational norm • Continuous transformation replaces periodic redesign • Stronger competitive advantage through agility and f

11. CONCLUSION

Competitive Intelligence (CI) emerges as a critical driver of successful organizational redesign by aligning external market insights with internal strategic imperatives. Key insights highlight that CI enhances foresight, supports data-driven decision-making, and mitigates risks during complex transformations. Integrating

CI into both strategic and operational redesign ensures that structures, processes, and cultures remain adaptive amid dynamic markets.

The indispensable role of CI lies in its ability to reveal emerging opportunities and threats, guide resource allocation, and facilitate proactive rather than reactive change. In mergers and acquisitions, CI informs target selection, due diligence, and post-merger integration by illuminating cultural fit, competitive responses, and synergy potentials.

For organizations embarking on M&A or large-scale transformation, we recommend establishing cross-functional CI teams, embedding intelligence workflows into strategic planning cycles, and investing in analytics platforms that combine real-time and predictive capabilities. Leadership should champion CI adoption, foster a culture of evidence-based decision-making, and ensure ethical governance of intelligence activities.

Finally, to advance both theory and practice, scholars and practitioners must collaborate on research that evaluates the impact of AI-driven CI tools, ethical frameworks, and dynamic capabilities on redesign outcomes. Such integration will deepen our understanding of how CI can sustainably empower organizations to navigate uncertainty and drive continuous transformation.

REFERENCES

Azoury, N., Subrahmanyam, S., & Sarkis, N. (2024). The influence of a data-driven culture on product development and organizational success through the use of business analytics. *Journal of Wireless Mobile Networks, Ubiquitous Computing and Dependable Applications, 15*(2), 123–134. DOI: 10.58346/JOWUA.2024.I2.009

Bughin, J., Seong, J., Manyika, J., Chui, M., & Joshi, R. (2019). *The future of work in Europe* (McKinsey Global Institute Discussion Paper). McKinsey & Company. https://www.mckinsey.com/~/media/mckinsey/featured%20insights/future%20of%20organizations/the%20future%20of%20work%20in%20europe/mgi-the-future-of-work-in-europe-discussion-paper.pdf

Cameron, E., & Green, M. (2019). *Making sense of change management: A complete guide to the models, tools and techniques of organizational change* (5th ed.). Kogan Page.

Casado Salguero, G., Fernández Gámez, M. Á., Aldeanueva Fernández, I., & Ruíz Palomo, D. (2019). Competitive intelligence and sustainable competitive advantage in the hotel industry. *Sustainability (Basel), 11*(6), 1597. DOI: 10.3390/su11061597

Cekuls, A. (2024). The complexity of competitive intelligence in the age of data ambiguity and artificial intelligence. *Journal of Intelligence Studies in Business, 14*(SI 1), 55–65. https://doi.org/DOI: 10.37380/jisib.v14.si1.2417

Fadhlurrahman, M. A., Riyanta, S., & Ras, A. R. (2024). The role of competitive intelligence in strategic decision-making: A literature review. *Asian Journal of Engineering. Socialism and Health, 3*(10), 2307–2324. DOI: 10.46799/ajesh.v3i9.411

Kotter, J. P. (2012). *Leading change*. Harvard Business Review Press.

Madiha, I. A., & Abdelaleem, M. M. (2024). The impact of using the competitive intelligence cycle on the structure of organizational DNA. *Journal of Contemporary Economics & Social Research, 15*(3), 2196–2219. DOI: 10.21608/jces.2024.391339

Madureira, L., Popović, A., & Castelli, M. (2021). Competitive Intelligence: A unified view and modular definition. *Technological Forecasting and Social Change, 173*, 121086. DOI: 10.1016/j.techfore.2021.121086

Maluleka, M. L., & Chummun, B. Z. (2023). Competitive intelligence and strategy implementation: Critical examination of present literature review. *South African Journal of Information Management, 25*(1), a1610. DOI: 10.4102/sajim.v25i1.1610

Markovich, A., Raban, D. R., & Efrat, K. (2022). Tailoring competitive information sources to the sequence of dynamic capabilities. *Journal of Management & Organization, 28*(3), 480–501. DOI: 10.1017/jmo.2022.35

Maurya, S., Shavkidinova, D., Shrivastava, V., & Subrahmanyam, S. (2025). Effects of Green Supply Chain Management Practices on Environmental and Firm Sustainability Performance. *ACTA INNOVATIONS*, 55, 13–22. https://www.actainnovations.com/index.php/pub/article/view/401

Peters, T. J., & Waterman, R. H. (1982). *In search of excellence: Lessons from America's best-run companies*. Harper & Row.

Porter, M. E. (2008). The five competitive forces that shape strategy. *Harvard Business Review, 86*(1), 78–93. https://hbr.org/2008/01/the-five-competitive-forces-that-shape-strategy PMID: 18271320

Rafique, M. (2021). *The human factor in mergers, acquisitions, and transformational change*. Business Expert Press.

Schein, E. H., & Schein, P. A. (2017). *Organizational culture and leadership* (5th ed.). Wiley.

Schilling, M. A. (2025). *Strategic management of technological innovation* (6th ed.). McGraw-Hill Education.

Schoemaker, P. J. H., Heaton, S., & Teece, D. (2018). Innovation, dynamic capabilities, and leadership. *California Management Review, 61*(1), 15–42. DOI: 10.1177/0008125618790246

Subrahmanyam, S. (2025). AI-Driven Leadership in the Modern Era for Revolutionizing Next-Generation Strategies: Organizational Impacts and Future Development. In Agnihotri, A., & Balusamy, B. (Eds.), *Leadership Paradigms and the Impact of Technology* (pp. 61–86). IGI Global Scientific Publishing., DOI: 10.4018/979-8-3693-7175-6.ch003

Subrahmanyam, S. (2025). Developing Mindful Leaders for Global Change: Cultivating Awareness and Resilience to Navigate a Complex World. In Baez, M. D. (Ed.), *Strategic Approaches to Mindful Leadership and Change Management* (pp. 1–34). IGI Global Scientific Publishing., DOI: 10.4018/979-8-3693-7066-7.ch001

Subrahmanyam, S. (2025). Strategic Collaboration and Partnerships in R&D for Innovation. In Martínez-Falcó, J., Sánchez-García, E., & Marco-Lajara, B. (Eds.), *Research and Development Practices in Innovation* (pp. 283–314). IGI Global Scientific Publishing., DOI: 10.4018/979-8-3373-0812-8.ch010

Subrahmanyam, S., & Sarkis, N. (2025). Mindfulness and Sustainability Leadership: Integrating Awareness and Action for a Resilient Future. In Baez, M. D. (Ed.), *Strategic Approaches to Mindful Leadership and Change Management* (pp. 349–382). IGI Global Scientific Publishing., DOI: 10.4018/979-8-3693-7066-7.ch012

Teixeira, A. R., Ferreira, J. V., & Ramos, A. L. (2024). Optimization of business processes through BPM methodology: A case study on data analysis and performance improvement. *Information (Basel)*, *15*(11), 724. DOI: 10.3390/info15110724

Ulrich, D., Brockbank, W., Johnson, D., Sandholtz, K., & Younger, J. (2017). *HR competencies: Mastery at the intersection of people and business*. Society for Human Resource Management.

Vantrappen, H., & Wirtz, F. (2023). *The organization design guide: A pragmatic framework for thoughtful, efficient and successful redesigns*. Routledge. DOI: 10.4324/9781003462811

Westerman, G., Bonnet, D., & McAfee, A. (2019). *Leading digital: Turning technology into business transformation* (2nd ed.). Harvard Business Review Press.

Worren, N. A. (2018). *Organization design: Simplifying complex systems* (2nd ed.). Routledge. DOI: 10.4324/9781315145112

Yang, M., & Ai, Q. (2025). Completion of high-tech M&As by Chinese firms: Knowledge distance, industry attractiveness and government involvement. *Asia Pacific Journal of Management*, *42*(1), 427–454. DOI: 10.1007/s10490-023-09923-3

Zhang, Q. (2025). Functions of PESTEL analysis in the assessment of enterprise environmental adaptability. In *Proceedings of the 2024 2nd International Conference on Economic Management, Financial Innovation and Public Service (EMFIPS 2024)* (pp. 340-349). Atlantis Press. https://doi.org/DOI: 10.2991/978-94-6463-706-9_31

Zhao, H. (2022). Management team cultural alignment and mergers and acquisitions. *Finance Research Letters, 46*(Part B). *Finance Research Letters*, *102448*, 102448. Advance online publication. DOI: 10.1016/j.frl.2021.102448

KEY TERMS & DEFINITIONS

Competitive Intelligence (CI): The systematic process of gathering, analyzing, and applying information about competitors, markets, technologies, and regulatory environments to support strategic decision-making and organizational advantage.

Market Intelligence: A subset of CI focusing on data and insights related to market trends, customer behaviors, pricing dynamics, and emerging opportunities or threats in a specific sector.

McKinsey 7S Framework: A diagnostic tool for organizational redesign that examines seven interdependent elements: strategy, structure, systems, shared values, skills, style, and staff.

Mergers and Acquisitions (M&A): Business activities where companies consolidate through merging with or acquiring other entities, often requiring careful strategic alignment, due diligence, and cultural integration supported by CI.

Nadler-Tushman Congruence Model: A framework for analyzing organizational performance by assessing the alignment (congruence) between key components such as tasks, people, structure, and culture.

Organizational Redesign: A strategic transformation of an organization's structure, processes, culture, or systems to enhance effectiveness, respond to external changes, or achieve new strategic goals.

Scenario Planning: A strategic method that helps organizations envision and prepare for multiple potential futures by developing and analyzing plausible scenarios based on key uncertainties.

Strategic Foresight: The ability to anticipate future market developments, industry shifts, and technological trends by analyzing patterns and signals to guide long-term strategy and innovation.

SWOT Analysis: A strategic planning tool used to identify an organization's internal Strengths and Weaknesses, as well as external Opportunities and Threats.

War-Gaming: A simulation technique used in strategic planning where teams assume the roles of competitors or stakeholders to anticipate moves, counter-moves, and the impact of strategic decisions.

Chapter 8
Short-Term Investments in the Context of Technology Integration

Filipa Martinho
ISLA Santarém, Portugal

Vasco Santos
ISLA Santarém, Portugal

Ruben Pinhal
http://orcid.org/0000-0002-0956-6698
University of Aveiro, Portugal

João Rodrigues
ISLA Santarém, Portugal

ABSTRACT

This paper examines how short-term technology investments support digital transformation and competitiveness in small and medium-sized enterprises (SMEs). Focusing on agile, low-capital technological solutions, it analyzes how SMEs improve operational efficiency, decision-making, and risk management under financial and resource constraints. Through a structured literature review and illustrative case studies, the study identifies key success factors, performance metrics, and limitations of short-term investments. The findings highlight how technology integration enables SMEs to achieve rapid returns while maintaining strategic flexibility and sustainable growth.

DOI: 10.4018/979-8-3373-5233-6.ch008

1. INTRODUCTION

Small and medium-sized enterprises (SMEs) play a crucial role in the global economy, accounting for a significant share of employment and gross domestic product (GDP) in many countries (OECD, 2019). Despite their importance, SMEs face considerable challenges in maintaining competitiveness, particularly in a rapidly evolving technological landscape. Digital transformation—driven by innovations such as artificial intelligence (AI), big data, the Internet of Things (IoT), and process automation—presents a significant opportunity for SMEs to differentiate themselves in the market (Brynjolfsson & McAfee, 2014; Chui et al., 2018). However, many SMEs lack the financial resources, technical expertise, and management capacity to implement large-scale technological changes, hindering their ability to adapt to the digital age (European Commission, 2020).

In this context, short-term technology investments emerge as a practical and attractive strategy for SMEs. Unlike long-term investments, which typically require substantial capital and involve considerable risk, short-term investments enable companies to adopt and test technological solutions in a more agile and cost-effective manner (Anderson, 2019). This approach is particularly relevant for SMEs, which often operate under tight budgetary constraints and must maintain flexibility in their innovation strategies (Brown, 2020). The capacity to implement new technologies quickly can not only improve operational efficiency but also provide a competitive advantage in increasingly dynamic and saturated markets (Green et al., 2022).

Technology adoption has become not only a strategic opportunity but a necessity for SME survival and growth. Integrating new technologies enhances core business operations—such as automation, real-time data analysis, communication, and customer service—and directly contributes to cost reduction, productivity gains, and innovation capacity (Davenport & Westerman, 2018; McKinsey & Company, 2021). Moreover, the digital economy facilitates globalization, enabling SMEs to reach broader markets and serve customers across borders (OECD, 2019). However, SME leaders still encounter barriers in evaluating feasibility and managing risks related to these investments, making it essential to study their effectiveness (Raymond, 2001).

This research analyzes the role of short-term technology investments in supporting SMEs as they pursue digital transformation. It investigates how these investments contribute to operational improvements and market competitiveness and explores the specific conditions under which they succeed or fail. By combining an extensive literature review with detailed case studies, this study aims to identify the factors that influence the outcome of such investments and how SMEs can optimize their strategies to maximize the return on investment (ROI).

Although the benefits of digital transformation for large enterprises are well documented, there remains a critical gap in understanding its effects on SMEs, particularly concerning short-term investment strategies. Much of the existing literature centers on long-term strategies or focuses exclusively on large firms, leaving the challenges and decision-making processes of SMEs underexplored (Levy & Powell, 2005). This paper addresses that gap by analyzing the implications of short-term investments and presenting actionable insights tailored to the unique needs of SMEs.

In volatile and competitive environments, SMEs must make swift, informed investment decisions, especially during periods of market disruption like the COVID-19 pandemic. Many SMEs had to adopt digital solutions rapidly to remain operational—highlighting the relevance of short-term technology strategies in crisis response and sustainable growth (European Commission, 2020; McKinsey & Company, 2021).

This study also evaluates the effectiveness of commonly used performance metrics—such as KPIs and ROI—in assessing the outcomes of technology investments in SMEs. Large organizations typically have sophisticated tools for tracking investment performance, but SMEs often lack such resources. Therefore, defining SME-appropriate evaluation models is another key goal of this study (Johnson & White, 2019).

The paper is structured as follows: Section 2 presents the literature review on short-term investment theory, the technological landscape in SMEs, and evaluation frameworks. Section 3 describes the research methodology, including case selection and data analysis procedures. Section 4 presents the case studies, followed by a discussion in Section 5. Section 6 concludes with a summary of findings, limitations, and directions for future research.

By exploring the intersection of short-term investments and technology integration in SMEs, this study provides valuable insights for SME leaders, policymakers, and researchers seeking to promote innovation and digital readiness in small businesses.

2. BACKGROUND

The integration of technology within small and medium-sized enterprises (SMEs) has been extensively studied, highlighting both the challenges and benefits associated with such endeavors. This literature review delves into the multifaceted aspects of short-term technology investments in SMEs, examining theoretical frameworks, determinants of adoption, benefits, challenges, and the role of external support mechanisms.

Several models have been developed to understand technology adoption in SMEs. The Technology Acceptance Model (TAM) posits that perceived usefulness and perceived ease of use are primary determinants of technology adoption (Davis, 1989). In the context of SMEs, these perceptions significantly influence decision-making processes regarding new technologies. Additionally, the Diffusion of Innovations (DOI) theory (Rogers, 2003) emphasizes factors such as relative advantage, compatibility, complexity, trialability, and observability in the adoption process. Expanding on these, the Unified Theory of Acceptance and Use of Technology (UTAUT) highlights additional factors like effort expectancy, social influence, and facilitating conditions, making it particularly relevant to understanding SME contexts (Venkatesh et al., 2003).

Research has identified various factors influencing technology adoption in SMEs. Organizational readiness, including the availability of financial resources, technological infrastructure, and skilled personnel, determines an SME's preparedness to adopt new technologies (Raymond, 2001). The alignment of new technology with existing processes and values within the organization—perceived compatibility—also affects adoption decisions (Rogers, 2003). Market competition and customer expectations can drive SMEs to invest in technology to maintain competitiveness, while the support and vision of top management are crucial in facilitating adoption (Levy & Powell, 2005).

Short-term technology investments offer several advantages to SMEs. Implementing technologies such as process automation and data analytics can streamline operations, reduce errors, and enhance productivity (Brynjolfsson & Hitt, 1996). These investments enable SMEs to quickly adapt to market changes and customer demands, providing a competitive edge (OECD, 2019). Additionally, short-term investments often require lower initial capital outlay, making them more accessible to SMEs with limited budgets (Levy & Powell, 2005).

Despite these benefits, SMEs face several challenges in adopting new technologies. Limited financial and human resources can hinder the adoption and effective utilization of new technologies (Raymond, 2001). Employees may resist new technologies due to fear of the unknown or concerns about job security, and a shortage of technical skills within the organization can further impede implementation (OECD, 2019).

External support can play a pivotal role in facilitating technology adoption in SMEs. Government policies and programs that provide financial assistance, training, and resources can alleviate some of the barriers SMEs face (European Commission, 2020). Collaborations with other businesses and industry associations can provide access to shared knowledge and resources (OECD, 2019).

Assessing the effectiveness of technology investments is crucial for SMEs. Developing customized key performance indicators (KPIs) aligned with business objectives can help measure the success of technology adoption (Brynjolfsson & Hitt, 1996). Calculating return on investment (ROI) provides insights into the financial benefits derived from technology investments (Levy & Powell, 2005).

Empirical studies have demonstrated the positive impact of technology adoption on SME performance. SMEs that adopted information technology reported significant improvements in productivity and operational efficiency (Brynjolfsson & Hitt, 1996). Technology adoption has also enabled SMEs to access new markets and customer segments, contributing to business growth.

To maximize the benefits of technology investments, SMEs should consider several strategies. Developing a clear technology adoption plan that aligns with business goals is essential (European Commission, 2020). Investing in training programs can enhance employee skills and reduce resistance to new technologies (Levy & Powell, 2005). Regularly assessing the performance of adopted technologies ensures that they continue to meet organizational needs.

While significant progress has been made in understanding technology adoption in SMEs, several areas warrant further investigation. These include examining the long-term effects of technology adoption on SME performance, investigating how technology adoption varies across different industries and sectors, and exploring the implications of advanced technologies such as artificial intelligence and blockchain on SMEs (McKinsey & Company, 2021).

In order to understand the underlying mechanisms that drive short-term technology investments in small and medium-sized enterprises (SMEs), it is essential to draw from established theoretical frameworks. This section explores two of the most relevant models for analyzing technology adoption, innovation, and strategic investment decisions in SMEs: the Technology Acceptance Model (TAM) and the Resource-Based View (RBV). Together, these frameworks offer valuable insights into how SMEs assess, adopt, and leverage technology to enhance competitiveness and operational effectiveness.

The Technology Acceptance Model (TAM), developed by Davis (1989), is one of the most widely applied frameworks for understanding user acceptance of new technologies. TAM proposes that two factors—perceived usefulness (PU) and perceived ease of use (PEOU)—determine the likelihood of technology adoption. Perceived usefulness refers to the extent to which individuals believe that a given technology will improve their job performance or productivity. For SMEs engaging in short-term technology investments, usefulness is often directly linked to efficiency gains, cost savings, or improved accuracy. For instance, if a small manufacturing firm considers adopting robotic process automation (RPA), managers will likely evaluate its utility based on how effectively it reduces processing time or labor costs (Brynjolfsson & Hitt, 1996).

Perceived ease of use reflects the degree to which users expect the technology to be free of effort. This is a critical factor for SMEs, which frequently lack internal IT support or training infrastructure. Technologies that are intuitive, quick to implement, and easily integrated into existing workflows are often prioritized in short-term investment decisions. For example, cloud-based platforms that require minimal installation and provide user-friendly interfaces are typically favored due to their minimal disruption to operations (Armbrust et al., 2010). When SMEs consider short-term investments, both perceived usefulness and ease of use are assessed rapidly, and decisions must often be made without the benefit of long pilot phases or extensive training periods.

The TAM has been extensively applied in the SME context because it aligns well with their operational constraints and decision-making patterns. It helps explain how SME managers and employees evaluate new technologies not just on functionality, but on immediate impact and simplicity. In scenarios involving short-term investments—such as adopting analytics dashboards or automating parts of the supply chain—TAM offers a useful lens to understand adoption behaviors, the speed of implementation, and the expected return on investment in the short term (Venkatesh et al., 2003).

Complementing TAM is the Resource-Based View (RBV), articulated by Barney (1991), which views technology as a strategic organizational resource. The RBV argues that firms can gain sustainable competitive advantages by acquiring and managing valuable, rare, inimitable, and non-substitutable (VRIN) resources. In the context of SMEs, short-term technology investments often represent an opportunity to strengthen internal capabilities quickly without committing large amounts of capital. These investments can serve as building blocks for longer-term strategic differentiation if they enhance the firm's productivity, responsiveness, or customer engagement (Grant, 1991).

The concept of resource heterogeneity within RBV is particularly relevant to SMEs, which often operate under resource constraints but may possess unique process knowledge, market insights, or agility. By strategically deploying limited resources toward high-impact technology, SMEs can build VRIN advantages. For example, implementing proprietary data analytics tools may help identify niche customer segments or optimize operations in a way that competitors cannot easily replicate (Teece, 2007).

By integrating TAM and RBV, SMEs can approach short-term technology investments holistically. While TAM informs the decision-making process at the adoption level—focusing on user experience and immediate operational benefits—RBV highlights how these investments can evolve into strategic assets. A technology that is easy to implement and improves performance today may also become a unique, embedded capability over time. This dual perspective enables SMEs to assess both the tactical and strategic value of their investments.

Through these theoretical lenses, we can better understand why SMEs may choose specific technological investments and how they navigate the balance between immediate returns and long-term strategic goals, offering insights into the broader phenomenon of technology adoption and its impact on organizational performance.

3. SHORT-TERM INVESTMENTS: DEFINITION AND IMPORTANCE

Short-term investments are a crucial aspect of financial strategy for businesses, particularly small and medium-sized enterprises (SMEs), as they aim to maintain flexibility and liquidity while pursuing technological advancements. These investments, while relatively short in duration compared to long-term investments, offer SMEs the opportunity to manage their capital efficiently, optimize operations, and respond swiftly to market dynamics. By understanding these factors, SMEs can make informed decisions that balance immediate operational improvements with long-term business sustainability (Jones & Smith, 2021; Brown, 2020).

In the context of business and finance, short-term investments refer to financial assets or expenditures that are expected to be liquidated or realized within a relatively short period, typically within one year or less. Unlike long-term investments, which are designed to generate returns over a prolonged period, short-term investments aim to achieve quick returns, address immediate needs, or fund specific, short-duration projects (Johnson & White, 2019). Key characteristics of short-term investments include high liquidity, relatively low risk, and moderate return expectations. Liquidity ensures that the invested capital can be easily converted into cash or utilized in operations without significant delays or penalties (Taylor, 2018). Although not without risk, short-term investments typically carry less exposure to market volatility compared to longer-term alternatives (Miller, 2020). Returns are often realized as cost savings, operational efficiencies, or incremental revenue growth rather than large capital gains (Anderson, 2019).

Short-term technology investments for SMEs might include software subscriptions, cloud computing services, automation tools, or enterprise resource planning (ERP) modules. These assets are typically implemented quickly and can lead to immediate productivity improvements or cost reductions. For example, implementing a cloud-based inventory management system can streamline supply chain operations, improve stock control, and reduce unnecessary expenses (Green, Taylor, & White, 2022).

Increased liquidity is another significant benefit, allowing SMEs to meet operational expenses and manage cash flow volatility more effectively. Investments such as money market funds or scalable digital tools help maintain cash availability without constraining broader financial obligations (Brown, 2020). In addition, short-term investments promote risk diversification. Piloting a customer relationship management (CRM) tool or launching a trial e-commerce platform, for instance, enables SMEs to assess their viability before committing to broader transformations (Johnson & White, 2019). This approach also fosters decision-making flexibility, especially in dynamic markets or periods of rapid technological change. A SaaSbased CRM tool, for example, enables rapid onboarding and adaptation without extensive infrastructure or capital expenditure (Taylor, 2018).

Despite their advantages, short-term investments also pose specific challenges. One major issue is the difficulty in balancing immediate operational improvements with long-term strategic goals. Investments that solve short-term problems may fail to align with broader digital transformation strategies, limiting their future value (Green et al., 2022). Moreover, overreliance on short-term investments can strain financial or human resources, especially if initial returns fall short of expectations. Incompatibilities with existing systems or workflows may result in inefficiencies, particularly in service-based industries where legacy systems are prevalent (Miller, 2020).

Technological risk is also a concern, particularly the possibility that tools will become obsolete or fail to scale with the business. A process automation solution, for example, might not deliver sustained value if it lacks integration capabilities or falls behind emerging standards (Anderson, 2019). Furthermore, while short-term solutions may offer operational efficiency, they often lack transformative potential. For instance, adopting a customer support platform might speed up response times but fail to strengthen long-term customer loyalty or retention strategies (Jones & Smith, 2021).

The strategic importance of liquidity and risk management is central to any discussion of short-term investment planning. Liquidity provides SMEs with the agility to meet obligations, capitalize on emerging opportunities, and withstand market shocks. Meanwhile, robust risk management practices can help avoid exposure to unanticipated financial or operational disruptions (Taylor, 2018; Brown, 2020).

Ultimately, short-term investments play a critical role in the financial and operational strategies of SMEs. When implemented thoughtfully, they offer tangible benefits including rapid returns, operational efficiency, and improved liquidity. However, SMEs must also be mindful of the potential pitfalls, such as misalignment with long-term goals and insufficient scalability. Those that succeed in navigating these trade-offs are better positioned to leverage short-term investments for sustainable growth and innovation (Green et al., 2022; Johnson & White, 2019).

4. TECHNOLOGY INTEGRATION: AN OVERVIEW

Technology integration plays a pivotal role in the modern business landscape, especially for small and medium-sized enterprises (SMEs) seeking to enhance operational efficiency, competitiveness, and overall business performance. In an increasingly digitized economy, the integration of new technologies into core business operations is essential for staying relevant, scalable, and agile (Brynjolfsson

& McAfee, 2014; Westerman, Bonnet, & McAfee, 2014). Successful integration not only supports day-to-day operations but also fosters innovation, accelerates decision-making, and positions firms for long-term growth.

Technology integration refers to the seamless embedding of digital tools and systems into existing organizational processes and infrastructure to improve efficiency, productivity, and customer value (Davenport & Westerman, 2018). For SMEs, such integration supports automation of repetitive tasks, better customer engagement, and real-time insights into operations. This digital shift allows SMEs to reduce costs, optimize workflows, and improve decision-making, especially when paired with effective data management strategies (OECD, 2021).

Several technologies are central to this transformation. Cloud computing, for instance, delivers scalable computing services—storage, software, and processing power—via the internet. It reduces the need for physical infrastructure and offers flexibility in how SMEs manage data and systems (Armbrust et al., 2010). Common applications include cloud-based enterprise resource planning (ERP) and customer relationship management (CRM) systems, which enhance collaboration and provide real-time access to critical business data.

Process automation is another key element, enabling SMEs to replace manual workflows with digital tools such as robotic process automation (RPA). These systems can streamline payroll, invoicing, and inventory management processes, ultimately reducing operational costs and human error (McKinsey & Company, 2020). AI and machine learning (ML) further expand these capabilities. These technologies help businesses deliver personalized customer experiences, forecast demand, and automate decision-making processes (Chui, Manyika, & Miremadi, 2018).

The Internet of Things (IoT) contributes to this ecosystem by connecting physical devices to digital networks, facilitating real-time data collection and analysis. SMEs in manufacturing, for example, use IoT to monitor equipment and implement predictive maintenance strategies, improving efficiency and reducing downtime (Atzori, Iera, & Morabito, 2010). Additionally, blockchain technology is gaining relevance due to its capacity for enhancing transparency and traceability in supply chains. Beyond cryptocurrencies, blockchain allows for secure and tamper-proof transaction records, which is critical for sectors where trust and compliance are essential (Tapscott & Tapscott, 2016).

Effective technology integration involves a structured process. First, businesses must identify their core challenges and set strategic objectives, ensuring that technology investments align with broader business goals (Kotter, 2012). Next, selecting appropriate technologies requires evaluating factors such as scalability, industry relevance, and vendor reliability. Implementation demands a collaborative approach that includes pilot testing, stakeholder engagement, and staff training (PMI, 2021). Post-implementation, businesses must monitor performance through well-defined key performance indicators (KPIs) and be prepared to iterate and upgrade systems as technologies evolve (Brynjolfsson & McAfee, 2014).

Ultimately, technology integration should support the enterprise's long-term strategy. When properly executed, it enables SMEs to expand market presence, enhance customer satisfaction, and foster innovation. However, without alignment to business goals, even the most advanced tools can fall short. Thus, integration must be approached holistically, combining digital capabilities with organizational readiness and strategic intent (Davenport & Westerman, 2018; Westerman et al., 2014).

5. CASE ANALYSIS

This section examines three detailed case studies of small and medium-sized enterprises (SMEs) from Europe and North America that successfully implemented short-term technology investments. The selected case studies cover different industries—services, industrial, and information technology (IT)—and explore the challenges faced, the specific technologies adopted, the key performance indicators (KPIs) utilized, and the financial and operational outcomes achieved. The section concludes with a comparative analysis to identify common success factors and contextual challenges.

Nucleus Financial, headquartered in Edinburgh, Scotland, operates in the financial services sector, providing digital platforms for independent financial advisors. By 2018, the company had grown to serve over 1,400 advisors across the UK, but this rapid expansion exposed inefficiencies in its back-office operations. Manual tasks, such as data reconciliation, transaction processing, and financial reporting, were time-intensive and prone to human error. These inefficiencies led to delays in service delivery, occasional discrepancies in client reports, and growing dissatisfaction among their user base (McKinsey & Company, 2020).

To modernize operations, Nucleus Financial invested £100,000 in Robotic Process Automation (RPA) technology. The automation solution targeted repetitive, rule-based tasks such as transaction reconciliation, customer request processing, and compliance reporting. Over a four-month implementation period, the company mapped workflows, configured the RPA tools to integrate with existing systems, and trained staff to use the new technology. As a result, transaction processing time was reduced by 40%, operational costs dropped by £200,000 annually, and error rates in reporting fell to under 1% (Brynjolfsson & Hitt, 1996).

TRUMPF GmbH, a German SME specializing in precision tools and industrial machinery, faced supply chain and production management challenges, including inventory misalignment and lack of real-time workflow visibility. These inefficiencies hampered production deadlines and profitability. To address these issues, the company invested €500,000 in a Microsoft Azure-powered cloud-based enterprise resource planning (ERP) system, integrating sensors and Internet of Things (IoT) devices for real-time monitoring (Atzori, Iera, & Morabito, 2010; Armbrust et al., 2010).

Following a 12-month deployment and pilot testing phase, TRUMPF achieved notable operational benefits. Inventory surplus was reduced by 30%, saving €1 million annually, while production traceability and downtime metrics improved significantly. Forecasting accuracy rose to 90%, reducing mismatches between supply and demand. These results highlight how cloud computing and IoT integration can enhance manufacturing SMEs' responsiveness and efficiency (OECD, 2019).

UiPath, a Romanian SME known for its automation software, faced growing pressure in 2016 due to its global customer base and limited support resources. To maintain service quality, the company invested $200,000 in AI-driven customer support tools, including chatbots, sentiment analysis systems, and automated ticket routing. The phased rollout began in high-traffic regions and allowed human support teams to concentrate on complex queries (Chui, Manyika, & Miremadi, 2018).

The results were substantial: average response times dropped below one minute, first-contact resolution rose to 85%, and customer satisfaction scores improved by 30%. The AI initiative also led to annual cost savings of $500,000. The success of this investment contributed to UiPath's rapid expansion and eventual IPO, showcasing how targeted short-term technology adoption can yield long-term strategic gains (He & Xie, 2021).

Despite differences in sectors and technologies, all three SMEs shared common success factors: clear strategic alignment of technology with business goals, employee training to ease adoption, and ongoing performance monitoring through KPIs (Davenport & Westerman, 2018). Challenges included change resistance, infrastructure dependence, and high upfront costs, although all firms achieved full ROI within a year, reinforcing the effectiveness of focused, short-term tech investments.

These case studies demonstrate how SMEs can overcome resource limitations and operational inefficiencies through agile and strategically aligned technology adoption. By investing in automation, cloud infrastructure, and AI, businesses can enhance productivity, reduce costs, and achieve sustainable growth.

6. THE INTERSECTION OF SHORT-TERM INVESTMENTS AND TECHNOLOGY INTEGRATION

In today's fast-paced and technology-driven business landscape, the intersection of short-term investments and technology integration has become a critical area of focus for small and medium-sized enterprises (SMEs). When effectively integrated into investment strategies, technology accelerates decision-making, enhances accuracy, improves risk management, and maximizes returns (He & Xie, 2021; Ghosh, 2020). Because short-term investments are time-sensitive, SMEs must act quickly and precisely. Leveraging tools such as data analytics, financial software, and automated trading systems allows for more agile, data-informed choices that improve investment performance (Neely & Weller, 2017).

Data analytics plays a pivotal role in enhancing the decision-making process for short-term investments. The ability to analyze large volumes of information in real time provides SMEs with deeper insights into market trends, consumer behavior, and economic indicators (Brynjolfsson & McAfee, 2014). Predictive analytics, for example, enables businesses to forecast price movements and identify opportunities or risks based on historical patterns (Ghosh, 2020). SMEs can act on these insights to make strategic trades, reducing the likelihood of impulsive decisions driven by incomplete information.

Another valuable analytical tool is sentiment analysis, which uses natural language processing (NLP) to evaluate public and investor sentiment from social media, news, and financial commentary. Understanding the market's psychological state helps SMEs anticipate shifts in asset value, guiding them to either capitalize on positive momentum or exit investments during downturns (Chui, Manyika, & Miremadi, 2018). This kind of market awareness is critical for making timely, informed decisions in short-term trading.

Real-time data analysis also supports robust risk management. Integrating live market data streams into investment platforms allows SMEs to monitor fluctuations and adjust their portfolios as needed. Risk metrics, such as value at risk (VaR), help quantify potential downsides and guide rebalancing strategies (Neely & Weller, 2017). These tools ensure investment decisions are grounded in the most current data available, an essential advantage in volatile markets.

In addition to analytics, financial software has transformed how SMEs manage short-term investments. Portfolio management systems (PMS) allow companies to track their holdings, analyze performance, and rebalance asset allocations with precision (Ang, 2014). These platforms provide real-time updates and simulate different investment scenarios, which help managers identify optimal strategies for reaching financial goals. Forecasting and modeling tools, often integrated into financial software suites, enable SMEs to evaluate projected returns and conduct scenario analysis based on dynamic market conditions (Ross, Westerfield, & Jaffe, 2016).

Automated trading systems, or algorithmic trading platforms, have also emerged as powerful assets for SMEs engaged in short-term investing. These systems execute trades automatically based on predefined rules, eliminating human error and emotional decision-making (Hull, 2017). Their speed allows SMEs to act on opportunities within milliseconds, which can be critical in fast-moving markets. Automated platforms also offer backtesting features, letting users test strategies against historical data and optimize their algorithms before deploying them in live markets.

The synergy of short-term investments and technology integration offers a compelling path for SMEs to navigate financial markets with agility and confidence. By embracing real-time analytics, intelligent software tools, and automated systems, businesses can make faster, more accurate investment decisions, better manage risk, and improve financial performance. As technological capabilities continue to evolve, SMEs that integrate these tools into their investment strategies will be better positioned to seize opportunities and maintain competitiveness in increasingly complex environments.

7. RECOMMENDATIONS

Based on the analysis of how technology can enhance short-term investment strategies, this section outlines practical recommendations for small and medium-sized enterprises (SMEs) seeking to optimize their investment decisions. The integration of technology into short-term investments has proven to be highly beneficial in improving decision-making, enhancing productivity, and better managing risk. The following recommendations are based on the findings of the study and aim to provide actionable insights for SMEs.

One of the most important recommendations for SMEs is to adopt predictive analytics and leverage data-driven decision-making. As demonstrated in previous chapters and aligned with findings by Ghosh (2020), predictive models can provide valuable insights into market trends and asset price movements, helping businesses forecast potential opportunities or risks in real-time. SMEs should invest in analytical tools that allow them to analyze historical and current market data, identify emerging patterns, and make more informed predictions about the future performance of their investments. By utilizing these tools, businesses can mitigate risks and capitalize on time-sensitive market opportunities. Furthermore, adopting a data-driven mindset across the organization—by incorporating data into everyday decision-making—will help businesses maintain a competitive edge in volatile markets (Davenport & Westerman, 2018).

Financial software plays a key role in managing investments effectively, particularly in short-term decision-making. SMEs should integrate financial portfolio management systems (PMS), which can help track and monitor investments, generate real-time market insights, and automate key processes (Hull, 2017; Ross et al., 2016). These tools enable businesses to have an up-to-date view of their investment portfolios, assess asset performance, and make timely adjustments based on market changes. Additionally, financial forecasting and modeling tools should be adopted to simulate various investment scenarios and assess potential returns and risks. These tools allow businesses to evaluate different strategies and ensure that their investment approach aligns with financial goals and market conditions. Investing in robust financial software not only enhances operational efficiency but also equips SMEs with the necessary tools to make data-backed decisions (Ang, 2014).

Sentiment analysis, which involves using natural language processing (NLP) to gauge market sentiment through social media, news, and reports, is a powerful tool that SMEs can integrate into their investment strategies. As noted by Tversky and Kahneman (1974), market psychology plays a substantial role in influencing investment behavior. SMEs should invest in tools that aggregate data from social media platforms, financial news outlets, and industry reports to gain real-time insights into market sentiment. This understanding can help businesses anticipate price fluctuations, improve timing for entry and exit points, and even adjust their investment portfolios based on changes in market mood (Akerlof & Shiller, 2015).

For businesses actively involved in short-term trading, automated trading systems or algorithmic trading can provide a significant edge. These systems allow businesses to execute trades based on predefined conditions, such as price movements, volume, or technical indicators, without requiring manual intervention. SMEs should consider adopting algorithmic trading platforms to execute trades efficiently and capitalize on opportunities faster than manual trading processes would allow (Neely & Weller, 2017; He & Xie, 2021). These systems enable businesses to respond to market changes in real-time, reduce human error, and ensure consistency in investment decisions. Additionally, SMEs should regularly backtest and optimize their algorithms to ensure that they are operating effectively under various market conditions.

Risk management is critical to the success of any investment strategy, especially in short-term markets where volatility is high. SMEs should invest in risk management tools and establish robust monitoring systems that track market changes in real-time. By integrating these tools into their investment strategies, businesses can identify high-risk positions early, assess the potential impact of negative market movements, and adjust their portfolios accordingly. Furthermore, businesses should use real-time market data and integrate risk metrics, such as value at risk (VaR), to quantify potential losses and ensure that investment decisions are made with a clear understanding of their risks (Anderson, 2019; Jones & Smith, 2021).

To fully leverage the power of technology in short-term investments, SMEs must foster a culture of continuous learning and adaptation within the organization. This includes regularly training staff to stay up-to-date with the latest technologies, tools, and trends in the investment landscape. As financial technologies and market conditions evolve, SMEs need to ensure that their teams are equipped with the knowledge and skills necessary to take full advantage of emerging opportunities. Additionally, SMEs should focus on developing a culture of adaptability, where quick decision-making and rapid response to market changes are prioritized. By combining cutting-edge technology with a responsive and knowledgeable team, SMEs can stay competitive in dynamic market environments (McKinsey & Company, 2021; OECD, 2019).

8. CONCLUSION AND FUTURE WORK

The integration of technology into short-term investment strategies has proven to be an indispensable element for small and medium-sized enterprises (SMEs) striving to remain competitive and maximize returns. This study has shown that leveraging digital tools—such as predictive analytics, financial software, and automated trading systems—can significantly enhance decision-making, improve productivity, and optimize risk management processes (Ghosh, 2020; Hull, 2017).

Case studies from different sectors, including finance, services, and technology, clearly demonstrated how SMEs can benefit from short-term technology investments to streamline operations and increase efficiency. These examples affirm that data-driven decision-making, supported by agile and scalable technological tools, is a key factor in achieving success in short-term investment environments (Brynjolfsson & McAfee, 2014; McKinsey & Company, 2021).

Additionally, the findings emphasized the importance of aligning technology investments with business objectives. SMEs that effectively integrate digital tools into their strategic planning are better positioned to adapt to market changes, manage risk, and sustain profitability. The research underscores the necessity for SMEs to tailor their technology choices to their unique operational contexts, ensuring that implementation leads to measurable performance improvements and enhanced competitiveness (Davenport & Westerman, 2018; OECD, 2019).

Future research should explore the long-term impacts of technology integration in SME investment strategies. While this study focused on short-term implementation, understanding the enduring effects on organizational growth and sustainability remains a critical next step. Additional studies could also examine how emerging technologies, such as blockchain, artificial intelligence, and quantum computing, may reshape short-term investment approaches and open new avenues for value creation (Tapscott & Tapscott, 2016; He & Xie, 2021).

In conclusion, the digitalization of short-term investment strategies presents both opportunities and challenges for SMEs. By fostering a culture of innovation, maintaining strategic alignment, and investing in scalable, data-driven solutions, SMEs can successfully navigate the complexities of today's financial landscape and build resilient, high-performing organizations.

ACKNOWLEDGEMENTS

The authors would like to express their sincere gratitude to Ricardo Marcão (ISLA Santarém, Polytechnic Institute & NECE-UBI, Portugal) and Vasco Ribeiro Santos (Polytechnic University of Tomar (IPT), Portugal) for their valuable editorial guidance, support, and contributions to the development of this chapter and the overall book project.

REFERENCES

Akerlof, G. A., & Shiller, R. J. (2015). *Phishing for phools: The economics of manipulation and deception*. Princeton University Press. DOI: 10.2307/j.ctvc777w8

Anderson, P. (2019). Short-term financial strategies for SMEs. *Business and Economics Journal, 12*(3), 45–58.

Ang, A. (2014). *Asset management: A systematic approach to factor investing*. Oxford University Press. DOI: 10.1093/acprof:oso/9780199959327.001.0001

Armbrust, M., Fox, A., Griffith, R., Joseph, A. D., Katz, R., Konwinski, A., Lee, G., Patterson, D., Rabkin, A., Stoica, I., & Zaharia, M. (2010). A view of cloud computing. *Communications of the ACM, 53*(4), 50–58. DOI: 10.1145/1721654.1721672

Atzori, L., Iera, A., & Morabito, G. (2010). The Internet of Things: A survey. *Computer Networks, 54*(15), 2787–2805. DOI: 10.1016/j.comnet.2010.05.010

Barney, J. (1991). Firm resources and sustained competitive advantage. *Journal of Management, 17*(1), 99–120. DOI: 10.1177/014920639101700108

Brown, T. (2020). Liquidity management in small enterprises. *Financial Insights, 8*(2), 120–135.

Brynjolfsson, E., & Hitt, L. M. (1996). Paradox lost? Firm-level evidence on the returns to information systems spending. *Management Science, 42*(4), 541–558. DOI: 10.1287/mnsc.42.4.541

Brynjolfsson, E., & McAfee, A. (2014). *The second machine age: Work, progress, and prosperity in a time of brilliant technologies*. W. W. Norton & Company.

Chui, M., Manyika, J., & Miremadi, M. (2018). *AI adoption advances, but foundational barriers remain*. McKinsey Insights.

Davenport, T. H., & Westerman, G. (2018). Why so many high-profile digital transformations fail. *Harvard Business Review*.

Davis, F. D. (1989). Perceived usefulness, perceived ease of use, and user acceptance of information technology. *Management Information Systems Quarterly*, *13*(3), 319–340. DOI: 10.2307/249008

European Commission. (2020). *Supporting small and medium-sized enterprises in the digital age*. European Commission Reports.

Ghosh, S. (2020). *Data analytics in finance: Applications in investments, risk management, and regulation*. Springer.

Grant, R. M. (1991). The resource-based theory of competitive advantage: Implications for strategy formulation. *California Management Review*, *33*(3), 114–135. DOI: 10.2307/41166664

Green, R., Taylor, J., & White, L. (2022). Technology investments and SME growth. *Journal of Business Innovation*, *14*(4), 233–245.

He, Z., & Xie, W. (2021). *Financial technology and applications in the global financial industry*. Elsevier.

Hull, J. C. (2017). *Options, futures, and other derivatives* (9th ed.). Pearson.

Johnson, D., & White, S. (2019). Strategic investment planning for SMEs. *Financial Strategies Quarterly*, *10*(1), 15–30.

Jones, M., & Smith, K. (2021). Risk mitigation in short-term investments. *The Journal of Economic Perspectives*, *25*(2), 89–105.

Kotter, J. P. (2012). *Leading change*. Harvard Business Review Press.

Levy, M., & Powell, P. (2005). *Strategies for growth in SMEs: The role of information and information systems*. Elsevier Science.

McKinsey & Company. (2020). *Automation in business operations*. McKinsey Insights.

McKinsey & Company. (2021). *How technology is driving SME growth*. McKinsey Insights.

Miller, A. (2020). Balancing short-term and long-term goals. *Strategic Management Review*, *7*(1), 67–80.

Neely, C. J., & Weller, P. A. (2017). *Short-term investments and risk management: A guide for practitioners*. Wiley.

OECD. (2019). *Digitalisation of SMEs: Policies to support SMEs in the digital transformation*. OECD.

PMI (Project Management Institute). (2021). *A guide to the project management body of knowledge* (7th ed.). PMI.

Raymond, L. (2001). Determinants of Web site implementation in small businesses. *Internet Research, 11*(5), 411–422. DOI: 10.1108/10662240110410363

Rogers, E. M. (2003). *Diffusion of innovations* (5th ed.). Free Press.

Ross, S. A., Westerfield, R., & Jaffe, J. (2016). *Corporate finance* (11th ed.). McGraw-Hill Education.

Tapscott, D., & Tapscott, A. (2016). *Blockchain revolution*. Portfolio.

Taylor, R. (2018). Flexibility in SME financial decisions. *Journal of Finance and Management, 6*(4), 101–118.

Teece, D. J. (2007). Explicating dynamic capabilities: The nature and microfoundations of (sustainable) enterprise performance. *Strategic Management Journal, 28*(13), 1319–1350. DOI: 10.1002/smj.640

Tversky, A., & Kahneman, D. (1974). Judgment under uncertainty: Heuristics and biases. *Science, 185*(4157), 1124–1131. DOI: 10.1126/science.185.4157.1124 PMID: 17835457

Venkatesh, V., Morris, M. G., Davis, G. B., & Davis, F. D. (2003). User acceptance of information technology: Toward a unified view. *Management Information Systems Quarterly, 27*(3), 425–478. DOI: 10.2307/30036540

Westerman, G., Bonnet, D., & McAfee, A. (2014). *Leading digital: Turning technology into business transformation*. Harvard Business Review Press.

Chapter 9
Strategic Realignment and Cultural Integration:
Human-Centric Approaches to Post-Merger Organizational Redesign

Muhammad Usman Tariq
http://orcid.org/0000-0002-7605-3040
Abu Dhabi University, UAE & University College Cork, Ireland

ABSTRACT

Strategic realignment and cultural integration are key to achieving post-merger success. Although finances and operational efficiencies may push firms to merge, neglecting to make strategic alignments and handle diverse company cultures can sabotage the results. Realignment brings the vision, values, and goals of merged firms together into one clear-cut plan. Cultural integration preserves the identity of each firm while creating a shared sense of purpose. This transformation requires leaders to be synchronized with one another, involve all important stakeholders, and create flexible, participative structures. Techniques such as design thinking, cultural audits, and managed change processes reduce resistance and build trust. In today's complex and networked world of business, sustained success after a merger depends on aligning plans with people's needs, using stories effectively, and engaging in ongoing feedback. This emphasizes the necessity of combining strategy and culture to create strong, effective, and meaningful organizations after a merger.

DOI: 10.4018/979-8-3373-5233-6.ch009

INTRODUCTION

Mergers and acquisitions are typically seen as giant steps forward, watershed moments that help companies gain an edge, grow their presence, or find new ways to be more efficient. On paper, everything makes sense: conserving resources by merging, swapping brains to spark innovation, or accelerating by cutting duplication in the marketplace. However, after the deal is cut and things start to settle down, organizations usually realize that the actual challenge is much tougher and more complex than anticipated. The actual test is not just a matter of numbers or legal audit; it is a matter of reconsidering how the new firm will function. Combining two disparate organizations, each with their own systems, the way things are done, people, and culture, establishes a massive disconnect between what was intended and what happens in day-to-day operations (Britsche & Fekete, 2022). The amount of work that needs to be done after a merger is staggering. It is not just a question of reorganizing the way the company is structured or eliminating duplicate jobs. It is a matter of beginning again to consider how the new organization will work. Who will make the decisions, and how? Which of the company's functions need to become more global, and which need to be localized? How must these roles change to achieve the new goals? There are no easy answers, and they keep changing as the merger progresses from the early phases to a steady growth phase. Many companies downplay the sheer amount of work that goes into it and think that a few press releases and some integration teams will make it happen. However, without a well-articulated, intentional, and people-centered plan, the new organization can get bogged down by confusion, conflict, and drain.

A large issue is caused by the disconnect between the intended strategy and reality in practice. Leaders may have well-defined, aggressive objectives, such as market leadership, innovation at speed, or efficiency. However, as these objectives cascade through the organization, they can become fuzzy or lost in translation. Lower-level workers do not know how these high-level abstractions apply to their daily work. Middle managers, who are the ones getting things done, get caught in the middle of conflicting messages or are asked to support strategies they had no input in. Overlooking these distinctions can lead to disappointment, distrust, and even loss of top talent. Even in so-called "mergers of equals," if there is no shared vision of how things get done or a shared leadership style, there will be hidden conflict and duplicated effort. Technically, everyone is now in the same company, but they may still act as two separate groups (Tariq, 2025). The secret to successful post-merger integration is to ensure that the strategy fits the people, structure, and culture of the merged company. These three factors are the foundation of any company, and if they do not collaborate, the plan will not deliver the projected results. People are not merely assets; they bring expertise, networks, and habits that are difficult to copy. Structure dictates how information flows, decisions are made, and groups come together. Culture, the most intangible yet powerful element, encompasses the behaviors, beliefs, and values that shape the way people interact with one another. If any of these elements do not sync with the new strategy, there will be trouble. If none of them sync, the whole organization begins to break down. It takes more than just redefining jobs or defining new performance targets to align people with the strategy. It involves explaining why changes are occurring, not only the changes themselves. Staff must be made aware of how the merger impacts their work, what new possibilities there are, and what their roles will be after the merger. Involve them at an early stage and keep them involved rather than simply issuing instructions at the top. This establishes ownership and minimizes the resistance. In addition, leaders must empower employees by helping them obtain new skills and stay current with any technology, process, or mode of operations alterations.

The alignment is also structured by analyzing how the business is organized to ensure that it facilitates the new strategy. This includes decisions regarding who reports to whom, the number of direct reports a manager has, how work is structured, and who gets to make what decisions. For example, an innovative strategy may require a less centralized structure, more flexible teams, and faster decision-making. A cost-cutting strategy may require more control at the center and more standardized processes. However, structural changes are often cosmetic types of changes, such as creating new titles or layering up, without analyzing how these structural changes affect work (Malik et al., 2023). While organizational charts might look different, if there are no changes in how people are motivated, how things get done, or what is held accountable to whom, then the changes do not amount to anything. Unclear structures can create confusion, slow progress, and result in duplication or conflicts. Cultural integration is probably the most challenging aspect of mergers. Culture cannot be imposed or mixed rapidly. It matures over time through shared experiences, leaders' actions, and the stories an organization shares about itself. In the months and weeks after a merger, cultural differences have the potential to create issues that are not necessarily obvious but can rock the boat and create problems for the merged company. Discrepancies in the manner people interact, their tolerance for risk, the speed at which they make decisions, or what they expect from performance can lead to confusion and mistrust of AI. If unresolved, these discrepancies can suppress morale, reduce teamwork, and push key individuals away from the organization. Therefore, leaders must take action to build a culture, starting with studying past cultures and deciding what to keep, change, or discard. It requires humility, flexibility, and a willingness to work together to forge a new cultural identity and look towards the future rather than just mashing together the past. It must fit the new strategy and future vision of the company.

The leadership's role in managing post-merger realities is imperative. Leaders establish the way things ought to be, show the behaviors they want to see, and make significant decisions that will determine whether the new culture will stick. However, most leadership teams are not well-prepared for the complexities of this process. They can be great at managing their previous organizations but not at managing uncertainty and change in the current organization. In addition, mergers bring in new leaders who have not collaborated before and whose values, views, goals, and loyalties may differ. Thus, a united leadership team is crucial. This includes ensuring that all stakeholders are on the same page regarding the overall image, integration guidelines, and as one entity that provides the rest of the company with clear leadership and continuity.

Communication is another key element of a successful merger. Mergers create a lot of uncertainty, rumors, and panic, especially when people do not know about their careers, where they will work, or to whom they will report. Without open and honest communication, these spaces are filled with rumors, which blunt trust and slow down productivity. Leaders must communicate frequently, regularly, and truthfully with their subordinates. They should provide people with information about what they know, what is still being figured out, and how they will keep people informed. They should not neglect listening. Tools such as feedback systems, quick surveys, and listening sessions can also help leaders understand how the changes are affecting people and where further support may be needed. Technology is helpful, but it is not a panacea. Computers can help people work together despite distances, make it easier to integrate processes, and provide more insight into how well things are going. AI can help solve what needs to be done in terms of skills, trying out structurally designing the firm, and predicting pitfalls via the merger. However, technology must be in service to the process, not drive it. Too much dependence on tools and not considering the human and strategic sides of the change will not yield real progress (Britsche & Fekete, 2022). At the end of the day, the problem after a merger is not just about systems or procedures; it is about people. It depends on leaders' willingness to tackle complexity instead of trying to reduce it. It is about establishing room for several perspectives and being willing to accept that integration is not about bringing two things together but creating something new, something neither of the current companies could create alone. By doing this, firms are more likely to succeed at what they want to accomplish with the merger, and they also position themselves for a more flexible, stronger, and more substantial future. Figure 1 provides overview of foundations of post-merger strategy.

Figure 1. Strategic alignment triad

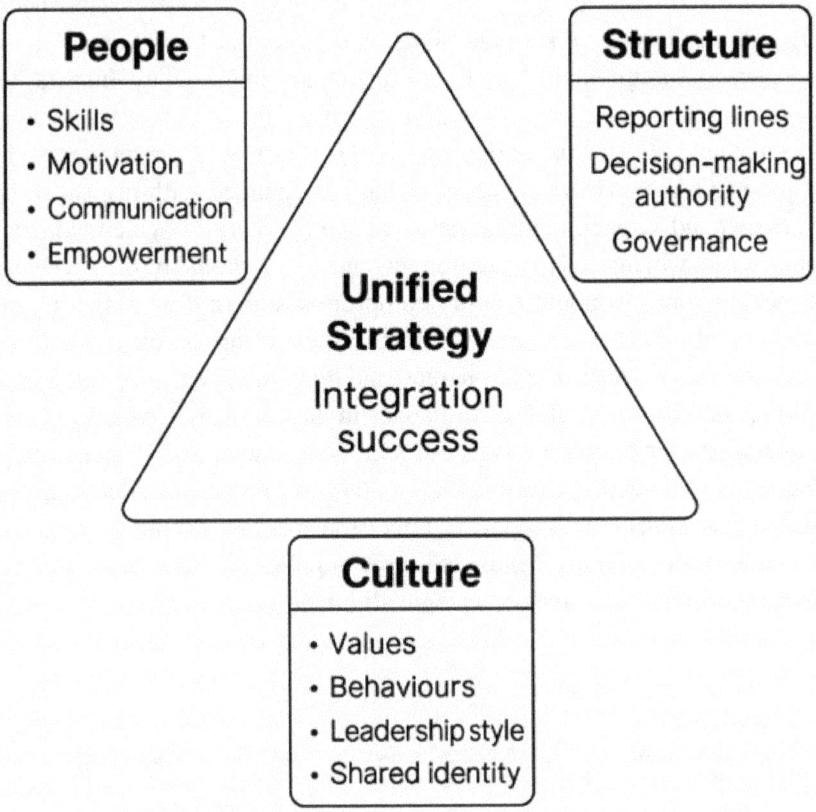

STRATEGIC ALIGNMENT IN POST-M&A REDESIGN

After a company merges or is acquired, the most important and difficult thing that leadership must do is to make strategic alignments. This means that the new company is not necessarily two companies spliced together but a single-minded, single, progressive unit. While financial rewards, cost savings, and turnaround time to merge are typically the areas of prime consideration in a merger, real value only exists if strategic harmony is the primary consideration for reconstructing the combined firm. Here, leaders need to do more than just implement one strategy on top of another. They need to intelligently blend diverse strategies before merging them into a uniform way of running the business that can achieve long-term performance, innovation, and competitiveness (Narassimhan et al., 2024). When two businesses combine, they both have their own strategic aims. These may include new growth in markets, adopting digital technologies, being price-efficient, innovation, or being more personalized as a customer service. However, these goals were established under varying circumstances, market conditions, and structural limitations. Attempting to keep them the same could lead to confusion and inefficiency. Instead, leadership needs to address this process with a reflective, intentional way of screening, synthesizing, and re-prioritizing these goals. This starts with conducting an honest evaluation of the new firm's situation: What has changed with respect to human resources on hand, capabilities, competition, and the market? Which old strategies still make sense, which need to be rethought, and which should be dropped entirely? This process is not just about making compromises or finding a middle ground; it is about creating clarity. A unified strategy must clearly explain what the new company stands for, where it will operate, and how it plans to succeed. Simplicity is the foundation on which all future changes in the company are made, whether in form, operations, or culture (Vaddepalli and Vishwanath, 2024). For example, if the strategy is grounded in fast innovation and fast product introduction, then the company's operations must support fast decision-making, simple governance, and cross-function teams. Figure 2 illustrates how aligning the value proposition of the firm is another important area of strategic alignment.

Figure 2. Post-merger strategic alignment process flow

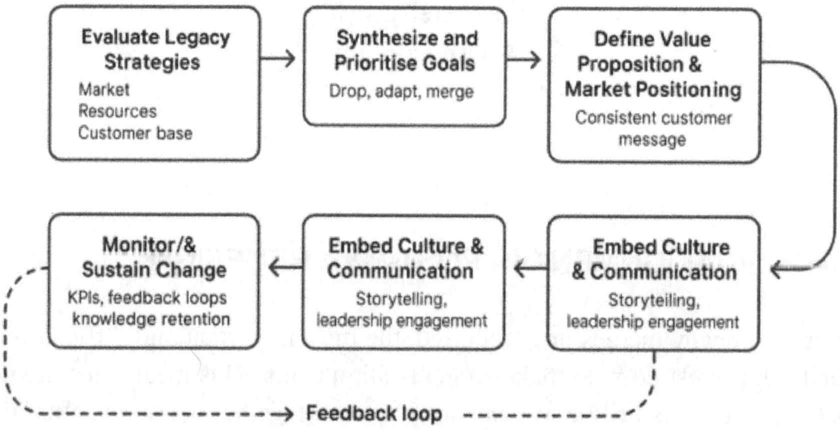

However, when it comes to making supply chains efficient or streamlining global operations, the organizational structure of the firm may need to be more process-driven and managed. This strong tie between strategy and the way the company is organized ensures that it is not only internally coherent but also robust in the market. Aligning the value proposition of the firm is another important area of strategic alignment. In all but the most atypical mergers, each company offered a particular promise to customers, exceptional service, high-technology products, low prices or customized experiences. The challenge in structuring the merged company is that the message to the market must be consistent (Zhang and Wei, 2024). Customers can quickly detect inconsistent information, lower quality of service, or product differences during the transition. Therefore, firms need to revisit and refine their value propositions to align with the new strategy and are appropriate considering what the combined firm can provide. This may involve paying more for certain items or services, dropping others, adjusting prices, or establishing various levels of service for customers. It could also mean rebranding the message to reference what the new entity has to offer while remaining faithful to what customers already appreciate (Prasetyo & Putro, 2024). Finally, the business markets must be reevaluated for their various customer segments. The merger likely combined two distinct sets of customers, each with its own behavior, expectations, and prior relationships. There may be some overlap, but the segments are quite disparate by industry, geography, or firm size. The new company should define which segments to pursue and how to tailor its products accordingly. This approach does not have to be based on past relationships but rather on market potential, compatibility with the company's goals, and profitability. With greater insight into customer needs, sales and marketing personnel can be reoriented, customer management programs can be re-engineered, and more sales opportunities can be addressed more precisely. This also enables product and service innovation to focus on areas where the company can clearly differentiate itself.

Market positioning, linked to value propositions and customer groups, must also change. The acquisition may have looked to it would become a market leader, grow into a new geography, or upend an industry leader. Whatever the aspiration, the firm must now possess a clear and believable position in the minds of customers and stakeholders. It is not branding; it is that every internal decision-making, how resources are utilized, and how talent is spent, must square with this new position (Britsche & Fekete, 2022). Positioning misalignment is especially dangerous in B2B markets, where trust and long-term relationships play crucial roles. Customers will lose perceived value at lightning speed if they see or feel disorientation inside the company. Therefore, it is vital that internal capabilities are matched with external messages to maintain a strong and consistent market presence.

To make sophisticated decisions about alignment and strategy, most successful organizations utilize tools such as strategic scorecards. Such structures, for instance, the Balanced Scorecard, help leaders convert high-level strategic goals into measurable goals in the domain of key significance, such as financial results, customer impact, internal processes, and growth. Scorecards are especially useful in post-mergers because they can track progress toward integration goals while keeping the organization focused on potential expansion (Miller & Verhoeven, 2019). For instance, one of the scorecard goals might be keeping 90% of year one's best customers, and another would measure how much cost reduction is provided by improved supply chain integration. By relating these goals to key performance measures (KPIs) and allocating them throughout the organization, leaders can ensure that strategy is no longer a solo inspiration for the top but a shared working goal for every department and team in the organization.

Aside from scorecards, design thinking is becoming increasingly popular as a means of aligning strategy and structure. Typically used in developing products and innovations, design thinking uses a user-centric iterative approach that is highly effective in redesigning complex systems with people, processes, and technology. With post-merger integration, design thinking enables companies to redesign their operations from a blank sheet. Instead of merely assembling existing models, this approach encourages teams to ask themselves how the company would work best to achieve strategic goals and meet stakeholder requirements. This entails practices such as ethnographic investigation, customer journey mapping, prototyping, and testing, which help identify problems, discover unserved needs, and create more adaptable and durable solutions (Watling & Wilén, 2024). For instance, if the combined firm finds that its frontline staff are spending too much time dealing with multiple older systems, a design thinking answer could involve shadowing the workers, observing their everyday activities, and creating a simpler interface or new job functions. Likewise, if customer support is disadvantaged because of incompatibility in service channels, design thinking can be used to design a novel support process that combines the capabilities of the two companies without any redundant processes. What is so useful about design thinking post-merger is that it focuses on human experience, whether for staff, customers, or partners, so that alignment is not merely theory but something that everyone lives and feels within the firm.

All these activities–obtaining strategies, crafting what the company does, splitting customers apart, setting performance measures, and reorganizing the firm–need to be supported with good execution and ongoing improvement. Note that merger changes are not a single plan imposed on the organization. It is a changing process that requires flexibility, feedback, and ongoing input from everyone involved. Markets change, new ideas displace old ones, and novel opportunities and challenges arise as mergers progress. Therefore, adequate mechanisms must be established to track alignment, adjust as needed, and maintain consistency in the strategy over time (Ayularas & Aulia Zaim, 2024). Integration groups, strategy groups, or hybrid committees can help enforce cohesion and establish a strategy-focused culture throughout the new company. Additionally, it is an important time for leaders to align. Without an overarching leadership message, the company may create mixed signals or internal competition. Leaders must not only agree on the strategy but also on how they act, act in favor of mutual goals, act together, and resolve disagreements positively. They also need to be out-in-front supporters of the new way of working, constantly articulating how the changes are for the benefit of the business meeting its goals and reinforcing actions that support the new vision.

Finally, strategic alignment after a merger is both a map and a measure of progress. It shows where the company is going and whether it is going in the right direction. Celebrating integration milestones along the way may be a success, but success does not lie in how quickly teams are integrated or how quickly costs are saved. It is not about whether the new organization can work as a shared purpose, provide value to customers, and respond quickly to a changing market. This requires more than astute planning; it requires transparency, creativity, and an ongoing emphasis on alignment across the entire organization.

ORGANIZATIONAL CULTURE AS A SUCCESS LEVER

In the high-stakes world of mergers and acquisitions, organizational culture is typically a key ingredient of success, but it is also one of the most overlooked. Cultural alignment must be assessed long before the merger agreement is signed. It is not enough to ask top management what they think of corporate values or to conduct a few employee polls. After a foundation is established, culture mapping can be useful. It gives leaders an eye for observing where the two firms are similar or dissimilar as far as key things like decision-making structures, how accountability is addressed, communication style, and how work gets done, either quickly or slowly. Mapping also helps to decide which cultural attributes are vital to each company and which may be more adaptable. After mapping, the next step is to create strategies to merge the cultures. A blatant example of a failed cultural integration is the merger of a major European engineering conglomerate with an American industrial technology corporation. From a business perspective, the merger is rational; it takes the offering into more markets, introduces variety to the products sold, and ought to be cost-efficient. However, from a cultural perspective, the two companies were substantially different. The European company stressed teamwork, long-term planning, and leaders regarded as equals by all. Americans, on the other hand, favor quick decisions, individual achievement, and tough top-down management. The differences were initially ignored for quick results and coordination of operations (Madhani,2019). It was not until these problems became extreme that the leaders became conscious that they needed to do something about the culture. While full cultural integration still proved elusive, the experience imparted one important lesson: cultural alignment is not something that just happens after consolidation; it is needed before any actual success can occur. This example demonstrates that while money and operations may seem more crucial than culture, it is what keeps a company together when change occurs. Unless there are comparable cultures, even the best-intentioned consolidations can fall apart. However, if leaders understand cultural differences, manage integration effectively, and lead ethically, culture can be a powerful ally. It can bring together disparate groups for a common purpose, create employees who are eager to build and work together, and create a simple merger as a transformative change. Understanding culture as not something to be avoided, but rather as an incredibly effective tool to be wielded, is the most critical change in thinking executives can do post-merger.

LEADERSHIP AND COMMUNICATION IN TIMES OF UNCERTAINTY

Post-merger leadership is one of the most essential elements that can cause a merged corporation to succeed or fail. Mergers and acquisitions are disruptors by nature, and the uncertainty they cause affects everyone within the organization (Britsche & Fekete, 2022). Workers are worried about their future as employees, customers are wondering if their service will continue to be available, and stakeholders are wondering if the new company will be an improvement over the two companies it was formed from. A leader who can handle ambiguous situations clearly, respond to change quickly, and stay plugged into real relationships is much more likely to achieve the trust and loyalty of the people they are leading.

Being agile in leadership during a merger means possessing the virtue of being able to turn quickly without losing focus on the bigger picture. It is open to new information, adapts when needed, and can think through things on multiple time scales. In a merger, it might mean a CEO pushing forward with integration plans but also being honest that not everything is nailed down. It may be a department leader shifting their team's objectives to suit a new organizational structure or a manager working with the emotional aspect of their team while still getting results (Wiegelmann and Glauerdt, 2025). An agile leader does not attempt to provide false comfort; rather, they provide a clear framework and stability without suggesting that they have all the answers. Being willing to say what is not known and remaining confident and calm in the doing of it enhances trust.

Open communication is critical to ensuring trust in the merger process. If information is scarce, people will start to guess, typically in a worst-case scenario. Mergers can easily become cultures where fears and rumors are fostered, especially if communication is not regular, consistent, or overly controlled. Communication needs to be clear, consistent, and follow a regular pattern to be effective. This requires setting up regular meetings in which employees can hear from leadership, not just what has been decided but what is still in the works and what is being contemplated (Britsche & Fekete, 2022). It also requires two-way communication. News itself is crucial. It needs to be fact-based yet empathetic towards people's feelings. It is necessary to recognize the confusion people are experiencing and lay out the reasons behind the merger and the benefits it offers. Leaders need to be transparent regarding what is changing and what is not, what is known and what is being negotiated. They should also be honest about the trade-offs and challenges. People will accept tough decisions, such as career changes or relocation, whenever they feel they are being told the truth and heard. If communication is honest, even difficult decisions can be made with greater resilience and faith.

Getting everyone involved is another essential area where leadership must take the helm under conditions of uncertainty. In a merger, the affected group is more diverse. Internal stakeholders include employees and managers, and external stakeholders include governments, customers, suppliers, and investors. They all have different goals, expectations and concerns. This requires a clear and structured way of communicating with all of them. The idea is that alignment starts at the top but must then filter down through everything in the company. Top-level leaders define the vision, but middle managers and team leaders are the ones who turn that vision into reality for employees. The middle layers connect high-level vision and day-to-day tasks (Pecis et al., 2025). If they are not adequately on board or resourced, the entire merger will collapse. For this type of alignment to be successful, leaders at all levels must have the right information, mindset, and tools. They must understand why the merger is taking place, what the change objectives are, and how long it will take before significant changes occur. Equally significant, they must be trained to communicate with their teams, deal with resistance, and listen empathetically. Equipping them with toolkits, FAQs, talking points, and training can make them effective communicators and change supporters. If not, messages may become confusing or deceptive, with the outcome being disunity rather than unity in the congregation.

This is underpinned using stories and narratives. People learn about change through stories, not through facts presented in a list. When a merger takes place, the story is the bridge that pulls people toward a shared identity and future. It tells them where the company has been, why it is merging, and what kind of organization they are now becoming part of. A compelling story brings the past and future together; it honors the history of the two companies merging and looks toward a new, positive future. This resonates with the values, hopes, and common aspirations of the team. It does so on an emotional basis, not a rational one. Leaders must tell stories in times of uncertainty. This does not mean creating happy endings or pretending that the world is always rosy (Tariq, 2025). This means telling real stories about what life was like within the company, stories of how the different groups worked together, how customers were served during the transition, and how new partnerships created new ideas. These stories are a sign that the merger is taking effect, that a new culture is being born, and that the future is here, not just what we imagine. It is also effective in coping with the messy bits of change. It can show the struggles and successes, losses, and lessons learned. It can be admitted that it is difficult to merge, but it is worth doing it properly. Storytelling is especially useful in creating a sense of who we are as members of the new company. When businesses merge, people are unclear about where they fit in. They may ask themselves, "Do I still work for my original team?" "Is this really a merger or is it just one company taking over?" "What are we about now?

These questions cannot be answered through papers or plans. They need stories to show that everyone is in, every idea matters, and everyone is part of building the new business. When leaders tell these stories of truth and heart, it makes people feel connected and ready to champion the future. The dynamic between leadership, communication, and uncertainty is a two-way street.". When the world is muddled, people seek guidance and reassurance from their leaders (Ansari, 2024). When leaders communicate in simple terms and with understanding, the company becomes stronger and more resilient in dealing with change. When a company is stronger, it is more likely to survive a merger and even emerge better and more unified. Leadership during these times is not about having all the answers. It is about creating an environment for individuals to discover their place, reawakened with a sense of purpose, and progress together. No single method for leading a merger exists. Each of these is unique, with its own problems, culture, and pressures. However, one thing remains the same: leaders must be present, always, clearly, and as real people. The greatest post-merger leaders do not view communication as something to be done but as a constant conversation. They realize that trust is built over time through a combination of small and large moments when honesty, compassion and vision intersect. They realize that when uncertainty is present, the most powerful assets they have are not necessarily plans or data but authenticity, connecting people, and picking the right stories to tell.

ESG AND HUMAN-CENTERED DESIGN IN RESTRUCTURING

Embedding ESG into a redesigning process entails considering what victory really means, beyond making extra money. On the environmental front, this could mean changing the way a company sources its supplies to reduce emissions and waste or using greener materials. When companies consolidate, there seems to be a lot of pressure to cut costs by laying people off and reducing operations. However, reducing it purely for financial motives hurts people a lot, such as losing jobs, morale, reputation, motivation, and competency (Britsche & Fekete, 2022). An HR-centric approach to restructuring tries to stay efficient while being kind. This includes being fair when deciding who is getting let go, being open and honest about what is happening, offering incentives such as payoffs, retraining, and counseling, enabling everyone in every walk of life to be involved in the decisions, and being honest about why decisions are being made. It is also important to keep people's sense of self and culture vibrant so that they do not lose their sense of history and values.

A good example of both how hard it is and how it can be done better is a merger between two global consumer products companies. Company A had aggressive environmental reporting and forward-looking staff engagement practices. Company B had more traditional hierarchies, fewer social governance agendas, and complex bureaucracy. Both post-merger companies planned to pool manufacturing, research and development, marketing, and support functions to reduce costs, invest in sustainable products, and reposition their brands in environmentally aware markets (Pesce et al., 2019). First, they quickly cut out redundant roles, merged factories, and reduced the number of management levels. However, several mistakes have left employees and stakeholders unhappy. The criteria for who to let go were not clearly communicated, and most felt unfairly targeted. In some places, cultural conventions surrounding employer duty created high resistance, as employees felt that the company was leaving them behind. Environmental upgrades were postponed because cost-cutting concentrated in areas that were viewed as "non-core" in nature and not as those that were most critical to the environment. Governance also suffered, with inadequate monitoring of how decisions were made locally, leading to inconsistency and injustice. The takeaways from this case are clear. It is all about transparency: workers should be informed about what is going on and why. Publication of information prematurely or excessively, using town hall meetings, small group discussions, frequently asked questions or just by word of mouth can lead to gossip, resentment and low morale. Explaining the packing-up and down and changing of places of factories and even decision making assistance assists in avoiding those issues and those rules should be put very clear and preferably modified with suggestions of the affected parties.

In reality, ESG-based redesign of an international consumer-goods merger is based on strategic planning and understanding. It starts with a diagnostic stage which charts the current culture, environmental performance, social relations and the sentiment of the employees. That evaluation predicts possible risks, vulnerable areas in the job, severe environmental policies, and high staff loyalty (Pippirs and Steckenbauer, 2022). In designing the new structure, put humanity first: consult employees, test new patterns of working and bring local flexibility rather than implementing a uniform template. What remains the same, what changes and frames the new identity are also important issues as values, symbols and shared stories. Governance must be robust. The decisions to be made concerning layoffs, role changes and allocation of resources must be reconsidered by the groups encompassing members of distinct segments, geographies, functions and backgrounds. Performance evaluation should include transparent ESG data, including carbon footprint, water impacts, waste, leadership gender diversity, staff turnover, well-being scores, even in restructuring leaders. Responsibility implies giving truthful explanations and in the case when the results are not good, it does not conceal problems. Firms neglecting individuals during change have bigger problems ahead of them: legal liability, reputation, loss of talent, decreased engagement and productivity. The organizational cost of integrating ESG into its structure is generally compensated by a higher reward (Iqbal et al., 2024). All this has to be weighed against business and financial urges: competition in the market, shareholder demands, and profitability objectives. These drivers are not meant to be disregarded but rather aligned with considerations of the dignity of people and the need to create trust, inclusiveness, and promote environmental care. Briefly, reconstructing an organization in the context of ESG and people-driven approach is not easy but still, absolutely necessary. Sharp reductions, layoffs, and cultural transitions may cause severe issues not just legal or accounting issues but also ethical and human-relations issues.

REDESIGNING ORGANIZATIONAL STRUCTURES AND ROLES

During company restructuring and mergers, changing how the organization is established and how jobs are defined is essential to achieving confidence, flexibility, and enhanced performance. What works in one firm will not necessarily work elsewhere unless it is redesigned well (Britsche & Fekete, 2022). One big trend is away from rigid hierarchies to more flexible, team-based structures: smaller, cross-functional teams, fewer management layers, more open communication styles, and jobs that can shift when the need arises. This is not restructuring for the sake of the show; it changes the way decisions are made, the way people work together, and how quickly and innovatively the company can react to new problems. However, changing the shape is not easy. It involves redesigning jobs so that everyone knows to whom they report, reshaping the amount of responsibility everyone has, mapping out who has what capabilities, planning for leadership in the future, and ensuring that the technology fits the new way of working.

Organizations used to operate with tall structures and many layers of managers, low spans of control, clear career paths for moving up, and formalized job definitions. This gave good direction and control but might slow things down, make it difficult to adapt, and reduce morale at times. Less contemporary arrangements kept decision-making centralized, minimized layers, had narrower spans of control, and fostered dependence on the teams. Although formal positions may remain, they are usually more adaptable to change. Individuals may have several positions, switch teams, and make decisions without consulting others (Amin et al., 2021). However, without proper guidelines, it can become confusing. Without proper coordination, teams may replicate efforts or lose touch. restructuring when companies restructure after a merger, managers usually prefer a compromise: having some form of structure to guarantee clarity and rule compliance, but with adaptable teams that can innovate and focus on the customer. Role clarity is especially important during these transitions. Mergers may result in duplication of work, some of which may not be required or poorly defined. Role redesigning involves returning to the fundamental nature of every job, what a person does, and to whom they report. It also includes determining which decisions must go up the line and which can be made locally. With no clear limits, people might end up duplicating work or doing nothing because they do not know what they are supposed to do. Even in informal agile applications, roles shift away from control-based to people collaborating, leading, and aligning rather than directing.

Another key element is changing the level of control that managers have. With fewer layers, managers would be able to manage more people. This means more effective delegation, good leadership skills, and support for more autonomous teams. Succession planning and talent mapping are also important aspects of this process. When jobs change, some people will not fit into the new organization, some will be too experienced, and others will need new skills (Britsche & Fekete, 2022). Companies need to understand how their current talent fits into the new setup: who will thrive under a flatter organization, who will need training, and who will need to be moved to another role. Succession planning is becoming increasingly dynamic. Instead of setting career tracks, executives must identify several potential successors across different teams and roles. This prevents problems when roles are changed, or people leave and shows that the company is interested in its people over merely cutting costs.

Technology plays an important role in reshaping today's world. Unless the right tools are available to enable collaboration, transparency, and real-time feedback, work will be affected. Communication tools, project tracking for collaborations, analytics for performance, and workflow automation must be integrated into daily work. The technology must adapt to the new organization, such as making it possible for teams to track their own goals and metrics without needing approval layers. If jobs are less formal, systems must show who is doing what at any given time and how that changes smoothly. Ensuring that new tools are compatible with existing tools is essential to prevent system failure. Sometimes, new positions for digital operations, change management, or aligning technology and jobs are necessary.

Deciding on the number of direct reports that one manager can effectively handle is another area that needs to be restructured. When managers have more direct reports, they need to be better at delegating and must have strong support. If a manager has too many employees or groups or complex projects, confusion, burnout, and poor communication can result. Leaders can try different configurations in pilot groups, see what works, and adjust along the way based on what they learn. Curving layers back can speed up decision-making but also requires stronger leadership at lower levels and clearer definitions of roles so that authority is not confused and action can be taken in time without waiting for approval from above. For integrated organizations, achieving a balance between centralized control and decentralized teams is often challenging. Some activities, such as finance or compliance, may require firm-level central control. Some, such as product development or customer engagement, can benefit from being more locally centered to accommodate local needs. A much-abused strategy is to apply a hybrid model, such as hubs and spokes or federated models. Networked teams can report to function leaders but can also organize locally. It avoids duplication, maintains consistency, and allows for flexibility where needed (Tariq, 2025).

Job redesign usually involves rethinking how jobs are performed, creating new mixed jobs, removing obsolete jobs, and inserting new changes, integration, and coordination jobs. Role definitions might shift from a task focus to results and contributions to overall goals. This might involve requesting employees to work across teams, contribute to shared objectives, and be willing to adapt to shifting priorities. Consequently, performance management must change to focus less on what people do and more on how well they work together, how they adapt, how rapidly they react, and how much they learn. Higher-level leadership must also change, with more focus on empowering autonomy, resolving team issues, and facilitating rather than directing. Talent mapping must look beyond current employees to find future leaders who can grow within the new system. They possess self-assurance, an intense passion to succeed, the ability to work with others, and the skills to leverage digital tools (Chowdhury et al., 2024). Succession planning cannot be solely concerned with who replaces current incumbents but with how to replace new requirements, such as roles that require new skills like driving digital transformation, building change, managing data, or enabling team development. Online tools can focus on the interdependence of people and processes, identify common risks, and support collaboration between teams. The automation of routine tasks enables managers to invest more time in training and planning. Software to support remote and distributed teams is especially required when a merger cut across different locations is required.

It is also important to develop mechanisms for learning and evolution. As new structures and roles are piloted, data are gathered on whether they are working how fast decisions are made, how well defined the roles are, how well employees like the changes, how long it takes to resolve issues, and whether there are overlaps or lost handoffs (Snell and Morris, 2021). Communication is required throughout the process. People need to understand not just what changes are happening, but why, how their role is positioned in the new form, what they are expected to do, and how they will be measured. Roles should be clearly defined, transparent, and live in organization charts, with clear lines of reporting, cross-functional collaboration, and expectations of collaboration clearly stated. Leaders also must actively champion the changes: commit resources for managing the transition, invest in training, listen to worries, and model the desired behaviors in the new structure, such as flexibility, cooperation, and accommodation of shared authority.

Finally, leaders must understand that reconsidering the organization's structure has risks: confusion, duplication of effort, unclear accountability, cultural differences, and slow decision-making. To deal with these, a phased approach is best: testing adjustments in some areas or zones, learning from what occurs, and disseminating those lessons, and modifying them before full implementation. In most mergers, the first six to twelve months are the most challenging (Britsche & Fekete, 2022). Jobs, work spans, and technical problems may require revisions, revisions, and solutions, respectively. Redesigning an organization is not an event but an ongoing process. Finally, restructuring jobs and buildings after a merger must balance structure and flexibility, clarity and flexibility, standardization and autonomy, and people-first and technology use. If managed correctly, this can be a major help in assisting merged teams, encouraging innovation, boosting morale, and improving performance within the new organization.

PERFORMANCE MONITORING AND CHANGE SUSTAINMENT

When a merger takes place, the real work begins, not just adding numbers or balancing books, but making the new entity work well, adapt, and live up to promises such as teamwork, efficiency, and growth. Tracking progress and making lasting changes is extremely important (Goolmeer et al., 2022). If there are no methods to monitor what works and what does not, even the best plans can dissipate or not yield the anticipated outcomes. This paper discusses how a group of corporations can use key performance indicators and early warning signs to keep track of their performance, how development programs can help keep changes in position, why it is important to keep knowledge and expertise on hand, and how a feedback culture helps improve strategies over time (Tariq, 2025).

Once a merger takes place, choosing the right key performance indicators is one of the first things to accomplish to track its progress. These numbers ought to reflect not only the money aspect, such as cost savings, revenue growth, and enhanced profits, but also other key areas such as staff engagement, customer loyalty, how the merger is going, team culture, how well things are done, regulatory compliance, and how happy stakeholders are. While numbers that deal with money are easier to measure, relying too much on them might mask problems. For example, cutting costs through employee dismissals can look great in the short run but result in problems such as losing seasoned minds and demoralization. Warning signs are of great benefit as they offer signs before things get worse. Examples include the volume of key people leaving, the rate at which decisions are being made in new team structures, the duration to bring in new teams or merge systems, the volume of customers that are complaining or having issues during the transition, and the rate at which the issues or duplicate work are fixed. All these KPIs and leading indicators in aggregate form the foundation of an early warning system or dashboard that keeps top management abreast of what parts of the merger are progressing, what is not, and where further support or tweaking might be needed (Chowdhury et al., 2024). It is advised that one checks how well processes are being linked, how engaged and content employees are, how many employees stick around, how quickly IT systems are being integrated, and how contented customers are, as all are vital parts of a good measure of how well the merger is going.

Organizational development provides the interventions and guidance needed to bring the culture, assess any resistance, and create more effective behaviors. It gets leaders on the same page and ensures that systems like performance reviews, rewards, and communications support the desired changes. Development and learning help with all of this by giving individuals and teams the skills they need, whether it is training for new technology, leadership development, working across teams, or dealing with change. In mergers, many people end up with new jobs, teams, and bosses; without proper training and support, confusion, inefficiency, and frustration can snowball. Organizational and learning development also support learning from experience by determining what is not working, testing new strategies, learning from what happens, and applying those lessons to make plans more robust. Maintaining knowledge and skills becomes especially important following a merger. Key people can leave, implied knowledge can be lost, best practices of the past company might not be transferred, and memory-based knowledge in people's minds can be lost if it is not documented (Skogland, 2017). To address this, the combined companies need to invest in knowledge management on a systematic basis, identifying the main areas of knowledge, documenting how things are done, creating opportunities for experienced people to pass on their expertise to others, ensuring that no single person has all the knowledge, creating a shared space in which to learn together, and enabling people to pass on what they know. Future leader planning also helps retain critical talent by determining who will be critical in the new company, developing them, and creating mechanisms so that when an individual departs or transitions, the business does not suffer. Talent retention is not financially driven; it is about making people aware of their role, being appreciated, being motivated, and knowing a clear purpose in the new company (Tariq, 2025).

A culture of appreciating feedback connects the use of KPIs, organizational development and learning, and knowledge sharing into an adaptive system that can be modified and improved upon. Feedback ensures that the data collected from measuring performance is truly followed through, not just sitting on a screen but resulting in genuine alterations by leaders, managers and teams. This means asking people regularly, through surveys, meetings, or casual conversations, what is working, what is not, and what they did not anticipate. Feedback also brings unexpected problems to the surface, such as productivity gains that produce burnout or falling customer satisfaction due to changes in service (Abdallah & Guhao Jr., 2025). A feedback culture must also be safe enough for people to feel free to report bad news, present suggestions for fixing things, or confess when they do not know. Leaders need to demonstrate that they respect this by doing something or at least explaining why some things simply cannot be altered right away. This helps build trust and the fact that the merger is not just a top-down initiative but a journey for everyone. Pulling all of this together, a solid plan for monitoring performance and maintaining changes made can proceed in a cycle: determine what success will look like in the short and long term, select a combination of KPIs and early warning indicators, establish systems for monitoring and reporting data frequently, design development programs to sustain skills, culture, and behavior change, develop systems to capture and retain knowledge, incorporate feedback loops, monitor progress frequently, and change structures, processes, or strategies as necessary based on what is learned.

Leadership commitment, ongoing support for individuals and systems, and proper management structures, such as steering committees and responsibility teams, maintain momentum. Finally, there are a couple of common pitfalls to avoid. One is keeping too many KPIs to track, which can create uncertainty, turn reporting into necessary evils, and cause it to be difficult to know what matters. It is better to set fewer, tightly defined, easily measured metrics that everyone who is familiar with these things is aware of. Failing to keep an eye on softer measures, such as the culture, identity, and morale of the staff, is another mistake (Chowdhury et al., 2024). These are harder to measure, but they have a significant influence on whether a merger is successful. Being too slow to respond to feedback also breaks trust and creates a negative attitude. Or waiting too long to take crucial knowledge that is already gone. It does not focus on enough middle managers, who are critical in bridging leaders' intentions and what happens on the ground. With good KPIs, first-class organizational development and learning facilitation, effective knowledge sharing, and a culture based on feedback, companies can minimize risks, leverage opportunities, retain the right employees, and achieve the anticipated advantages of the merged organization.

CONCLUSION AND FUTURE IMPLICATIONS

In the complex world of mergers and acquisitions, it comes down to being able to integrate strategy, people, and sustainability into a consistent and cohesive plan. It is not so much a matter of surviving the integration process as coming out stronger, more supple, and more in tune with both market developments and moral norms. A Commercial Survival Plan. The future of this field is to think not merely about the mechanics of integration but also about building models for organizations that can adapt to change, preserve human values, and maintain performance consistently over time. This study describes how these pieces can fit together, what new models are promising, and what researchers, consultants, and business leaders should adopt (Setyadi et al., 2025). To achieve successful post-merger integration, it is essential to understand that strategic goals, human capital and environmental, social, and governance (ESG) sustainability should be inseparably related. People need not be ignored in a strategy because people with no direction cannot do anything. Sustainability without having a standpoint approach is superficial. The issue is to shift to the thinking of restructuring as a stylistic cost-cutting tool instead of regarding it as a potential to reconsider the purpose of the company, its value creation, and its role in society. Therefore, strategic alignment needs to encompass market position, financial goals but culture, values, incentives, functions and governance as well so that the combined business can do its work with a common purpose, keep learning and be credible to its employees, communities, regulating bodies and investors (Chowdhury et al., 2024). The redesign is integrated and sustainable behaviors become the main performance measures based on carbon reduction, ethical sourcing, inclusion and equity is the priority and not an afterthought. Here, individuals are not considered resources but important stakeholders whose safety, wellbeing, identity, and aspirations are important. With these elements at the center, then the integration will build sustained value, will diminish conflict, will increase retention, reputation and will withstand uncertainty.

New models of organization design reveal that the old hierarchies are being supplanted by the nimble, networked and responsive structures. The so-called adaptive operating model, which was discussed in consulting communities and in academia, approaches structural redesign as a continuing capability: shifting the decision rights, reporting, allocation of resources, and workflows with the varying conditions. Triggers Organizations can preprogram decision structures to make triggers (market changes, customer response, performance alarm) and enable fine-grained adjustments instead of complete restructuring once every few years. The focus of these models are on agility, role definition, responsibility, and outward orientation so that the flexible and networked organization still has individuals on the ground, guidance to provide to employees and definite team goals. Experimental organizational design is another trend which is being seen and where small pilots and tests are conducted to experiment with various team designs, reporting relationships, and decision-making processes. The objective is learning, exploration and expansion of successful ideas. This will minimize the risk as teams can experiment with new approaches, get feedback, monitor outcomes, and repeat. It also engages people in the change making them co-creators of the future organization. These experiments when paired with data analysis and real-time monitoring can tell what structural or process modifications will produce more morale, faster decisions, and greater collaboration in one and what will not (Hakim and Putra Pratama, 2024). These new forms have major impacts to scientists, professionals and corporate leaders. There is a lot to research: what design models can be applied to mergers of various scale, location, cultural diversity, industry, how can indicators of adaptive capacity be measured and tested, how ESG performance is related to the strategies of adaptation over time, how AI and real-time used platform can contribute to its adaptivity, and how the results can be provided by psychological factors, by identity factors. Long term research that extends past the initial-year follow ups of M&A integrations can reveal what choices made in design survive, and what do not. There are as important as quantitative indicators, such as KPIs and organizational data, qualitative analyses are made on culture, identity, and storytelling.

REFERENCES

Abdallah, J. C., & Guhao, E. S.Jr. (2025). Filipino graduate students in foreign universities: A phenomenological inquiry. *European Journal of Education Studies, 12*(2), 271–289. DOI: 10.46827/ejes.v12i2.5827

Amin, R. U., Awan, G. M., & Raheem, F. (2021). Critical analyses of Pak-Afghan Transit Trade Agreement: Pakistan's perspective. *Research Journal of Social Sciences and Economics Review, 1*(4), 418–426. DOI: 10.36902/rjsser-vol1-iss4-2020(418-426)

Ansari, W. M. (2024). Integrating Pathology and Laboratory Medicine into the Transitional Clerkship Model: A Strategic Educational Realignment. *Journal of HBS M&DC, 4*(1), 32–38. DOI: 10.70394/jhbsmdc.v4i1.70

Ayularas, B., & Aulia Zaim, I. (2024). Business Strategic Realignment for a Sustainable Fashion Brand. *Journal of Business and Management Review, 5*(2), 105–123. DOI: 10.47153/jbmr52.8952024

Britsche, A., & Fekete, M. (2022). Strategic Management for the Realignment of Risk Determination of the Supply Chain in Electric Car Production. *International Scientific Conference EMAN – Economics and Management: How to Cope with Disrupted Times*. (pp. 44–50) DOI: 10.31410/EMAN.2022.97

Chowdhury, S., Budhwar, P., & Wood, G. (2024). Generative artificial intelligence in business: Towards a strategic human resource management framework. *British Journal of Management, 35*(4), 1680–1691. DOI: 10.1111/1467-8551.12824

Goolmeer, T., Skroblin, A., Grant, C., van Leeuwen, S., Archer, R., Gore-Birch, C., & Wintle, B. A. (2022). Recognizing culturally significant species and Indigenous-led management is key to meeting international biodiversity obligations. *Conservation Letters, 15*(6), e12899. DOI: 10.1111/conl.12899

Hakim, H. A., & Putra Pratama, A. (2024). Internalization strategies of company culture: A case study of ex-employees of Chevron Pacific Indonesia transitioning to Pertamina WK Rokan. *International Journal of Current Science Research and Review, 7*(4), 4767–4775. DOI: 10.47191/ijcsrr/V7-i5-45

Iqbal, M. S., Abdul Rahim, Z., Alshammari, A. M. K., & Iftikhar, H. (2024). Innovative strategies for overcoming barriers to technology adoption in small and medium-sized enterprises. *Journal of the International Council for Small Business, 5*(4), 331–344. DOI: 10.1080/26437015.2024.2367440

Madhani, P. M. (2019). Strategic supply chain management for enhancing competitive advantages: Developing a business value added framework. *International Journal of Value Chain Management, 10*(3), 189–212. DOI: 10.1504/IJVCM.2019.103270

Malik, A., Sinha, P., Budhwar, P., & Pereira, V. (2023). Managing legitimacy in a cross-border post-merger integration context: The role of language strategies. *International Journal of Human Resource Management, 34*(21), 4144–4174. DOI: 10.1080/09585192.2023.2237878

Miller, R., & Verhoeven, H. (2019). Overcoming smallness: Qatar, the United Arab Emirates and strategic realignment in the Gulf. *International Politics, 57*(1), 1–20. DOI: 10.1057/s41311-019-00180-0

Narassimhan, E., Myslikova, Z., & Gallagher, K. S. (2024). Strategies for green industrial and innovation policy: An analysis of alignment, misalignment, and realignment around dominant designs in the EV sector. *Environmental Research Letters, 19*(1), 014019. DOI: 10.1088/1748-9326/ad101e

Pecis, L., Ge, B., & Bauer, F. (2025). The strategic realignment of paradoxical family and business goals in family business: A rhetorical history perspective. *Business History, 67*(2), 577–607. DOI: 10.1080/00076791.2024.2317938

Pesce, D., Neirotti, P., & Paolucci, E. (2019). When culture meets digital platforms: Value creation and stakeholders' alignment in big data use. *Current Issues in Tourism, 22*(15), 1883–1903. DOI: 10.1080/13683500.2019.1591354

Pippirs, C., & Steckenbauer, G. C. (2022). Case study—Spa destination branding—A strategic realignment process of five Bavarian thermal spas. *International Journal of Spa and Wellness, 5*(3–4), 308–319. DOI: 10.1080/24721735.2022.2117009

Prasetyo, B., & Putro, U. S. (2024). Strategic analysis of international oil and gas companies' response to global carbon emission reduction initiatives. *Applied Quantitative Analysis, 3*(2), 45–59. DOI: 10.31098/quant.2038

Setyadi, A., Pawirosumarto, S., & Damaris, A. (2025). Rethinking Sustainable Operations: A Multi-Level Integration of Circularity, Localization, and Digital Resilience in Manufacturing Systems. *Sustainability (Basel), 17*(15), 6929. DOI: 10.3390/su17156929

Skogland, M. A. C. (2017). A spatial approach to transformational change: Strategic alignment of the spatial and cultural environment. *Journal of Corporate Real Estate, 19*(4), 285–299. DOI: 10.1108/JCRE-09-2016-0030

Snell, S. A., & Morris, S. S. (2021). Time for realignment: The HR ecosystem. *The Academy of Management Perspectives, 35*(2), 219–236. DOI: 10.5465/amp.2018.0069

Tariq, M. U. (2025). Green FinTech-Driving Sustainable Finance and Empowering Underserved Communities. In Masri, M., Sait, M., & Anshari, M. (Eds.), *Promoting Inclusivity and Accessibility With FinTech* (pp. 279–306). IGI Global Scientific Publishing., DOI: 10.4018/979-8-3373-1112-8.ch010

Tariq, M. U. (2025). AI Tools and Technologies for Management Education: Enhancing Learning Through Innovation. In M. R. & S. R. (Eds.), *Integrating AI and Machine Learning into Business and Management Education* (pp. 105-132). IGI Global Scientific Publishing. DOI: 10.4018/979-8-3373-2150-9.ch005

Tariq, M. U. (2025). AI-Driven Digital Nomads: Transforming Labor Markets and Industrial Growth in the Digital Economy. In Ordóñez de Pablos, P., Zhang, X., Anshari, M., & Almunawar, M. (Eds.), *AI and Digital Nomads Shaping Global Industrial Technology Transitions* (pp. 113–138). IGI Global Scientific Publishing., DOI: 10.4018/979-8-3373-0159-4.ch004

Tariq, M. U. (2025). The Influence of Leadership Styles on Innovation: Driving Change Through Effective Leadership. In Paradiso-Testa, M. (Ed.), *The Impact of Innovation in Leadership* (pp. 249–274). IGI Global Scientific Publishing., DOI: 10.4018/979-8-3373-2402-9.ch010

Tariq, M. U. (2025). Building Green-Crafting Sustainable Business Models for a Resilient Future. In Mehra, P., & Kumar, P. (Eds.), *Incentives and Benefits for Adopting Green Entrepreneurship Practices* (pp. 37–64). IGI Global Scientific Publishing., DOI: 10.4018/979-8-3693-9306-2.ch002

Vaddepalli, S., & Vishwanath, B. (2024). Mergers and acquisitions: Drivers, challenges, and performance outcomes in GCC nations. *International Journal of Central Banking*, *20*(1), 298–310.

Watling, J., & Wilén, N. (2024). Assessing the causes of strategic realignment in Sahelian states. *RUSI Journal*, *169*(4), 64–77. DOI: 10.1080/03071847.2024.2395563

Wiegelmann, T., & Glauerdt, R. (2025). Practice Briefing: Mergers and Acquisitions in real estate asset management (Part 1)–strategic motivations, valuation and transaction structuring. *Journal of Property Investment & Finance*, *43*(4), 454–468. DOI: 10.1108/JPIF-02-2025-0033

Zhang, M., & Wei, X. (2024). Resource efficiency, cultural industry, and green economic growth: A synergistic approach. *Resources Policy*, *90*, 104769. DOI: 10.1016/j.resourpol.2024.104769

KEY TERMS AND DEFINITIONS

Cultural Integration: Merging values, behaviors, and organizational norms.

Identity Continuity: Preserving the core resolution through organizational transition.

Strategic Alignment: Coordinating objectives, structures, and performance expectations.

Chapter 10
The Technological Transformation of Competitive Intelligence Through AI, Big Data, and ML

Ricardo Marcão
http://orcid.org/0000-0003-3277-3078
ISLA Santarém, Portugal & NECE, University of Beira Interior, Portugal

Vasco Santos
ISLA Santarém, Portugal & Polytechnic University of Tomar, Portugal, & NECE, University of Beira Interior, Portugal

ABSTRACT

In increasingly competitive and data-intensive markets, organizations rely on competitive intelligence (CI) to support strategic decision-making and sustain competitive advantage. This paper examines the evolution of CI from traditional, manually driven approaches to digital and data-driven models. It analyzes how artificial intelligence, big data analytics, and machine learning enhance information collection, filtering, and analysis, improving decision relevance and strategic insight. The paper also discusses key challenges related to information overload, data quality, and ethical boundaries, highlighting the importance of structured CI processes in modern organizations.

DOI: 10.4018/979-8-3373-5233-6.ch010

INTRODUCTION

Nowadays, organizations need to know about their competitors for survival in the modern narrow markets, which consider factors like the rise in several organizations that include competitive intelligence in operations. The development in technology and internet advancements allows all organizations to use competitive intelligence (CI) techniques (Attaway, 1999). Competitive intelligence is habitually misjudged, as it's a kind of business surveillance, because they both have similar activities. Industrial surveillance is restricted in most countries, which restricts the growth of competitive intelligence.

Apart from the legal regulations, it's clear how competitive intelligence can be evaluated and how it will work effectively. In this confused field, the available data is only a little about the results of the application in the competitive business, and despite the wide knowledge disclosed, there is a long path to illuminate the domain. The normal CI consists of three parts, which explore the collection of raw data, processing of raw data, and obtaining the target in a concise as well as organized manner. The gathering of raw data is easy with the support of internet, the real challenge in CI is to focus on a limited number of topics and filtering out as the irrelevant documents as possible (Dan, 2000)

AI, big data, and machine learning enhance competitive intelligence by enabling organizations to analyze vast amounts of data, derive insights, and improve decision-making. These technologies help mitigate risks and improve the customer experience, which ultimately leads to a competitive advantage. Competitive intelligence influences the decision-making and acquisition of competitive advantages. Organizations must leverage data, AI, and social capital for effective competitive intelligence. (Cekuls,2023).

EVOLUTION OF CI: FROM TRADITIONAL TO DIGITAL APPROACHES

Competitive intelligence traces its intellectual origins to Harvard Professor Michael E. Porter's 1998 work, Competitive Strategy: Techniques for Analyzing Industries and Competitors. (Porter, 1998) highlights about the creation of "competitor analysis system" (Porter, 1998: 368–82), which connects the concept of CI in the development of corporate strategy. Competitive intelligence traces much of its operational origins to retired US government intelligence community officials who, at about the same time, helped transfer the concept of governmental intelligence to business

(McGonagle, 2007). For example, Motorola was early recognized as the home of one of the first full-time modern competitive intelligence units: (Muller,2008)

(Galvin,1997), since that time, competitive intelligence has been adopted by numerous private organizations, both businesses and non-profits, has been offered in universities, some at graduate-level, has been nurtured by numerous professional organisations, including the Strategic and Competitive Intelligence Professionals (SCIP, formerly the Society of Competitive Intelligence Professionals) and the International Association for Intelligence Education (IAFIE), and closely studied by research groups including the APQC (formerly the American Productivity and Quality Center) (Nikolaos & Evangelia, 2012). Today, competitive intelligence, at least formally, still retains elements of its government intelligence origins, first among them the importance of the CI cycle, as well as the implicit given that competitive intelligence is a product to be transmitted from an analyst to an end-user, rather than a process to be in corporated into management wherever it can help (McGonagle & Misner-Elias, 2016)

DIGITAL DISRUPTORS AND THE RECONFIGURATION OF COMPETITIVE LANDSCAPES

The digital interruption has constantly modified the e-business competitive perspective, accompanying a prototype shift which is characterized by advanced technology and the transformation of the market. As defined by (Westerman et al., 2014), digital disruption refers to "the rapid transformation of traditional industries and markets through the adoption and integration of digital technologies." This case sparked the intense modifications across diverse sectors by creating the innovation of new business models that challenge the top to democratize markets. Recently, research has shown the extensive implications of digital interruption in e-businesses. For example, (Arora et al., 2020) highlight the wild impact of blockchain technology on the e-commerce supply chains. Blockchain is one of the decentralized ledger systems that offers security in supply chain management and unprecedented transparency, which enables e-businesses to streamline their operations and mitigate the risks to enhance the stakeholders' trust. It highlights the essentials for online businesses to adopt blockchain technology to stay competitive in the growing digital marketplace According to a study by (Nerbel & Kreutzer, 2023), ecosystems platform have emerged as key drivers of digital interruptions which enables the e-businesses to tackle the network effects and seize values across the interconnected markets.

This platform-based e-business creates exceptional value propositions and refines the industry dynamics by attaining the co-innovation and collaboration among the participant ecosystem. It also emphasizes the importance of strategy in platformization in traversing the digital interruptions and achieving sustainable growth in the digital economy. In addition to the development of artificial intelligence technologies has transformed the competitive e-business perspective. Research by (Gao & Liu, 2023) elucidates the transformative potential of AI-driven personalization in e-commerce platforms. The e-businesses can able to deliver hyper-personalized experiences through customization for customers' preferences and behavior patterns with the influence of machine learning algorithms and big data analytics.

AI plays a major role in boosting customer engagement, driving conversions, and encouraging long-term loyalty in the age of digital interruption. Recently, research has explored the importance of the agility of an organization and strategic foresight in steering the digital disruption. (Amajuoyi et al., 2024) emphasizes the critical role of agile methodologies in enabling e-businesses to adapt swiftly to changing market conditions and customer expectations. By encouraging an innovative culture, experimentation, and continuous improvement, agile methods in companies can tap the opportunities, mitigate the risks, and outflank competitors in the digital era. The transformative impact of digital interruption on the competitive e-business perspective, as the transition from blockchain-enabled supply chains and platform ecosystems to AI-driven customization in agile organizations, e-businesses must enfold innovation and strategic planning to thrive in the striking technological change. By leveraging innovative technologies, fostering collaboration, and cultivating a culture of agility, e-businesses can position themselves for sustained success amidst the relentless forces of digital disruption (Baskoro, 2024)

SUCCESSFUL STORIES OF DATA-DRIVEN CI FOR BUSINESS AND TECHNOLOGY LEADERS

One notable example is Netflix, a company that has revolutionized the entertainment industry through its data-driven approach. Based on the customer views analysis, preferences, and their interactions, it can able to customize the suggestions for its users, and the customer experience and engagement can be boosted on the platform, which helps Netflix in its content creation strategies. For example, the hit series "House of Cards" originates from deep data analysis, which indicates a strong customer interest in political dramas. As a result, Netflix can effectively align in offering the content according to its viewers' preferences, which led to an improvement in subscriptions and customer loyalty.

Amazon also employed data-driven decision-making to optimize its logistics operations and customer experience. It engaged with the refined algorithms to analyze the buying behaviour of the consumer and stock levels to predict the demand proactively. This helps them to manage their star products always in the inventory stocks and enables them to manage their logistics operations efficiently by reducing costs and focusing on on-time delivery. This data-driven penetration is the foundation of Amazon's strategy of business strategy, which enables it to maintain its leading position in the e-commerce market. This illustrates how data-driven decision-making empowers an organization to make informed decisions about strategic decisions (Gade, 2021)

TECHNOLOGICAL FOUNDATIONS

Overview of Artificial Intelligence: Key Capabilities in Automation, Reasoning, and Language Processing

Nowadays, we live in a technological age, the Fourth Industrial Revolution, known as Industry 4.0 or 4IR (Maynard, 2015; Ślusarczyk,2018), which envisions fast change in technology, industries, societal patterns, and processes as a consequence of enhanced interconnectivity and smart automation. In every country, this revolution impacts each sector and causes an immense change in an undirected manner at a striking rate, with implications for all industry sectors. The application of the latest smart technologies enables more intelligent, quicker decision-making for the business process, which leads to an increase in the productivity and profitability of the business with the help of Artificial Intelligence (AI) technology. The AI revolution, which launched tremendous economic growth activity in the field of manufacturing, commerce, transportation, and other areas, is leading the way in the progress of growth. The impact of AI in the Industrial Revolution 4.0 focuses more on in-depth "AI-based modeling". Artificial intelligence is a field of computer science that helps build the make smart machines which is capable of delivering tasks that typically require human intelligence. AI focuses on making smart computers and intelligent by providing them with all the capabilities to learn and think by using computer programs or machines that can independently think and work like humans can. Therefore, AI-based modeling is the key to building automated, intelligent, and smart systems (Sarker, 2022)

The Big Data Landscape: Characteristics (Volume, Velocity, Variety, Veracity, Value) and Data Ecosystems

The term Big Data is commonly thought to have been coined by John R. Mashey in 1998 at Silicon Graphics (Mashey,1999; Parmar & Yadav, 2017). However, its true origin may extend back to the early 90s (Gullberg, 1991). Since then, its popularity has grown in parallel with the exponential increase of the amount of data being produced, to the point where, in the present day, everyone in the IT world wants 'to do Big Data' (Lohr, 2012; Pepper & Garrity, 2014; Hartmann et al., 2014; Hirsch, 2013; Kiran et al., 2015; Sieben, 2016; Alexander & Lyytinen, 2017; Columbus, 2017).

The term Big Data suffers from a 'buzz word' effect, which led to widespread imprecise definitions, however it is typically understood as an umbrella term encompassing a variety of techniques applied to the analysis of large amounts of data within a defined timeframe (Kiran et al., 2025; Dave, & Gianey, 2016; Wingerath et al.,2016). It poses substantial multidisciplinary challenges like high-performance computing, parallel computing, statistics, machine learning, non-structured data treatment, networking, and database design. In light of the lack of a precise and consensual definition (Gattiker et al., 2013; Chen et al., 2014; Zheng et al., 2015), for this article, we consider 'Big Data processing' to include any operations conducted on a dataset resulting in a process too voluminous to be handled efficiently and in a tractable way on a single machine.

This is consistent with a previously used definition (Li & Cheng, 2012), and can be extended to include data acquisition, management, and storage, all of which are aspects that became critical to the way data is processed, often in serverless contexts. Despite these semantic considerations, this new field has had a striking impact on industries and institutions, which suddenly realized the value of the data they had been collecting without a clear purpose (Alexander & Lyytinen, 2017). The thorough analysis of that information enabled many organisations to optimize their business strategies and more efficiently target potential opportunities (Lohr, 2012; Chen & Zhang, 2014)

This trend also led to the emergence of 'Big Data' consultancies that offered support and services to companies that wanted to use 'Big Data' but did not have the appropriate expertise or resources to do so. (Columbus, 2017; Assunção et al.,2015; Hashem et al., 2015). As established companies navigate this new and growing technological landscape, the number of industry-specific issues grows alongside the number of technological solutions available, and this upward trend leaves newcomers with the difficult task of understanding and assessing the available Big Data tools based on their characteristics (Dubuc et al., 2020)

Machine Learning Prototype: CI Task Using Supervised, Unsupervised, and Reinforcement Learning

Supervised Learning

Supervised learning is one of the eminent categories of ML (Sarker, 2021). It provides a dataset and labels it with the support of a supervised dataset. It is focused on how the inputs are interconnected to the outputs to generalize when faced with new data. For example, one of the most familiar supervised learning applications is in email filtering systems (Jáñez-Martino et al., 2023). In the model training, the pre-labelled email sets were employed. Based on the features like specific word occurrence, sender's details, and email layout, it helps them to evaluate whether the received messages are spam or not. It also helps to detect fraudulent occurrences in the financial transactions. Supervised learning is trained based on past transaction history characterized by fraud detection (Aschi et al., 2022)

Unsupervised Learning

In unsupervised learning systems, the model deals with data with no labels, and the system's objective is to find patterns or structures or construct groups in the data (Morales & Escalante, 2022). These techniques help us to understand how the data structures and relationships are entwined. For example, in marketing, the application of unsupervised learning for a group of customers based on their behaviour pattern, preferences, and past purchase history (Ebrahimi et al.,2022). The Customers can be segregated based on their resemblance and ensure a customized marketing message is sent to each group in the Unsupervised learning. For deploying the customer segmentation, K-means and hierarchical clustering can be used. The unsupervised learning technique can also identify when data displays abnormality in patterns (Verma et al.,2022).

Semi-Supervised Learning

It employs both labelled and unlabelled data to utilize the combination of supervised and unsupervised learning. It is very helpful in obtaining the labelled data, which is very exigent and expensive, while offering better access to a huge volume of valuable data, which is unrelated. It utilizes the labeled data set as well as the unlabelled data set to boost the reliability and generalization. For instance, semi-supervised learning is heavily employed in different fields, such as computer vision, especially in image annotation (Mamat et al.,2023). Meanwhile, semi-supervised learning has also been applied to speech recognition systems where a large set of unlabelled speech data augments a small, labeled set of audio samples (Torre et al.,2021).

Reinforcement Learning

The core agent learns by interacting with its environment to learn how to optimize a premium function through the trial-and-error approach in the reinforcement learning approach. The agent adapts from the surroundings and aligns its performance to modify whenever the feedback is unfavourable. Whenever the decision maker deals with a problem, RL is commonly used in a scenario where an agent identifies the best sequence of actions. RL is applied to robotics, most of the time to autonomous robots (Wesselhöft et al.,2022), which require the completion of tasks or missions, such as moving around an area, picking up an object, or joining parts together.

Moreover, RL has been studied and incorporated in the gaming industry with much focus (Jain et al.,2024). RL was employed in programmes and algorithms such as AlphaGo and half of OpenAI's Dota 2 agents that won over people in games such as Go and Dota 2. Another example of RL is the actor–critic model, which joins actors with critics to enhance learning capability (Li et al., 2025).

In this analysis, Proximal Policy Optimization and Deep Q-Network are the versatile, applicable methods. It is the latest actor–critic method that helps us to improve the policies while sustaining consistency by controlling tremendous policy updates. However, Deep Q-Network is a value-based approach that integrates Deep NNs with Q-learning (Zhang & Zhu, 2024).

In e-commerce and marketing, ML is used in recommendation systems to provide individual customer offers, for example, those used by Amazon or Netflix, as well as customer segmentation for advertising purposes, like in Facebook Ads or Google AdWords (Bhardwaj et al., 2024). Tesla and Waymo's self-driving cars use ML to guide systems and come to decisions (Sriram et al., 2024). Today, finance is one of the most significant sectors that use ML, as it can detect fraud; it is used in PayPal and American Express (Ridzuan et al.,2024).

ML is also critically important in manufacturing; predictive maintenance models help decrease the time that equipment is out of service due to failure, exemplified by products like GE Predix and Siemens MindSphere (Azeem et al.,2022). Organisations like Walmart and Target use ML to track their stocks and enhance the restocking processes (Pasupuleti et al.,2024; Ntakolia et al.,2021). In education, personal collectable learning systems like Duolingo and Coursera are flexible depending on the learner (Kabudi et al.,2021; Gheibi et al.,2021; Strielkowski et al.,2024). Sample use of agriculture involves using environmental data to predict crop yields using ML, which John Deere and the Climate Corporation have implemented (Elbasi et al.,2023; Trentin et al.,2024). Finally, entertainment hiring ML, with music or video streaming services, like Spotify or YouTube, provides recommendations to make the utilisation more engaging (Raj & Renumol,2022)

Integration of AI, Big Data, and ML in the Lifecycle of CI

Employed in the Data Collection and Monitoring

Web Scraping Techniques: Web scraping has gained more traction in recent years due to the increasing growth of online content for its automated data extraction method from websites. Many strategies have been developed to enable web scraping, scaling from basic rule analysis to highly enhanced methods for examining web scraping libraries like Beautiful Soup and Scrapy.

Figure 1. Overview of web scraping

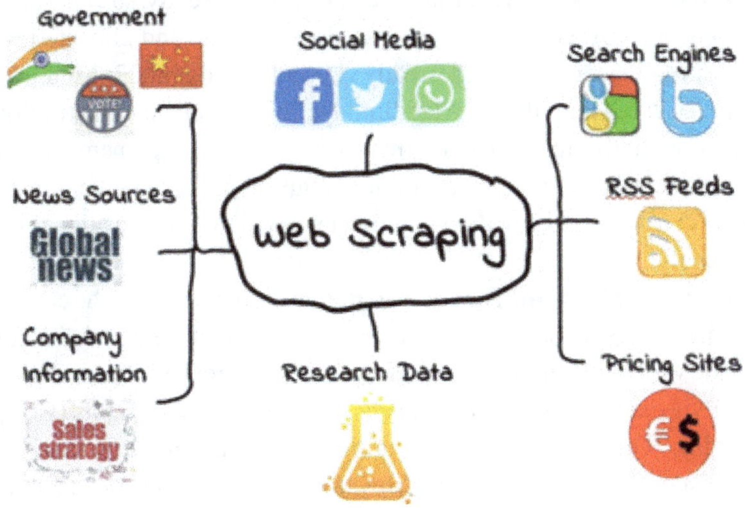

(Pichiyan et al., 2023)

Natural Language Processing in Text Analysis: Many applications in language processing, such as text categorization and sentiment analysis, have benefited greatly from this embedding strategy (Yu et al.,2023). It enables context-aware text representations and improves performance in NLP tasks (Ai et al.,2023). For example, Chatbots and sentiment analysis are employed on how NLP can transform the doctor-patient relationship by training the computers to respond and understand human language (Lenin et al,2023)

Integration of Web Scraping and NLP: Integrating web scraping techniques with NLP has opened up new avenues for researchers and practitioners in the data science domain. By integrating web scraping's data acquisition capabilities with Natural Language Processing, it is able to examine unstructured data that requires strong structural development for extracting valuable data from online platforms. It showcases the integration of web scraping and NLP in the context of social media analysis (Vijayaragavan et al., 2020).

DATA ANALYSIS AND PATTERN RECOGNITION

ML has become an essential component, helping to improve operational processes, decision-making frameworks, and paradigms for interacting with customers (Chirra,2021; Chirra,2022; Maddireddy & Maddireddy,2020)

Predictive Analytics: One prominent application of ML is predictive analytics, which involves looking at past data to guess what will happen next (Chirra,2021; Maddireddy & Maddireddy, 2021; Maddireddy & Maddireddy,2021). This allows businesses to better foresee customer needs, identify risks, and allocate inventory resources with more accuracy (Maddireddy & Maddireddy, 2022; Maddireddy & Maddireddy, 2022; Maddireddy & Maddireddy, 2022). Financial institutions employ the use of predictive analytics to analyze credit risk management and discover activities like fraudulent activity by examining unusual patterns in the transactions, while retailers can utilize this method to predict sales direction and align their stock levels accordingly.

Customer Personalisation: The complexities in the behaviour of the customer are very important for marketing campaigns customization. Machine learning algorithms examine a wide variety of data sources to create detailed profiles of consumers based on their social media activity, purchase history, and web surfing habits (Goriparthi, 2022). Nowadays, Organizations are providing the personalized experiences which help them boost customer happiness and loyalty. Notable companies like Amazon and Netflix utilise machine learning-powered recommendation systems to enhance user engagement metrics and boost revenues by suggesting products and content that match individual tastes (Goriparthi, 2021; Goriparthi, 2022). In healthcare, it helps to analyze a huge volume of data known as Big Data through electronic health records for diagnosis and preventing the disease (Chattu, 2021)

Enhanced Decision-Making: ML provides a vital instrument in enabling data-informed decision-making processes by extracting actionable insights from convoluted datasets (Goriparthi, 2021). With the use of ML models, company executives may analyse internal performance metrics, competition moves, and market dynamics to create more nuanced strategic plans (Goriparthi, 2020)

Robotic process automation, brought together by RPA combined with ML approaches, allows for the automation of repetitive processes, such as data entry, invoice processing, and contacts with customer support (Chirra, 2022; Maddireddy & Maddireddy, 2020; Maddireddy & Maddireddy, 2020).

Advanced logistical operations can enhance the demand forecasting and inventory level control. ML encourages the supply chain efficacy and ensures the product delivery of the product and cost restraint by examining the supplier's data, logistics networks, and market demand to recognize the operational congestions and forecast the interference. Walmart and DHL have simplified their operating matrix by combining the Machine learning driven supply chain structure. By improving logistical operations, enhancing demand forecasting, and controlling inventory levels, ML enhances supply chain efficacy (Maddireddy & Maddireddy, 2022). Machine learning algorithms can ensure the timely delivery of the product and IoT-enabled smart packaging proactively detects the deviations from storage and conditions of transportation, which helps us to reduce the product degradation by collecting and analyzing the data in real-time (Raman et al.,2023)

Google and Tesla are spearheading in using the ML to innovate and launch innovative products and services, which sets a unique benchmark within their competitive sectors. Strategic planning efforts to alleviate the risk, which depend on forecasting the financial aspects, which is the basis for developing strong management of finance. Machine learning has refined financial management by making exact assumptions based on the past and present market trends. These models make it easier to optimise budgets, forecast cash flows, and assess investment opportunities (Goriparthi, 2022).

INSIGHT GENERATION AND VISUALIZATION: THE ROLE OF AI IN ENHANCING MARKET ANALYSIS (JACK, 2024)

Market analysis is a crucial component of business strategy, enabling companies to understand industry trends, customer needs, and competitive dynamics. Traditionally, this process relied on manual analysis of data, often resulting in slower insights and less accurate predictions. The integration of Artificial Intelligence has acutely transformed this aspect and enables businesses to gain deeper insights, quick responses, and more accurate forecasting.

AI and Predictive Analytics: At the core of AI-driven market analysis recline on predictive analytics, which uses past data and machine learning algorithms to predict future trends and behavior patterns. Predictive models allow businesses to forecast market movements, consumer behavior, and potential risks with high accuracy. For example, AI can analyze purchasing patterns, customer demographics, and external factors like economic measures to predict the demand for products or services. This entitles the businesses to make more predictive decisions about the inventory management, pricing strategies, and new product launches. AI algorithms, particularly those based on deep learning, can also identify hidden patterns in complex datasets, providing valuable insights that would otherwise be difficult to detect through traditional methods. By using advanced models like neural networks, AI can process large-scale data, identify correlations, and generate forecasts that align more closely with real-world outcomes.

Real-Time Data Processing: The process of real-time data in market analysis is an advantage of AI. Unlike the traditional market research approach, which often depends on delayed data, AI-powered systems can analyze real-time data, which streamlines the activities in social media, customer reviews of customers, and online transactions. This enables businesses to detect emerging trends, identify consumer sentiment, and monitor competitor strategies in real time. To quickly manage the market shifts can significantly enhance a company's competitive advantage, enabling faster product development, marketing adjustments, and customer engagement.

Applications in a Real-Time Scenario

Case Study 1: Social Media Sentiment Analysis for Product Launch Planning

The application of Data Analytics and AI is to analyze and examine the multiple product reviews on social media. Its primary purpose is to discover underlying patterns to assess more accurately certain capabilities and drawbacks of products or services (Chan et al.,2016; Fader & Winer 2012). The utmost interest of a product review is to support a company through AI in identifying and obtaining the characteristics or attributes of the product, know the subjective comments of the user, extract comments and collocations, and distinguish the user's tendency (Singh et al.,2017) so that the company can plan and tailor the production strategy analogously. Extracting the data of market research, customers' requests data, and selection of strategy helps in the new product development. The extraction of information and figuring out the product reviews are based on the data mining techniques of AI. However, since the subject of the product review is the name of the product, the focus of the product review is to extract information around the specific characteristics of the product and the corresponding emotional words (Bruns & Stieglitz 2013).

Case Study 2: AI-Driven Supply Chain Intelligence in Manufacturing

AI can automate reasoning and forecasting for complex, uncertain choices (Baryannis et al.,2019). Elasticity to the supply chain interference required for the intrusive environment and flexibility with response to reconfiguring the physical and intangible resources to deal with the interference (Ralston & Blackhurst, 2020; Dohale et al., 2024) have combined the voting, analytical process of hierarchy, Bayesian network, and machine learning to forecast and recognize the possible success factors which is necessary to achieve the optimal production elasticity. (Belhadi et al., 2022) discussed about the fuzzy logic programming, techniques in machine learning, and agent-based systems employed to develop a decision-making framework that helps industry practitioners to adopt AI efficiently for achieving supply chain resilience.

(Lerch et al.,2022) collected the data from the 237 manufacturing organizations to explain about the adoption of AI in production decision-making would boost the capabilities of resilience in the organisations, where the organisations have already exceeded a specific level of digital readiness to realize the benefits. The recent literature has also shown the positive impact of AI capabilities within SMEs on SC re-engineering, risk management, and the ability to react in an uncertain and dynamic business environment with agility that will enhance cost efficiency (Wong et al.,2022).

The role of AI adoption and digital transformation in the organic food supply chain to enhance supply chain visibility, transparency, and security, which will lead to SC resiliency and sustainable practices, was explored by (Bechtsis et al.,2022). Furthermore, (Dora et al.,2021) showed that digital readiness within organisations, demand volatility, regulatory compliance, customer satisfaction, pressure from continuous innovation from competitors, and information sharing within the SC networks with collaborators are critical success factors that will drive AI adoption in food supply chains which will subsequently improve SC traceability, and reduce food waste, making SC operations both robust and lean.

CHALLENGES AND LIMITATIONS: SECURITY AND PRIVACY CONCERNS

In the era of data-driven technologies, AI devices significantly rely upon large volumes of individual records, the capacity for personal privacy infractions ends up being substantial (Couture et al., 2023).

Figure 2. Customized manufacturing by artificial intelligence

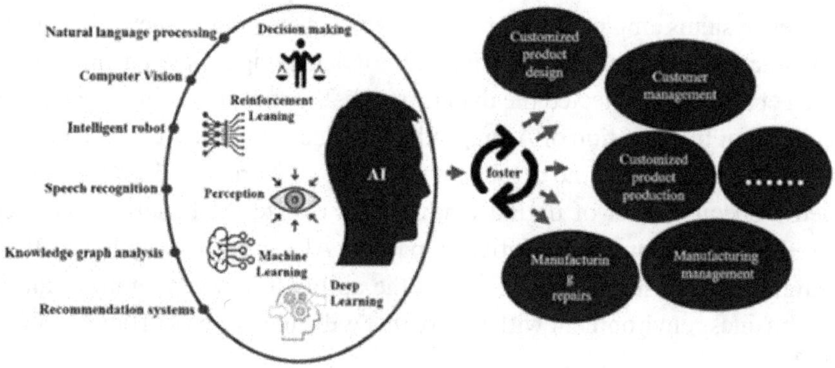

(Shafik, 2025)

Managing the Bias and Fairness in Artificial Intelligence

Predisposition and justness in AI bodies pose considerable obstacles that can easily affect people as well as areas that are overmuch. AI formulas are taught on historical records, and if this information shows prejudices, the AI designs can easily sustain and intensify those predispositions in decision-making procedures (Currie & Hawk, 2021). It will appear in the contrasting domain names, from screening the attributes of formulas, the sex, or even genetic prejudices, to face awareness by showing the errors from overall diverse market teams. The justness worry is twofold: making certain that AI applications in settings certainly do not victimize teams and assuring reasonable results for all individuals (Butterworth, 2018).

Further, these types of risks were analysed by the researchers as being progressively constrained in their capacity to experiment with such algorithms and having a poor comprehension of the implications in real-world settings. Also, the machine learning algorithms bear from the risk to automation bias (where bias occurs in training the data, development of the model, or the algorithm leads to lumping on human judgment), the secondary outcomes from the AI competencies also need to be examined. First, as mentioned, they may be employed to bypass security settings or disable safety systems, which implies a need for controlling sensitive system settings (Couture et al., 2023).

Transparency and Explainability

The lack of transparency highlights the issues regarding the "black box" attribute of AI formulas, where the internal processes are not logical as well as nor explainable. This opacity may lead to a shortage of obligation, particularly in vulnerable requests like health care, money, and unlawful fair treatment (Jobson et al., 2022). Explainability is important for customers and stakeholders to understand the purpose responsible for AI-driven selections, guaranteeing they align with ethical criteria as well as legal needs (Gerlick & Liozu, 2020).

Developing and deploying a process with transparency, in the direction of intellectual property rights and national security concerns, will be paramount to safeguard future deployments and societal trust. Some AI systems specifically focus on employing the administrative agencies in the decision making about an individual's rights, which should be considered as the most required standards of transparency. Finally, AI systems can create harm, they should be liable (Couture et al., 2023).

Ethical AI Decision-Making

This barrier depends on a broadly accepted AI ethical platform, focusing on different points of view, social subtleties, and developing social rules. This entails resolving problems, including focusing on worth, staying clear of damage, and promoting justice (Ford et al., 2023; Jun et al., 2021).

Figure 3. Demystifying artificial intelligence in the medical tourism case study

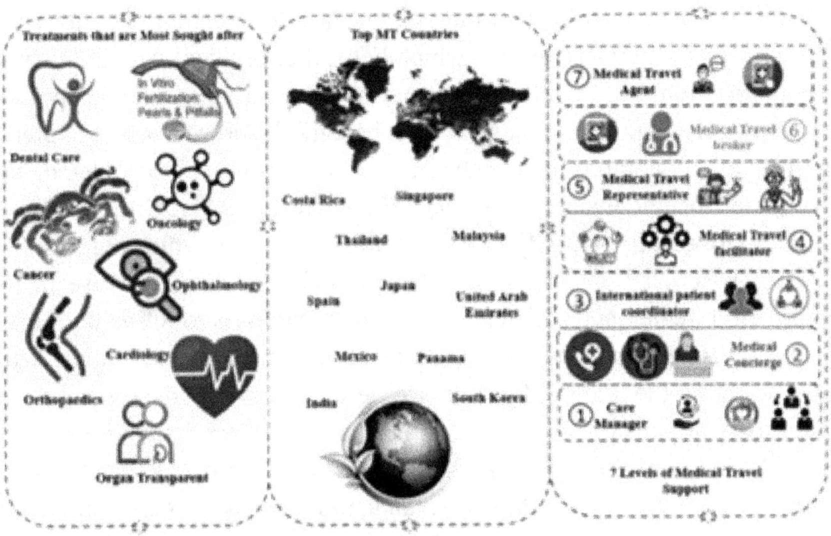

(Shafik, 2025)

Attacking the ideal harmony between advancement and moral points to consider includes combining moral guidelines right into AI protocols, setting up reliable testimonial panels, and nurturing social discourse on AI's reliable ramifications (Butterworth, 2018). The effect of ethical AI decision-making expands past specific requests to form a wider popular understanding of AI as pressure for beneficial modification (Dave et al., 2023; Kalinaki et al., 2023).

STEPS FOR THE STRATEGIC IMPLEMENTATION FRAMEWORK USING AI AND ML IN CI FUNCTIONS

Automation of spotting the anomalies and data analysis: Machine learning algorithms help us to automate the complex data analysis processes like extraction of features, data transformation, and refinement, which leads to supporting the productivity and streamlining their operations in the organization. This automation expedites the data processing cycle, facilitating swifter insights into business processes while diminishing reliance on human labor (Mungoli, 2023). These technologies are outstandingly employed in detecting the anomalies, discovering the untapped patterns, and refining the invaluable insights for enhancing the procedure. Machine learning efficacy methodologies in handling the huge and complex datasets, which are greater than the capabilities of human analysts, enable organizations to recognize relevant trends and manage the data repositories in an effective manner. Automated data analysis algorithms offer real-time surveillance and alerts for anomaly detection, empowering companies to promptly identify fraud or errors and undertake pre-emptive measures (Kilanko, 2022). By screening the diverse data sources, automated systems which support the organization in screening the inefficiencies and restrictions of their operations, which helps them to facilitate in adapting the resource allocation and monitor the operations. Proactive maintenance planning and anticipation of equipment malfunctions become feasible through the predictive capabilities of autonomous data analysis, enabling businesses to reduce downtime and facilitate strategic maintenance scheduling (West & Allen, 2020).

Demand forecasting and dynamic pricing: Machine learning algorithms have tackled the past sales data, organizational apprehension, and diverse factors to forecast the future demand accurately, enabling businesses to refine their resource allocation, inventory management, and strategies for production schedules. Artificial intelligence drives the pricing algorithms to fiercely align with the pricing strategies in response to the shift in the demand of the customer, market situations, and other factors, which optimize the generation of profit in real-time. Demand forecasting powered by machine learning algorithms analyses the past sales data, market shifts, and behavior of the consumer to accurately predict the demand for the future. This enables organizations to streamline their supply chains, boost manufacturing efficiency, and optimize the inventory levels (Sahija, 2021).

By adopting artificial intelligence and machine learning-driven pricing techniques and forecasting the demand, which is always dynamic, an organization can clinch valuable insights into customer demand and boost their strategies of pricing strategies. Accurate demand forecasting, efficient inventory management, and dynamic pricing methods enable businesses to increase sales, optimize profitability, and sustain market leadership (Babatunde,2024)

TECHNOLOGY CONSIDERATIONS IN DECISION MAKING (AI, ML, AND DATA LAKES, ETC.)

Table 1. AI and machine learning integration in data lakes for the financial sector (Kothandapani, 2023)

Feature	Benefits	Demonstration
Predictive Modeling	AI and machine learning are employed to improve the models that forecast the future trends, Consumer behaviors, and market activity based on the past data. This kind of prediction is very important for making decisions in areas like investment plans and credit risk management	With the help of machine learning, financial institutions can forecast stock price movements by examining the previous trading data, economic measures. This model helps the portfolio managers to make data-driven investment decisions.
Assessing Risk	Machine learning algorithms can examine the wide datasets to identify the patterns that prudent the possible risks. It accesses the real-time risk assessment by allowing the organization to respond to the emerging threats more quickly.	AI monitors the transactions in the bank for different patterns that reveal the fraudulent activity. By screening these risks earlier, which helps the bank to prevent fraudulent activities and reduce financial losses.
Data Automation	The processes of data ingestion, cleaning, and preparation within data lakes with the help of AI-driven automation are streamlined. It helps to reduce the manual effort and quickens the overall workflow in data processing.	A company can automate the data cleaning process in its data lake by employing AI to detect and precisely identify the instability in the customer records. It ensures the data used for the analysis is accurate and contemporary, which improves the reliability of the intuition generated.

Security, Governance, and Compliance (John,2025)

A. Access Control and Authentication

Granularity of Access: Data warehouses offer the sturdy, fine-grained access control mechanisms, integrates with an enterprise IAM systems. Data lakes have originated with the tools like Apache Ranger and AWS Lake Formation which enables the comparable security enforcement. Warehouses typically integrate with the SSO, LDAP, or cloud IAMs. Data lakes require more complex configurations which depends on the technology stack.

B. Data Lineage and Auditing

Metadata and Lineage Tracking: Data warehouses have supported the lineage tracking and auditing. In contrast, data lakes depend on the external metadata services like Apache Atlas, Amundsen to ensure about traceability.

C. Compliance with Regulations

HIPAA, GDPR, etc: These frameworks support the regulatory compliance also the implementation in the complexity is differs when compare to others. Warehouses provides unique compliance features, while data lakes request for custom policy implementation. Cloud-native solutions like Azure Purview, Google DLP are helps to bridging this gap in the lake environments.

FUTURE DIRECTIONS: THE RISE OF AUTONOMOUS CI AGENTS

The evolution of autonomous competitive intelligence agents stems from their cognitive capabilities, permits them to understand, analyze, and learn from their environment. This evolution allows them to decide and executes the actions which is fundamentally reshaping the competitive dynamics across diverse industries (Naqvi, 2017). Autonomous competitive intelligence agents are constructed to act independently, prioritizing the responses, and adapting to the dynamic environment. Their proactive and reactive approach enable them to manage the overloaded information, enhancing the business processes and effective strategies within their problem domains (Iyengar, 2006). Intelligent agents are increasingly utilized for competitive intelligence, autonomously managing vast data, reducing user workload, and continuously adapting to environmental changes. Their ability to operate without breaks positions them as essential tools for organizations navigating information overload in today's digital landscape (Desouza, 2001)

Quantum Computing and CI.

Quantum computing can enhance AI and machine learning, potentially improving competitive intelligence through advanced algorithms for optimization, pattern recognition, and data classification, enabling more efficient processing of vast data compared to classical methods. Quantum algorithms is used for optimization, pattern recognition, and data classification. Quantum annealing and optimization techniques for complex decision-making problems (Acampora, 2020). Quantum computing can enhance AI algorithms, potentially impacting various fields, including competitive intelligence, by providing faster data analysis and improved decision-making capabilities through advanced computational techniques (Hadap & Patil, 2024)

Human-AI Collaboration and Augmented Intelligence in Strategic Foresight

Human-AI Collaboration uses the cases that boosts the strategic forethought by enabling the organizations to predict and react to the AI's impact, highlighting the importance of systematically mapping these cases along with the support of value chain analysis (Sudeeptha et al.,2024). Large Pre-trained Models (LPtMs) enhances the Human-AI Teaming, human capabilities augmentation in the strategic anticipation. This collaboration enhances the decision-making processes and problem-solving, also highlights the transformative impact of LPtMs in diverse sectors for the effective and ethical applications (Vats et al.,2024). Human-machine collaboration in the field like cybersecurity, highlights about how augmented intelligence boosts the threat detection. By collaborating the human expertise with machine learning, it enhances the effective decision-making and strategic foresight, particularly in labeling the complex cyber threats through an interactive interfaces and automated analysis (Gore et al.,2023).

CONCLUSION

The integration of AI, big data, and machine learning in the competitive intelligence has reviewed about how organizations collect, process, and utilizing the information. These technologies encourage not only efficient data management but also strategic practices and innovation which enables the businesses to adapt the rapidly switching the digital environments. By intensifying the decision-making, personalizing customer experience, and optimizing the supply chains, AI and ML allowing the firms to secure the sustainable competitive advantages. However, these advancements also present challenges which is related to the privacy, bias, and transparency that should be addressed through the ethical frameworks and robust governance. Future directions like autonomous CI agents, quantum computing, and human-AI collaboration signal which are all the continued evolution of the CI field, which emphasize the need for proactive, adaptable, and ethical foundation strategies in the using data-driven intelligence.

REFERENCES

Acampora, G. (2020, February). Quantum computing meets artificial intelligence. In *AISEM annual conference on sensors and microsystems* (pp. 151-155). Cham: Springer International Publishing.DOI: 10.1007/978-3-030-69551-4_21

Ai, Q., Bai, T., Cao, Z., Chang, Y., Chen, J., Chen, Z., Cheng, Z., Dong, S., Dou, Z., Feng, F., Gao, S., Guo, J., He, X., Lan, Y., Li, C., Liu, Y., Lyu, Z., Ma, W., Ma, J., & Zhu, X. (2023). Information retrieval meets large language models: A strategic report from Chinese IR community. *AI Open*, *4*, 80–90. DOI: 10.1016/j.aiopen.2023.08.001

. Alexander, D. T., & Lyytinen, K. (2017). Organizing successfully for big data to transform organizations.

Amajuoyi, P., Benjamin, L. B., & Adeusi, K. B. (2024). Agile methodologies: Adapting product management to rapidly changing market conditions. *GSC Advanced Research and Reviews*, *19*(2), 249–267. DOI: 10.30574/gscarr.2024.19.2.0181

Arora, A., Sharma, M., & Bhaskaran, S. (2020). Blockchain technology transforms E-commerce for enterprises. In *Data Science and Analytics: 5th International Conference on Recent Developments in Science, Engineering and Technology, REDSET 2019, Gurugram, India, November 15–16, 2019, Revised Selected Papers, Part II 5* (pp. 26-34). Springer Singapore.DOI: 10.1007/978-981-15-5830-6_3

Aschi, M., Bonura, S., Masi, N., Messina, D., & Profeta, D. (2022). Cybersecurity and fraud detection in financial transactions. In *Big data and artificial intelligence in digital finance: Increasing personalization and trust in digital finance using big data and AI* (pp. 269–278). Springer International Publishing., DOI: 10.1007/978-3-030-94590-9_15

Assunção, M. D., Calheiros, R. N., Bianchi, S., Netto, M. A., & Buyya, R. (2015). Big Data computing and clouds: Trends and future directions. *Journal of Parallel and Distributed Computing*, *79*, 3–15. DOI: 10.1016/j.jpdc.2014.08.003

Attaway, M. C. (1999). Competitive intelligence. *Internal auditor, 56*(6), 48-48.

Azeem, M., Haleem, A., Bahl, S., Javaid, M., Suman, R., & Nandan, D. (2022). Big data applications to take up major challenges across manufacturing industries: A brief review. *Materials Today: Proceedings*, *49*, 339–348. DOI: 10.1016/j.matpr.2021.02.147

Babatunde, A. T. (2024). Driving Innovation through AI and Machine Learning: Exploring the Opportunities of Integrating Artificial Intelligence in Business Intelligence. *Academic Journal of Global Who is who in Academia, 5*(1), 1-14.

. Baryannis, G., Dani, S., Validi, S., & Antoniou, G. (2019). Decision support systems and artificial intelligence in supply chain risk management. *Revisiting supply chain risk*, 53-71. DOI: 10.1007/978-3-030-03813-7_4

Baskoro, T. (2024). Digital Disruption: Landscape of E-Business for Competitive Advantage. *Advances in Business & Industrial Marketing Research*, *2*(1), 1–14. DOI: 10.60079/abim.v2i1.218

Bechtsis, D., Tsolakis, N., Iakovou, E., & Vlachos, D. (2022). Data-driven Secure, Resilient and Sustainable Sup-ply Chains: Gaps, Opportunities, and a New Generalized Data Sharing and Data Monetization Framework. *International Journal of Production Research, 60*(14), 4397–4417. DOI: 10.1080/00207543.2021.1957506

Belhadi, A., Kamble, S., Fosso Wamba, S., & Queiroz, M. M. (2022). Building supply-chain resilience: An artificial intelligence-based technique and decision-making framework. *International Journal of Production Research, 60*(14), 4487–4507. DOI: 10.1080/00207543.2021.1950935

Bhardwaj, S., Sharma, N., Goel, M., Sharma, K., & Verma, V. (2024). Enhancing customer targeting in e-commerce and digital marketing through AI-driven personalization strategies. *Advances in Digital Marketing in the Era of Artificial Intelligence*, 41-60. *Machine learning and deep learning paradigms: From techniques to practical applications and research frontiers. Computers, 14*(3), 93. DOI: 10.1201/9781003450443-4

Bruns, A., & Stieglitz, S. (2013). Towards more systematic Twitter analysis: Metrics for tweeting activities. *International Journal of Social Research Methodology, 16*(2), 91–108. DOI: 10.1080/13645579.2012.756095

Butterworth, M. (2018). The ICO and artificial intelligence: The role of fairness in the GDPR framework. *Computer Law & Security Review, 34*(2), 257–268. DOI: 10.1016/j.clsr.2018.01.004

Cekuls, A. (2023). Unveiling the value of competitive intelligence: Coordinated communication and added value. *Journal of Intelligence Studies in Business, 13*(1), 4–5. DOI: 10.37380/jisib.v13i1.987

Chan, H. K., Wang, X., Lacka, E., & Zhang, M. (2016). A mixed-method approach to extracting the value of social media data. *Production and Operations Management, 25*(3), 568–583. DOI: 10.1111/poms.12390

Chattu, V. K. (2021). A review of artificial intelligence, big data, and blockchain technology applications in medicine and global health. *Big Data and Cognitive Computing*, *5*(3), 41. DOI: 10.3390/bdcc5030041

Chen, C. P., & Zhang, C. Y. (2014). Data-intensive applications, challenges, techniques and technologies: A survey on Big Data. *Information Sciences*, *275*, 314–347. DOI: 10.1016/j.ins.2014.01.015

Chen, M., Mao, S., & Liu, Y. (2014). Big data: A survey. *Mobile Networks and Applications*, *19*(2), 171–209. DOI: 10.1007/s11036-013-0489-0

Chirra, B. R. (2021). AI-Driven Security Audits: Enhancing Continuous Compliance through Machine Learning. *International Journal of Machine Learning Research in Cybersecurity and Artificial Intelligence*, *12*(1), 410–433.

Chirra, B. R. (2021). Enhancing Cyber Incident Investigations with AI-Driven Forensic Tools. *International Journal of Advanced Engineering Technologies and Innovations*, *1*(2), 157–177.

Chirra, D. R., & Collaborative, A. I. Blockchain Models for Enhancing Data Privacy in IoMT Networks. (2022). *International Journal of Machine Learning Research in Cybersecurity and Artificial Intelligence*, *13*(1), 482-504.

Columbus, L. (2017). IBM predicts demand for data scientists will soar 28% by 2020. *IBM White Paper*

Couture, V., Roy, M. C., Dez, E., Laperle, S., & Bélisle-Pipon, J. C. (2023). Ethical implications of artificial intelligence in population health and the public's role in its governance: Perspectives from a citizen and expert panel. *Journal of Medical Internet Research*, *25*, e44357. DOI: 10.2196/44357 PMID: 37104026

Currie, G., & Hawk, K. E. (2021, March). Ethical and legal challenges of artificial intelligence in nuclear medicine. In *Seminars in Nuclear Medicine* (Vol. 51, No. 2, pp. 120-125). WB Saunders.DOI: 10.1053/j.semnuclmed.2020.08.001

Dan, S. (2000). Eye on the Competition. *Intelligent Enterprise*.

Dave, M., & Gianey, H. (2016, November). Different clustering algorithms for Big Data analytics: A review. In *2016 International Conference System Modeling & Advancement in Research Trends (SMART)* (pp. 328-333). IEEE.DOI: DOI: 10.1109/SYSMART.2016.7894544

Dave, T., Athaluri, S. A., & Singh, S. (2023). ChatGPT in medicine: An overview of its applications, advantages, limitations, future prospects, and ethical considerations. *Frontiers in Artificial Intelligence*, *6*, 1169595. DOI: 10.3389/frai.2023.1169595 PMID: 37215063

Desouza, K. C. (2001). Intelligent agents for competitive intelligence: Survey of applications. *Competitive Intelligence Review*, *12*(4), 57–63. DOI: 10.1002/cir.1032

Dohale, V., Akarte, M., Gunasekaran, A., & Verma, P. (2024). Exploring the role of artificial intelligence in building production resilience: Learnings from the COVID-19 pandemic. *International Journal of Production Research*, *62*(15), 5472–5488. DOI: 10.1080/00207543.2022.2127961

Dora, M., Kumar, A., Mangla, S. K., Pant, A., & Kamal, M. M. (2021). Critical Success Factors Influencing Artificial Intelligence Adoption in Food Supply Chains. *International Journal of Production Research*, *60*(14), 4621–4640. DOI: 10.1080/00207543.2021.1959665

Dubuc, T., Stahl, F., & Roesch, E. B. (2020). Mapping the big data landscape: Technologies, platforms and paradigms for real-time analytics of data streams. *IEEE Access : Practical Innovations, Open Solutions*, *9*, 15351–15374. DOI: 10.1109/ACCESS.2020.3046132

Ebrahimi, P., Basirat, M., Yousefi, A., Nekmahmud, M., Gholampour, A., & Fekete-Farkas, M. (2022). Social networks marketing and consumer purchase behavior: The combination of SEM and unsupervised machine learning approaches. *Big Data and Cognitive Computing*, *6*(2), 35. DOI: 10.3390/bdcc6020035

Elbasi, E., Zaki, C., Topcu, A. E., Abdelbaki, W., Zreikat, A. I., Cina, E., Shdefat, A., & Saker, L. (2023). Crop prediction model using machine learning algorithms. *Applied Sciences (Basel, Switzerland)*, *13*(16), 9288. DOI: 10.3390/app13169288

Fader, P. S., & Winer, R. S. (2012). Introduction to the special issue on the emergence and impact of user-generated content. *Marketing Science*, *31*(3), 369–371. DOI: 10.1287/mksc.1120.0715

Ford, E., Milne, R., & Curlewis, K. (2023). Ethical issues when using digital biomarkers and artificial intelligence for the early detection of dementia. *Wiley Interdisciplinary Reviews. Data Mining and Knowledge Discovery*, *13*(3), e1492. DOI: 10.1002/widm.1492 PMID: 38439952

Gade, K. R. (2021). Data-driven decision making in a complex world. *Journal of Computational Innovation*, *1*(1).

Galvin, R. H. (1997). Competitive intelligence at Motorola. *Competitive Intelligence Review*, *8*(1), 3–6. DOI: 10.1002/cir.3880080104

Gao, Y., & Liu, H. (2023). Artificial intelligence-enabled personalization in interactive marketing: A customer journey perspective. *Journal of Research in Interactive Marketing*, *17*(5), 663–680. DOI: 10.1108/JRIM-01-2022-0023

Gattiker, A., Gebara, F. H., Hofstee, H. P., Hayes, J. D., & Hylick, A. (2013). Big Data text-oriented benchmark creation for Hadoop. *IBM Journal of Research and Development*, *57*(3/4), 10–11. DOI: 10.1147/JRD.2013.2240732

Gerlick, J. A., & Liozu, S. M. (2020). Ethical and legal considerations of artificial intelligence and algorithmic decision-making in personalized pricing. *Journal of Revenue and Pricing Management*, *19*(2), 85–98. DOI: 10.1057/s41272-019-00225-2

Gheibi, O., Weyns, D., & Quin, F. (2021). Applying machine learning in self-adaptive systems: A systematic literature review. [TAAS]. *ACM Transactions on Autonomous and Adaptive Systems*, *15*(3), 1–37. DOI: 10.1145/3469440

Gore, S., Hamsa, S., Roychowdhury, S., Patil, G., Gore, S., & Karmode, S. (2023, August). Augmented Intelligence in Machine Learning for Cybersecurity: Enhancing Threat Detection and Human-Machine Collaboration. In *2023 Second International Conference on Augmented Intelligence and Sustainable Systems (ICAISS)* (pp. 638-644). IEEE.DOI: 10.1109/ICAISS58487.2023.10250514

Goriparthi, R. G. (2021). AI-Driven Natural Language Processing for Multilingual Text Summarization and Translation. *Revista de Inteligencia Artificial en Medicina*, *12*(1), 513–535.

Goriparthi, R. G. (2022). AI-Powered Decision Support Systems for Precision Agriculture: A Machine Learning Perspective. *International Journal of Advanced Engineering Technologies and Innovations*, *1*(3), 345–365.

Gullberg, A. (1991). Den samhälleliga självreflexionens möjligheter: Big data på 1980-talet. https://urn.kb.se/resolve?urn=urn:nbn:se:kth:diva-149318

. Hadap, S., & Patil, M. (2024). Quantum computing in artificial intelligence: A paradigm shift. *Int. J. Adv. Res. Sci. Commun. Technol*, 530-534.

. Hartmann, P., Zaki, M., Feldmann, N., & Neely, A. (2014). Big data for big business? A taxonomy of data-driven business models used by start-up firms. https://doi.org/DOI: 0.1108/IJOPM-02-2014-0098

Hashem, I. A. T., Yaqoob, I., Anuar, N. B., Mokhtar, S., Gani, A., & Khan, S. U. (2015). The rise of "big data" on cloud computing: Review and open research issues. *Information Systems*, *47*, 98–115. DOI: 10.1016/j.is.2014.07.006

Hirsch, D. D. (2013). The glass house effect: Big Data, the new oil, and the power of analogy. *Me. L. Rev.*, *66*, 373.

Iyengar, J. (2006). Intelligent software agents and the creation of competitive advantage. In *Competition Forum* (Vol. 4, No. 1, p. 66). American Society for Competitiveness.

Jack, H. (2024). Leveraging AI and Data Analytics: Revolutionizing Competitive Intelligence for Market Insights.DOI: 10.13140/RG.2.2.25148.76166

Jain, G., Kumar, A., & Bhat, S. A. (2024). Recent developments of game theory and reinforcement learning approaches: A systematic review. *IEEE Access : Practical Innovations, Open Solutions*, *12*, 9999–10011. DOI: 10.1109/ACCESS.2024.3352749

Jáñez-Martino, F., Alaiz-Rodríguez, R., González-Castro, V., Fidalgo, E., & Alegre, E. (2023). A review of spam email detection: Analysis of spammer strategies and the dataset shift problem. *Artificial Intelligence Review*, *56*(2), 1145–1173. DOI: 10.1007/s10462-022-10195-4

Jobson, D., Mar, V., & Freckelton, I. (2022). Legal and ethical considerations of artificial intelligence in skin cancer diagnosis. *The Australasian Journal of Dermatology*, *63*(1), e1–e5. DOI: 10.1111/ajd.13690 PMID: 34407234

John, B. (2025). *Comparative Analysis of Data Lakes and Data Warehouses for Machine Learning Workflows: Architecture*. Performance, and Scalability Considerations.

Jun, Y., Craig, A., Shafik, W., & Sharif, L. (2021). Artificial intelligence application in cybersecurity and cyberdefense. *Wireless Communications and Mobile Computing*, *2021*(1), 3329581. DOI: 10.1155/2021/3329581

Kabudi, T., Pappas, I., & Olsen, D. H. (2021). AI-enabled adaptive learning systems: A systematic mapping of the literature. *Computers and education. Artificial Intelligence*, *2*, 100017. DOI: 10.1016/j.caeai.2021.100017

Kalinaki, K., Fahadi, M., Alli, A. A., Shafik, W., Yasin, M., & Mutwalibi, N. (2023). Artificial intelligence of internet of medical things (AIoMT) in smart cities: a review of cybersecurity for smart healthcare. *Handbook of security and privacy of ai-enabled healthcare systems and internet of medical things*, 271-292.https://doi .org/DOI: 10.1201/9781003370321-11

Kilanko, V. (2022). Turning Point: Policymaking in the Era of Artificial Intelligence, by Darrell M. West and John R. Allen, Washington, DC: Brookings Institution Press, 2020, 297 pp., hardcover 24.99, paperback 19.99. DOI: 10.1002/pam.22374

Kiran, M., Murphy, P., Monga, I., Dugan, J., & Baveja, S. S. (2015, October). Lambda architecture for cost-effective batch and speed big data processing. In *2015 IEEE International Conference on Big Data (Big Data)* (pp. 2785-2792). IEEE.DOI: 10.1109/BigData.2015.7364082

Kothandapani, H. P. (2023). Emerging trends and technological advancements in data lakes for the financial sector: An in-depth analysis of data processing, analytics, and infrastructure innovations. *Quarterly Journal of Emerging Technologies and Innovations*, *8*(2), 62–75.

Lenin, J., Komathi, A., Vijayan, H., Rathinam, A. R., Kasthuri, A., & Srinivasan, C. (2023, December). Revolutionizing Healthcare With Cloud Computing: The Impact of Clinical Decision Support Algorithm. In *2023 International Conference on Artificial Intelligence for Innovations in Healthcare Industries (ICAIIHI)* (Vol. 1, pp. 1-6). IEEE. DOI: 10.1109/ICAIIHI57871.2023.10489022

Lerch, C. M., Heimberger, H., Jäger, A., Horvat, D., & Schultmann, F. (2022). AI-readiness and Production Resilience: Empirical Evidence from German Manufacturing in Timesof the Covid-19 Pandemic. *International Journal of Production Research*, •••, 1–22. DOI: 10.1080/00207543.2022.2141906

Li, G. J., & Cheng, X. Q. (2012). Research status and scientific thinking of big data. *Bulletin of Chinese Academy of Sciences*, *27*(6), 647–657.

Li, Z., Ji, Q., Ling, X., & Liu, Q. (2025). A Comprehensive Review of Multi-Agent Reinforcement Learning in Video Games. *Authorea Preprints*.DOI: 10.36227/techrxiv.173603149.94954703/v1

Lohr, S. (2012). Big data's impact on the world. *The New York Times, 11*(1), 1.

Maddireddy, B. R., & Maddireddy, B. R. (2020). AI and Big Data: Synergizing to Create Robust Cybersecurity Ecosystems for Future Networks. *International Journal of Advanced Engineering Technologies and Innovations*, *1*(2), 40–63.

Maddireddy, B. R., & Maddireddy, B. R. (2020). Proactive Cyber Defense: Utilizing AI for Early Threat Detection and Risk Assessment. *International Journal of Advanced Engineering Technologies and Innovations*, *1*(2), 64–83.

Maddireddy, B. R., & Maddireddy, B. R. (2021). Cyber security Threat Landscape: Predictive Modelling Using Advanced AI Algorithms. *Revista Española de Documentación Científica*, *15*(4), 126–153.

Maddireddy, B. R., & Maddireddy, B. R. (2022). AI-Based Phishing Detection Techniques: A Comparative Analysis of Model Performance. *Unique Endeavor in Business & Social Sciences, 1*(2), 63–77.

Maddireddy, B. R., & Maddireddy, B. R. (2022). Blockchain and AI Integration: A Novel Approach to Strengthening Cybersecurity Frameworks. *Unique Endeavor in Business & Social Sciences, 1*(2), 27–46.

Maddireddy, B. R., & Maddireddy, B. R. (2022). Real-Time Data Analytics with AI: Improving Security Event Monitoring and Management. *Unique Endeavor in Business & Social Sciences, 1*(2), 47–62.

Mamat, N., Othman, M. F., Abdulghafor, R., Alwan, A. A., & Gulzar, Y. (2023). Abdulgha for, R., Alwan, A. A., & Gulzar, Y. (2023). *Enhancing Image Annotation Technique of Fruit Classification Using a Deep Learning Approach. Sustainability (Basel), 15*(2), 901. DOI: 10.3390/su15020901

Mashey, J. R. (1999). Big data and the next wave of {InfraStress} problems, solutions, opportunities. In *1999 USENIX annual technical conference (USENIX ATC 99).*

Maynard, A. D. (2015). Navigating the fourth industrial revolution. *Nature Nanotechnology, 10*(12), 1005–1006. DOI: 10.1038/nnano.2015.286 PMID: 26632281

. McGonagle, J. J. (2007). An examination of the classic CI model. *Journal of competitive intelligence and management, 4*(2), 71-86.

McGonagle, J. J., & Misner-Elias, M. (2016). The changing landscape of competitive intelligence: Two critical issues investigated. *Salus Journal, 4*(1), 13–24.

Morales, E. F., & Escalante, H. J. (2022). A brief introduction to supervised, unsupervised, and reinforcement learning. In *Biosignal processing and classification using computational learning and intelligence* (pp. 111–129). Academic Press., DOI: 10.1016/B978-0-12-820125-1.00017-8

Muller, M. L. (2008). How and what others are doing in competitive intelligence: The Motorola case study. *South African Journal of Information Management, 10*(4). Advance online publication. DOI: 10.4102/sajim.v10i4.333

Mungoli, N. (2023). Adaptive ensemble learning: Boosting model performance through intelligent feature fusion in deep neural networks. *arXiv preprint arXiv:2304. 02653.https://doi.org//arXiv.2304.02653*DOI: 10.48550

Naqvi, A. (2017). Competitive dynamics of artificial intelligence economy: The Wicked Problem of cognitive competition. *Journal of Economics Library, 4*(2), 187–193. DOI: 10.1453/jel.v4i2.1319

Nerbel, J. F., & Kreutzer, M. (2023). Digital platform ecosystems in flux: From proprietary digital platforms to wide-spanning ecosystems. *Electronic Markets, 33*(1), 6. DOI: 10.1007/s12525-023-00625-8

Nikolaos, T., & Evangelia, F. (2012). Competitive intelligence: Concept, context and a case of its application. *Science Journal of Business Management, 2*(15), 1–15. DOI: 10.7237/sjbm/261

Ntakolia, C., Kokkotis, C., Karlsson, P., & Moustakidis, S. (2021). An explainable machine learning model for material backorder prediction in inventory management. *Sensors (Basel), 21*(23), 7926. DOI: 10.3390/s21237926 PMID: 34883930

Parmar, V., & Yadav, J. (2017). Big Data: Meaning, Challenges, Opportunities, Tools. *International Journal of Advanced Research in Computer Science, 8*(1).

Pasupuleti, V., Thuraka, B., Kodete, C. S., & Malisetty, S. (2024). Enhancing supply chain agility and sustainability through machine learning: Optimization techniques for logistics and inventory management. *Logistics (Basel), 8*(3), 73. DOI: 10.3390/logistics8030073

. Pepper, R., & Garrity, J. (2014). The internet of everything: How the network unleashes the benefits of big data. *Global Information Technology Report 2014*.

Pichiyan, V., Muthulingam, S., Nalajala, S. Ch. A., & Das, M. N. (2023). Web scraping using natural language processing: Exploiting unstructured text for data extraction and analysis. *Procedia Computer Science, 230*, 193–202. DOI: 10.1016/j.procs.2023.12.074

. Porter, E. M. (1998). Competitive strategy: Techniques for analyzing industries and competitors.

Raj, N. S., & Renumol, V. G. (2022). A systematic literature review on adaptive content recommenders in personalized learning environments from 2015 to 2020. *Journal of Computers in Education, 9*(1), 113–148. DOI: 10.1007/s40692-021-00199-4

Ralston, P., & Blackhurst, J. (2020). Industry 4.0 and Resilience in the Supply Chain: A Driver of Capability Enhancement or Capability Loss? *International Journal of Production Research, 58*(16), 5006–5019. DOI: 10.1080/00207543.2020.1736724

Raman, R., Dhivya, K., Sapra, P., Gurpur, S., Maniraj, S. P., & Murugan, S. (2023, December). IoT-driven Smart Packaging for Pharmaceuticals: Ensuring Product Integrity and Patient Safety. In *2023 International Conference on Artificial Intelligence for Innovations in Healthcare Industries (ICAIIHI)* (Vol. 1, pp. 1-6). IEEE. DOI: 10.1109/ICAIIHI57871.2023.10489420

Ridzuan, N. N., Masri, M., Anshari, M., Fitriyani, N. L., & Syafrudin, M. (2024). AI in the financial sector: The line between innovation, regulation and ethical responsibility. *Information (Basel), 15*(8), 432. DOI: 10.3390/info15080432

Sahija, D. (2021). *Critical review of machine learning integration with augmented reality for discrete manufacturing*. Independent Researcher and Enterprise Solution Manager in Leading Digital Transformation Agency., DOI: 10.2015/IJIRMF.2455.0620/202112017

Sarker, I. H. (2021). Machine learning: Algorithms, real-world applications and research directions. *SN Computer Science, 2*(3), 160. DOI: 10.1007/s42979-021-00592-x PMID: 33778771

Sarker, I. H. (2022). AI-based modeling: Techniques, applications and research issues towards automation, intelligent and smart systems. *SN Computer Science, 3*(2), 158. DOI: 10.1007/s42979-022-01043-x PMID: 35194580

. Shafik, W. (2025). Ethical and legal considerations in artificial intelligence. *AI-Enabled Threat Intelligence and Cyber Risk Assessment*, 90.

. Sieben, K. C. (2016). Labor markets in 2040: big data could be a big deal for jobseekers. *Monthly Labor Review*.

Singh, J. P., Irani, S., Rana, N. P., Dwivedi, Y. K., Saumya, S., & Roy, P. K. (2017). Predicting the "helpfulness" of online consumer reviews. *Journal of Business Research, 70*, 346–355. DOI: 10.1016/j.jbusres.2016.08.008

Ślusarczyk, B. (2018). Industry 4.0: Are we ready? *Polish Journal of Management Studies, 17*(1), 232–248. Advance online publication. DOI: 10.17512/pjms.2018.17.1.19

. Sriram, G. K., Malini, A., & Santhosh, K. M. R. (2024). State of the art of artificial intelligence approaches toward driverless technology. *Artificial Intelligence for Autonomous Vehicles*, 55-74. DOI: 10.1002/9781119847656.ch3

Strielkowski, W., Grebennikova, V., Lisovskiy, A., Rakhimova, G., & Vasileva, T. (2024). AI-driven adaptive learning for sustainable educational transformation. *Sustainable Development (Bradford)*. Advance online publication. DOI: 10.1002/sd.3221

Sudeeptha, I., Müller, W., Leyer, M., Richter, A., & Nolte, F. (2024). Use Cases for Prospective Sensemaking of Human-AI-Collaboration. *arXiv preprint arXiv:2408.10812*. https://doi.org//arXiv.2408.10812DOI: 10.48550

Torre, I. G., Romero, M., & Álvarez, A. (2021). Improving aphasic speech recognition by using novel semi-supervised learning methods on aphasiabank for english and spanish. *Applied Sciences (Basel, Switzerland), 11*(19), 8872. DOI: 10.3390/app11198872

Trentin, C., Ampatzidis, Y., Lacerda, C., & Shiratsuchi, L. (2024). Tree crop yield estimation and prediction using remote sensing and machine learning: A systematic review. *Smart Agricultural Technology, 100556*, 100556. Advance online publication. DOI: 10.1016/j.atech.2024.100556

Vats, V., Nizam, M. B., Liu, M., Wang, Z., Ho, R., Prasad, M. S., . . . Davis, J. (2024). A survey on human-ai teaming with large pre-trained models. *arXiv preprint arXiv:2403.04931*. https://doi.org//arXiv.2403.04931DOI: 10.48550

Verma, K. K., Singh, B. M., & Dixit, A. (2022). A review of supervised and unsupervised machine learning techniques for suspicious behavior recognition in the intelligent surveillance system. *International Journal of Information Technology : an Official Journal of Bharati Vidyapeeth's Institute of Computer Applications and Management, 14*(1), 397–410. DOI: 10.1007/s41870-019-00364-0

Vijayaragavan, P., Ponnusamy, R., & Aramudhan, M. (2020). An optimal support vector machine-based classification model for sentimental analysis of online product reviews. *Future Generation Computer Systems, 111*, 234–240. DOI: 10.1016/j.future.2020.04.046

Wesselhöft, M., Hinckeldeyn, J., & Kreutzfeldt, J. (2022). Controlling fleets of autonomous mobile robots with reinforcement learning: A brief survey. *Robotics (Basel, Switzerland), 11*(5), 85. DOI: 10.3390/robotics11050085

West, D. M., & Allen, J. R. (2020). *Turning point: Policymaking in the era of artificial intelligence*. Brookings Institution Press. DOI: 10.5040/9780815751113

Westerman, G., Bonnet, D., & McAfee, A. (2014). *Leading digital: Turning technology into business transformation*. Harvard Business Press.

. Wingerath, W., Gessert, F., Friedrich, S., & Ritter, N. (2016). Real-time stream processing for Big Data. *it-Information Technology, 58*(4), 186-194.DOI: 10.1515/itit-2016-0002

Wong, L. W., Tan, G. W. H., Ooi, K. B., Lin, B., & Dwivedi, Y. K. (2022). Artificial Intelligence-Driven Risk Management for Enhancing Supply Chain Agility: A Deep-Learning-Based Dual-Stage PLS-SEM-ANN Analysis. *International Journal of Production Research*, •••, 1–21. DOI: 10.1080/00207543.2022.2063089

Yu, S., Liu, Z., Xiong, C., & Liu, Z. (2023, July). Openmatch-v2: An all-in-one multi-modality plm-based information retrieval toolkit. In *Proceedings of the 46th International ACM SIGIR Conference on Research and Development in Information Retrieval* (pp. 3160-3164). DOI: 10.1145/3539618.3591813

Zhang, X., & Zhu, G. Y. (2024). A literature review of reinforcement learning methods applied to job-shop scheduling problems. *Computers & Operations Research, 106929*. Advance online publication. DOI: 10.1016/j.cor.2024.106929

Zheng, Z., Wang, P., Liu, J., & Sun, S. (2015). Real-time big data processing framework: Challenges and solutions. *Applied Mathematics & Information Sciences, 9*(6), 3169. DOI: 10.12785/amis/090646

KEY TERMS AND DEFINITIONS

Artificial Intelligence: Artificial Intelligence is the ability of a computer or machine to perform tasks that require human intelligence, like learning, reasoning, problem-solving, and perception view of analysis. It aims to replicate the human intelligence processes in machines, particularly in computer systems, while performing the task.

Big Data: Big data is defined as the vast and complex collections of structured, unstructured, and semi-structured data that are too large and it is very critical to process the in traditional systems to handle.

Competitive Intelligence: Competitive intelligence is defined as the process of data gathering, analyzing, and employing the data about the competitors, market trends, and external factors in order to strengthen their strategic advantage. It helps the businesses to understand more about their competitive landscape, expected market shifts, and make informed decisions to develop their market position.

Machine Learning: Machine learning is one of the subsets of artificial intelligence that focuses on enabling computers to learn from data without being explicitly programmed. It creates the algorithms to analyze the patterns in data and generate the models for specific tasks, which allows them for predictions and deliver intelligent behavior.

Natural Language Processing: Natural Language Processing is one of the subsets of artificial intelligence that empower computers to understand, interpret, and generate language like humans. Its focus is on making computers which is capable of communicating with human beings in their natural language, whether it's spoken or written.

Predictive Analytics: Predictive analytics is defined as the process of analyzing data to predict future outcomes. It utilizes data analysis, machine learning, artificial intelligence, and statistical models to find patterns that might predict future behavior.

Chapter 11
Digital Marketing and Globalization

Ricardo Marcão
http://orcid.org/0000-0003-3277-3078
ISLA Santarém, Portugal & NECE, University of Beira Interior, Portugal

Vasco Santos
ISLA Santarém, Portugal

Rúben Pinhal
http://orcid.org/0000-0002-0956-6698
University of Aveiro, Portugal

ABSTRACT

This article examines the growing influence of digital marketing in a global-ized economy, highlighting how technology and sociocultural changes have reshaped traditional marketing. With widespread internet access and digital platforms, businesses engage consumers through real-time, personalized, and socially driven interactions. The study explores the evolution of digital strategies, their role in customer loyalty, and their impact on traditional re-tail. Drawing from academic literature and market trends, it shows how digi-tal marketing supports global reach via precise segmentation, cultural adap-tation, and analytics. It also addresses glo-balization's challenges, such as competition and ethical concerns, offering insights for brands aiming to stay relevant.

DOI: 10.4018/979-8-3373-5233-6.ch011

INTRODUCTION

The 21st century has ushered in a dramatic transformation in how organizations communicate, operate, and compete. At the heart of this transformation is the digital revolution, a multifaceted phenomenon driven by rapid advancements in information and communication technologies. This digital revolution has redefined business practices across sectors, none more profoundly than marketing. As globalization breaks down geographical and cultural barriers, the strategic role of marketing has expanded from promoting goods and services to facilitating real-time interactions, cultivating relationships, and delivering value through personalized and data-driven experiences. In this context, digital marketing emerges as a contemporary necessity and a strategic asset for navigating and thriving in a hyper-connected, competitive global marketplace.

Traditionally, marketing has been defined by the American Marketing Association (2009) as a set of activities aimed at creating, communicating, delivering, and exchanging offerings that have value for customers, clients, partners, and society. These offerings were typically disseminated in earlier decades through mass media, television, radio, newspapers, and billboards. However, these channels offered limited interactivity and personalization. Communication was unidirectional: brands spoke, and consumers listened. This static model has since been dismantled by digital media, empowering consumers to participate actively in the marketing conversation. Marketing is no longer about merely reaching audiences but engaging them, understanding their behaviors, and co-creating meaningful experiences.

The shift from traditional to digital marketing coincided with broader economic and cultural changes brought on by globalization. Companies no longer operate within fixed local markets; instead, they compete internationally, addressing culturally diverse, geographically dispersed, and technologically savvy consumer bases. Globalization has accelerated the integration of economies and markets, allowing businesses to scale operations and access customers across borders. Digital technologies, in parallel, have made it possible to reach these customers efficiently and affordably. The convergence of globalization and digitalization has thus created an ecosystem where digital marketing becomes essential for brand survival and growth.

One of the defining characteristics of this new marketing paradigm is interactivity. Unlike traditional advertising, digital marketing enables two-way communication between brands and consumers. Social media platforms, in particular, have become arenas for real-time interaction, reputation management, and consumer feedback. Companies can respond to queries, address complaints, and gather insights instantaneously. These capabilities enhance customer satisfaction and loyalty, particularly when accompanied by personalized and contextually relevant messaging.

Moreover, digital marketing supports advanced segmentation and targeting strategies. Through tools such as Google Analytics, Meta Business Suite, and CRM systems, marketers can analyze customer data to develop tailored campaigns that speak directly to user needs and preferences. This precision enhances conversion rates and fosters deeper emotional connections between brands and consumers. As Behera et al. (2020) assert, personalization in digital marketing leads to increased engagement and loyalty by making consumers feel recognized and valued.

The increasing prevalence of mobile devices and social networks has further expanded the reach and relevance of digital marketing. Platforms such as Instagram, TikTok, and YouTube have redefined content consumption patterns, especially among younger demographics. These platforms emphasize visual storytelling, short-form content, and user-generated interactions, allowing marketers to experiment creatively and engage organically. The rise of influencer marketing, which leverages individuals' social capital to promote brands, has added another dimension to digital strategy. Through their perceived authenticity and relatability, influencers serve as intermediaries between companies and consumers, facilitating trust and community-building (Vieira, 2024; Pereira Jr. & Porto, 2021).

Despite its promise, digital marketing also introduces significant challenges. In a saturated digital environment, brands must compete not only with direct competitors but also with the constant influx of content that floods users' feeds and attention spans. The challenge is to stand out, not through volume, but through value. Brands must create relevant, ethical, and engaging content that resonates with the lived experiences of diverse audiences. As Santos (2021) highlighted, contemporary consumers are increasingly socially conscious, placing value on transparency, corporate responsibility, and authenticity.

Another crucial challenge lies in the ethical and regulatory implications of data use. Digital marketing thrives on demographic, behavioral, psychographic, and transactional data. However, its collection and usage must comply with privacy laws such as the General Data Protection Regulation (GDPR) and the California Consumer Privacy Act (CCPA). Consumers today demand not only personalization but also data security and transparency. Companies must find the right balance between relevance and respect, ensuring that personalization does not become an intrusion.

Furthermore, digital marketing is intrinsically linked to the crisis of traditional retail. As e-commerce platforms provide convenience, choice, and price transparency, brick-and-mortar businesses must reinvent themselves. The integration of proximity marketing technologies, such as geo-fencing and beacon systems, enables physical stores to digitize in-store experiences, offer real-time promotions, and collect behavioral insights, creating a hybrid retail environment that bridges the online and offline divide (Giridhararajan et al., 2020).

Given these developments, the strategic imperative for businesses is to adopt a holistic and agile approach to digital marketing. This means not merely adopting new technologies, but cultivating a consumer-centric culture grounded in empathy, responsiveness, and innovation. It also entails understanding cultural variability, how consumers in different regions perceive value, respond to messaging, and interact with brands. As Sousa (2025) and Laice (2024) note, global marketing success depends not on uniformity but on adaptive communication that respects local norms and identities.

In summary, this article examines digital marketing as both a product and an enabler of globalization. It seeks to answer critical questions: How has digital marketing evolved in response to global pressures? What are the mechanisms through which digital marketing fosters customer loyalty and engagement across borders? What strategies can businesses adopt to align technological capability with consumer expectations ethically and culturally sensitively? By addressing these questions, the study aims to contribute to the theoretical understanding and practical application of digital marketing strategies in a rapidly evolving global economy.

1 RESEARCH BACKGROUND

The evolution of marketing from a product-centric function to a consumer-oriented and technology-integrated discipline mirrors the broader socioeconomic shifts of the past century. Initially conceptualized as a mechanism for facilitating the exchange of goods and services, marketing has historically served to bridge the gap between producers and consumers through structured and linear communication processes. As articulated by the American Marketing Association (2009), early definitions of marketing emphasized its transactional nature, focusing on the movement of products from production to consumption. This traditional view aligned with the industrial era's focus on mass production, distribution, and standardization, where marketing campaigns were essentially unidirectional and non-interactive, broadcast through media such as newspapers, radio, and television.

However, with the dawn of the digital era in the late 20th century, marketing began to undergo a profound transformation. The rise of the internet, followed by mobile technologies, social networks, and data analytics, created new opportunities for two-way communication, audience segmentation, and personalization. The term "digital marketing" emerged during the 1990s, marking the initial phase in which businesses began leveraging online tools such as email campaigns, banner advertisements, and early e-commerce platforms to reach consumers directly (Fierro et al., 2017). This shift coincided with increased consumer access to information, and gradually, the balance of power began to tilt from the marketer to the consumer.

This transformation is marked by a change in medium and a paradigmatic shift in the underlying logic of marketing itself. Traditional marketing followed a push strategy, where messages were distributed broadly to influence consumer attitudes and behaviors. In contrast, digital marketing follows a pull logic, where the objective is to attract, engage, and convert consumers through relevance, interaction, and value-added content (Kannan & Li, 2017). This transformation reflects a broader societal movement toward decentralization, democratization of information, and user empowerment. Consumers are no longer passive targets but active participants in the marketing process.

The academic literature has recognized this shift. Kannan and Li (2017) define digital marketing as "an adaptive, technology-enabled process" that allows businesses to co-create value with customers and partners. This definition departs from earlier frameworks by emphasizing adaptability, collaboration, and technological integration. It also introduces the notion that marketing is no longer confined to a single department but is an organization-wide capability that involves IT, customer service, operations, and strategic management.

Social media has played a central role in this evolution. Platforms such as Facebook, Twitter, Instagram, LinkedIn, TikTok, and YouTube have become vital components of marketing strategy, offering businesses direct access to millions of users across the globe. According to Saura, Palos-Sanchez, and Herráez (2020), these platforms enable real-time, bidirectional communication, allowing brands to interact with consumers, solicit feedback, and adjust campaigns based on audience sentiment. This interactivity fosters higher trust, engagement, and loyalty than traditional advertising. Moreover, the data generated through social media, likes, shares, comments, and views provides valuable insights into consumer preferences and behavior.

One significant offshoot of social media is influencer marketing, which leverages the credibility and reach of individuals with established followings to promote products or services. Influencers operate at various scales, from global celebrities to micro-influencers with niche audiences. Pereira Jr. and Porto (2021) note that influencer marketing is effective because it is perceived as more authentic than corporate advertising. Influencers build trust over time through consistent content, personal storytelling, and engagement, creating an emotional connection with their audience. As Vieira (2024) emphasizes, this perceived authenticity is central to the success of influencer campaigns, particularly among younger consumers who are skeptical of traditional advertising.

The rise of personalization is another hallmark of digital marketing. Unlike mass marketing, which assumes homogeneity, digital marketing is predicated on differentiation. Collecting, analyzing, and acting on consumer data allows for tailored messaging, offers, and experiences. Behera et al. (2020) argue that personalization enhances relevance and fosters loyalty by making consumers feel seen and understood. Examples include personalized email campaigns, dynamic website content, product recommendations, and retargeting ads. Tools such as Customer Relationship Management (CRM) systems, marketing automation platforms, and AI-powered analytics engines facilitate this level of customization by integrating data from multiple touchpoints to form a unified customer profile.

The convergence of digital marketing and globalization has added new layers of complexity and opportunity. Ramos et al. (2024) describe that the intensification of cross-border goods, services, capital, and cultural flows characterizes globalization. This process has expanded the potential reach of businesses and introduced challenges related to cultural sensitivity, market segmentation, and regulatory compliance. Marketing strategies that succeed in one country may falter in another due to differences in language, values, media consumption habits, and social norms. As such, digital marketing in a global context demands a delicate balance between standardization. maintaining a coherent brand identity, and localization, adapting content to local cultures.

Silva (2024) asserts that effective market segmentation in the digital age goes beyond basic demographics. It involves psychographic, behavioral, and contextual factors that provide deeper insights into consumer motivations, needs, and values. Advanced segmentation strategies use data analytics to group consumers into meaningful clusters, enabling businesses to craft content that speaks directly to each segment. This approach is critical in global markets where consumer behavior varies significantly by region.

Similarly, brand positioning in international markets requires cultural adaptation. Correia et al. (2025) stress that global brands must communicate value propositions that align with local cultural codes. This might involve adjusting tone, color schemes, humor, or symbols to avoid misinterpretation. Abreu (2024) adds that companies must manage their global digital presence across multiple platforms, ensuring that core messages remain consistent while being sensitive to regional variations.

Technological tools have become indispensable for managing these complexities. AI, machine learning, and big data analytics allow businesses to forecast trends, identify opportunities, and optimize campaigns in real time. Zanon (2024) explains that these technologies enable predictive analytics to anticipate customer behavior based on historical data and contextual cues. For instance, AI algorithms can determine the best time to send an email, the optimal channel for a message, or the likelihood of a customer making a purchase.

One of the most significant disruptions driven by digital marketing has been the decline of traditional retail. The rise of e-commerce platforms like Amazon, Alibaba, and Shopify has fundamentally altered the retail landscape, shifting consumer expectations toward convenience, choice, and speed. Brick-and-mortar stores have struggled to compete, leading many to either close or pivot toward hybrid models. Giridhararajan et al. (2020) propose that digital tools such as location-based marketing, augmented reality, and interactive displays can help revitalize physical stores by creating immersive and personalized experiences. These innovations blur the boundaries between the digital and physical, allowing retailers to integrate online and offline channels seamlessly.

The COVID-19 pandemic further accelerated the digitization of marketing. Lockdowns and social distancing measures forced many businesses to move operations online, making digital marketing the primary means of reaching customers. This period highlighted the importance of agility, as companies had to adapt quickly to changing consumer behaviors, supply chain disruptions, and market uncertainties. As Campos et al. (2021) observed, firms already invested in digital infrastructure were better positioned to respond to the crisis and sustain market presence.

An additional dimension in the evolution of digital marketing is the growing importance of platform-centric ecosystems. Technology conglomerates such as Google, Meta, Amazon, TikTok, and Tencent have created environments where businesses operate, advertise, and analyze user behavior using the platform's tools and algorithms. These ecosystems centralize access to audiences and user data, often shaping the entire strategic framework of brand communication. Francato et al. (2024) argue that understanding these ecosystems is essential for visibility and reach, given that algorithms now determine whether content is shown, when, and to whom.

Cultural adaptation in digital marketing has also gained strategic importance. Laice (2024) highlights that adapting visual identity, tone, and language to local semiotics is critical to avoid brand misalignment or cultural offense. For example, a color or gesture with positive connotations in one culture may be offensive in another. Marketers must go beyond linguistic translation to ensure emotional and symbolic resonance in each region.

Behavioral analytics now includes decision psychology, behavioral economics, and neuromarketing to study how consumers respond to different stimuli online. Techniques like A/B testing, heat mapping, and eye-tracking help optimize content layout, CTA design, and message framing (Pinto, 2023). This scientific approach has elevated marketing into an evidence-driven field where hypotheses are continually tested and refined.

Content marketing has also matured, with SEO, storytelling, and user-generated content (UGC) forming its backbone. Oliveira et al. (2024) state that valuable content that educates or entertains builds authority and engagement, especially when algorithmically discoverable. Personalization, meanwhile, has been advanced through machine learning models that segment audiences by sentiment, behavior, and engagement level in real-time (Caravantes & Weiler, 2024).

AI has become a cornerstone, enabling intelligent recommendation engines, dynamic pricing, sentiment analysis, and predictive lead scoring. Coutinho (2021) highlights AI's growing role in real-time decision-making and automated communication, including chatbots and adaptive landing pages.

Lifecycle email automation and CRM integration allow businesses to track and nurture leads from awareness to advocacy (Pimenta, 2025). Meanwhile, social commerce, selling directly through social platforms, shortens purchase journeys and boosts conversion through impulse marketing and influencer integration (Costa, 2025).

Voice search optimization, privacy ethics (Teixeira & Macedo, 2023), and value-based consumer preferences (Carvalho, 2025) all signal an expanding scope. Ethical marketing now demands compliance with regulations like GDPR and CCPA and proactive transparency, fairness, and social alignment. Brands that thrive in this space adopt glocal strategies (Requião & Costa, 2023) and cultivate community through UGC, review engagement, and participatory content (Ribeiro et al., 2025).

2 METHODS

This study employs an integrative literature review methodology as its foundational research approach, chosen for its ability to synthesize diverse theoretical perspectives and empirical findings across disciplines. The aim is to construct a comprehensive understanding of how digital marketing has evolved in conjunction with globalization and to identify the strategies, tools, and frameworks that businesses employ to foster engagement and consumer loyalty across digital environments. The integrative review approach is especially suited to this objective, as it enables the consolidation of heterogeneous sources into a coherent analytical narrative, allowing for the evaluation of both conceptual developments and applied practices in the field.

The review draws from a wide range of scholarly materials, including peer-reviewed journal articles, academic theses, published books, and relevant industry studies, with a particular focus on works published between 2015 and 2025. While contemporary sources dominate the selection to reflect recent trends and technological advancements, foundational texts and theoretical contributions that shaped the trajectory of marketing research were included where necessary to provide historical context and theoretical grounding. Data sources were selected from high-impact academic databases such as Scopus, Web of Science, Google Scholar, and SciELO, ensuring the credibility and relevance of all literature considered. The criteria for inclusion were based on academic rigor, thematic relevance to digital marketing or globalization, and methodological clarity. Texts that lacked theoretical contribution, empirical support, or relevance to marketing strategy were excluded to maintain focus and analytical depth.

The process of literature selection employed strategic keyword combinations such as "digital marketing," "globalization," "consumer behavior," "market segmentation," "social media marketing," "influencer marketing," "personalization," and "CRM," among others. Boolean operators were used to refine and filter search results to identify studies that explicitly addressed the interplay between digital marketing tools and cross-border strategic communication. Each selected source was carefully read, coded, and analyzed according to its methodological design, conceptual contributions, and findings related to technology integration, market behavior, cultural adaptation, and ethical implications.

The interpretive process followed a thematic analytical framework to identify recurring patterns, converging arguments, and contrasting viewpoints across the literature. In doing so, the review illuminated the multifaceted roles played by technology, data analytics, mobile platforms, AI, and user-generated content in shaping global marketing strategies. At the same time, particular attention was paid to the socio-cultural dimensions of marketing, how culture, language, and norms mediate the perception of brand messages in diverse markets. This dual emphasis on technological and cultural variables ensures that the findings reflect the full scope of complexity that digital marketing encompasses in an era of globalization.

While this integrative method provides valuable insights and offers a high-level synthesis of current knowledge, it is not without limitations. The exclusion of non-English sources may have narrowed the cultural and geographical diversity of perspectives included, particularly from regions undergoing rapid digital transformation. Moreover, the reliance on published literature necessarily excludes grey literature and emergent industry practices that may not yet have been documented academically but are nonetheless influential in the field. Despite these constraints, the methodology offers a rigorous foundation for articulating the strategic, technological, and cultural imperatives of digital marketing in a global context and serves as a solid platform for the critical discussion that follows.

3 DISCUSSION

The ongoing transformation of marketing practices under the influence of digital technologies and globalization has produced a profound reconfiguration of strategic thinking within organizations. Digital marketing, once considered an extension of traditional advertising into electronic media, has become an essential strategic pillar through which firms communicate value, build relationships, and sustain competitive advantage. At its core, digital marketing enables firms to engage with consumers in interactive, data-driven, and responsive ways, features that are particularly valuable in the fast-evolving global economic environment. As markets expand across borders and consumers become more technologically literate and socially engaged, the traditional paradigms of marketing communication have proven insufficient to address the complexities and demands of the contemporary business landscape. Instead, a new marketing model has emerged, centered on personalization, participatory engagement, and continuous adaptation.

At the heart of this transformation is the consumer, who has shifted from a passive recipient of brand messaging to an active co-creator of brand meaning and value. Empowered by social media platforms, mobile connectivity, and on-demand content, consumers now expect real-time responses, relevant experiences, and ethical accountability from the brands they engage with. This shift has required marketers to reimagine their strategies, moving from mass appeal to individual resonance. Through behavioral data, geolocation tools, CRM systems, and AI-powered analytics, businesses can now understand consumers' unique preferences, values, and behaviors at a granular level and craft hyper-personalized messages and offers that foster deeper emotional and psychological bonds. In this way, personalization ceases to be a functional tactic and becomes a strategic imperative tied to brand differentiation and loyalty.

Moreover, the digitalization of marketing has not occurred in isolation but in tandem with the intensification of globalization. The convergence of these two forces has amplified the reach of brands while simultaneously exposing them to heightened levels of cultural diversity and sociopolitical scrutiny. In global digital environments, consumers are not only exposed to a broader array of choices. However, they can also share experiences and form collective narratives about brands across platforms, languages, and national boundaries. This dynamic has heightened the need for cultural competence in marketing strategy. Brands must now navigate multiple cultural codes, symbolic systems, and communication styles to connect authentically with audiences in varied contexts. Translating campaigns linguistically is no longer sufficient; brands must localize them emotionally and symbolically, ensuring relevance and resonance within specific socio-cultural settings.

Such cultural adaptation is especially critical when considering the rise of influencer marketing, which exemplifies the move toward authentic, peer-mediated communication. Influencers serve not merely as promotional tools but as trusted intermediaries whose voices shape consumer perceptions and influence decision-making. Their ability to generate trust lies in their perceived authenticity and ability to speak in the vernacular of their community. Brands that align with the right influencers gain access to deeply engaged audiences and can benefit from the credibility transferred through these relationships. However, the exact authenticity that makes influencer marketing powerful also demands that brands relinquish a degree of control. Influencer partnerships must be managed with transparency, ethical clarity, and brand alignment to avoid backlash and reputational damage.

Alongside these cultural and relational dynamics, the technological infrastructure of digital marketing continues to evolve rapidly. Social commerce, AI-driven content generation, voice search, and recommendation algorithms transform how consumers discover, evaluate, and purchase products. These technologies allow for unprecedented personalization and predictive precision but also introduce new ethical dilemmas regarding privacy, data sovereignty, and algorithmic bias. Consumers, while often enthusiastic about the convenience and personalization these technologies provide, are increasingly aware of how their data is being used and are demanding greater transparency and control. Regulatory frameworks such as the GDPR and CCPA have emerged in response to these demands, compelling marketers to integrate privacy by design into their strategies. Ethical marketing is not simply a legal compliance issue but a reputational and strategic necessity in this environment.

The global pandemic further accelerated the adoption of digital marketing tools, forcing organizations to pivot quickly to online channels for both communication and commerce. Businesses with established digital infrastructures were able to respond more agilely, maintaining engagement and capturing market share, while those reliant on traditional models experienced disruption and decline. The pandemic highlighted the critical role of agility and resilience in marketing strategy—qualities embedded in digital ecosystems that allow for rapid testing, feedback loops, and cross-channel integration. These qualities are now repurposed for post-pandemic recovery and long-term competitiveness, as brands invest in scalable digital infrastructures and data capabilities to support sustainable growth in uncertain environments.

This analysis reveals that marketing is not merely about transmitting a brand's message but cultivating meaningful, reciprocal relationships that transcend transactional logic. Brands must operate not as monologues but as active participants in digital dialogue, co-creating experiences, narratives, and values in partnership with consumers. This requires continuous listening, iterative learning, and authentic communication. It also necessitates a shift in organizational culture, where marketing is integrated not as a standalone department but as a strategic capability embedded across all functions.

Simultaneously, the boundaries between marketing, technology, and social responsibility are becoming increasingly porous. Consumers today evaluate brands not only by the quality of their products or the creativity of their campaigns but also by their environmental impact, inclusivity, and corporate ethics. Therefore, marketing in the digital era must extend its focus to encompass the social and ecological dimensions of brand action, embedding ESG (Environmental, Social, Governance) principles into storytelling, stakeholder engagement, and campaign execution. This broader role of marketing as a vehicle for social influence and systemic change underscores its strategic centrality in the 21st century.

In conclusion, the discussion affirms that digital marketing in the age of globalization is characterized by complexity, interdependence, and accelerated change. The tools and platforms are important, but what defines success is the ability to apply them with strategic insight, cultural sensitivity, and ethical responsibility. Digital marketing is not a neutral set of techniques; it is a dynamic practice that reflects and shapes global consumers' values, expectations, and identities. To succeed in this evolving landscape, brands must move beyond short-term metrics and adopt a long-term vision rooted in empathy, innovation, and trust. Only by doing so can they survive and lead in a digital economy of human connection and global interconnectivity.

CONCLUSION

This study has explored the intricate relationship between digital marketing and globalization, emphasizing the strategic, technological, and cultural transformations that define modern consumer engagement. As digital platforms proliferate and market boundaries dissolve, organizations face the dual challenge of remaining technologically agile while culturally sensitive. The evidence synthesized from contemporary literature and industry practices demonstrates that digital marketing is no longer merely a promotional function but a critical strategic enabler of value creation, customer loyalty, and global competitiveness. This evolution underscores the need for marketing to be reconceptualized as a dynamic, adaptive, and ethically grounded capability embedded within the broader architecture of the firm.

A core conclusion drawn from this analysis is that digital marketing's power lies in its ability to humanize technology. Through real-time data analytics, AI-driven personalization, and interactive digital environments, firms can increasingly create individualized and emotionally resonant consumer experiences. However, this capability must be deployed with ethical integrity, as consumers have become more vigilant about privacy, consent, data usage, and algorithmic manipulation. Transparency, accountability, and fairness in deploying digital strategies are not optional but strategic imperatives.

Another critical insight pertains to the cultural complexity of global markets. Brands that succeed internationally do so not by replicating standardized models across borders, but by cultivating glocal strategies, preserving a consistent core identity while adapting expression and interaction to local sociocultural contexts. This requires investment in cultural intelligence, local partnerships, and platform-specific nuances, particularly as engagement increasingly occurs in decentralized, user-generated content ecosystems such as TikTok, Instagram, and regional social platforms.

The study also reveals that while technological tools such as CRM systems, automation software, and machine learning algorithms enable strategic precision, their effectiveness ultimately depends on organizational alignment. Digital marketing must transcend functional silos to inform strategic decision-making at every level, from product development and branding to customer service and corporate communication. This calls for cross-functional collaboration and the upskilling of marketing professionals to become fluent not only in creative execution but also in data analytics, ethical reasoning, and consumer psychology.

Theoretically, this research contributes to the expanding literature on marketing as a socially embedded, technology-mediated practice. It challenges the traditional dichotomy between mass and relationship marketing by positioning digital marketing as a hybrid model: scalable yet personalized, automated yet interactive, and global yet local. The integrative approach taken here also supports the evolution of marketing theory toward a systems-based, multi-disciplinary paradigm that intersects communication theory, behavioral science, and information technology.

The managerial implications are equally significant. Executives must view digital marketing not simply as a toolkit of tactics, but as a strategic orientation that informs every customer-facing aspect of the enterprise. Organizations should prioritize the development of agile, data-literate teams capable of executing and iterating across platforms while maintaining a consistent and meaningful brand narrative. Managers should invest in analytics capabilities beyond performance metrics to capture sentiment, intent, and behavioral context. Moreover, firms operating across borders must allocate resources to market research, localization, and cultural adaptation, areas often underfunded in pursuit of scale.

Nevertheless, this study is not without limitations. While the integrative literature review method enables a broad synthesis of existing knowledge, it lacks empirical data from fieldwork, case studies, or experimental design. Additionally, excluding non-English sources may have restricted access to perspectives from non-Western contexts, where digital adoption and behavior may follow different trajectories. The rapidly changing nature of digital platforms and consumer expectations also challenges temporal validity; what is accurate today may become obsolete as new technologies and norms emerge.

Future research should address these limitations by conducting longitudinal studies and real-time case analyses that examine how digital marketing strategies evolve in specific industries, geographies, and organizational contexts. Comparative studies across different regulatory environments (e.g., Europe's GDPR vs. China's PIPL) would also provide valuable insight into how legal frameworks shape marketing practice. Moreover, research into the unintended consequences of hyper-personalization, including digital fatigue, exclusionary targeting, and algorithmic reinforcement of biases, would deepen our understanding of digital marketing's societal impacts.

Finally, future work could expand on the intersection between sustainability and digital marketing, exploring how ESG commitments can be communicated authentically in digital spaces and how consumer engagement can drive economic value and environmental and social progress.

In summary, this study reaffirms the centrality of digital marketing in shaping the future of global commerce. It is a response to changing consumer behaviors and technological possibilities and a catalyst for how organizations think, act, and evolve. Firms that embrace their complexity with strategic clarity, cultural sensitivity, and ethical responsibility will not merely survive in the digital economy, but they will lead it.

REFERENCES

Abreu, J. (2024). Marketing global de produtos: Impactos dos fatores culturais nas decisões estratégicas das corporações.

Behera, R. K., Bala, P. K., Rana, N. P., & Khorana, S. (2020). Personalization in marketing: A review of technologies, approaches, and effectiveness. *Journal of Business Research, 116*, 147–161.

Campos, A. C., de Rezende, D. C., Leme, P. H. M. V., de Brito, M. J., & Antonialli, L. M. (2021). Marketing digital em tempos de crise. *Revista Gestão e Desenvolvimento, 18*(3), 102–130. DOI: 10.25112/rgd.v18i3.2784

Caravantes, C. B., & Weiler, T. K. R. (2024). *Empresas na era digital: Uma análise das mudanças e implicações na administração moderna*. Editora Manual.

Carvalho, P. V. (2025). Globalização da produção e desenvolvimento tecnológico: Ascensão chinesa e a disputa no setor de telecomunicações.

Correia, J. F., de Sousa, J. D., Macedo, K. G., da Silva, L. A. B., de Godoy, L. R. B., & Maschio, P. A. S. (2025). A relevância das estratégias do marketing digital para as organizações contemporâneas. *Revista FOCO, 18*(4), e8157. DOI: 10.54751/revistafoco.v18n4-108

Costa, O. R. (2025). O impacto das estratégias de marketing digital no branding: Um estudo de caso do Bar Chico em Parintins/AM.

Coutinho, D. A. (2021). O consumidor e modulação algorítmica de comportamento: A influência da inteligência artificial por meio de algoritmos no poder decisório do consumidor.

Fierro, I., Arbelaez, A., & Gavilanes, M. (2017). Digital marketing: A framework, review and research agenda. *International Journal of Research in Marketing, 34*(1), 22–43. DOI: 10.1016/j.ijresmar.2016.11.006

Francato, F. C., da Costa, W. D., & de Souza, R. O. P. (2024). Estratégias de marketing digital na era atual: Desafios e oportunidades. *Prospectus, 6*(2), 21–36.

Giridhararajan, A., Prasad, S., & Ranjith, K. (2020). Retail store transformation using digital marketing proximity sensors. *Journal of Retailing and Consumer Services, 52*, 101903.

Kannan, P. K., & Li, H. (2017). Digital marketing: A framework, review and research agenda. *International Journal of Research in Marketing, 34*(1), 22–45. DOI: 10.1016/j.ijresmar.2016.11.006

Laice, H. C. F. (2024). Estratégias de adaptação cultural na identidade visual de marcas globalizadas: Um estudo de caso da Sumol Compal.

Oliveira, J. P. M., Ramos, L. S., & Rosada, V. C. (2024). A importância do marketing digital para micro e pequenas empresas para potencializar os resultados do negócio.

Pereira, S.Jr, & Porto, A. P. S. (2021). *Entre posts e parcerias: Práticas de marketing de influência em agência de viagem receptiva*. Ateliê do Turismo.

Pimenta, K. C. L. (2025). A integração de tecnologias digitais no ensino do direito: Inovação e desafios na formação jurídica.

Pinto, M. F. (2023). Análise de público-alvo e comportamento do consumidor no contexto digital. *Revista Brasileira de Marketing*, *22*(1), 55–73.

Requião, A. R., & Costa, H. M. (2023). Estratégias de posicionamento e adaptação cultural em marketing global. *Revista Brasileira de Estratégia de Marketing*, *17*(2), 80–102.

Ribeiro, A., Eloi, D. L. C., & Rodrigues, R. V. M. (2025). Engajamento através de conteúdo gerado pelo usuário (UGC). *Revista Base Científica*, *3*, 1–20. DOI: 10.52832/rbc541

Santos, E. A. (2021). A responsabilidade social nas empresas de cosméticos: Uma análise das relações raciais e de gênero.

Saura, J. R., Palos-Sanchez, P. R., & Herráez, B. R. (2020). The digital marketing strategy: A review and research agenda. *Journal of Innovation & Knowledge*, *5*(4), 266–273.

Silva, C. F. (2024). Alternativas entre o luxo e o lixo: A publicidade no contexto da moda sustentável.

Sousa, K. S. (2025). Biblioteca Pública Municipal Antônio Luís Marcelo Antunes a partir do marketing digital: Estratégias de integração.

Teixeira, J. S., & Macedo, M. F. (2023). Plano de marketing: Lançamento da Starlight Makeup.

Vieira, J. P. (2024). Influência do padrão de beleza transmitido pelos influencers no consumismo das jovens na indústria de cosméticos.

Zanon, P. H. (2024). Análise de dados e inovação no marketing digital para a área de saúde.

Chapter 12
Optimizing Financial Decision Making for Strategic Planning Success

Bruno Barbosa Sousa
http://orcid.org/0000-0002-8588-2422
UNIAG, Polytechnic University of Cávado and Ave, Portugal

Tiago Rodrigues
http://orcid.org/0009-0007-6455-3877
ISLA Santarém, Portugal

ABSTRACT

This chapter examines the optimization of financial decision-making as a foundation for strategic planning success. It explores how structured tools – such as the Balanced Scorecard, Monte Carlo simulations, and decision trees – enhance scenario evaluation, risk mitigation, and resource allocation. Emphasis is placed on integrating financial and strategic planning, leveraging data analytics, and embedding sustainability and human capital considerations. By aligning financial decisions with long-term goals, organizations can boost competitiveness, resilience, and sustainable growth in volatile markets. The chapter offers a comprehensive theoretical framework and practical insights for decision-makers.

DOI: 10.4018/979-8-3373-5233-6.ch012

1. INTRODUCTION TO FINANCIAL DECISION MAKING

Financial decision-making is an essential process for ensuring the sustainability and development of organizations, particularly in a business environment characterized by constant changes and economic uncertainties. This process involves selecting the best alternatives for allocating financial resources – often scarce – with the goal of maximizing economic value and ensuring long-term competitiveness. As noted by Ross et al. (2019), financial decision-making is grounded in a thorough analysis of economic and financial data, risk assessment, and consideration of future outcomes to support strategic decisions. The role of financial management as a support mechanism for strategic decision-making has been widely recognized in literature. According to Gitman and Zutter (2020), financial decisions directly influence organizational performance by determining the efficient allocation of capital, whether for investments, operations, or acquisitions. In this context, adopting analytical and structured approaches is imperative, enabling companies to adapt to the dynamics of the global market. The integration of analytical models into the decision-making process is a crucial aspect discussed in contemporary studies. The Balanced Scorecard, for instance, is widely used as a strategic tool to align financial decisions with organizational goals. Kaplan and Norton (1996), the creators of this model, emphasize the importance of linking financial and non-financial indicators to provide a holistic view of organizational performance. Additionally, methods such as Monte Carlo Simulation have demonstrated their utility in predicting potential outcomes of decisions under conditions of uncertainty (Pritchard et al. 2024). One of the central challenges in financial decision-making is market volatility, which requires constant revision of the strategies adopted by organizations. Studies such as those by Brealey et al. (2020) indicate that there is no universal solution to address these fluctuations. Instead, there is a need to develop flexible and customized approaches tailored to the specificities of each company and sector. The increasing complexity of financial markets has driven the adoption of advanced technologies to enhance analysis and decision-making. Tools such as artificial intelligence and big data analytics have enabled a deeper understanding of financial trends and patterns, as highlighted by Agrawal et al. (2018). These technologies not only accelerate decision-making processes but also increase their accuracy, contributing to more informed decisions aligned with strategic objectives. In addition to technological tools, risk management plays a pivotal role in shaping financial decisions. Recent studies emphasize that identifying, assessing, and mitigating risks are fundamental to avoiding significant financial losses and ensuring long-term viability (Svetlova & Thielmann 2020). Techniques such as sensitivity analysis and decision trees help map potential consequences and probabilities associated with different scenarios, assisting managers in choosing more robust strategies. This article aims to provide a comprehensive review of the foundations of financial decision-making, highlighting its theoretical underpinnings, practical tools, and strategic implications. Based on an analysis of existing literature and empirical studies, it seeks to present an integrated perspective on the subject, contributing to advancing knowledge in this field. The relevance of this study lies in offering models that can be applied in practice by managers, promoting a more efficient and sustainable approach to decision-making in a challenging business environment.

1.1. Making Financial Decisions

Financial decision-making is a crucial component of organizational success, directly influencing resource allocation, sustainability, and competitiveness in the market. In an economic environment characterized by rapid change and uncertainty, the ability to make informed financial decisions is essential for aligning short-term goals with long-term strategic objectives. According to Van Horne and Wachowicz (2008), effective financial decision-making is fundamental to ensuring the viability and sustainable growth of companies, even in highly volatile conditions. The use of structured approaches is indispensable for optimizing the decision-making process. Tools such as Economic Value Added (EVA) have proven effective in measuring economic value creation and aligning financial decisions with organizational goals. Stern, Shiely, and Ross (2001) emphasize that EVA provides a powerful metric for evaluating financial performance by considering the cost of capital, offering a robust foundation for decision-making that maximizes value generation. Risk management plays a central role in financial decision-making, especially in uncertain markets. Hull (2018) argues that financial instruments such as futures contracts and options allow companies to mitigate risks associated with price fluctuations, exchange rates, and interest rates. Additionally, frameworks such as Risk-Adjusted Return on Capital (RAROC) help organizations incorporate risk analysis into decision-making processes, promoting more balanced and sustainable strategies. Technology has also transformed financial decision-making, increasing efficiency and accuracy. Davenport and Harris (2007) demonstrate that predictive analytics tools based on data enable companies to uncover patterns and trends, providing valuable insights to support strategic decisions. The application of big data and machine learning in the financial sector not only improves forecasting precision but also reduces the costs associated with analyzing large datasets. Another critical aspect of financial decision-making is strategic flexibility, which allows companies to adapt quickly to rapidly changing market conditions. Mintzberg, Ahlstrand, and Lampel (1998) emphasize that organizations adopting adaptive approaches are better positioned to adjust their financial strategies effectively, capitalizing on emerging opportunities while mitigating risks. This adaptability is essential for maintaining competitiveness in environments marked by high uncertainty. In addition to flexibility, financial sustainability is increasingly relevant in modern business practices. Studies conducted by Freeman, Harrison, and Wicks (2007) show that integrating stakeholder interests into financial decision-making strengthens organizational relationships and promotes long-term growth. Companies that incorporate environmental, social, and governance (ESG) factors into their strategies can balance financial performance with social impact, enhancing their reputation and attracting sustainability-focused investors. The integration of financial and non-financial indicators is also crucial for effective decision-making. Hope and Fraser (2003) advocate for performance management systems that extend beyond traditional financial metrics, enabling a broader view of organizational performance. These systems help companies align operational actions with broader strategic goals, ensuring better overall outcomes. The adoption of advanced quantitative methods, such as linear programming, has also proven useful in financial decision making. Winston (2004) highlights that linear programming optimizes resource allocation problems, helping organizations find ideal solutions to complex financial challenges. This approach is particularly valuable for companies operating in highly regulated sectors or facing significant financial constraints. In addition, investor confidence is directly influenced by the quality of an organization's financial practices. Damodaran (2012) asserts that companies with strong, transparent financial structures can reduce their cost of capital and attract greater market interest. This underscores the importance of well-informed financial practices supported by rigorous analysis in strengthening an organization's reputation and competitiveness. The importance of financial decision-making extends beyond direct economic impact, encompassing a company's ability to innovate and adapt continuously. Christensen, Raynor, and McDonald (2015) argue that well-founded financial strategies enable businesses to fund disruptive innovations, ensuring their leadership in increasingly competitive markets. Thus, the combination of analytical tools, advanced technology, and sustainable practices positions companies for long-term growth, even in challenging scenarios. Financial decision-making is a complex process requiring robust analytical approaches, strategic flexibility, and the use of advanced technologies. Tools like EVA, RAROC, and linear programming, along with the consideration of ESG factors and the integration of non-financial metrics, provide a solid foundation for informed financial decisions. As market conditions become more uncertain, companies that adopt optimized financial practices not only ensure their viability but also drive innovation, growth, and long-term competitiveness.

1.2. Strategic Planning

Strategic planning is an essential practice in organizational management, providing a structured framework to achieve long-term objectives and maintain competitiveness in dynamic markets. It involves developing a clear vision for the future, identifying necessary resources, available opportunities, and potential challenges. According to Ansoff (1965), strategic planning is fundamental for aligning organizations with their external environments, enabling proactive responses to market changes and maximizing performance. The essence of strategic planning lies in its ability to connect short-term actions with long-term organizational goals. Mintzberg (1994) argues that while planning is often associated with rigid processes, its true effectiveness lies in adaptability. He highlights that the most successful organizations balance deliberate planning with emergent strategies, allowing flexibility to adjust to constantly changing market conditions. Analyzing the external environment is a critical component of strategic planning, helping organizations better understand the factors that influence their operations. Porter (1980) identifies his Five Forces framework – threat of new entrants, bargaining power of suppliers, bargaining power of buyers, threat of substitute products, and competitive rivalry – as an indispensable tool for uncovering market opportunities and threats. Applying this framework enables organizations to identify strategic positions that foster sustainability and growth. Formulating effective strategies requires a detailed understanding of an organization's internal resources and capabilities. Barney (1991) introduced the Resource-Based View (RBV), emphasizing that sustainable competitive advantages are achieved through the possession and effective utilization of resources that are valuable, rare, inimitable, and organized. This perspective encourages companies to focus on their core competencies and invest in building unique capabilities that differentiate them in the market. Furthermore, strategic planning plays a crucial role in managing organizational change. Kotter (1996) argues that success in dynamic environments depends on the ability to align strategic initiatives with necessary transformations within the organization. He proposes an eight-step model for change management, emphasizing the importance of creating a shared vision, effective communication, and consolidating gains throughout the process. Leadership also plays a central role in strategic planning. Yukl (2010) notes that effective leaders are essential in developing and implementing organizational strategies. They are responsible for articulating a clear vision, motivating teams, and aligning daily operations with strategic objectives. Visionary leadership is often cited as a determining factor in the success of strategic initiatives. The integration of technology into strategic planning has become increasingly relevant. According to Teece (2018), the digital era has introduced new opportunities and challenges, requiring managers to consider the impact of disruptive technologies when formulating strategies. He highlights the importance of dynamic capabilities – the ability to identify and respond quickly to technological changes – as a key competitive differentiator. Sustainability also plays an increasingly significant role in contemporary strategic planning. Elkington (1997) introduced the concept of the Triple Bottom Line, suggesting that organizations should balance financial performance with social and environmental impacts. This approach not only enhances a company's reputation but also better positions it to meet the demands of increasingly conscious stakeholders. Besides, continuous monitoring and evaluation are crucial for the success of strategic planning. Kaplan and Norton (2008) propose using the Balanced Scorecard as a tool to translate strategy into clear operational metrics, enabling organizations to track progress toward their goals. This method ensures that strategic plans are reviewed and adjusted as needed, enhancing their relevance and effectiveness over time. Implementing strategic planning requires alignment across all levels of the organization. Hambrick and Fredrickson (2001) emphasize that strategy must be consistent and integrated throughout the organization, from formulation to execution. They argue that a sound strategy is not merely a set of objectives but rather an interdependent combination of elements that define how a company competes, allocates resources, and creates value. Strategic planning is a multifaceted process that combines environmental analysis, resource management, visionary leadership, and adaptation to technological and social changes. It enables organizations to navigate dynamic markets, maximize performance, and achieve long-term sustainability. By integrating concepts such as competitive analysis, dynamic capabilities, and social impact, companies can develop effective and flexible strategies, ensuring their relevance and competitiveness in the future.

1.3. Integration Between Financial Decision-Making and Strategic Planning

The integration between financial decision-making and strategic planning is a key factor for organizational sustainability and growth. Financial decisions often serve as the foundation for executing business strategies, as the financial resources needed to implement strategic objectives relieve robust financial planning. According to Schilling (2017), effective resource management is crucial for the success of strategic initiatives, as it allows companies to leverage their assets and maximize value creation. For strategies to be successfully implemented, financial decisions must be aligned with the organization's long-term goals, creating a continuous cycle of evaluation and adaptation. The connection between financial decisions and strategic planning is rooted in the idea that financial decisions should support the organization's growth goals. One of the main functions of strategic financial management is ensuring that resources are allocated effectively and efficiently, considering both short-term and long-term priorities. Mintzberg et al. (2005) argue that for strategic planning to be effective, it must consider the limitations and opportunities presented by available financial resources. This means that financial resource allocation should be made carefully, based on financial projections, but also considering the need for continuous adaptation to changes in the business environment. Another crucial aspect of the integration between financial decision-making and strategic planning is risk assessment. Business strategy should be formulated with a clear understanding of the financial risks that may affect the organization. Companies need to assess the financial viability of their strategies, considering economic uncertainties, market fluctuations, and regulatory changes. Risk management theories, such as those proposed by Kaplan and Mikes (2012), show that integrating rigorous financial analysis with risk mitigation strategies can help organizations make more informed decisions and reduce susceptibility to unexpected surprises. The use of tools such as sensitivity analysis and simulation models can predict the financial impacts of various scenarios, thus assisting in the strategic decision-making process. Financial decision-making in a strategic context also involves the need for long-term planning, especially for companies aiming to sustain their growth over time. Harrison et al. (2014) discuss the importance of combining financial planning with long-term strategies, emphasizing that anticipating financing needs and allocating investments to long-term projects are vital for any strategy's success. Companies must be able to adjust their investment strategies to reflect changes in market conditions but always maintain a long-term vision that can sustain the business's future viability. Additionally, the integration between financial decision-making and strategic planning requires a flexible approach, as both market conditions and internal organizational needs can change over time. Porter (1991) emphasizes that market competitiveness depends on an organization's ability to adjust its financial and operational strategies as circumstances change. Companies that adopt an agile approach to strategic planning are better positioned to respond quickly to unexpected opportunities or threats, adjusting their financial resources to support these changes. This is particularly important in highly volatile sectors, where the ability to adjust financial strategies quickly can make the difference between success and failure. Technology plays an increasing role in the integration between financial decision-making and strategic planning. The use of management information systems and advanced analytical tools has allowed managers to integrate financial and operational data more efficiently, creating a solid foundation for informed decisions. According to Brynjolfsson and McAfee (2014), digitalization and the use of big data can generate valuable insights that allow companies to adjust their strategies in real-time, responding quickly to changes in the business environment and optimizing resource allocation. The integration of information technology in strategic and financial processes makes organizations more agile and adaptable, enabling more efficient planning and better resource allocation. The importance of financial sustainability should also be considered in the integration between financial decisions and strategic planning. Organizations must increasingly incorporate social and environmental responsibility practices into their financial strategies. Freeman et al. (2007) argue that companies that align their financial decisions with social and environmental goals have a competitive advantage in the long run. This happens because stakeholders, including consumers, investors, and regulators, are increasingly demanding that companies adopt practices that respect the environment and promote social well-being. The ability to integrate these concerns into financial decisions helps ensure that companies can grow sustainably and compete effectively in the long term. Another area where the integration of financial decisions and strategic planning is crucial is in human capital management. Companies need to ensure that their investments in people are sustainable and aligned with organizational strategies. In the context of strategic planning, it is necessary for human resource costs to be appropriately planned and for investments in skill development and talent retention to be considered as part of the strategic investment portfolio. Pfeffer (1998) suggests that companies that treat their employees as strategic assets, investing in their continuous development, gain a significant competitive advantage. Therefore, financial management should include human resource planning as part of its long-term strategy. Financial analysis is also critical to ensure that strategic planning is executed within budgetary limits and with the necessary resources. According to Koller et al. (2010), continuous performance evaluation and reassessment of budget projections over time help companies maintain control over their finances and ensure that strategic goals are achieved. Without rigorous cost control and constant monitoring of cash flows, even the best strategies can be undermined by a lack of financial resources. Integration between financial decision-making and strategic planning is fundamental for the long-term success of organizations. This requires companies to implement a holistic approach that considers all aspects of their operations and the external environment. As Hitt et al. (2012) argue, the effective implementation of strategies depends on the ability to align financial decisions with the organization's strategic objectives, ensuring that resources are directed in a way that maximizes return and sustainability. When this integration is successfully achieved, companies can not only meet their strategic goals but also build a solid foundation for sustainable and lasting growth.

2. THE IMPORTANCE OF OPTIMIZING FINANCIAL DECISION-MAKING IN BUSINESS STRATEGY

Optimizing financial decision-making has emerged as one of the most critical pillars for the success of business strategies in increasingly competitive and volatile markets. This process is essential for ensuring the efficient allocation of resources and aligning financial decisions with long-term organizational objectives. As Brigham and Ehrhardt (2022) emphasize, the ability to make informed financial decisions based on rigorous analysis not only maximizes a company's value but also strengthens its resilience in uncertain environments. A structured approach to decision-making is indispensable for navigating the complexities of modern markets. Merchant and Van der Stede (2017) highlight that well-implemented management control systems enable managers to access integrated financial and operational information, thereby fostering clearer strategic insights. Analytical tools and robust methodologies, such as Activity-Based Costing (ABC), empower organizations to identify high-impact financial areas and prioritize resources efficiently. Furthermore, optimizing financial decision-making is closely linked to organizational sustainability. Research by Khan, Serafeim, and Yoon (2016) demonstrates that companies incorporating environmental, social, and governance (ESG) factors into their financial strategies achieve higher long-term profitability. This approach not only enhances risk management but also attracts investors who prioritize responsible business practices. Risk management is another critical element in optimizing financial decision-making. Elliot & Elliot (2020) argue that implementing integrated risk frameworks, such as Enterprise Risk Management (ERM), allows organizations to identify and mitigate risks with greater precision.

These frameworks are often complemented by quantitative tools, such as scenario analysis and Value at Risk (VaR) models, which help quantify risks and forecast potential impacts on financial outcomes. Technology has revolutionized financial decision-making by providing advanced tools that enhance analytical capabilities. In a study by Brynjolfsson and McAfee (2017), the authors highlight that businesses leveraging predictive analytics can identify patterns within large volumes of financial data, enabling faster and more accurate decisions. Emerging technologies not only improve decision quality but also enhance organizational agility in responding to sudden market shifts. Another key factor in financial optimization is the integration of non-financial indicators, such as customer satisfaction and operational efficiency, to complement traditional metrics. Chenhall and Moers (2015) argue that adopting more comprehensive performance measurement systems provides a holistic view of the impact of financial decisions on operations and competitiveness. This approach is particularly relevant in industries where competitive differentiation relies not only on financial performance but also on qualitative factors. Strategic flexibility is also vital for coping with the volatility of global markets. Porter and Kramer (2011) emphasize that the ability to swiftly adjust financial strategies to market changes enables companies to seize new opportunities while minimizing potential losses. Their concept of "creating shared value" suggests that financial decisions should balance short-term priorities with long-term impacts on all stakeholders. A clear example of the importance of optimizing financial decision-making is the adoption of methodologies such as real options analysis, which evaluates the value of future options in strategic decisions. As Amram and Kulatilaka (1999) argue, this approach is particularly valuable in highly uncertain environments, as it allows for greater flexibility and dynamic assessment of investment projects. Financial optimization not only improves resource management efficiency but also builds investor and stakeholder confidence in organizational leadership. Studies by La Porta et al. (1998) reveal that companies with sound financial practices tend to have lower capital costs and greater access to investments. As a result, optimized financial management enhances operational performance while strengthening the company's reputation and credibility in the market. In summary, optimizing financial decision-making is a vital component in the formulation and execution of effective business strategies. Advanced analytical tools, the integration of non-financial indicators, and the adoption of emerging technologies have enabled organizations to balance operational efficiency, risk management, and long-term sustainability. While the process is complex, it provides businesses with a crucial competitive advantage in an ever-evolving business landscape.

2.1. Advantages and Benefits of Optimization

The optimization of financial decision-making has become an essential element for the effective management of organizations, providing a solid foundation for achieving strategic goals and ensuring long-term sustainability. The ability to make well-founded financial decisions allows companies to leverage their resources efficiently, maximizing returns and minimizing risks. According to Jorion (2007), optimizing financial decisions is not just about maximizing profits but also involves the strategic allocation of resources to ensure the organization's future viability. This process is crucial in a business environment characterized by uncertainty and volatility, enabling companies to face market challenges with greater security and confidence. One of the main advantages of optimizing financial decisions is the improvement in resource allocation. With an optimized approach, companies can direct their resources more efficiently, prioritizing investments that offer the highest possible returns. According to Modigliani and Miller (1958), the efficient allocation of capital is crucial to maximizing the value of a company, as it ensures that resources are invested in areas with the greatest potential for profit. This practice not only improves short-term financial performance but also contributes to the company's sustainable growth in the long term. Additionally, optimization allows companies to avoid investments in low-return areas, minimizing waste and increasing market competitiveness. Another significant benefit of optimizing financial decisions is the improved risk management. Companies are constantly exposed to various types of risks, such as market risks, operational risks, and financial risks. Optimization enables a more accurate assessment of these risks, helping organizations identify and mitigate potential threats before they materialize. The modern portfolio theory, as proposed by Markowitz (1952), highlights the importance of diversifying investments to reduce the overall risk of a portfolio. By optimizing financial decisions, organizations can build more balanced investment portfolios that are less susceptible to market fluctuations, resulting in greater financial stability. Optimizing financial decisions also provides greater flexibility and the ability to adapt to changes in the economic environment. Companies that adopt optimization practices can adjust their financial strategies quickly in response to unexpected market or economic changes. The real options theory, discussed by Black and Scholes (1973), argues that flexibility in financial decision-making is a value-added factor, allowing companies to seize new opportunities or adjust strategies according to circumstances. This is particularly important in volatile markets, where the ability to adapt can be the key to long-term survival and success. Moreover, optimizing financial decisions contributes to greater operational efficiency. Companies that make optimized financial decisions typically see improvements in productivity and efficiency across their operations. Detailed financial analysis and accurate cash flow forecasting allow organizations to better plan their activities and use their resources more effectively. According to Jensen (1986), the efficient allocation of financial resources is directly related to maximizing organizational efficiency because it ensures that resources are used to support the areas of highest performance and profitability. This not only improves the company's competitiveness but also contributes to reduced operational costs. Financial optimization also has a positive impact on human capital management within organizations. By optimizing financial processes, companies can more effectively invest in training, development, and talent retention, ensuring that resources are allocated to initiatives that promote sustainable growth. Pfeffer (1998) argues that investing in human capital is one of the most effective ways to ensure long-term competitive advantages.

With optimized financial decision-making, organizations have more resources available to invest in the continuous development of their teams, improving organizational performance and ensuring that the company is prepared to face future challenges. Furthermore, optimizing financial decisions can lead to greater stakeholder satisfaction and confidence. Transparency and effectiveness in financial decision-making convey trust to investors, shareholders, and other stakeholders, who perceive the company as well-managed and capable of delivering sustainable results. According to Kaplan and Norton (1992), creating value for stakeholders is one of the main goals of organizational strategy, and optimizing financial decisions contributes to this objective by ensuring that resources are employed in a way that benefits both financial goals and stakeholder interests. Another important benefit of financial optimization is the improvement in strategic planning capacity. Companies that make optimized financial decisions have a clearer view of their financial position and available options, which facilitates the development of effective strategies. The use of tools such as the Balanced Scorecard, as suggested by Kaplan and Norton (2008), enables companies to integrate financial and nonfinancial information into their strategic process, ensuring that financial decisions are aligned with organizational goals. This facilitates strategy implementation and improves the execution of strategic planning. Optimizing financial decisions also contributes to maximizing the company's value over the long term. As Stewart (1991) asserts, maximizing company value should be the central goal of any financial strategy. Optimizing financial decisions enables companies to invest more effectively, leverage their capabilities better, and generate value for shareholders. With efficient financial management, companies can achieve sustainable growth and increase their competitiveness in the market. Additionally, optimizing financial decisions fosters innovation within organizations. By ensuring that financial resources are allocated appropriately, companies can invest in new technologies, research and development, and other innovative projects that drive growth. Christensen et al. (2004) emphasize that innovation is essential for the long-term survival of companies, and optimizing financial decisions is a key enabler of these investments. ptimizing financial decision-making is an essential practice for ensuring organizational resilience. Companies that adopt optimized financial practices are better able to face economic crises or financial difficulties, as they have a solid foundation to make quick and effective decisions. According to Fama (1980), the efficiency of financial markets directly reflects the ability of companies to make informed decisions, and optimizing these decisions contributes to the organization's financial and operational stability.

2.2. Negative Impacts of Inefficient Financial Decisions

Inefficient financial decisions can have profoundly negative impacts on the sustainability, competitiveness, and overall health of organizations. Poorly considered financial strategies often lead to misallocation of resources, which hampers organizational growth and diminishes shareholder value. According to Hillier et al. (2021), inefficient capital allocation often results in excessive costs, underutilized resources, and diminished profitability. Companies that fail to align their financial decisions with strategic objectives may also struggle to maintain a competitive edge in dynamic markets, as their inefficiencies allow competitors to outperform them. A key consequence of inefficient financial decision-making is the mismanagement of risk, which can expose organizations to significant vulnerabilities. Poor risk assessment and mitigation strategies may lead to catastrophic losses, especially in industries prone to market volatility. As argued by Hull (2018), inadequate risk management stemming from suboptimal financial decisions increases the likelihood of exposure to financial shocks, which can severely disrupt operations. Companies that fail to integrate robust risk management frameworks into their financial decision-making are often left unprepared to cope with crises, thereby jeopardizing their long-term viability.Inefficient financial decisions also frequently result in poor cash flow management, which can lead to liquidity crises. Insufficient liquidity constrains a company's ability to meet its short-term obligations, damaging its creditworthiness and straining relationships with suppliers and creditors. According to Brigham and Daves (2021), poorly managed cash flows arising from ineffective financial decisions often cause organizations to lose access to favorable credit terms, further exacerbating financial instability. This creates a cycle of financial distress that can ultimately lead to bankruptcy if not addressed promptly. Another negative impact of inefficient financial decision-making is the inability to seize growth opportunities. Poor allocation of financial resources can prevent organizations from investing in promising ventures, new technologies, or expansion initiatives. Rajan and Zingales (2001) highlight that financial inefficiencies limit a firm's capacity to innovate and adapt, which are critical for maintaining competitiveness in fast-evolving markets.

Organizations that are unable to allocate capital effectively are often outpaced by competitors who leverage strategic investments to gain market share and enhance profitability. Moreover, inefficient financial decisions often undermine employee morale and organizational culture. When financial resources are mismanaged, companies may be forced to implement layoffs, wage cuts, or benefit reductions to offset losses. These actions create a sense of instability among employees, reducing job satisfaction and productivity. As noted by Cascio (2021), financial distress resulting from poor decision-making negatively affects workforce engagement and retention, which, in turn, further impacts organizational performance and increases recruitment and training costs. The erosion of investor confidence is another significant repercussion of inefficient financial decision-making. Investors are drawn to organizations that demonstrate sound financial management and the ability to generate consistent returns. However, when financial missteps lead to declining profitability or missed earnings targets, investor trust is eroded, leading to decreased stock prices and limited access to capital markets. As documented by Damodaran (2020), organizations with a history of poor financial decisionmaking often face higher costs of capital, which hinders their ability to finance future projects and maintain operational efficiency. In the context of mergers and acquisitions (M&A), inefficient financial decisions can be particularly detrimental. Overpaying for acquisitions or failing to realize anticipated synergies can lead to significant financial losses and erode shareholder value. Gaughan (2020) observes that M&A transactions driven by poor financial analysis or misaligned strategic objectives often fail to deliver the expected benefits, leaving companies with excessive debt and integration challenges. Such failures can tarnish a company's reputation and diminish its standing in the market. Environmental, social, and governance (ESG) considerations are increasingly influencing financial decision-making, and inefficiencies in this area can have severe reputational consequences. Organizations that neglect ESG factors or fail to allocate resources toward sustainable practices often face backlashes from stakeholders, including consumers, regulators, and investors. According to Eccles et al. (2020), inefficient financial decisions that disregard sustainability not only damage a company's reputation but also increase regulatory risks and reduce access to ESG-focused investment funds, thereby limiting growth opportunities. The long-term financial health of an organization can also be jeopardized by inefficient decisions regarding debt management. Excessive borrowing or poor structuring of debt can lead to unsustainable leverage ratios, making it difficult for companies to meet their repayment obligations. As Moyer et al. (2022) explain, high debt levels resulting from ineffective financial decisions increase the risk of default, restrict financial flexibility, and reduce the organization's ability to navigate economic downturns. This financial fragility often discourages potential investors and limits the company's growth prospects. Inefficient financial decisions can negatively affect corporate governance, creating a misalignment between the interests of management and shareholders. Poor financial oversight can result in agency problems, where managers prioritize personal or short-term gains over long-term value creation. Bebchuk and Fried (2004) argue that ineffective financial decisionmaking exacerbates governance issues, reducing shareholder trust and increasing scrutiny from regulators. Addressing these governance challenges often requires significant time and resources, further straining the organization. These decisions can have far-reaching consequences that extend beyond immediate financial performance. From resource misallocation and risk mismanagement to diminished investor confidence and weakened corporate governance, the adverse impacts of poor financial decision-making are profound and multifaceted. To mitigate these risks, organizations must prioritize the integration of robust financial analysis, effective governance frameworks, and strategic alignment in their decisionmaking processes. By addressing inefficiencies proactively, companies can protect their financial health, enhance competitiveness, and ensure long-term sustainability.

3. TOOLS AND METHODS FOR OPTIMIZING FINANCIAL DECISIONS

Optimizing financial decisions is a critical aspect of organizational success, as it ensures the efficient allocation of resources, minimizes risks, and maximizes value creation. To achieve these objectives, organizations leverage a variety of tools and methods designed to enhance decision-making processes and improve outcomes. Among the most widely used tools is the Net Present Value (NPV) method, which evaluates the profitability of an investment by calculating the present value of future cash flows. According to Berk and DeMarzo (2020), NPV is a fundamental tool in corporate finance, as it provides a clear metric for assessing whether investment will add value to the organization. Another powerful method is the Internal Rate of Return (IRR), which identifies the discount rate at which the present net value of an investment is zero. IRR is particularly useful for comparing multiple investment opportunities, as it provides a standardized measure of expected returns. Damodaran (2015) highlights that IRR, when used alongside NPV, enables decision-makers to prioritize projects based on both profitability and scale, ensuring that financial resources are allocated effectively to maximize returns. Monte Carlo simulation is another critical tool for optimizing financial decisions, particularly in environments characterized by uncertainty. This method uses probability distributions to model potential outcomes of financial decisions, allowing organizations to evaluate risks and identify optimal strategies. Glasserman (2004) notes that the Monte Carlo simulation is especially valuable in risk management and portfolio optimization, as it provides a detailed analysis of potential scenarios and their associated probabilities. Scenario analysis is another method that supports financial decision-making by examining the potential outcomes of different strategic choices under varying conditions. By testing multiple scenarios, organizations can better understand the implications of their decisions and develop strategies to mitigate risks. Koller et al. (2020) argue that scenario analysis is an essential tool for stress testing financial strategies, particularly in industries exposed to economic volatility or regulatory changes. The use of financial ratios is also instrumental in optimizing financial decisions. Ratios such as the current ratio, debt-to-equity ratio, and return on equity provide critical insights into an organization's financial health and operational efficiency. These metrics help decision-makers evaluate performance, identify areas for improvement, and align financial strategies with organizational goals. Higgins (2016) emphasizes that financial ratios are indispensable for monitoring performance over time and ensuring that financial strategies remain aligned with market conditions. Advanced analytical tools, including big data and machine learning, are increasingly being integrated into financial decision-making processes. These technologies enable organizations to analyze vast amounts of data, uncovering patterns and insights that support more informed decisions. According to Brynjolfsson and McAfee (2017), the use of predictive analytics and artificial intelligence enhances the precision of financial forecasts, reduces uncertainty, and supports the development of more robust financial strategies. Linear programming is another quantitative method frequently employed to optimize financial decisions, particularly in resource allocation. This technique identifies the optimal allocation of resources subject to constraints such as budget limits or production capacity. Winston and Venkataramanan (2003) note that linear programming is particularly useful in optimizing supply chain operations, investment portfolios, and production schedules, ensuring that organizations achieve maximum efficiency. Risk-adjusted metrics, such as the Sharpe Ratio, are also widely used to evaluate the performance of financial decisions by measuring returns relative to risk.

The Sharpe Ratio enables decision-makers to compare investments with differing risk profiles, ensuring that resources are allocated to projects that offer the highest risk-adjusted returns. According to Bodie et al. (2014), incorporating risk-adjusted metrics into decision-making processes helps organizations balance risk and return, fostering more sustainable financial strategies. The Balanced Scorecard (BSC) is another valuable tool that integrates financial and non-financial metrics to align strategic objectives with operational activities. By providing a holistic view of organizational performance, the BSC helps decision-makers ensure that financial strategies support broader business goals. Kaplan and Norton (2004) argue that the BSC is particularly effective in aligning financial decisions with long-term objectives, promoting organizational cohesion and improving overall performance. The use of sensitivity analysis allows organizations to understand how changes in key variables, such as interest rates or market demand, affect financial outcomes. This method enables decision-makers to identify the most significant drivers of financial performance and develop strategies to mitigate risks. Truong et al. (2008) highlights that sensitivity analysis is a critical tool for evaluating the robustness of financial decisions, particularly in capital-intensive industries where small changes in assumptions can have significant impacts. Optimizing financial decisions requires the integration of various tools and methods that provide insights, reduce uncertainty, and improve resource allocation. From traditional techniques like NPV and IRR to advanced technologies such as machine learning and big data analytics, these tools empower organizations to make more informed and effective decisions. By leveraging these methods, companies can enhance their financial performance, mitigate risks, and align their strategies with long-term objectives, ensuring sustained growth and competitiveness in a dynamic business environment.

3.1. Balance Scorecard, Monte Carlo Simulation and Decision Trees on the base for decision making

The integration of the Balanced Scorecard (BSC) model with advanced analytical tools such as Monte Carlo Simulation and Decision Trees represents a powerful approach to optimizing organizational performance by evaluating potential outcomes under varying scenarios. The Balanced Scorecard, developed by Kaplan and Norton, is designed to link strategic objectives with measurable performance indicators across financial, customer, internal processes, and learning dimensions. According to Niven (2006), the BSC serves as a bridge between long-term strategic planning and day-to-day operational management, allowing organizations to align resource allocation with overarching business goals effectively. By incorporating Monte Carlo

Simulation, organizations can enhance the predictive capabilities of the Balanced Scorecard, enabling them to evaluate a broad range of possible outcomes based on resource allocation and investment decisions. Monte Carlo Simulation uses probabilistic modeling to account for uncertainty, simulating thousands of scenarios to provide a comprehensive understanding of potential risks and opportunities. Glasserman (2004) emphasizes that this technique is particularly effective in environments with complex and interdependent variables, as it helps decision-makers quantify the likelihood of different outcomes and optimize resource allocation for maximum profitability. Decision Trees further complement the Balanced Scorecard and Monte Carlo Simulation by enabling organizations to evaluate the potential consequences of their decisions systematically. A Decision Tree is a graphical representation of choices and their potential outcomes, helping organizations map out possible paths and associated probabilities. According to Clemen and Reilly (2013), Decision Trees are invaluable tools for incorporating uncertainty into the decision-making process, allowing organizations to weigh the expected value of various strategies and identify the optimal course of action. The combination of these tools facilitates a more nuanced approach to resource distribution, ensuring that investments are directed toward areas with the highest potential returns. For instance, the Balanced Scorecard provides a strategic framework for identifying critical performance areas, while Monte Carlo Simulation and Decision Trees offer quantitative support for evaluating and refining these strategies. As stated by Hubbard (2014), integrating quantitative models into strategic planning enhances the precision and reliability of financial forecasts, enabling organizations to make better-informed decisions that align with their strategic objectives. Moreover, this integrated approach allows organizations to simulate different investment levels and assess their impact on performance outcomes. By doing so, companies can identify diminishing returns or areas where additional resources may yield exponential benefits. Parnell et al. (2013) highlight that such analyses are critical for ensuring that resource allocation decisions are not only aligned with strategic priorities but also grounded in empirical data that maximize overall profitability. The inclusion of Monte Carlo Simulation also enhances risk management by allowing organizations to evaluate the impact of uncertainty on resource distribution and investment decisions. By modeling various risk scenarios, companies can develop strategies that mitigate potential downsides while capitalizing on opportunities. As described by Chapman and Ward (2011), incorporating probabilistic methods into resource planning reduces uncertainty and enables organizations to implement risk-adjusted strategies that enhance long-term resilience. Similarly, Decision Trees support organizations in evaluating trade-offs between competing priorities by visually mapping the potential outcomes of different choices. This method not only clarifies the decision-making process but also helps organizations prioritize investments based on expected returns and associated risks.

According to Taylor (2013), Decision Trees are particularly effective in multi-criteria decision-making contexts, where organizations must balance financial objectives with operational and strategic goals. The integration of these tools into the Balanced Scorecard model also facilitates continuous performance monitoring and improvement. By simulating scenarios and evaluating outcomes, organizations can refine their strategies iteratively, ensuring that resource allocation remains aligned with evolving business needs. Bititci et al. (2016) argue that performance management systems that incorporate advanced analytics are more adaptable to changing market conditions, enabling organizations to maintain a competitive edge by proactively addressing emerging challenges and opportunities. Another critical advantage of this integrated approach is its ability to foster alignment between organizational strategy and operational execution. By linking strategic objectives to measurable outcomes through the Balanced Scorecard and leveraging Monte Carlo Simulation and Decision Trees for scenario analysis, organizations can create a cohesive framework that aligns all levels of the organization toward shared goals. As noted by Bourne et al. (2013), alignment between strategy and operations is essential for achieving long-term success, as it ensures that every resource is utilized efficiently to drive organizational performance. This methodology supports the creation of a culture of data-driven decision-making within organizations. By relying on quantitative tools to inform strategic planning and resource allocation, organizations can instill a mindset that values evidence-based approaches to achieving business objectives. Provost and Fawcett (2013) emphasize that leveraging data-driven methodologies enhances organizational learning and promotes more effective decision-making, ultimately leading to improved performance and profitability. Integrating the Balanced Scorecard with Monte Carlo Simulation and Decision Trees provides organizations with a robust framework for optimizing resource allocation and maximizing profitability. This approach enables companies to account for uncertainty, evaluate potential outcomes, and align investments with strategic objectives. By combining qualitative insights from the Balanced Scorecard with quantitative analysis from Monte Carlo Simulation and Decision Trees, organizations can enhance their decision-making processes, mitigate risks, and drive sustainable growth in an increasingly complex business environment.

3.2. Financial Performance Indicators

Financial performance indicators (FPIs) are essential tools for evaluating the financial health and operational efficiency of organizations. These metrics provide critical insights into profitability, liquidity, solvency, and overall financial stability, enabling stakeholders to make informed decisions. According to Palepu et al. (2020), FPIs play a central role in financial analysis by offering a comprehensive view of an organization's financial position, which is crucial for assessing performance trends and guiding strategic planning. The accurate interpretation of these indicators allows companies to identify strengths and weaknesses, optimizing their decision-making processes to enhance long-term sustainability. Profitability indicators, such as gross profit margin, operating profit margin, and return on equity (ROE), are among the most widely used metrics for assessing an organization's ability to generate income relative to its expenses and investments. These metrics offer valuable insights into the efficiency and effectiveness of a company's operations. As Brigham and Houston (2021) note, profitability ratios are fundamental for evaluating how well a company utilizes its resources to create value, making them indispensable for investors and managers aiming to enhance financial performance. Higher profitability ratios typically indicate better operational efficiency and financial stability. Liquidity indicators, including the current ratio and quick ratio, are critical for understanding an organization's ability to meet short-term obligations. These ratios measure the company's capacity to convert assets into cash to cover liabilities. A strong liquidity position signals financial health and stability, allowing organizations to manage unexpected expenses and maintain operational continuity. Atrill and McLaney (2020) emphasize that liquidity ratios are especially important in volatile economic environments, as they provide a buffer against unforeseen challenges and ensure the smooth functioning of daily operations. Solvency indicators, such as the debt-to-equity ratio and interest coverage ratio, assess a company's longterm financial health by examining its ability to meet long-term debt obligations. These metrics are vital for evaluating the risk associated with a company's capital structure and determining its financial resilience. Gitman et al. (2018) argue that solvency ratios are key for investors and lenders, as they reflect the level of financial risk an organization is exposed to and its capacity to sustain operations in the long term. Maintaining an optimal solvency ratio is essential for fostering investor confidence and securing favorable financing terms. Efficiency indicators, like inventory turnover and asset turnover ratios, measure how effectively an organization utilizes its resources to generate revenue. These metrics provide insights into operational efficiency and the effectiveness of resource management. According to Hillier et al. (2021), high efficiency ratios often indicate that a company is maximizing its asset utilization and minimizing waste, which contributes to improved profitability. These indicators are particularly useful for identifying areas where processes can be streamlined to enhance performance. Market performance indicators, such as earnings per share (EPS) and price-to-earnings (P/E) ratio, assess a company's valuation and attractiveness to investors. These metrics are essential for understanding how the market perceives a company's performance and growth potential. Damodaran (2016) highlights that market-based indicators provide a forward-looking perspective, enabling investors to gauge prospects and make informed decisions about equity investments. Companies with strong market performance metrics typically enjoy higher investor confidence and greater access to capital markets. Cash flow indicators, including operating cash flow and free cash flow, are crucial for evaluating the financial flexibility and sustainability of an organization. These metrics provide insights into a company's ability to generate cash from its core operations and fund future growth. As Parrino et al. (2020) explain, strong cash flow performance is indicative of a company's operational strength and its capacity to withstand financial challenges. Free cash flow is a critical metric for assessing a company's ability to invest in expansion initiatives while maintaining liquidity. Economic value added (EVA) is another important financial performance indicator that measures a company's ability to generate value beyond the cost of capital. EVA provides a clear picture of whether a company's operations are truly creating shareholder wealth. According to Young and O'Byrne (2001), EVA is particularly useful for assessing long-term financial performance and aligning managerial incentives with shareholder interests. Companies with positive EVA are efficiently utilizing their resources to generate value. Integrated performance indicators, such as the balanced scorecard (BSC), combine financial and non-financial metrics to provide a holistic view of organizational performance. The BSC aligns financial performance with broader strategic objectives, offering a comprehensive framework for performance management. Kaplan and Norton (2004) argue that the integration of financial and non-financial indicators ensures that organizations maintain a balanced approach to achieving long-term goals while addressing immediate financial priorities. Sustainability indicators, which include metrics related to environmental, social, and governance (ESG) performance, are becoming increasingly important for assessing financial performance in a broader context. These indicators help organizations evaluate their commitment to sustainable practices and their impact on stakeholder value. Eccles et al. (2014) note that companies with strong ESG performance often experience improved financial outcomes, as they attract socially responsible investors and enhance their reputation in the market. Incorporating sustainability metrics into financial performance analysis is crucial for addressing the evolving expectations of stakeholders. Comparative financial performance analysis through benchmarking provides valuable insights into an organization's relative performance within its industry. By comparing key financial indicators with industry peers, companies can identify areas of improvement and competitive advantages. Robinson et al. (2020) emphasize that benchmarking helps organizations stay competitive by fostering a culture of continuous improvement and innovation. This approach allows companies to set realistic performance targets and implement strategies to achieve them effectively. These indicators are indispensable tools for evaluating organizational performance and guiding strategic decisions. From profitability and liquidity metrics to market-based and sustainability indicators, these metrics provide a comprehensive framework for understanding a company's financial health and operational efficiency. Leveraging these indicators enables organizations to optimize resource allocation, improve risk management, and enhance stakeholder confidence, ultimately ensuring long-term success and sustainability.

4. CHALLENGES AND OBSTACLES IN OPTIMIZING FINANCIAL DECISION-MAKING

Optimizing financial decision-making is a complex process that faces numerous challenges and obstacles, stemming from the dynamic nature of financial markets, organizational limitations, and external uncertainties. One of the primary challenges is the inherent uncertainty in predicting future economic conditions, such as interest rates, inflation, and market demand, which significantly influence financial decisions. As noted by Damodaran (2012), financial decision-making often relies on forecasts and assumptions that are inherently uncertain, making it difficult to achieve precise predictions. This uncertainty creates risks that can undermine even the most well-thought-out strategies. Another obstacle is the issue of information asymmetry, which occurs when decision-makers lack access to complete or accurate data necessary for making informed financial decisions. This problem is particularly prevalent in large organizations where communication gaps can hinder the flow of critical information. According to Akerlof (2003), information asymmetry can lead to adverse selection and moral hazard, resulting in suboptimal financial decisions. Bridging these information gaps requires the implementation of robust data collection and management systems, which can be resourceintensive and time-consuming. The complexity of financial markets also presents significant challenges for optimizing decision-making. Financial markets are influenced by a myriad of interconnected factors, including geopolitical events, regulatory changes, and technological advancements. These factors create a dynamic environment where financial decision-makers must continuously adapt their strategies. As highlighted by Bodie et al. (2014), the rapid pace of change in financial markets demands that organizations maintain a high level of agility, which can be difficult to achieve given the often-rigid structures of financial planning processes. A lack of adequate technological infrastructure is another common obstacle in optimizing financial decisions. Advanced analytical tools, such as big data analytics, artificial intelligence, and machine learning, are increasingly being used to enhance financial decision-making. However, many organizations face challenges in adopting these technologies due to high implementation costs, insufficient expertise, or resistance to change. According to Brynjolfsson and McAfee (2014), the digital divide in technological adoption exacerbates disparities in decision-making capabilities between organizations, leaving less technologically advanced firms at a disadvantage. Human biases also pose a significant challenge to optimizing financial decisionmaking. Cognitive biases, such as overconfidence, anchoring, and confirmation bias, can lead to suboptimal decisions by distorting judgment and reasoning. These biases are particularly problematic in high-stakes financial decisions where objectivity is crucial. Kahneman and Tversky (2000) emphasize that overcoming these biases requires the implementation of structured decision-making frameworks and the use of quantitative models to counteract subjective influences. Another challenge lies in balancing short-term financial objectives with long-term strategic goals. Organizations often face pressure from stakeholders to deliver immediate results, which can lead to decisions that prioritize short-term gains over sustainable growth. Kaplan and Norton (2004) argue that this misalignment of objectives undermines the effectiveness of financial decision-making and hampers the organization's ability to achieve its long-term vision. Striking the right balance requires a cohesive strategy that integrates financial performance with broader organizational goals. Resource constraints also hinder the optimization of financial decisions. Limited financial, human, and technological resources can restrict an organization's ability to conduct thorough analyses or implement advanced decisionmaking tools. Parnell et al. (2013) suggest that resource limitations often force organizations to rely on simplified models or heuristic approaches, which may fail to capture the complexity of financial decisions. Addressing these constraints requires prioritizing investments in decisionmaking capabilities and ensuring that resources are allocated effectively. Regulatory and compliance requirements add another layer of complexity to financial decision-making. Organizations must navigate an increasingly stringent regulatory landscape, which often imposes constraints on their financial strategies. According to Chapman and Ward (2011), the need to comply with complex regulations can slow down the decision-making process and limit the range of viable financial options. This challenge is further compounded by the variability in regulatory frameworks across different regions, making it difficult for multinational organizations to harmonize their financial strategies. The lack of effective risk management frameworks is another significant obstacle in optimizing financial decisions. Organizations often struggle to quantify and mitigate risks effectively, leaving them vulnerable to adverse outcomes. As noted by Hubbard (2014), traditional risk management approaches may be inadequate for addressing the complexities of modern financial decision-making, necessitating the adoption of more sophisticated methods such as probabilistic modeling and scenario analysis. Organizational culture and resistance to change can impede efforts to optimize financial decision-making. A culture that prioritizes maintaining the status quo over embracing innovation often stifles the adoption of new tools and methodologies. According to Cameron and Quinn (2011), fostering a culture of adaptability and continuous improvement is essential for overcoming resistance and enabling the successful implementation of optimized financial decision-making practices. Optimizing financial decision-making is fraught with challenges ranging from uncertainty and information asymmetry to technological barriers and cognitive biases. Addressing these obstacles requires a multifaceted approach that includes adopting advanced analytical tools, implementing robust risk management frameworks, fostering a culture of adaptability, and aligning financial decisions with long-term organizational goals. By overcoming these challenges, organizations can enhance their decision-making processes, reduce risks, and achieve sustainable financial performance in an increasingly complex business environment.

5. CONCLUSIONS AND EVALUATIONS

The integration between financial management and strategic planning is a crucial factor for the success of organizations, especially in a volatile and dynamic economic environment. Aligning financial decisions with strategic objectives is a fundamental pillar to ensure long-term sustainability and competitiveness. Financial tools such as the Balanced Scorecard, Monte Carlo simulation, and decision trees provide a robust framework for scenario evaluation and risk management, allowing for efficient resource allocation. These tools, combined with the use of advanced technologies and data analysis, are vital for developing strategies that maximize organizational value while mitigating the impacts of market uncertainties and fluctuations. Strategic flexibility in financial management is an essential condition for organizational success. Mintzberg et al. (2005) emphasize that strategic planning, to be effective, must be adaptable to rapid and unpredictable changes in the external environment. In highly volatile markets, the ability to quickly adapt financial resources can determine the survival and competitiveness of companies, seizing new opportunities while minimizing risks. Continuous adaptation of financial strategies is, therefore, crucial for ensuring long-term viability. Additionally, integrating sustainability practices into financial planning, as stated by Khan et al. (2016), is becoming increasingly relevant, as investors and stakeholders are prioritizing companies committed to social and environmental responsibility. However, despite being initially planned, it was not possible to conduct surveys with companies to validate the information and hypotheses proposed in the study. This challenge prevented the collection of empirical data directly from organizations, which would limit the ability to validate financial models in a more practical and specific context. Nevertheless, the study heavily relies on evidence from literature, offering a comprehensive theoretical perspective on how financial management tools can be applied in different organizational scenarios. The difficulty in applying these tools in real companies does not invalidate the recommendations but limits the depth of the practical analysis that could have been conducted. The recommendations remain, as already outlined in the theoretical practices. It is imperative for companies to invest in financial management systems that provide an integrated view of their indicators, both financial and non-financial. The implementation of the Balanced Scorecard, as suggested by Kaplan and Norton (2004), should be a standard practice in organizations to ensure that financial performance is aligned with strategic objectives. Adopting new technologies, such as artificial intelligence and big data, also becomes a priority, as these tools not only accelerate decision-making but also increase the accuracy of financial forecasts, as evidenced by Brynjolfsson and McAfee (2017). The use of these technologies represents a significant advantage for companies by providing more robust predictive analysis, which contributes to more efficient resource allocation and better-informed decision-making. Risk management also needs to be more rigorous. The use of tools such as Monte Carlo simulation and sensitivity analysis, as noted by Glasserman (2004) and Truong et al. (2008), can help companies predict the impacts of different economic scenarios and identify vulnerability points. Furthermore, implementing financial models that consider not only financial returns but also the social and environmental impact of decisions, as proposed by Elkington (1997), becomes increasingly essential. Companies that enter this area of analysis not only meet stakeholders' expectations but position themselves as leaders in social and environmental responsibility, gaining greater respect and trust in the market. Regarding human resources, continuous investment in talent development should also be a priority within financial strategic planning. Pfeffer (1998) argues that companies that treat employees as strategic assets have a significant competitive advantage. Investing in human capital, especially in training and talent retention, ensures the effective execution of financial decisions, aligning employees with the organization's strategic goals. Therefore, financial management must integrate people management as part of its long-term strategy, ensuring that human resources also contribute to the organization's sustainable growth. Finally, despite the limitations in using surveys directly with companies, the analysis remains valid, based on robust theoretical models that demonstrate the importance of integrating financial decisions with strategic planning. Organizations that adopt a flexible approach, aligned with advanced technologies, sustainable practices, and effective human resource management, will be better positioned to face future challenges and ensure their competitiveness in the global market.

ACKNOWLEDGEMENT

The authors would like to express their sincere gratitude to Ricardo Marcão (ISLA Santarém, Polytechnic Institute & NECE-UBI, Portugal) and Vasco Ribeiro Santos (Polytechnic University of Tomar (IPT), Portugal) for their valuable editorial guidance, support, and contributions to the development of this chapter and the overall book project.

REFERENCES

Agrawal, A., Gans, J., & Goldfarb, A. (2018). *Prediction machines: The simple economics of artificial intelligence*. Harvard Business Review Press.

Akerlof, G. A. (2003). Behavioral macroeconomics and macroeconomic behavior. *The American Economic Review, 92*(3), 411–433. DOI: 10.1257/00028280260136192

Amram, M., & Kulatilaka, N. (1999). *Real options: Managing strategic investment in an uncertain world*. Harvard Business School Press.

Ansoff, H. I. (1965). *Corporate strategy: An analytic approach to business policy for growth and expansion*. McGraw-Hill.

Atrill, P., & McLaney, E. (2020). *Accounting and finance for non-specialists*. Pearson.

Barney, J. (1991). Firm resources and sustained competitive advantage. *Journal of Management, 17*(1), 99–120. DOI: 10.1177/014920639101700108

Bebchuk, L. A., & Fried, J. M. (2004). *Pay without performance: The unfulfilled promise of executive compensation*. Harvard University Press.

Berk, J., & DeMarzo, P. (2020). *Corporate finance*. Pearson.

Bititci, U. S., Bourne, M., Cross, J. A., & Nudurupati, S. S. (2016). Integrated performance measurement systems: Structure and dynamics. *International Journal of Operations & Production Management, 36*(5), 575–601.

Black, F., & Scholes, M. (1973). The pricing of options and corporate liabilities. *Journal of Political Economy, 81*(3), 637–654. DOI: 10.1086/260062

Bodie, Z., Kane, A., & Marcus, A. J. (2014). *Investments*. McGraw-Hill Education.

Bourne, M., Neely, A., Mills, J., & Platts, K. (2013). *The impact of performance measurement on organizational success*. Cambridge University Press.

Brigham, E. F., & Daves, P. R. (2021). *Intermediate financial management*. Cengage Learning.

Brigham, E. F., & Ehrhardt, M. C. (2022). *Financial management: Theory and practice*. Cengage Learning.

Brigham, E. F., & Houston, J. F. (2021). *Fundamentals of financial management*. Cengage Learning.

Brynjolfsson, E., & McAfee, A. (2014). *The second machine age: Work, progress, and prosperity in a time of brilliant technologies*. W. W. Norton & Company.

Brynjolfsson, E., & McAfee, A. (2017). *Machine, platform, crowd: Harnessing our digital future*. W. W. Norton & Company.

Cameron, K. S., & Quinn, R. E. (2011). *Diagnosing and changing organizational culture: Based on the competing values framework*. Jossey-Bass.

Cascio, W. F. (2021). *Managing human resources: Productivity, quality of work life, profits*. McGraw-Hill Education.

Chapman, C., & Ward, S. (2011). *How to manage project opportunity and risk: Why uncertainty management can be a much better approach than risk management*. Wiley.

Chenhall, R. H., & Moers, F. (2015). The role of innovation in the evolution of management accounting and its integration into management control. *Accounting, Organizations and Society*, *47*, 1–13. DOI: 10.1016/j.aos.2015.10.002

Christensen, C. M., Raynor, M. E., & McDonald, R. (2004). *The innovator's solution: Creating and sustaining successful growth*. Harvard Business School Press.

Christensen, C. M., Raynor, M. E., & McDonald, R. (2015). What is disruptive innovation? *Harvard Business Review*, *93*(12), 44–53. PMID: 17183796

Clemen, R. T., & Reilly, T. (2013). *Making hard decisions with decision tools*. Cengage Learning.

Damodaran, A. (2012). *Investment valuation: Tools and techniques for determining the value of any asset*. Wiley.

Damodaran, A. (2015). *Applied corporate finance: A user's manual*. Wiley.

Damodaran, A. (2016). *Damodaran on valuation: Security analysis for investment and corporate finance*. Wiley.

Damodaran, A. (2020). *Narrative and numbers: The value of stories in business*. Columbia University Press.

Davenport, T. H., & Harris, J. G. (2007). *Competing on analytics: The new science of winning*. Harvard Business Review Press.

Eccles, R. G., Ioannou, I., & Serafeim, G. (2014). The impact of corporate sustainability on organizational processes and performance. *Management Science, 60*(11), 2835–2857. DOI: 10.1287/mnsc.2014.1984

Eccles, R. G., Ioannou, I., & Serafeim, G. (2020). The impact of corporate sustainability on organizational processes and performance. *Management Science, 60*(11), 2835–2857. DOI: 10.1287/mnsc.2014.1984

Elkington, J. (1997). *Cannibals with forks: The triple bottom line of 21st century business*. Capstone Publishing.

Fama, E. F. (1980). Agency problems and the theory of the firm. *Journal of Political Economy, 88*(2), 288–307. DOI: 10.1086/260866

Freeman, R. E., Harrison, J. S., & Wicks, A. C. (2007). *Managing for stakeholders: Survival, reputation, and success*. Yale University Press.

Gaughan, P. A. (2020). *Mergers, acquisitions, and corporate restructurings*. Wiley.

Gitman, L. J., & Zutter, C. J. (2020). *Principles of managerial finance*. Pearson.

Gitman, L. J., Zutter, C. J., & Joehnk, M. D. (2018). *Personal financial planning*. Cengage Learning.

Glasserman, P. (2004). *Monte Carlo methods in financial engineering*. Springer.

Hambrick, D. C., & Fredrickson, J. W. (2001). Are you sure you have a strategy? *The Academy of Management Perspectives, 15*(4), 48–59. DOI: 10.5465/ame.2001.5897655

Harrison, J. R., Carroll, G. R., & Tosi, H. L. (2014). The impact of capital structure on business strategy. *Academy of Management Review, 39*(4), 413–436.

Higgins, R. C. (2016). *Analysis for financial management*. McGraw-Hill Education.

Hillier, D., Ross, S. A., Westerfield, R. W., Jaffe, J., & Jordan, B. D. (2021). *Corporate finance*. McGraw-Hill Education.

Hitt, M. A., Ireland, R. D., & Hoskisson, R. E. (2012). *Strategic management: Concepts and cases: Competitiveness and globalization*. Cengage Learning.

Hope, J., & Fraser, R. (2003). *Beyond budgeting: How managers can break free from the annual performance trap*. Harvard Business School Press.

Hubbard, D. W. (2014). *How to measure anything: Finding the value of intangibles in business*. Wiley.

Hubbard, D. W. (2014). *The failure of risk management: Why it's broken and how to fix it*. Wiley.

Hull, J. C. (2018). *Risk management and financial institutions*. Wiley.

Jensen, M. C. (1986). Agency costs of free cash flow, corporate finance, and takeovers. *The American Economic Review*, *76*(2), 323–329.

Jorion, P. (2007). *Financial risk manager handbook*. Wiley.

Kahneman, D., & Tversky, A. (2000). *Choices, values, and frames*. Cambridge University Press. DOI: 10.1017/CBO9780511803475

Kaplan, R. S., & Mikes, A. (2012). Managing risks: A new framework. *Harvard Business Review*, *90*(6), 48–60.

Kaplan, R. S., & Norton, D. P. (1992). The balanced scorecard: Measures that drive performance. *Harvard Business Review*, *70*(1), 71–79. PMID: 10119714

Kaplan, R. S., & Norton, D. P. (1996). *The balanced scorecard: Translating strategy into action*. Harvard Business Review Press.

Kaplan, R. S., & Norton, D. P. (2004). *Strategy maps: Converting intangible assets into tangible outcomes*. Harvard Business School Press.

Kaplan, R. S., & Norton, D. P. (2008). *The execution premium: Linking strategy to operations for competitive advantage*. Harvard Business Review Press.

Khan, M., Serafeim, G., & Yoon, A. (2016). Corporate sustainability: First evidence on materiality. *The Accounting Review*, *91*(6), 1697–1724. DOI: 10.2308/accr-51383

Koller, G., Goedhart, M., & Wessels, D. (2010). *Valuation: Measuring and managing the value of companies*. Wiley.

Koller, T., Goedhart, M., & Wessels, D. (2020). *Valuation: Measuring and managing the value of companies*. McKinsey & Company.

Kotter, J. P. (1996). *Leading change*. Harvard Business Review Press.

La Porta, R., Lopez-de-Silanes, F., Shleifer, A., & Vishny, R. W. (1998). Law and finance. *Journal of Political Economy*, *106*(6), 1113–1155. DOI: 10.1086/250042

Markowitz, H. M. (1952). Portfolio selection. *The Journal of Finance*, *7*(1), 77–91.

Merchant, K. A., & Van der Stede, W. A. (2017). *Management control systems: Performance measurement, evaluation and incentives*. Pearson.

Mintzberg, H. (1994). *The rise and fall of strategic planning*. Free Press.

Mintzberg, H., Ahlstrand, B. W., & Lampel, J. (1998). *Strategy safari: A guided tour through the wilds of strategic management*. Free Press.

Mintzberg, H., Ahlstrand, B. W., & Lampel, J. (2005). *Strategy safari: A guided tour through the wilds of strategic management*. Free Press.

Modigliani, F., & Miller, M. H. (1958). The cost of capital, corporation finance and the theory of investment. *The American Economic Review*, *48*(3), 261–297.

Moyer, R. C., McGuigan, J. R., & Rao, R. P. (2022). *Contemporary financial management*. Cengage Learning.

Niven, P. R. (2006). *Balanced scorecard step-by-step: Maximizing performance and maintaining results*. Wiley.

Palepu, K. G., Healy, P. M., & Peek, E. (2020). *Business analysis and valuation: IFRS edition*. Cengage Learning.

Parnell, G. S., Driscoll, P. J., & Henderson, D. L. (2013). *Decision making in systems engineering and management*. Wiley.

Parrino, R., Kidwell, D. S., & Bates, T. W. (2020). *Fundamentals of corporate finance*. Wiley.

Pfeffer, J. (1998). *The human equation: Building profits by putting people first*. Harvard Business School Press.

Porter, M. E. (1980). *Competitive strategy: Techniques for analyzing industries and competitors*. Free Press.

Porter, M. E. (1991). *Competitive advantage: Creating and sustaining superior performance*. Free Press.

Porter, M. E., & Kramer, M. R. (2011). Creating shared value. *Harvard Business Review*, *89*(1–2), 62–77.

Pritchard, A., Taylor, D., & Belford, M. (2024). Teaching data-driven decision making for inventory analysis with Monte Carlo simulation. *Decision Sciences Journal of Innovative Education*.

Provost, F., & Fawcett, T. (2013). *Data science for business: What you need to know about data mining and data-analytic thinking*. O'Reilly Media.

Rajan, R. G., & Zingales, L. (2001). The great reversals: The politics of financial development in the twentieth century. *Journal of Financial Economics, 69*(1), 5–50. DOI: 10.1016/S0304-405X(03)00125-9

Ross, S., Westerfield, R., Jaffe, J., & Jordan, B. (2019). *Corporate finance*. McGraw-Hill Education.

Schilling, M. A. (2017). *Strategic management of technological innovation*. McGraw-Hill Education.

Stern, J. M., Shiely, J. S., & Ross, I. (2001). *The EVA challenge: Implementing value-added change in an organization*. Wiley.

Stewart, G. B. (1991). *The quest for value: A guide for senior managers*. Harper-Business.

Svetlova, E., & Thielmann, K. (2020). Financial risks and management. In *International Encyclopedia of Human Geography* (2nd ed.). DOI: 10.1016/B978-0-08-102295-5.10065-4

Taylor, B. W. (2013). *Introduction to management science*. Pearson.

Teece, D. J. (2018). *Dynamic capabilities and strategic management: Organizing for innovation and growth*. Oxford University Press.

Truong, G., Partington, G., & Peat, M. (2008). Cost-of-capital estimation and capital-budgeting practice in Australia. *Australian Journal of Management, 33*(1), 95–121. DOI: 10.1177/031289620803300106

Van Horne, J. C., & Wachowicz, J. M. (2008). *Fundamentals of financial management*. Pearson.

Winston, W. L. (2004). *Operations research: Applications and algorithms*. Cengage Learning.

Winston, W. L., & Venkataramanan, M. (2003). *Introduction to mathematical programming: Applications and algorithms*. Cengage Learning.

Young, S. D., & O'Byrne, S. F. (2001). *EVA and value-based management: A practical guide to implementation*. McGraw-Hill Education.

Yukl, G. (2010). *Leadership in organizations* (7th ed.). Pearson.

Compilation of References

Abdallah, J. C., & Guhao, E. S.Jr. (2025). Filipino graduate students in foreign universities: A phenomenological inquiry. *European Journal of Education Studies*, *12*(2), 271–289. DOI: 10.46827/ejes.v12i2.5827

Abreu, J. (2024). Marketing global de produtos: Impactos dos fatores culturais nas decisões estratégicas das corporações.

Acampora, G. (2020, February). Quantum computing meets artificial intelligence. In *AISEM annual conference on sensors and microsystems* (pp. 151-155). Cham: Springer International Publishing.DOI: 10.1007/978-3-030-69551-4_21

Agence Francaise Anticorruption. (2021). Anti-corruption due diligence for mergers and acquisitions: Practical guide. https://www.agence-francaise-anticorruption.gouv.fr/files/files/Practical%20Guide%202021%20FUSACQ.pdf

Agrawal, A., Gans, J., & Goldfarb, A. (2018). *Prediction machines: The simple economics of artificial intelligence*. Harvard Business Review Press.

Ahammad, M. F., Tarba, S. Y., Liu, Y., & Glaister, K. W. (2016). Knowledge transfer and cross-border acquisition performance: The impact of cultural distance and employee retention. *International Business Review*, *25*(1), 66–75. DOI: 10.1016/j.ibusrev.2014.06.015

Ahlawat., & Associates. (2024). Anti-corruption due diligence in India transactions. https://www.ahlawatassociates.com/blog/anti-corruption-due-diligence-in-india-transactions

Ai, Q., Bai, T., Cao, Z., Chang, Y., Chen, J., Chen, Z., Cheng, Z., Dong, S., Dou, Z., Feng, F., Gao, S., Guo, J., He, X., Lan, Y., Li, C., Liu, Y., Lyu, Z., Ma, W., Ma, J., & Zhu, X. (2023). Information retrieval meets large language models: A strategic report from Chinese IR community. *AI Open*, *4*, 80–90. DOI: 10.1016/j.aiopen.2023.08.001

Akerlof, G. A. (2003). Behavioral macroeconomics and macroeconomic behavior. *The American Economic Review, 92*(3), 411–433. DOI: 10.1257/00028280260136192

Akerlof, G. A., & Shiller, R. J. (2015). *Phishing for phools: The economics of manipulation and deception*. Princeton University Press. DOI: 10.2307/j.ctvc777w8

Al-Laham, A., Schweizer, L., & Amburgey, T. (2018). Post-acquisition reorganization: The role of timing and integration depth. *European Management Review, 15*(2), 205–221. DOI: 10.1111/emre.12138

Allee, T., & Yohn, T. L. (2018). A yardstick approach to merger retrospectives. *The Journal of Finance, 73*(2), 887–914. DOI: 10.1111/jofi.12589

Alqahtani, F., Alhassan, A., & Alshammari, M. (2025). The role of artificial intelligence in enhancing ESG outcomes: Insights from Saudi Arabia. *Journal of Risk and Financial Management, 18*(10), 572.

Amajuoyi, P., Benjamin, L. B., & Adeusi, K. B. (2024). Agile methodologies: Adapting product management to rapidly changing market conditions. *GSC Advanced Research and Reviews, 19*(2), 249–267. DOI: 10.30574/gscarr.2024.19.2.0181

Amaral, O. (2022). NLP-based automated compliance checking of data processing agreements. *arXiv*. https://arxiv.org/abs/2209.09722

Amin, R. U., Awan, G. M., & Raheem, F. (2021). Critical analyses of Pak-Afghan Transit Trade Agreement: Pakistan's perspective. *Research Journal of Social Sciences and Economics Review, 1*(4), 418–426. DOI: 10.36902/rjsser-vol1-iss4-2020(418-426)

Amram, M., & Kulatilaka, N. (1999). *Real options: Managing strategic investment in an uncertain world*. Harvard Business School Press.

Anderson, P. (2019). Short-term financial strategies for SMEs. *Business and Economics Journal, 12*(3), 45–58.

Ang, A. (2014). *Asset management: A systematic approach to factor investing*. Oxford University Press. DOI: 10.1093/acprof:oso/9780199959327.001.0001

Ang, S., Van Dyne, L., Koh, C., Ng, K. Y., Templer, K. J., Tay, C., & Chandrasekar, N. A. (2007). Cultural intelligence: Its measurement and effects on cultural judgment and decision making, cultural adaptation and task performance. *Management and Organization Review, 3*(3), 335–371. DOI: 10.1111/j.1740-8784.2007.00082.x

Angwin, D., & Meadows, M. (2015). Human integration following M&A: Synthesizing different M&A research streams. *Journal of Management Studies, 52*(7), 1141–1167.

Ansari, W. M. (2024). Integrating Pathology and Laboratory Medicine into the Transitional Clerkship Model: A Strategic Educational Realignment. *Journal of HBS M&DC, 4*(1), 32–38. DOI: 10.70394/jhbsmdc.v4i1.70

Ansoff, H. I. (1965). *Corporate strategy: An analytic approach to business policy for growth and expansion*. McGraw-Hill.

Armbrust, M., Fox, A., Griffith, R., Joseph, A. D., Katz, R., Konwinski, A., Lee, G., Patterson, D., Rabkin, A., Stoica, I., & Zaharia, M. (2010). A view of cloud computing. *Communications of the ACM, 53*(4), 50–58. DOI: 10.1145/1721654.1721672

Arnold & Porter. (2011). Anti-corruption due diligence in mergers and acquisitions. https://www.arnoldporter.com/-/media/files/perspectives/publications/2011/07/anticorruption-due-diligence-in-mergers-and-acqu__/files/newsletter-item/fileattachment/advisory_anticorruption_due_diligence_in_mergers__.pdf?rev=7c55fc285ac941848313327d92b8df42&sc_lang=en&hash=6EC5DB12BD540827ABEF32AA6D932F54

Arora, A., Sharma, M., & Bhaskaran, S. (2020). Blockchain technology transforms E-commerce for enterprises. In *Data Science and Analytics: 5th International Conference on Recent Developments in Science, Engineering and Technology, REDSET 2019, Gurugram, India, November 15–16, 2019, Revised Selected Papers, Part II 5* (pp. 26-34). Springer Singapore.DOI: 10.1007/978-981-15-5830-6_3

Aschi, M., Bonura, S., Masi, N., Messina, D., & Profeta, D. (2022). Cybersecurity and fraud detection in financial transactions. In *Big data and artificial intelligence in digital finance: Increasing personalization and trust in digital finance using big data and AI* (pp. 269–278). Springer International Publishing., DOI: 10.1007/978-3-030-94590-9_15

Ashiedu, B. I., Ogbuefi, E., Nwabekee, U. S., Ogeawuchi, J. C., & Abayomi, A. A. (2024). The silent dealbreaker: Why organizational culture should be a due diligence priority. *International Journal of Scientific Research in Science and Technology, 11*(4), 565–586. DOI: 10.32628/IJSRST241151214

Assunção, M. D., Calheiros, R. N., Bianchi, S., Netto, M. A., & Buyya, R. (2015). Big Data computing and clouds: Trends and future directions. *Journal of Parallel and Distributed Computing, 79*, 3–15. DOI: 10.1016/j.jpdc.2014.08.003

Atrill, P., & McLaney, E. (2020). *Accounting and finance for non-specialists*. Pearson.

Attaway, M. C. (1999). Competitive intelligence. *Internal auditor, 56*(6), 48-48.

Atzori, L., Iera, A., & Morabito, G. (2010). The Internet of Things: A survey. *Computer Networks, 54*(15), 2787–2805. DOI: 10.1016/j.comnet.2010.05.010

Avrillia, S., Hakim, L., Sulfia, S., & Anshori, M. I. (2025). Hybrid leadership and organizational performance: A literature review approach. *Implementasi Manajemen & Kewirausahaan*, *5*(1), 14–30. DOI: 10.38156/imka.v5i1.540

Ayularas, B., & Aulia Zaim, I. (2024). Business Strategic Realignment for a Sustainable Fashion Brand. *Journal of Business and Management Review*, *5*(2), 105–123. DOI: 10.47153/jbmr52.8952024

Azeem, M., Haleem, A., Bahl, S., Javaid, M., Suman, R., & Nandan, D. (2022). Big data applications to take up major challenges across manufacturing industries: A brief review. *Materials Today: Proceedings*, *49*, 339–348. DOI: 10.1016/j.matpr.2021.02.147

Azoury, N., Subrahmanyam, S., & Sarkis, N. (2024). The influence of a data-driven culture on product development and organizational success through the use of business analytics. *Journal of Wireless Mobile Networks, Ubiquitous Computing and Dependable Applications*, *15*(2), 123–134. DOI: 10.58346/JOWUA.2024.I2.009

Babatunde, A. T. (2024). Driving Innovation through AI and Machine Learning: Exploring the Opportunities of Integrating Artificial Intelligence in Business Intelligence. *Academic Journal of Global Who is who in Academia, 5*(1), 1-14.

Babu, S. R., & Jagadish, A. (2022). ESG compliance and firm value: Evidence from emerging markets. *Journal of International Financial Management & Accounting*, *33*(3), 345–372. DOI: 10.1111/jifm.12123

Barney, J. (1991). Firm resources and sustained competitive advantage. *Journal of Management*, *17*(1), 99–120. DOI: 10.1177/014920639101700108

Basel Institute on Governance. (2021). Recommendation of the Council for OECD Further Combating Bribery of Foreign Public Officials in International Business Transactions (2021 Anti-Bribery Recommendation). *OECD*. https://baselgovernance.org/publications/recommendation-council-oecd-further-combating-bribery-foreign-public-officials

Baskoro, T. (2024). Digital Disruption: Landscape of E-Business for Competitive Advantage. *Advances in Business & Industrial Marketing Research*, *2*(1), 1–14. DOI: 10.60079/abim.v2i1.218

Bauer, F., & Matzler, K. (2012). Antecedents of M&A success: The role of strategic complementarity, cultural fit, and degree and speed of integration. *Strategic Management Journal*, *33*(5), 517–539. DOI: 10.1002/smj.1957

Bebchuk, L. A., & Fried, J. M. (2004). *Pay without performance: The unfulfilled promise of executive compensation*. Harvard University Press.

Bechtsis, D., Tsolakis, N., Iakovou, E., & Vlachos, D. (2022). Data-driven Secure, Resilient and Sustainable Sup-ply Chains: Gaps, Opportunities, and a New Generalized Data Sharing and Data Monetization Framework. *International Journal of Production Research, 60*(14), 4397–4417. DOI: 10.1080/00207543.2021.1957506

Behera, R. K., Bala, P. K., Rana, N. P., & Khorana, S. (2020). Personalization in marketing: A review of technologies, approaches, and effectiveness. *Journal of Business Research, 116*, 147–161.

Bekaert, G., Harvey, C. R., Lundblad, C. T., & Siegel, S. (2021). Global growth opportunities and market integration. *Journal of International Economics, 132*, 103533. DOI: 10.1016/j.jinteco.2021.103533

Belhadi, A., Kamble, S., Fosso Wamba, S., & Queiroz, M. M. (2022). Building supply-chain resilience: An artificial intelligence-based technique and decision-making framework. *International Journal of Production Research, 60*(14), 4487–4507. DOI: 10.1080/00207543.2021.1950935

Bellis, A., De Stefano, V., & Zaninotto, E. (2024). Digital leadership and hybrid work: Organizational agility in the digital era. *Journal of Business Research, 172*, 114412. DOI: 10.1016/j.jbusres.2023.114412

Bhardwaj, S., Sharma, N., Goel, M., Sharma, K., & Verma, V. (2024). Enhancing customer targeting in e-commerce and digital marketing through AI-driven personalization strategies. *Advances in Digital Marketing in the Era of Artificial Intelligence*, 41-60. *Machine learning and deep learning paradigms: From techniques to practical applications and research frontiers. Computers, 14*(3), 93. DOI: 10.1201/9781003450443-4

Birkinshaw, J., Bresman, H., & Håkanson, L. (2000). Managing the post-acquisition integration process: How the human integration and task integration processes interact to foster value creation. *Journal of Management Studies, 37*(3), 395–425. DOI: 10.1111/1467-6486.00186

Bititci, U. S., Bourne, M., Cross, J. A., & Nudurupati, S. S. (2016). Integrated performance measurement systems: Structure and dynamics. *International Journal of Operations & Production Management, 36*(5), 575–601.

Black, F., & Scholes, M. (1973). The pricing of options and corporate liabilities. *Journal of Political Economy, 81*(3), 637–654. DOI: 10.1086/260062

Bodie, Z., Kane, A., & Marcus, A. J. (2014). *Investments*. McGraw-Hill Education.

Botta, E., & Kozul-Wright, R. (2021). Industrial policy and institutional capacity in the global South. *Development Policy Review, 39*(S1), O7–O27. DOI: 10.1111/dpr.12560

Bourne, M., Neely, A., Mills, J., & Platts, K. (2013). *The impact of performance measurement on organizational success.* Cambridge University Press.

Bozos, K., Filatotchev, I., & Goergen, M. (2025). Corporate governance, finance, and global strategy. *International Business Review, 34*(6), 102499. DOI: 10.1016/j.ibusrev.2025.102499

Brigham, E. F., & Daves, P. R. (2021). *Intermediate financial management.* Cengage Learning.

Brigham, E. F., & Ehrhardt, M. C. (2022). *Financial management: Theory and practice.* Cengage Learning.

Brigham, E. F., & Houston, J. F. (2021). *Fundamentals of financial management.* Cengage Learning.

Bristol-Alagbariya, B., Ayanponle, L. O., & Ogedengbe, D. E. (2022). Integrative HR approaches in mergers and acquisitions ensuring seamless organizational synergies. Magna Scientia Advanced Research and Reviews, 6(1), 078–085. DOI: 10.30574/msarr.2022.6.1.0070

Britsche, A., & Fekete, M. (2022). Strategic Management for the Realignment of Risk Determination of the Supply Chain in Electric Car Production. *International Scientific Conference EMAN – Economics and Management: How to Cope with Disrupted Times.* (pp. 44–50) DOI: 10.31410/EMAN.2022.97

Broome, A., & Quigley, F. (2021). Harmonizing merger control: A global comparative analysis. *The Journal of Law & Economics, 64*(3), 387–420. DOI: 10.1086/714431

Brouthers, K. D., & Brouthers, L. E. (2020). Acquisition or greenfield investment: An institutional perspective. *Strategic Management Journal, 41*(9), 1679–1697. DOI: 10.1002/smj.3139

Brown, T. (2020). Liquidity management in small enterprises. *Financial Insights, 8*(2), 120–135.

Bruns, A., & Stieglitz, S. (2013). Towards more systematic Twitter analysis: Metrics for tweeting activities. *International Journal of Social Research Methodology, 16*(2), 91–108. DOI: 10.1080/13645579.2012.756095

Brynjolfsson, E., & Hitt, L. M. (1996). Paradox lost? Firm-level evidence on the returns to information systems spending. *Management Science, 42*(4), 541–558. DOI: 10.1287/mnsc.42.4.541

Brynjolfsson, E., & McAfee, A. (2014). *The second machine age: Work, progress, and prosperity in a time of brilliant technologies.* W. W. Norton & Company.

Brynjolfsson, E., & McAfee, A. (2017). *Machine, platform, crowd: Harnessing our digital future.* W. W. Norton & Company.

Budhiraja, S. (2021). Can continuous learning amplify employees' change-efficacy and contextual performance? Evidence from post-merger Indian organizations. *International Journal of Manpower, 42*(6), 1144–1158. DOI: 10.1108/IJM-05-2020-0208

Bughin, J., Seong, J., Manyika, J., Chui, M., & Joshi, R. (2019). *The future of work in Europe* (McKinsey Global Institute Discussion Paper). McKinsey & Company. https://www.mckinsey.com/~/media/mckinsey/featured%20insights/future%20of%20organizations/the%20future%20of%20work%20in%20europe/mgi-the-future-of-work-in-europe-discussion-paper.pdf

Butterworth, M. (2018). The ICO and artificial intelligence: The role of fairness in the GDPR framework. *Computer Law & Security Review, 34*(2), 257–268. DOI: 10.1016/j.clsr.2018.01.004

Cameron, E., & Green, M. (2019). *Making sense of change management: A complete guide to the models, tools and techniques of organizational change* (5th ed.). Kogan Page.

Cameron, K. S., & Quinn, R. E. (2011). *Diagnosing and changing organizational culture: Based on the competing values framework.* Jossey-Bass.

Campos, A. C., de Rezende, D. C., Leme, P. H. M. V., de Brito, M. J., & Antonialli, L. M. (2021). Marketing digital em tempos de crise. *Revista Gestão e Desenvolvimento, 18*(3), 102–130. DOI: 10.25112/rgd.v18i3.2784

Caravantes, C. B., & Weiler, T. K. R. (2024). *Empresas na era digital: Uma análise das mudanças e implicações na administração moderna.* Editora Manual.

Cartwright, S., & Schoenberg, R. (2006). Thirty years of mergers and acquisitions research: Recent advances and future opportunities. *British Journal of Management, 17*(S1), S1–S5. DOI: 10.1111/j.1467-8551.2006.00475.x

Carvalho, P. V. (2025). Globalização da produção e desenvolvimento tecnológico: Ascensão chinesa e a disputa no setor de telecomunicações.

Casado Salguero, G., Fernández Gámez, M. Á., Aldeanueva Fernández, I., & Ruíz Palomo, D. (2019). Competitive intelligence and sustainable competitive advantage in the hotel industry. *Sustainability (Basel), 11*(6), 1597. DOI: 10.3390/su11061597

Cascio, W. F. (2021). *Managing human resources: Productivity, quality of work life, profits*. McGraw-Hill Education.

Cekuls, A. (2024). The complexity of competitive intelligence in the age of data ambiguity and artificial intelligence. *Journal of Intelligence Studies in Business, 14*(SI 1), 55–65. https://doi.org/DOI: 10.37380/jisib.v14.si1.2417

Cekuls, A. (2023). Unveiling the value of competitive intelligence: Coordinated communication and added value. *Journal of Intelligence Studies in Business, 13*(1), 4–5. DOI: 10.37380/jisib.v13i1.987

Chan, H. K., Wang, X., Lacka, E., & Zhang, M. (2016). A mixed-method approach to extracting the value of social media data. *Production and Operations Management, 25*(3), 568–583. DOI: 10.1111/poms.12390

Chan, Y. E., & Reich, B. H. (2007). IT alignment: What have we learned? *Journal of Information Technology, 22*(4), 297–315. DOI: 10.1057/palgrave.jit.2000109

Chapman, C., & Ward, S. (2011). *How to manage project opportunity and risk: Why uncertainty management can be a much better approach than risk management*. Wiley.

Chatterjee, S., Lubatkin, M. H., Schweiger, D. M., & Weber, Y. (1992). Cultural differences and shareholder value in related mergers: Linking equity and human capital. *Strategic Management Journal, 13*(5), 319–334. DOI: 10.1002/smj.4250130502

Chattu, V. K. (2021). A review of artificial intelligence, big data, and blockchain technology applications in medicine and global health. *Big Data and Cognitive Computing, 5*(3), 41. DOI: 10.3390/bdcc5030041

Chen, C. P., & Zhang, C. Y. (2014). Data-intensive applications, challenges, techniques and technologies: A survey on Big Data. *Information Sciences, 275*, 314–347. DOI: 10.1016/j.ins.2014.01.015

Chenhall, R. H., & Moers, F. (2015). The role of innovation in the evolution of management accounting and its integration into management control. *Accounting, Organizations and Society, 47*, 1–13. DOI: 10.1016/j.aos.2015.10.002

Chen, M., Mao, S., & Liu, Y. (2014). Big data: A survey. *Mobile Networks and Applications, 19*(2), 171–209. DOI: 10.1007/s11036-013-0489-0

Chen, W., & Liu, W. (2025). Digital M&A triggers innovation: When the going gets tough, the tough get going. *Research in International Business and Finance, 78*, 102957. DOI: 10.1016/j.ribaf.2025.102957

Chen, Y., Liu, H., & Tang, J. (2022). Post-merger integration and innovation upgrading: Evidence from knowledge-intensive acquisitions. *Technovation, 113*, 102450. DOI: 10.1016/j.technovation.2021.102450

Chirra, B. R. (2021). AI-Driven Security Audits: Enhancing Continuous Compliance through Machine Learning. *International Journal of Machine Learning Research in Cybersecurity and Artificial Intelligence, 12*(1), 410–433.

Chirra, B. R. (2021). Enhancing Cyber Incident Investigations with AI-Driven Forensic Tools. *International Journal of Advanced Engineering Technologies and Innovations, 1*(2), 157–177.

Chirra, D. R., & Collaborative, A. I. Blockchain Models for Enhancing Data Privacy in IoMT Networks. (2022). *International Journal of Machine Learning Research in Cybersecurity and Artificial Intelligence, 13*(1), 482-504.

Chowdhury, S., Budhwar, P., & Wood, G. (2024). Generative artificial intelligence in business: Towards a strategic human resource management framework. *British Journal of Management, 35*(4), 1680–1691. DOI: 10.1111/1467-8551.12824

Christensen, C. M., Raynor, M. E., & McDonald, R. (2004). *The innovator's solution: Creating and sustaining successful growth*. Harvard Business School Press.

Christensen, C. M., Raynor, M. E., & McDonald, R. (2015). What is disruptive innovation? *Harvard Business Review, 93*(12), 44–53. PMID: 17183796

Chui, M., Manyika, J., & Miremadi, M. (2018). *AI adoption advances, but foundational barriers remain*. McKinsey Insights.

Ciampi, F., Faraoni, M., Ballerini, J., & Meli, F. (2021). The co evolutionary relationship between digitalization and organizational agility. arXiv.

Čirjevskis, A. (2020). Valuing reciprocal synergies in merger and acquisition deals using the real option analysis. *Administrative Sciences, 10*(2), 27. DOI: 10.3390/admsci10020027

Claessens, S., & Yafeh, Y. (2019). How does corporate governance affect emerging market M&As? *Corporate Governance, 27*(5), 343–364. DOI: 10.1111/corg.12266

Clemen, R. T., & Reilly, T. (2013). *Making hard decisions with decision tools*. Cengage Learning.

Columbus, L. (2017). IBM predicts demand for data scientists will soar 28% by 2020. *IBM White Paper*

Correia, J. F., de Sousa, J. D., Macedo, K. G., da Silva, L. A. B., de Godoy, L. R. B., & Maschio, P. A. S. (2025). A relevância das estratégias do marketing digital para as organizações contemporâneas. *Revista FOCO, 18*(4), e8157. DOI: 10.54751/revistafoco.v18n4-108

Costa, O. R. (2025). O impacto das estratégias de marketing digital no branding: Um estudo de caso do Bar Chico em Parintins/AM.

Coutinho, D. A. (2021). O consumidor e modulação algorítmica de comportamento: A influência da inteligência artificial por meio de algoritmos no poder decisório do consumidor.

Couture, V., Roy, M. C., Dez, E., Laperle, S., & Bélisle-Pipon, J. C. (2023). Ethical implications of artificial intelligence in population health and the public's role in its governance: Perspectives from a citizen and expert panel. *Journal of Medical Internet Research, 25*, e44357. DOI: 10.2196/44357 PMID: 37104026

Crane, A., & Matten, D. (2021). *Business ethics: Managing corporate citizenship and sustainability in the age of globalization.* Oxford University Press., https://global.oup.com/academic/product/business-ethics-9780198810070?cc=in&lang=

Csaszar, F. A., Ketkar, H., & Kim, H. (2024). Artificial intelligence and strategic decision-making: Evidence from entrepreneurs and investors. *arXiv*. https://arxiv.org/abs/2408.08811

Currie, G., & Hawk, K. E. (2021, March). Ethical and legal challenges of artificial intelligence in nuclear medicine. In *Seminars in Nuclear Medicine* (Vol. 51, No. 2, pp. 120-125). WB Saunders.DOI: 10.1053/j.semnuclmed.2020.08.001

Damodaran, A. (2012). *Investment valuation: Tools and techniques for determining the value of any asset*. Wiley.

Damodaran, A. (2015). *Applied corporate finance: A user's manual*. Wiley.

Damodaran, A. (2016). *Damodaran on valuation: Security analysis for investment and corporate finance*. Wiley.

Damodaran, A. (2020). *Narrative and numbers: The value of stories in business.* Columbia University Press.

Dan, S. (2000). Eye on the Competition. *Intelligent Enterprise*.

Datta, D. K. (1991). Organizational fit and acquisition performance: Effects of post-acquisition integration. *Strategic Management Journal*, *12*(4), 281–297. DOI: 10.1002/smj.4250120404

Dave, M., & Gianey, H. (2016, November). Different clustering algorithms for Big Data analytics: A review. In *2016 International Conference System Modeling & Advancement in Research Trends (SMART)* (pp. 328-333). IEEE.DOI: DOI: 10.1109/SYSMART.2016.7894544

Davenport, T. H., & Harris, J. G. (2007). *Competing on analytics: The new science of winning*. Harvard Business Review Press.

Davenport, T. H., & Westerman, G. (2018). Why so many high-profile digital transformations fail. *Harvard Business Review*.

Dave, T., Athaluri, S. A., & Singh, S. (2023). ChatGPT in medicine: An overview of its applications, advantages, limitations, future prospects, and ethical considerations. *Frontiers in Artificial Intelligence*, *6*, 1169595. DOI: 10.3389/frai.2023.1169595 PMID: 37215063

Davis, F. D. (1989). Perceived usefulness, perceived ease of use, and user acceptance of information technology. *Management Information Systems Quarterly*, *13*(3), 319–340. DOI: 10.2307/249008

Debevoise & Plimpton. (2018). FCPA update: Successor liability and post-acquisition risk. https://www.debevoise.com/~/media/files/insights/publications/2018/12/201812_fcpa_update_december_2018.pdf

Denison, D. R., & Ko, I. (2016). Cultural due diligence in mergers and acquisitions. In *Advances in Mergers and Acquisitions* (pp. 53–72). Emerald Group Publishing Limited., DOI: 10.1108/S1479-361X20160000015004

Department of Information Systems and Security 6178 College Station Drive Williamsburg KY 40769 United States of America, U. of the C., Mohammed, M. H. S., Khan, M. S. A., Syed, M. M., Prosis Technologies Inc TX United States of America, D., & Cloud Resources - Irving United States of America, T. X. 75038. (2023). Remote work culture: The impact of digital transformation on workforce productivity. Journal of E-Science Letters, 4(1), 1–5. DOI: 10.51470/eSL.2023.4.1.01

Desouza, K. C. (2001). Intelligent agents for competitive intelligence: Survey of applications. *Competitive Intelligence Review*, *12*(4), 57–63. DOI: 10.1002/cir.1032

Devoteam. (2023). Devoteam announces strategic partnership with solutions by stc in the Middle East. https://www.devoteam.com

Dissanaike, G., Liu, Y., & Sturm, A. (2021). The dynamic effects of antitrust policy on growth and welfare. *Journal of Development Economics, 157*, 102719. DOI: 10.1016/j.jdeveco.2021.102719

Dohale, V., Akarte, M., Gunasekaran, A., & Verma, P. (2024). Exploring the role of artificial intelligence in building production resilience: Learnings from the COVID-19 pandemic. *International Journal of Production Research, 62*(15), 5472–5488. DOI: 10.1080/00207543.2022.2127961

Donaldson, T., & Walsh, J. P. (2015). Toward a theory of business ethics and governance. *Academy of Management Review, 40*(3), 436–457. https://repository.upenn.edu/handle/20.500.14332/38342

Dora, M., Kumar, A., Mangla, S. K., Pant, A., & Kamal, M. M. (2021). Critical Success Factors Influencing Artificial Intelligence Adoption in Food Supply Chains. *International Journal of Production Research, 60*(14), 4621–4640. DOI: 10.1080/00207543.2021.1959665

Drori, I., Wrzesniewski, A., & Ellis, S. (2011). Cultural clashes in a "merger of equals": The case of high-tech start-ups. *Human Resource Management, 50*(5), 625–649. DOI: 10.1002/hrm.20446

Dubuc, T., Stahl, F., & Roesch, E. B. (2020). Mapping the big data landscape: Technologies, platforms and paradigms for real-time analytics of data streams. *IEEE Access : Practical Innovations, Open Solutions, 9*, 15351–15374. DOI: 10.1109/ACCESS.2020.3046132

Ebrahimi, P., Basirat, M., Yousefi, A., Nekmahmud, M., Gholampour, A., & Fekete-Farkas, M. (2022). Social networks marketing and consumer purchase behavior: The combination of SEM and unsupervised machine learning approaches. *Big Data and Cognitive Computing, 6*(2), 35. DOI: 10.3390/bdcc6020035

Eccles, R. G., Ioannou, I., & Serafeim, G. (2014). The impact of corporate sustainability on organizational processes and performance. *Management Science, 60*(11), 2835–2857. DOI: 10.1287/mnsc.2014.1984

Eisenhardt, K. M., & Martin, J. A. (2000). Dynamic capabilities: What are they? *Strategic Management Journal, 21*(10–11), 1105–1121. DOI: 10.1002/1097-0266(200010/11)21:10/11<1105::AID-SMJ133>3.0.CO;2-E

Elbasi, E., Zaki, C., Topcu, A. E., Abdelbaki, W., Zreikat, A. I., Cina, E., Shdefat, A., & Saker, L. (2023). Crop prediction model using machine learning algorithms. *Applied Sciences (Basel, Switzerland), 13*(16), 9288. DOI: 10.3390/app13169288

Elkington, J. (1997). *Cannibals with forks: The triple bottom line of 21st century business*. Capstone Publishing.

European Commission. (2020). *Supporting small and medium-sized enterprises in the digital age*. European Commission Reports.

Fader, P. S., & Winer, R. S. (2012). Introduction to the special issue on the emergence and impact of user-generated content. *Marketing Science*, *31*(3), 369–371. DOI: 10.1287/mksc.1120.0715

Fadhlurrahman, M. A., Riyanta, S., & Ras, A. R. (2024). The role of competitive intelligence in strategic decision-making: A literature review. *Asian Journal of Engineering. Socialism and Health*, *3*(10), 2307–2324. DOI: 10.46799/ajesh.v3i9.411

Fama, E. F. (1980). Agency problems and the theory of the firm. *Journal of Political Economy*, *88*(2), 288–307. DOI: 10.1086/260866

Fang, X., & Liu, M. (2024). How does digital transformation drive digital technology innovation of enterprises? Evidence from Chinese listed firms. *Technological Forecasting and Social Change*, *204*, 123428. DOI: 10.1016/j.techfore.2024.123428

Feng, Y., & Liu, Z. (2024). Digital transformation and firm adaptive performance: Evidence from emerging markets. *Journal of Business Research*, *169*, 114215. DOI: 10.1016/j.jbusres.2023.114215

Fierro, I., Arbelaez, A., & Gavilanes, M. (2017). Digital marketing: A framework, review and research agenda. *International Journal of Research in Marketing*, *34*(1), 22–43. DOI: 10.1016/j.ijresmar.2016.11.006

Firk, S., Gehrke, Y., Meier, J., & Wolff, M. (2025). Fooled by the hype? The influence of technology hype on acquisition premiums in digital M&As. *Long Range Planning*, *58*(6), 102589. DOI: 10.1016/j.lrp.2025.102589

Ford, E., Milne, R., & Curlewis, K. (2023). Ethical issues when using digital biomarkers and artificial intelligence for the early detection of dementia. *Wiley Interdisciplinary Reviews. Data Mining and Knowledge Discovery*, *13*(3), e1492. DOI: 10.1002/widm.1492 PMID: 38439952

Francato, F. C., da Costa, W. D., & de Souza, R. O. P. (2024). Estratégias de marketing digital na era atual: Desafios e oportunidades. *Prospectus*, *6*(2), 21–36.

Frantz, T. L., & Center, D. T. I. (2014). A behavioral theory of the merger: Dynamics of the post-merger integration process. DOI: 10.21236/ADA606347

Freeman, R. E., Harrison, J. S., & Wicks, A. C. (2007). *Managing for stakeholders: Survival, reputation, and success*. Yale University Press.

Gade, K. R. (2021). Data-driven decision making in a complex world. *Journal of Computational Innovation, 1*(1).

Gallagher, K. P., & Pisani, N. (2019). State as global capitalist: FDI screening and national security. *International Affairs, 95*(3), 685–707. DOI: 10.1093/ia/iiz095

Galvin, R. H. (1997). Competitive intelligence at Motorola. *Competitive Intelligence Review, 8*(1), 3–6. DOI: 10.1002/cir.3880080104

Gao, X., & Johnston, D. (2021). Legal infrastructure and cross-border deal success. *International Business Review, 30*(1), 101751. DOI: 10.1016/j.ibusrev.2020.101751

Gao, Y., & Liu, H. (2023). Artificial intelligence-enabled personalization in interactive marketing: A customer journey perspective. *Journal of Research in Interactive Marketing, 17*(5), 663–680. DOI: 10.1108/JRIM-01-2022-0023

Gattiker, A., Gebara, F. H., Hofstee, H. P., Hayes, J. D., & Hylick, A. (2013). Big Data text-oriented benchmark creation for Hadoop. *IBM Journal of Research and Development, 57*(3/4), 10–11. DOI: 10.1147/JRD.2013.2240732

Gaughan, P. A. (2020). *Mergers, acquisitions, and corporate restructurings*. Wiley.

Gerlick, J. A., & Liozu, S. M. (2020). Ethical and legal considerations of artificial intelligence and algorithmic decision-making in personalized pricing. *Journal of Revenue and Pricing Management, 19*(2), 85–98. DOI: 10.1057/s41272-019-00225-2

Gheibi, O., Weyns, D., & Quin, F. (2021). Applying machine learning in self-adaptive systems: A systematic literature review. [TAAS]. *ACM Transactions on Autonomous and Adaptive Systems, 15*(3), 1–37. DOI: 10.1145/3469440

Ghosh, S. (2020). *Data analytics in finance: Applications in investments, risk management, and regulation*. Springer.

Giridhararajan, A., Prasad, S., & Ranjith, K. (2020). Retail store transformation using digital marketing proximity sensors. *Journal of Retailing and Consumer Services, 52*, 101903.

Gitman, L. J., & Zutter, C. J. (2020). *Principles of managerial finance*. Pearson.

Gitman, L. J., Zutter, C. J., & Joehnk, M. D. (2018). *Personal financial planning*. Cengage Learning.

Glasserman, P. (2004). *Monte Carlo methods in financial engineering*. Springer.

Godwin, A., & Osei, K. A. (2022). Investment treaty obligations and national security reviews in M&As. *Journal of International Economic Law, 25*(4), 983–1006. DOI: 10.1093/jiel/jgac047

Gomes, E., Angwin, D. N., Weber, Y., & Tarba, S. (2019). The challenge of HR integration: A review of the M&A HR integration literature. *Journal of Change Management*.

Goolmeer, T., Skroblin, A., Grant, C., van Leeuwen, S., Archer, R., Gore-Birch, C., & Wintle, B. A. (2022). Recognizing culturally significant species and Indigenous-led management is key to meeting international biodiversity obligations. *Conservation Letters*, *15*(6), e12899. DOI: 10.1111/conl.12899

Gore, S., Hamsa, S., Roychowdhury, S., Patil, G., Gore, S., & Karmode, S. (2023, August). Augmented Intelligence in Machine Learning for Cybersecurity: Enhancing Threat Detection and Human-Machine Collaboration. In *2023 Second International Conference on Augmented Intelligence and Sustainable Systems (ICAISS)* (pp. 638-644). IEEE.DOI: 10.1109/ICAISS58487.2023.10250514

Goriparthi, R. G. (2021). AI-Driven Natural Language Processing for Multilingual Text Summarization and Translation. *Revista de Inteligencia Artificial en Medicina*, *12*(1), 513–535.

Goriparthi, R. G. (2022). AI-Powered Decision Support Systems for Precision Agriculture: A Machine Learning Perspective. *International Journal of Advanced Engineering Technologies and Innovations*, *1*(3), 345–365.

Graebner, M. E., Heimeriks, K. H., Huy, Q. N., & Vaara, E. (2017). The process of postmerger integration: A review and agenda for future research. *The Academy of Management Annals*, *11*(1), 1–32. DOI: 10.5465/annals.2014.0078

Grant, R. M. (1991). The resource-based theory of competitive advantage: Implications for strategy formulation. *California Management Review*, *33*(3), 114–135. DOI: 10.2307/41166664

Green, R., Taylor, J., & White, L. (2022). Technology investments and SME growth. *Journal of Business Innovation*, *14*(4), 233–245.

Gullberg, A. (1991). Den samhälleliga självreflexionens möjligheter: Big data på 1980-talet. https://urn.kb.se/resolve?urn=urn:nbn:se:kth:diva-149318

Hakim, H. A., & Putra Pratama, A. (2024). Internalization strategies of company culture: A case study of ex-employees of Chevron Pacific Indonesia transitioning to Pertamina WK Rokan. *International Journal of Current Science Research and Review*, *7*(4), 4767–4775. DOI: 10.47191/ijcsrr/V7-i5-45

Hambrick, D. C., & Fredrickson, J. W. (2001). Are you sure you have a strategy? *The Academy of Management Perspectives*, *15*(4), 48–59. DOI: 10.5465/ame.2001.5897655

Handley, M. (2012). Anti-corruption due diligence in M&A. *Gibson Dunn*. https://www.gibsondunn.com/wp-content/uploads/documents/publications/Handley-AntiCorruptionDueDiligenceInMA.pdf

Han, J., & Lee, W. (2023). ESG disclosure and acquisition premiums in Asia. *Sustainability Accounting. Management and Policy Journal*, *14*(1), 34–51. DOI: 10.1108/SAMPJ-04-2021-0121

Harrison, J. R., Carroll, G. R., & Tosi, H. L. (2014). The impact of capital structure on business strategy. *Academy of Management Review*, *39*(4), 413–436.

Hashem, I. A. T., Yaqoob, I., Anuar, N. B., Mokhtar, S., Gani, A., & Khan, S. U. (2015). The rise of "big data" on cloud computing: Review and open research issues. *Information Systems*, *47*, 98–115. DOI: 10.1016/j.is.2014.07.006

Haspeslagh, P., & Jemison, D. (1991). *Managing acquisitions: Creating value through corporate renewal*. Free Press.

Haunschild, P. R., & Beckman, C. M. (2020). Vertical integration and market power in emerging economies. *Strategic Management Journal*, *41*(12), 2360–2388. DOI: 10.1002/smj.3120

Henderson, J. C., & Venkatraman, N. (1993). Strategic alignment: Leveraging information technology for transforming organizations. *IBM Systems Journal*, *32*(1), 4–16. DOI: 10.1147/sj.382.0472

He, Z., & Xie, W. (2021). *Financial technology and applications in the global financial industry*. Elsevier.

Higgins, R. C. (2016). *Analysis for financial management*. McGraw-Hill Education.

Hirsch, D. D. (2013). The glass house effect: Big Data, the new oil, and the power of analogy. *Me. L. Rev.*, *66*, 373.

Hitt, M. A., Ireland, R. D., & Hoskisson, R. E. (2012). *Strategic management: Concepts and cases: Competitiveness and globalization*. Cengage Learning.

Hope, J., & Fraser, R. (2003). *Beyond budgeting: How managers can break free from the annual performance trap*. Harvard Business School Press.

Huang, X., Yang, H., & Yang, P. (2024). The impact of cross-border mergers and acquisitions on organisational resilience. *Sustainability*, *16*(6), 2242. DOI: 10.3390/su16062242

Hubbard, D. W. (2014). *How to measure anything: Finding the value of intangibles in business*. Wiley.

Hubbard, D. W. (2014). *The failure of risk management: Why it's broken and how to fix it.* Wiley.

Hull, J. C. (2017). *Options, futures, and other derivatives* (9th ed.). Pearson.

Hull, J. C. (2018). *Risk management and financial institutions.* Wiley.

Hutasoit, A. W., Yusuf Sirat, M., & Erisusanto, R. (2023). Company performance and achievements post merger case study of pt Indosat Tbk (ioh). International Journal of Social Science, Educational, Economics [IJSET]. *Agricultural Research & Technology: Open Access Journal, 2*(7), 203–210. DOI: 10.54443/ijset.v2i7.174

Iqbal, M. S., Abdul Rahim, Z., Alshammari, A. M. K., & Iftikhar, H. (2024). Innovative strategies for overcoming barriers to technology adoption in small and medium-sized enterprises. *Journal of the International Council for Small Business, 5*(4), 331–344. DOI: 10.1080/26437015.2024.2367440

Itan, I., Sylvia, S., Septiany, S., & Chen, R. (2025). The influence of environmental, social, and governance disclosure on market reaction: Evidence from emerging markets. *Discover Sustainability, 6*(1), 347. Advance online publication. DOI: 10.1007/s43621-025-01085-0

Iyengar, J. (2006). Intelligent software agents and the creation of competitive advantage. In *Competition Forum* (Vol. 4, No. 1, p. 66). American Society for Competitiveness.

Jack, H. (2024). Leveraging AI and Data Analytics: Revolutionizing Competitive Intelligence for Market Insights.DOI: 10.13140/RG.2.2.25148.76166

Jain, G., Kumar, A., & Bhat, S. A. (2024). Recent developments of game theory and reinforcement learning approaches: A systematic review. *IEEE Access : Practical Innovations, Open Solutions, 12*, 9999–10011. DOI: 10.1109/ACCESS.2024.3352749

Jáñez-Martino, F., Alaiz-Rodríguez, R., González-Castro, V., Fidalgo, E., & Alegre, E. (2023). A review of spam email detection: Analysis of spammer strategies and the dataset shift problem. *Artificial Intelligence Review, 56*(2), 1145–1173. DOI: 10.1007/s10462-022-10195-4

Jarvenpaa, S. L., & Leidner, D. E. (2006). Communication and trust in global virtual teams. Journal of Computer-Mediated Communication: JCMC, 3(4), 0–0. DOI: 10.1111/j.1083-6101.1998.tb00080.x

Jensen, M. C. (1986). Agency costs of free cash flow, corporate finance, and takeovers. *The American Economic Review, 76*(2), 323–329.

Jha, J. K. (2016). Effect of cultural differences on performance of merger and acquisition via psychological safety: A framework. OPUS HR Journal, 6(2).

Jobson, D., Mar, V., & Freckelton, I. (2022). Legal and ethical considerations of artificial intelligence in skin cancer diagnosis. *The Australasian Journal of Dermatology*, *63*(1), e1–e5. DOI: 10.1111/ajd.13690 PMID: 34407234

John, B. (2025). *Comparative Analysis of Data Lakes and Data Warehouses for Machine Learning Workflows: Architecture*. Performance, and Scalability Considerations.

Johnson, D., & White, S. (2019). Strategic investment planning for SMEs. *Financial Strategies Quarterly*, *10*(1), 15–30.

Jones, M., & Smith, K. (2021). Risk mitigation in short-term investments. *The Journal of Economic Perspectives*, *25*(2), 89–105.

Jorion, P. (2007). *Financial risk manager handbook*. Wiley.

Jorzik, P., Klein, S. P., Kanbach, D. K., & Kraus, S. (2024). AI-driven business model innovation: A systematic review and research agenda. *Journal of Business Research*, *182*, 114764. DOI: 10.1016/j.jbusres.2024.114764

Joseph, J. (2014). Managing change after the merger: The value of pre-merger ingroup identities. *Journal of Organizational Change Management*, *27*(3), 430–448. DOI: 10.1108/JOCM-10-2013-0184

Jun, Y., Craig, A., Shafik, W., & Sharif, L. (2021). Artificial intelligence application in cybersecurity and cyberdefense. *Wireless Communications and Mobile Computing*, *2021*(1), 3329581. DOI: 10.1155/2021/3329581

Kabudi, T., Pappas, I., & Olsen, D. H. (2021). AI-enabled adaptive learning systems: A systematic mapping of the literature. *Computers and education. Artificial Intelligence*, *2*, 100017. DOI: 10.1016/j.caeai.2021.100017

Kahneman, D., & Tversky, A. (2000). *Choices, values, and frames*. Cambridge University Press. DOI: 10.1017/CBO9780511803475

Kalinaki, K., Fahadi, M., Alli, A. A., Shafik, W., Yasin, M., & Mutwalibi, N. (2023). Artificial intelligence of internet of medical things (AIoMT) in smart cities: a review of cybersecurity for smart healthcare. *Handbook of security and privacy of ai-enabled healthcare systems and internet of medical things*, 271-292.https://doi.org/DOI: 10.1201/9781003370321-11

Kaplan, R. S., & Mikes, A. (2012). Managing risks: A new framework. *Harvard Business Review*, *90*(6), 48–60.

Kaplan, R. S., & Norton, D. P. (1992). The balanced scorecard: Measures that drive performance. *Harvard Business Review*, *70*(1), 71–79. PMID: 10119714

Kaplan, R. S., & Norton, D. P. (1996). *The balanced scorecard: Translating strategy into action*. Harvard Business Review Press.

Kaplan, R. S., & Norton, D. P. (2004). *Strategy maps: Converting intangible assets into tangible outcomes*. Harvard Business School Press.

Kaplan, R. S., & Norton, D. P. (2008). *The execution premium: Linking strategy to operations for competitive advantage*. Harvard Business Review Press.

Karavadi, A. K. (2014). Committees under the Companies Act, 2013. *Lakshmikumaran Sridharan Attorneys*. https://www.lakshmisri.com/insights/articles/committees-under-the-companies-act-2013/#

Kayser, C., & Zülch, H. (2024). Understanding the relevance of sustainability in mergers and acquisitions: A systematic literature review on sustainability and its implications throughout deal stages. *Sustainability (Basel)*, *16*(2), 613. DOI: 10.3390/su16020613

Khan, R., & Khan, M. (2024, March 30). Legal challenges of mergers and acquisitions in global markets. https://lawresearchreview.com/index.php/Journal/article/view/52

Khan, M., Serafeim, G., & Yoon, A. (2016). Corporate sustainability: First evidence on materiality. *The Accounting Review*, *91*(6), 1697–1724. DOI: 10.2308/accr-51383

Khare, P. (2025). Integrating the SDGs Into Corporate Governance: A Legal Imperative for Global Sustainability. *IGI Global*, 391-416. https://doi.org/DOI: 10.4018/979-8-3373-4192-7.ch015

Kilanko, V. (2022). Turning Point: Policymaking in the Era of Artificial Intelligence, by Darrell M. West and John R. Allen, Washington, DC: Brookings Institution Press, 2020, 297 pp., hardcover 24.99, paperback 19.99. DOI: 10.1002/pam.22374

Killingsworth, B., Xue, Y., & Liu, Y. (2016). Factors influencing knowledge sharing among global virtual teams. *Team Performance Management*, *22*(5/6), 284–300. DOI: 10.1108/TPM-10-2015-0042

Kim, S., & Park, T. (2020). Hart–Scott–Rodino notification compliance and fill delays. *Journal of Competition Law & Economics*, *16*(2), 255–277. DOI: 10.1093/joclec/nhaa004

Kiran, M., Murphy, P., Monga, I., Dugan, J., & Baveja, S. S. (2015, October). Lambda architecture for cost-effective batch and speed big data processing. In *2015 IEEE International Conference on Big Data (Big Data)* (pp. 2785-2792). IEEE.DOI: 10.1109/BigData.2015.7364082

Knittel, C. R., & Stango, V. (2021). Industrial organization and competition in digital M&As. *The Journal of Industrial Economics*, *69*(2), 229–260. DOI: 10.1111/joie.12210

Koller, G., Goedhart, M., & Wessels, D. (2010). *Valuation: Measuring and managing the value of companies*. Wiley.

Koopman, A., & van Tongeren, F. (2021). FDI screening & competition law interplay in the EU. *International Review of Law and Economics*, *65*, 105952. DOI: 10.1016/j.irle.2020.105952

Kothandapani, H. P. (2023). Emerging trends and technological advancements in data lakes for the financial sector: An in-depth analysis of data processing, analytics, and infrastructure innovations. *Quarterly Journal of Emerging Technologies and Innovations*, *8*(2), 62–75.

Kotsantonis, S., Pinney, C., & Serafeim, G. (2020). ESG integration in M&A deal-making: Global evidence. *Journal of Corporate Finance*, *65*, 101760. DOI: 10.1016/j.jcorpfin.2020.101760

Kotter, J. P. (2012). *Leading change*. Harvard Business Review Press.

Kovela, S., Annandale, A., Annandale, B., & Jackson, P. N. (2023). Post merger IT integration in banking: Literature review. *International Journal of Business and Management*, *18*(6), 77–92. DOI: 10.5539/ijbm.v18n6p77

Kurthalanathan, C. S. M. (2016). Whistle-Blowing/ Vigil Mechanism Under Companies Act, 2013. *Taxguru*. https://taxguru.in/company-law/whistleblowing-vigil-mechanism-companies-act-2013.html

La Porta, R., Lopez-de-Silanes, F., & Shleifer, A. (2021). Corporate ownership around the world. *Review of Financial Studies*, *34*(3), 107–161. DOI: 10.1093/rfs/hhaa130

La Porta, R., Lopez-de-Silanes, F., Shleifer, A., & Vishny, R. W. (1998). Law and finance. *Journal of Political Economy*, *106*(6), 1113–1155. DOI: 10.1086/250042

Laice, H. C. F. (2024). Estratégias de adaptação cultural na identidade visual de marcas globalizadas: Um estudo de caso da Sumol Compal.

Leadership development strategies of human resources in digital era. (2023). Journal of Human Resource Development, 5(6). DOI: 10.23977/jhrd.2023.050620

Lenin, J., Komathi, A., Vijayan, H., Rathinam, A. R., Kasthuri, A., & Srinivasan, C. (2023, December). Revolutionizing Healthcare With Cloud Computing: The Impact of Clinical Decision Support Algorithm. In *2023 International Conference on Artificial Intelligence for Innovations in Healthcare Industries (ICAIIHI)* (Vol. 1, pp. 1-6). IEEE. DOI: 10.1109/ICAIIHI57871.2023.10489022

Lerch, C. M., Heimberger, H., Jäger, A., Horvat, D., & Schultmann, F. (2022). AI-readiness and Production Resilience: Empirical Evidence from German Manufacturing in Timesof the Covid-19 Pandemic. *International Journal of Production Research*, •••, 1–22. DOI: 10.1080/00207543.2022.2141906

Lestari, H. D. (2022). Cross-border platform mergers in ASEAN's digital market. *Singapore Academy of Law Journal, 34*, 768–794.

Levy, B. (2024). Global M&A Industry Trends. *PWC*. https://www.pwc.com/gx/en/services/deals/trends/2024.html

Levy, M., & Powell, P. (2005). *Strategies for growth in SMEs: The role of information and information systems*. Elsevier Science.

Liang, S., Ullrich, J., Dick, R., & Lupina-Wegener, A. (2021). The intergroup sensitivity effect in mergers and acquisitions: Testing the role of merger motives. *Journal of Applied Social Psychology*, *51*(8), 769–778. DOI: 10.1111/jasp.12785

Li, G. J., & Cheng, X. Q. (2012). Research status and scientific thinking of big data. *Bulletin of Chinese Academy of Sciences*, *27*(6), 647–657.

Lins, K. V., Servaes, H., & Tamayo, A. (2017). Social capital, trust, and firm performance: The value of CSR. *The Journal of Finance*, *72*(4), 1785–1824. DOI: 10.1111/jofi.12505

Liu, X., Fang, J., Hu, X., & Lv, Y. (2024). Cross-border M&As and productivity: Technology absorption. *Systems*, *12*(5), 161. DOI: 10.3390/systems12050161

Li, Y., & Li, X. (2026). Digital economy and high-quality enterprise development: Evidence from emerging markets. *Technological Forecasting and Social Change*, *210*, 124501. DOI: 10.1016/j.techfore.2025.124501

Li, Z., Ji, Q., Ling, X., & Liu, Q. (2025). A Comprehensive Review of Multi-Agent Reinforcement Learning in Video Games. *Authorea Preprints*.DOI: 10.36227/techrxiv.173603149.94954703/v1

Lohr, S. (2012). Big data's impact on the world. *The New York Times, 11*(1), 1.

Madan, A. K. (2024). *10 lessons for unlocking post-merger integration success*. Technology Consultant Insights.

Maddireddy, B. R., & Maddireddy, B. R. (2020). AI and Big Data: Synergizing to Create Robust Cybersecurity Ecosystems for Future Networks. *International Journal of Advanced Engineering Technologies and Innovations, 1*(2), 40–63.

Maddireddy, B. R., & Maddireddy, B. R. (2020). Proactive Cyber Defense: Utilizing AI for Early Threat Detection and Risk Assessment. *International Journal of Advanced Engineering Technologies and Innovations, 1*(2), 64–83.

Maddireddy, B. R., & Maddireddy, B. R. (2021). Cyber security Threat Landscape: Predictive Modelling Using Advanced AI Algorithms. *Revista Española de Documentación Científica, 15*(4), 126–153.

Maddireddy, B. R., & Maddireddy, B. R. (2022). AI-Based Phishing Detection Techniques: A Comparative Analysis of Model Performance. *Unique Endeavor in Business & Social Sciences, 1*(2), 63–77.

Maddireddy, B. R., & Maddireddy, B. R. (2022). Blockchain and AI Integration: A Novel Approach to Strengthening Cybersecurity Frameworks. *Unique Endeavor in Business & Social Sciences, 1*(2), 27–46.

Maddireddy, B. R., & Maddireddy, B. R. (2022). Real-Time Data Analytics with AI: Improving Security Event Monitoring and Management. *Unique Endeavor in Business & Social Sciences, 1*(2), 47–62.

Madhani, P. M. (2019). Strategic supply chain management for enhancing competitive advantages: Developing a business value added framework. *International Journal of Value Chain Management, 10*(3), 189–212. DOI: 10.1504/IJVCM.2019.103270

Madiha, I. A., & Abdelaleem, M. M. (2024). The impact of using the competitive intelligence cycle on the structure of organizational DNA. *Journal of Contemporary Economics & Social Research, 15*(3), 2196–2219. DOI: 10.21608/jces.2024.391339

Madureira, L., Popović, A., & Castelli, M. (2021). Competitive Intelligence: A unified view and modular definition. *Technological Forecasting and Social Change, 173*, 121086. DOI: 10.1016/j.techfore.2021.121086

Maisenhelder, F., Rapp, M. S., & Wolff, M. (2025). Digital acquisitions and corporate innovation: Evidence from global technology markets. *Research Policy, 54*(3), 104873. DOI: 10.1016/j.respol.2024.104873

Malik, A., Sinha, P., Budhwar, P., & Pereira, V. (2023). Managing legitimacy in a cross-border post-merger integration context: The role of language strategies. *International Journal of Human Resource Management, 34*(21), 4144–4174. DOI: 10.1080/09585192.2023.2237878

Malmqvist, L. (2025). Enhancing post merger integration planning through AI assisted dependency analysis. arXiv.

Maluleka, M. L., & Chummun, B. Z. (2023). Competitive intelligence and strategy implementation: Critical examination of present literature review. *South African Journal of Information Management*, *25*(1), a1610. DOI: 10.4102/sajim.v25i1.1610

Mamat, N., Othman, M. F., Abdulghafor, R., Alwan, A. A., & Gulzar, Y. (2023). Abdulgha for, R., Alwan, A. A., & Gulzar, Y. (2023). *Enhancing Image Annotation Technique of Fruit Classification Using a Deep Learning Approach. Sustainability (Basel)*, *15*(2), 901. DOI: 10.3390/su15020901

Markovich, A., Raban, D. R., & Efrat, K. (2022). Tailoring competitive information sources to the sequence of dynamic capabilities. *Journal of Management & Organization*, *28*(3), 480–501. DOI: 10.1017/jmo.2022.35

Markowitz, H. M. (1952). Portfolio selection. *The Journal of Finance*, *7*(1), 77–91.

Mashey, J. R. (1999). Big data and the next wave of {InfraStress} problems, solutions, opportunities. In *1999 USENIX annual technical conference (USENIX ATC 99)*.

Maulana, S., Nurhayati, P., Sumarwan, U., & Sukmawati, A. (2024). Managing organizational culture integration post-acquisition: Lessons from PT "X" in the oil and gas sector. *Evolutionary Studies in Imaginative Culture*, •••, 1611–1620. DOI: 10.70082/esiculture.vi.1486

Maurya, S., Shavkidinova, D., Shrivastava, V., & Subrahmanyam, S. (2025). Effects of Green Supply Chain Management Practices on Environmental and Firm Sustainability Performance. *ACTA INNOVATIONS*, 55, 13–22. https://www.actainnovations.com/index.php/pub/article/view/401

Maynard, A. D. (2015). Navigating the fourth industrial revolution. *Nature Nanotechnology*, *10*(12), 1005–1006. DOI: 10.1038/nnano.2015.286 PMID: 26632281

McGonagle, J. J., & Misner-Elias, M. (2016). The changing landscape of competitive intelligence: Two critical issues investigated. *Salus Journal*, *4*(1), 13–24.

McKinsey & Company. (2020). *Automation in business operations*. McKinsey Insights.

McKinsey & Company. (2021). *How technology is driving SME growth*. McKinsey Insights.

McKinsey. (2019, March 26). Organizational culture in mergers: Addressing the unseen forces. McKinsey & Company.

Meglio, O., King, D. R., & Risberg, A. (2025). Mergers and acquisitions as service ecosystems: Toward a value co-creation perspective. *Journal of Management Studies*, *62*(1), 98–125. DOI: 10.1111/joms.12910

Merchant, K. A., & Van der Stede, W. A. (2017). *Management control systems: Performance measurement, evaluation and incentives*. Pearson.

Miczka, S., & Größler, A. (2010). Merger dynamics. Kybernetes. The International Journal of Cybernetics. *Kybernetes*, *39*(9/10), 1491–1512. DOI: 10.1108/03684921011081132

Miller, A. (2020). Balancing short-term and long-term goals. *Strategic Management Review*, *7*(1), 67–80.

Miller, R., & Verhoeven, H. (2019). Overcoming smallness: Qatar, the United Arab Emirates and strategic realignment in the Gulf. *International Politics*, *57*(1), 1–20. DOI: 10.1057/s41311-019-00180-0

Mintzberg, H. (1994). *The rise and fall of strategic planning*. Free Press.

Mintzberg, H., Ahlstrand, B. W., & Lampel, J. (1998). *Strategy safari: A guided tour through the wilds of strategic management*. Free Press.

Mockaitis, A. I., Rose, E. L., & Zettinig, P. (2012). The power of individual cultural values in global virtual teams. *International Journal of Cross Cultural Management*, *12*(2), 193–210. DOI: 10.1177/1470595812439868

Modigliani, F., & Miller, M. H. (1958). The cost of capital, corporation finance and the theory of investment. *The American Economic Review*, *48*(3), 261–297.

Morales, E. F., & Escalante, H. J. (2022). A brief introduction to supervised, unsupervised, and reinforcement learning. In *Biosignal processing and classification using computational learning and intelligence* (pp. 111–129). Academic Press., DOI: 10.1016/B978-0-12-820125-1.00017-8

Moyer, R. C., McGuigan, J. R., & Rao, R. P. (2022). *Contemporary financial management*. Cengage Learning.

Muller, M. L. (2008). How and what others are doing in competitive intelligence: The Motorola case study. *South African Journal of Information Management*, *10*(4). Advance online publication. DOI: 10.4102/sajim.v10i4.333

Mungoli, N. (2023). Adaptive ensemble learning: Boosting model performance through intelligent feature fusion in deep neural networks. *arXiv preprint arXiv:2304.02653.https://doi.org//arXiv.2304.02653*DOI: 10.48550

Musandu, G., & Schoombee, A. (2019). Building antitrust capacity in Africa: Challenges and opportunities. *Journal of Competition Law & Economics, 15*(3), 433–462. DOI: 10.1093/joclec/nhz007

Napier, N. K. (1989). Mergers and acquisitions, human resource issues and outcomes: A review and suggested typology. *Journal of Management Studies, 26*(3), 271–290. DOI: 10.1111/j.1467-6486.1989.tb00728.x

Naqvi, A. (2017). Competitive dynamics of artificial intelligence economy: The Wicked Problem of cognitive competition. *Journal of Economics Library, 4*(2), 187–193. DOI: 10.1453/jel.v4i2.1319

Narassimhan, E., Myslikova, Z., & Gallagher, K. S. (2024). Strategies for green industrial and innovation policy: An analysis of alignment, misalignment, and realignment around dominant designs in the EV sector. *Environmental Research Letters, 19*(1), 014019. DOI: 10.1088/1748-9326/ad101e

Neely, C. J., & Weller, P. A. (2017). *Short-term investments and risk management: A guide for practitioners*. Wiley.

Nerbel, J. F., & Kreutzer, M. (2023). Digital platform ecosystems in flux: From proprietary digital platforms to wide-spanning ecosystems. *Electronic Markets, 33*(1), 6. DOI: 10.1007/s12525-023-00625-8

Nikolaos, T., & Evangelia, F. (2012). Competitive intelligence: Concept, context and a case of its application. *Science Journal of Business Management, 2*(15), 1–15. DOI: 10.7237/sjbm/261

Niven, P. R. (2006). *Balanced scorecard step-by-step: Maximizing performance and maintaining results*. Wiley.

Norton Rose Fulbright. (2020). Divergent diligence? Uncovering M&A anti-corruption risks. https://www.nortonrosefulbright.com/en-in/knowledge/publications/9b8dfb45/divergent-diligence-uncovering-ma-anticorruption-risks-in-asia-pacific

Ntakolia, C., Kokkotis, C., Karlsson, P., & Moustakidis, S. (2021). An explainable machine learning model for material backorder prediction in inventory management. *Sensors (Basel), 21*(23), 7926. DOI: 10.3390/s21237926 PMID: 34883930

Oberoi, J. K. (2025). Future of work: Will hybrid work culture become the norm in MNCs? *INTERNATIONAL JOURNAL OF SCIENTIFIC RESEARCH IN ENGINEERING AND MANAGEMENT, 09*(05), 1–9. DOI: 10.55041/IJSREM48958

OECD. (2017). OECD guidelines for multinational enterprises. *OECD Publishing*. https://www.oecd.org/en/publications/2017/07/oecd-transfer-pricing-guidelines-for-multinational-enterprises-and-tax-administrations-2017_g1g71100.html

OECD. (2019). *Digitalisation of SMEs: Policies to support SMEs in the digital transformation*. OECD.

OECD. (2022). *OECD Merger Control Guidelines*. OECD Publishing.

OECD. (2023). *Competition policy in Latin America and the Caribbean*. OECD Publishing.

Oh, J.-H., & Johnston, W. J. (2021). How post-merger integration duration affects merger outcomes. *Journal of Business and Industrial Marketing*, *36*(5), 807–820. DOI: 10.1108/JBIM-11-2019-0476

Oliveira, J. P. M., Ramos, L. S., & Rosada, V. C. (2024). A importância do marketing digital para micro e pequenas empresas para potencializar os resultados do negócio.

Oludapo, S., Carroll, N., & Helfert, M. (2024). Why do so many digital transformations fail? A bibliometric analysis and future research agenda. *Journal of Business Research, 174*, 114528. DOI: 10.1016/j.jbusres.2024.114528

Palepu, K. G., Healy, P. M., & Peek, E. (2020). *Business analysis and valuation: IFRS edition*. Cengage Learning.

Pantazi, T. (2012). The legal framework for mergers and acquisitions in the European Union and the United States. In *Palgrave Macmillan US eBooks* (pp. 195–205). https://doi.org/DOI: 10.1057/9781137031556_11

Parmar, V., & Yadav, J. (2017). Big Data: Meaning, Challenges, Opportunities, Tools. *International Journal of Advanced Research in Computer Science*, *8*(1).

Parnell, G. S., Driscoll, P. J., & Henderson, D. L. (2013). *Decision making in systems engineering and management*. Wiley.

Parrino, R., Kidwell, D. S., & Bates, T. W. (2020). *Fundamentals of corporate finance*. Wiley.

Pasupuleti, V., Thuraka, B., Kodete, C. S., & Malisetty, S. (2024). Enhancing supply chain agility and sustainability through machine learning: Optimization techniques for logistics and inventory management. *Logistics (Basel)*, *8*(3), 73. DOI: 10.3390/logistics8030073

Pecis, L., Ge, B., & Bauer, F. (2025). The strategic realignment of paradoxical family and business goals in family business: A rhetorical history perspective. *Business History, 67*(2), 577–607. DOI: 10.1080/00076791.2024.2317938

Pereira, S.Jr, & Porto, A. P. S. (2021). *Entre posts e parcerias: Práticas de marketing de influência em agência de viagem receptiva.* Ateliê do Turismo.

Pesce, D., Neirotti, P., & Paolucci, E. (2019). When culture meets digital platforms: Value creation and stakeholders' alignment in big data use. *Current Issues in Tourism, 22*(15), 1883–1903. DOI: 10.1080/13683500.2019.1591354

Peteraf, M. (1993). The cornerstones of competitive advantage: A resource-based view. *Strategic Management Journal, 14*(3), 179–191. DOI: 10.1002/smj.4250140303

Peters, T. J., & Waterman, R. H. (1982). *In search of excellence: Lessons from America's best-run companies.* Harper & Row.

Pfeffer, J. (1998). *The human equation: Building profits by putting people first.* Harvard Business School Press.

Phillips, T. (2015). The federal common law of successor liability and the FCPA. *William & Mary Business Law Review, 6*(1). https://scholarship.law.wm.edu/wmblr/vol6/iss1/4/

Pichiyan, V., Muthulingam, S., Nalajala, S. Ch. A., & Das, M. N. (2023). Web scraping using natural language processing: Exploiting unstructured text for data extraction and analysis. *Procedia Computer Science, 230*, 193–202. DOI: 10.1016/j.procs.2023.12.074

Pimenta, K. C. L. (2025). A integração de tecnologias digitais no ensino do direito: Inovação e desafios na formação jurídica.

Pinto, M. F. (2023). Análise de público-alvo e comportamento do consumidor no contexto digital. *Revista Brasileira de Marketing, 22*(1), 55–73.

Piper, D. L. A. (2022). The new OECD Anti-Bribery Recommendation. https://www.dlapiper.com/en/insights/publications/global-anti-corruption-perspective/global-anticorruption-perspective-q1-2022/the-new-oecd-anti-bribery-recommendation

Pippirs, C., & Steckenbauer, G. C. (2022). Case study—Spa destination branding—A strategic realignment process of five Bavarian thermal spas. *International Journal of Spa and Wellness, 5*(3–4), 308–319. DOI: 10.1080/24721735.2022.2117009

PMI (Project Management Institute). (2021). *A guide to the project management body of knowledge* (7th ed.). PMI.

Porter, M. E. (1980). *Competitive strategy: Techniques for analyzing industries and competitors*. Free Press.

Porter, M. E. (1991). *Competitive advantage: Creating and sustaining superior performance*. Free Press.

Porter, M. E. (2008). The five competitive forces that shape strategy. *Harvard Business Review, 86*(1), 78–93. https://hbr.org/2008/01/the-five-competitive-forces-that-shape-strategy PMID: 18271320

Porter, M. E., & Kramer, M. R. (2011). Creating shared value. *Harvard Business Review*, *89*(1–2), 62–77.

Pot, L., Friedman, D., Rosiello, M., Meyer, T., & Brocca, M. (2022). *Organization design will make or break a deal*. BCG.

Prasetyo, B., & Putro, U. S. (2024). Strategic analysis of international oil and gas companies' response to global carbon emission reduction initiatives. *Applied Quantitative Analysis*, *3*(2), 45–59. DOI: 10.31098/quant.2038

Presbitero, A. (2020). Task performance in global virtual team. *Personnel Review*, *49*(5), 1091–1105. DOI: 10.1108/PR-10-2018-0415

Pritchard, A., Taylor, D., & Belford, M. (2024). Teaching data-driven decision making for inventory analysis with Monte Carlo simulation. *Decision Sciences Journal of Innovative Education*.

Provost, F., & Fawcett, T. (2013). *Data science for business: What you need to know about data mining and data-analytic thinking*. O'Reilly Media.

Rafique, M. (2021). *The human factor in mergers, acquisitions, and transformational change*. Business Expert Press.

Raitis, J., Szczepanska-Woszczyna, K., & Sroka, W. (2018). Cultural integration challenges in mergers and acquisitions: Central and Eastern European perspective. *The Engineering Economist*, *29*(2), 215–222. DOI: 10.5755/j01.ee.29.2.20345

Rajan, R. G., & Zingales, L. (2001). The great reversals: The politics of financial development in the twentieth century. *Journal of Financial Economics*, *69*(1), 5–50. DOI: 10.1016/S0304-405X(03)00125-9

Raj, N. S., & Renumol, V. G. (2022). A systematic literature review on adaptive content recommenders in personalized learning environments from 2015 to 2020. *Journal of Computers in Education*, *9*(1), 113–148. DOI: 10.1007/s40692-021-00199-4

Ralston, P., & Blackhurst, J. (2020). Industry 4.0 and Resilience in the Supply Chain: A Driver of Capability Enhancement or Capability Loss? *International Journal of Production Research*, *58*(16), 5006–5019. DOI: 10.1080/00207543.2020.1736724

Raman, R., Dhivya, K., Sapra, P., Gurpur, S., Maniraj, S. P., & Murugan, S. (2023, December). IoT-driven Smart Packaging for Pharmaceuticals: Ensuring Product Integrity and Patient Safety. In *2023 International Conference on Artificial Intelligence for Innovations in Healthcare Industries (ICAIIHI)* (Vol. 1, pp. 1-6). IEEE. DOI: 10.1109/ICAIIHI57871.2023.10489420

Ranajee, R., Naik, K. R., & Iyengar, S. R. (2025). Unlocking long-term value in M&A: The role of HR strategies. *The International Journal of Organizational Analysis*, *33*(11), 4117–4135. DOI: 10.1108/IJOA-05-2024-4492

Ranft, A. L., & Lord, M. D. (2010). Acquiring new technologies and capabilities: A grounded model of acquisition implementation. *Organization Science*, *21*(1), 197–215. DOI: 10.1287/orsc.1080.0367

Ravikumar, & Aarthi, S. (2025a). Natural Language Processing in conversational AI tutors. In Advances in Computational Intelligence and Robotics (pp. 275–306). IGI Global Scientific Publishing. DOI: 10.4018/979-8-3373-4217-7.ch011

Ravikumar, A. Olimbaevich, I. R., Mashkhura, S., & Musayeva, S. (2025). Transforming Healthcare with Large Language Models and AI agents. In Advances in Computational Intelligence and Robotics (pp. 51–82). IGI Global Scientific Publishing. DOI: 10.4018/979-8-3373-2008-3.ch003

Ravikumar, R. N., & Aarthi, S. (2025b). Climate data without borders. In *Cross-Border Cooperation in the Age of Climate Change* (pp. 61–90). IGI Global Scientific Publishing., DOI: 10.4018/979-8-3373-3972-6.ch003

Ravikumar, R. N., & Aarthi, S. (2025c). Federated Learning for cross-enterprise supply chain collaboration. In *Advances in Computational Intelligence and Robotics* (pp. 47–84). IGI Global Scientific Publishing., DOI: 10.4018/979-8-3373-2833-1.ch002

Raymond, L. (2001). Determinants of Web site implementation in small businesses. *Internet Research*, *11*(5), 411–422. DOI: 10.1108/10662240110410363

Reddy, K. S. (2016). Regulatory framework of mergers and acquisitions. *International Journal of Law and Management*, *58*(2), 197–215. DOI: 10.1108/IJLMA-03-2015-0013

Requião, A. R., & Costa, H. M. (2023). Estratégias de posicionamento e adaptação cultural em marketing global. *Revista Brasileira de Estratégia de Marketing*, *17*(2), 80–102.

Ribeiro, A., Eloi, D. L. C., & Rodrigues, R. V. M. (2025). Engajamento através de conteúdo gerado pelo usuário (UGC). *Revista Base Científica, 3*, 1–20. DOI: 10.52832/rbc541

Richter, N. F., Martin, J., Hansen, S. V., Taras, V., & Alon, I. (2021). Motivational configurations of cultural intelligence, social integration, and performance in global virtual teams. *Journal of Business Research, 129*, 351–367. DOI: 10.1016/j.jbusres.2021.03.012

Ridzuan, N. N., Masri, M., Anshari, M., Fitriyani, N. L., & Syafrudin, M. (2024). AI in the financial sector: The line between innovation, regulation and ethical responsibility. *Information (Basel), 15*(8), 432. DOI: 10.3390/info15080432

Rodríguez-Sánchez, J.-L., Ortiz-de-Urbina-Criado, M., & Mora-Valentín, E.-M. (2019). Thinking about people in mergers and acquisitions processes. *International Journal of Manpower, 40*(4), 643–657. DOI: 10.1108/IJM-05-2018-0143

Rogers, E. M. (2003). *Diffusion of innovations* (5th ed.). Free Press.

Rose, J. M. (2023). Evaluating the effects of organizational culture on post-merger integration. Doctoral dissertation, Pepperdine University.

Rosendale, J., Wilkie, L., & Lowry, W. (2024). On strategic communication during mergers & acquisitions: A pragmatic perspective to improve outcomes. *Development and Learning in Organizations, 38*(5), 1–4. DOI: 10.1108/DLO-10-2023-0226

Ross, S. A., Westerfield, R., & Jaffe, J. (2016). *Corporate finance* (11th ed.). McGraw-Hill Education.

Rottig, D., Schappert, J., & Starkman, E. (2017). Successfully managing the sociocultural integration process in international acquisitions: A qualitative analysis of canon's acquisition of océ. *Thunderbird International Business Review, 59*(2), 187–208. DOI: 10.1002/tie.21831

Ruiz, J., López-Cabrales, Á., & Valle-Cabrera, R. (2024). Digital human resource strategies and firm performance in the digital era. *Human Resource Management Journal, 34*(2), 451–468. DOI: 10.1111/1748-8583.12480

Safavi, M. (2021). Organizational routines and post-merger integration: A dynamic capabilities perspective. *Journal of Management & Organization, 27*(5), 982–1002. DOI: 10.1017/jmo.2019.73

Sahija, D. (2021). *Critical review of machine learning integration with augmented reality for discrete manufacturing*. Independent Researcher and Enterprise Solution Manager in Leading Digital Transformation Agency., DOI: 10.2015/IJIRMF.2455.0620/202112017

Sales, A., Roth, S., Grothe-Hammer, M., & Azambuja, R. (2022). From play to pay: A multifunctional approach to the role of culture in post-merger integration. *Management Decision*, *60*(7), 1922–1946. DOI: 10.1108/MD-01-2021-0136

Santos, E. A. (2021). A responsabilidade social nas empresas de cosméticos: Uma análise das relações raciais e de gênero.

Sarala, R. M., & Vaara, E. (2010). Cultural differences, convergence, and crossvergence as explanations of knowledge transfer in international acquisitions. *Journal of International Business Studies*, *41*(8), 1365–1390. DOI: 10.1057/jibs.2009.89

Sarker, I. H. (2021). Machine learning: Algorithms, real-world applications and research directions. *SN Computer Science*, *2*(3), 160. DOI: 10.1007/s42979-021-00592-x PMID: 33778771

Sarker, I. H. (2022). AI-based modeling: Techniques, applications and research issues towards automation, intelligent and smart systems. *SN Computer Science*, *3*(2), 158. DOI: 10.1007/s42979-022-01043-x PMID: 35194580

Saura, J. R., Palos-Sanchez, P. R., & Herráez, B. R. (2020). The digital marketing strategy: A review and research agenda. *Journal of Innovation & Knowledge*, *5*(4), 266–273.

Schein, E. H., & Schein, P. A. (2017). *Organizational culture and leadership* (5th ed.). Wiley.

Schilling, M. A. (2025). *Strategic management of technological innovation* (6th ed.). McGraw-Hill Education.

Schoemaker, P. J. H., Heaton, S., & Teece, D. (2018). Innovation, dynamic capabilities, and leadership. *California Management Review*, *61*(1), 15–42. DOI: 10.1177/0008125618790246

Screpante, M. S. (2021). OECD anti-bribery convention. Implications on corporate criminal liability in Latin America. *Business Law Review*, *42*(1), 26–38. DOI: 10.54648/BULA2021003

SEBI. (2021). Business responsibility and sustainability reporting guidelines. Securities and Exchange Board of India. https://www.sebi.gov.in/legal/circulars/may-2021/business-responsibility-and-sustainability-reporting-by-listed-entities_50096.html

Setyadi, A., Pawirosumarto, S., & Damaris, A. (2025). Rethinking Sustainable Operations: A Multi-Level Integration of Circularity, Localization, and Digital Resilience in Manufacturing Systems. *Sustainability (Basel)*, *17*(15), 6929. DOI: 10.3390/su17156929

Sherwood, M. W., & Pollard, J. (2018). The risk-adjusted return potential of integrating ESG strategies into emerging market equities. *Journal of Sustainable Finance & Investment*, *8*(1), 26–44. DOI: 10.1080/20430795.2017.1331118

Silva, C. F. (2024). Alternativas entre o luxo e o lixo: A publicidade no contexto da moda sustentável.

Singhal, A., & Sharma, K. (2024). Companies Act 2013, Procedures for constitution of audit committee and vigil mechanism policy. *Lawrbit*. https://www.lawrbit.com/companies-act-procedures/constitution-of-audit-committee-and-vigil-mechanism-policy/

Singh, J. P., Irani, S., Rana, N. P., Dwivedi, Y. K., Saumya, S., & Roy, P. K. (2017). Predicting the "helpfulness" of online consumer reviews. *Journal of Business Research*, *70*, 346–355. DOI: 10.1016/j.jbusres.2016.08.008

Siri, M., & Zhu, S. (2024). Embedding sustainability in EU corporate governance codes. In *Sustainable Finance in Europe* (pp. 211–262). Springer., DOI: 10.1007/978-3-031-53696-0_7

Skogland, M. A. C. (2017). A spatial approach to transformational change: Strategic alignment of the spatial and cultural environment. *Journal of Corporate Real Estate*, *19*(4), 285–299. DOI: 10.1108/JCRE-09-2016-0030

Ślusarczyk, B. (2018). Industry 4.0: Are we ready? *Polish Journal of Management Studies*, *17*(1), 232–248. Advance online publication. DOI: 10.17512/pjms.2018.17.1.19

Snell, S. A., & Morris, S. S. (2021). Time for realignment: The HR ecosystem. *The Academy of Management Perspectives*, *35*(2), 219–236. DOI: 10.5465/amp.2018.0069

solutions by stc. (2024). solutions by stc completes acquisition of Devoteam Middle East. https://solutions.com.sa

Song, Y., Mi, L., Bian, Z., Tu, W., & He, J. (2025). How does artificial intelligence impact corporate ESG performance? The catching-up effect of digital technological innovation. *Journal of Innovation & Knowledge*, *10*(6), 100843. DOI: 10.1016/j.jik.2025.100843

Sousa, K. S. (2025). Biblioteca Pública Municipal Antônio Luís Marcelo Antunes a partir do marketing digital: Estratégias de integração.

Stahl, G. K., Angwin, D. N., Very, P., Gomes, E., Weber, Y., Tarba, S. Y., Noorderhaven, N., Benyamini, H., Bouckenooghe, D., Chreim, S., Durand, M., Hassett, M. E., Kokk, G., Mendenhall, M. E., Mirc, N., Miska, C., Park, K. M., Reynolds, N.-S., Rouzies, A., & Yildiz, H. E. (2013). Sociocultural integration in mergers and acquisitions: Unresolved paradoxes and directions for future research. *Thunderbird International Business Review*, *55*(4), 333–356. DOI: 10.1002/tie.21549

Stahl, G. K., Larsson, R., Kremershof, I., & Sitkin, S. B. (2011). Trust dynamics in acquisitions: A case survey. *Human Resource Management*, *50*(5), 575–603. DOI: 10.1002/hrm.20448

Stahl, G. K., & Voigt, A. (2008). Do cultural differences matter in mergers and acquisitions? A tentative model and examination. *Organization Science*, *19*(1), 160–176. DOI: 10.1287/orsc.1070.0270

Steigenberger, N. (2017). The challenge of integration: A review of the M&A integration literature. *International Journal of Management Reviews*, *19*(4), 408–431. DOI: 10.1111/ijmr.12099

Stephenson, M. (2021). The new FCPA Resource Guide wisely suggests a more flexible approach to successor liability. *Global Anticorruption Blog*. https://globalanticorruptionblog.com/2021/02/15/the-new-fcpa-resource-guide-wisely-suggests-a-more-flexible-approach-to-successor-liability/

Stern, J. M., Shiely, J. S., & Ross, I. (2001). *The EVA challenge: Implementing value-added change in an organization*. Wiley.

Stewart, G. B. (1991). *The quest for value: A guide for senior managers*. HarperBusiness.

Strielkowski, W., Grebennikova, V., Lisovskiy, A., Rakhimova, G., & Vasileva, T. (2024). AI-driven adaptive learning for sustainable educational transformation. *Sustainable Development (Bradford)*. Advance online publication. DOI: 10.1002/sd.3221

Subrahmanyam, S. (2025). AI-Driven Leadership in the Modern Era for Revolutionizing Next-Generation Strategies: Organizational Impacts and Future Development. In Agnihotri, A., & Balusamy, B. (Eds.), *Leadership Paradigms and the Impact of Technology* (pp. 61–86). IGI Global Scientific Publishing., DOI: 10.4018/979-8-3693-7175-6.ch003

Subrahmanyam, S. (2025). Developing Mindful Leaders for Global Change: Cultivating Awareness and Resilience to Navigate a Complex World. In Baez, M. D. (Ed.), *Strategic Approaches to Mindful Leadership and Change Management* (pp. 1–34). IGI Global Scientific Publishing., DOI: 10.4018/979-8-3693-7066-7.ch001

Subrahmanyam, S. (2025). Strategic Collaboration and Partnerships in R&D for Innovation. In Martínez-Falcó, J., Sánchez-García, E., & Marco-Lajara, B. (Eds.), *Research and Development Practices in Innovation* (pp. 283–314). IGI Global Scientific Publishing., DOI: 10.4018/979-8-3373-0812-8.ch010

Sun, A. (2024). Talent management and organizational change in corporate mergers and acquisitions. *Frontiers in Business, Economics and Management, 12*(3), 99–102. DOI: 10.54097/dcjd4ghk

Svetlova, E., & Thielmann, K. (2020). Financial risks and management. In *International Encyclopedia of Human Geography* (2nd ed.). DOI: 10.1016/B978-0-08-102295-5.10065-4

Tangwaragorn, P., Dhir, A., & Kaur, P. (2024). Digital transformation and corporate strategy: A systematic review and research agenda. *Technological Forecasting and Social Change, 199*, 122995. DOI: 10.1016/j.techfore.2023.122995

Tao, Q., Li, S., & Liu, Y. (2026). Digital transformation and corporate diversification: Evidence from emerging markets. *Journal of Business Research, 175*, 114526. DOI: 10.1016/j.jbusres.2024.114526

Tapscott, D., & Tapscott, A. (2016). *Blockchain revolution*. Portfolio.

Tariq, M. U. (2025). AI Tools and Technologies for Management Education: Enhancing Learning Through Innovation. In M. R. & S. R. (Eds.), *Integrating AI and Machine Learning into Business and Management Education* (pp. 105-132). IGI Global Scientific Publishing. DOI: 10.4018/979-8-3373-2150-9.ch005

Tariq, M. U. (2025). AI-Driven Digital Nomads: Transforming Labor Markets and Industrial Growth in the Digital Economy. In Ordóñez de Pablos, P., Zhang, X., Anshari, M., & Almunawar, M. (Eds.), *AI and Digital Nomads Shaping Global Industrial Technology Transitions* (pp. 113–138). IGI Global Scientific Publishing., DOI: 10.4018/979-8-3373-0159-4.ch004

Tariq, M. U. (2025). Building Green-Crafting Sustainable Business Models for a Resilient Future. In Mehra, P., & Kumar, P. (Eds.), *Incentives and Benefits for Adopting Green Entrepreneurship Practices* (pp. 37–64). IGI Global Scientific Publishing., DOI: 10.4018/979-8-3693-9306-2.ch002

Tariq, M. U. (2025). Green FinTech-Driving Sustainable Finance and Empowering Underserved Communities. In Masri, M., Sait, M., & Anshari, M. (Eds.), *Promoting Inclusivity and Accessibility With FinTech* (pp. 279–306). IGI Global Scientific Publishing., DOI: 10.4018/979-8-3373-1112-8.ch010

Tariq, M. U. (2025). The Influence of Leadership Styles on Innovation: Driving Change Through Effective Leadership. In Paradiso-Testa, M. (Ed.), *The Impact of Innovation in Leadership* (pp. 249–274). IGI Global Scientific Publishing., DOI: 10.4018/979-8-3373-2402-9.ch010

Taylor, B. W. (2013). *Introduction to management science*. Pearson.

Taylor, R. (2018). Flexibility in SME financial decisions. *Journal of Finance and Management*, *6*(4), 101–118.

Teece, D. J. (2007). Explicating dynamic capabilities: The nature and microfoundations of sustainable enterprise performance. *Strategic Management Journal*, *28*(13), 1319–1350. DOI: 10.1002/smj.640

Teece, D. J. (2018). *Dynamic capabilities and strategic management: Organizing for innovation and growth*. Oxford University Press.

Teece, D. J. (2022). Dynamic capabilities, digital platforms, and M&As. *Strategic Management Journal*, *43*(6), 1102–1122. DOI: 10.1002/smj.3334

Teece, D. J., Pisano, G., & Shuen, A. (1997). Dynamic capabilities and strategic management. *Strategic Management Journal*, *18*(7), 509–533. DOI: 10.1002/(SICI)1097-0266(199708)18:7<509::AID-SMJ882>3.0.CO;2-Z

Teerikangas, S., & Very, P. (2011). Culture in mergers and acquisitions: A critical review and future research agenda. *International Journal of Cross Cultural Management*, *11*(2), 143–156. DOI: 10.1177/1470595811413107

Teixeira, J. S., & Macedo, M. F. (2023). Plano de marketing: Lançamento da Starlight Makeup.

Teixeira, A. R., Ferreira, J. V., & Ramos, A. L. (2024). Optimization of business processes through BPM methodology: A case study on data analysis and performance improvement. *Information (Basel)*, *15*(11), 724. DOI: 10.3390/info15110724

Thelisson, A.-S. (2023). Coopetition in a failed merger project: Why two French companies called it quits. *The Journal of Business Strategy*, *44*(1), 44–49. DOI: 10.1108/JBS-06-2021-0102

Torre, I. G., Romero, M., & Álvarez, A. (2021). Improving aphasic speech recognition by using novel semi-supervised learning methods on aphasiabank for english and spanish. *Applied Sciences (Basel, Switzerland), 11*(19), 8872. DOI: 10.3390/app11198872

Transparency International UK. (2012). Anti-bribery due diligence for transactions. https://archive.transparency.org.uk/sites/default/files/pdf/publications/Anti-Bribery_Due_Diligence_for_Transactions_1.pdf

Trentin, C., Ampatzidis, Y., Lacerda, C., & Shiratsuchi, L. (2024). Tree crop yield estimation and prediction using remote sensing and machine learning: A systematic review. *Smart Agricultural Technology, 100556*, 100556. Advance online publication. DOI: 10.1016/j.atech.2024.100556

Tripathi, A. A. (2018). Factors affecting effective mergers and acquisition: An empirical investigation. *INFORMATION TECHNOLOGY IN INDUSTRY, 6*(3). Advance online publication. DOI: 10.17762/itii.v6i3.823

Truong, G., Partington, G., & Peat, M. (2008). Cost-of-capital estimation and capital-budgeting practice in Australia. *Australian Journal of Management, 33*(1), 95–121. DOI: 10.1177/031289620803300106

Tversky, A., & Kahneman, D. (1974). Judgment under uncertainty: Heuristics and biases. *Science, 185*(4157), 1124–1131. DOI: 10.1126/science.185.4157.1124 PMID: 17835457

U.S. Department of Justice. (2008). Siemens AG and Three Subsidiaries Plead Guilty to Foreign Corrupt Practices Act Violations and Agree to Pay $450 Million in Combined Criminal Fines. https://www.justice.gov/archive/opa/pr/2008/December/08-crm-1105.html

Ulrich, D., Brockbank, W., Johnson, D., Sandholtz, K., & Younger, J. (2017). *HR competencies: Mastery at the intersection of people and business*. Society for Human Resource Management.

Umashankar, N., Bahadir, S. C., & Bharadwaj, S. (2022). M&As hurt customer satisfaction and firm value. *Journal of Marketing, 86*(2), 66–86. DOI: 10.1177/00222429211024255

UNCTAD. (2023). *World Investment Report: Institutional Capacity Building*. United Nations.

United Nations. (2015). Transforming our world: The 2030 Agenda for Sustainable Development. https://sdgs.un.org/2030agenda

Vaddepalli, S., & Vishwanath, B. (2024). Mergers and acquisitions: Drivers, challenges, and performance outcomes in GCC nations. *International Journal of Central Banking, 20*(1), 298–310.

Vantrappen, H., & Wirtz, F. (2023). *The organization design guide: A pragmatic framework for thoughtful, efficient and successful redesigns.* Routledge. DOI: 10.4324/9781003462811

Venkatesh, V., Morris, M. G., Davis, G. B., & Davis, F. D. (2003). User acceptance of information technology: Toward a unified view. *Management Information Systems Quarterly, 27*(3), 425–478. DOI: 10.2307/30036540

Verma, K. K., Singh, B. M., & Dixit, A. (2022). A review of supervised and unsupervised machine learning techniques for suspicious behavior recognition in the intelligent surveillance system. *International Journal of Information Technology : an Official Journal of Bharati Vidyapeeth's Institute of Computer Applications and Management, 14*(1), 397–410. DOI: 10.1007/s41870-019-00364-0

Vieira, J. P. (2024). Influência do padrão de beleza transmitido pelos influencers no consumismo das jovens na indústria de cosméticos.

Vijayaragavan, P., Ponnusamy, R., & Aramudhan, M. (2020). An optimal support vector machine-based classification model for sentimental analysis of online product reviews. *Future Generation Computer Systems, 111*, 234–240. DOI: 10.1016/j.future.2020.04.046

Wang, Y., Chen, X., & Zhang, L. (2024). Digital transformation and cross-border mergers and acquisitions: Evidence from emerging economies. *International Business Review, 33*(5), 102123. DOI: 10.1016/j.ibusrev.2023.102123

Wang, Y., Xu, Y., & Zhong, Y. (2025). Does artificial intelligence invariably enhance ESG performance? *Journal for Economic Forecasting, 2*, 24–40.

Wang, Z., Luo, X., & Li, J. (2025). Digital innovation ecosystems and strategic collaboration: A network perspective. *Technovation, 128*, 102741. DOI: 10.1016/j.technovation.2024.102741

Watling, J., & Wilén, N. (2024). Assessing the causes of strategic realignment in Sahelian states. *RUSI Journal, 169*(4), 64–77. DOI: 10.1080/03071847.2024.2395563

Weber, Y., Rachman-Moore, D., & Tarba, S. Y. (2012). HR practices during post-merger conflict and merger performance. *International Journal of Cross Cultural Management, 12*(1), 73–99. DOI: 10.1177/1470595811413111

Weber, Y., & Tarba, S. Y. (2017). Strategic agility in M&A: A dynamic capabilities perspective. *Human Resource Management Review*, *27*(3), 316–329. DOI: 10.1016/j.hrmr.2016.09.010

Weber, Y., & Tarba, S. Y. (2020). Strategic agility in M&A integration: The role of continuous organizational redesign. *Journal of Organizational Change Management*, *33*(6), 1231–1250.

Weber, Y., & Yedidia Tarba, S. (2012). Mergers and acquisitions process: The use of corporate culture analysis. *Cross Cultural Management*, *19*(3), 288–303. DOI: 10.1108/13527601211247053

Wengel, J. (2023). Cultural intelligence and trust in global virtual teams. *Business and Professional Communication Quarterly*. Advance online publication. DOI: 10.1177/23294906231179915

Wernerfelt, B. (1984). A resource-based view of the firm. *Strategic Management Journal*, *5*(2), 171–180. DOI: 10.1002/smj.4250050207

Wesselhöft, M., Hinckeldeyn, J., & Kreutzfeldt, J. (2022). Controlling fleets of autonomous mobile robots with reinforcement learning: A brief survey. *Robotics (Basel, Switzerland)*, *11*(5), 85. DOI: 10.3390/robotics11050085

West, D. M., & Allen, J. R. (2020). *Turning point: Policymaking in the era of artificial intelligence*. Brookings Institution Press. DOI: 10.5040/9780815751113

Westerman, G., Bonnet, D., & McAfee, A. (2019). *Leading digital: Turning technology into business transformation* (2nd ed.). Harvard Business Review Press.

Wiegelmann, T., & Glauerdt, R. (2025). Practice Briefing: Mergers and Acquisitions in real estate asset management (Part 1)–strategic motivations, valuation and transaction structuring. *Journal of Property Investment & Finance*, *43*(4), 454–468. DOI: 10.1108/JPIF-02-2025-0033

Williams, N., Ved, K., & Lim, N. (2022). Anti-bribery, corruption and risk diligence recommendations for M&A activity in Asia. *Financier Worldwide*. https://www.financierworldwide.com/anti-bribery-corruption-and-risk-diligence-recommendations-for-ma-activity-in-asia

Winston, W. L. (2004). *Operations research: Applications and algorithms*. Cengage Learning.

Winston, W. L., & Venkataramanan, M. (2003). *Introduction to mathematical programming: Applications and algorithms*. Cengage Learning.

Wong, L. W., Tan, G. W. H., Ooi, K. B., Lin, B., & Dwivedi, Y. K. (2022). Artificial Intelligence-Driven Risk Management for Enhancing Supply Chain Agility: A Deep-Learning-Based Dual-Stage PLS-SEM-ANN Analysis. *International Journal of Production Research*, •••, 1–21. DOI: 10.1080/00207543.2022.2063089

Worren, N. A. (2018). *Organization design: Simplifying complex systems* (2nd ed.). Routledge. DOI: 10.4324/9781315145112

WTO. (2021). *Trade and Investment Policy Measures Report*. WTO Secretariat.

Wu, C.-C., Liu, T.-Y., & Yang, T.-H. (2025). Unraveling the dynamics of cross-border mergers and acquisitions: Motivations and performance implications. *SAGE Open*, *15*(2), 21582440251338684. Advance online publication. DOI: 10.1177/21582440251338684

Wu, J., Li, H., & Zhao, X. (2026). Platform alignment and value co-creation in digital supply chains. *Industrial Marketing Management*, *118*, 213–225. DOI: 10.1016/j.indmarman.2025.09.004

Xie, H., & Wu, F. (2025). Artificial intelligence technology and corporate ESG performance: Empirical evidence from Chinese-listed firms. *Sustainability (Basel)*, *17*(2), 420. DOI: 10.3390/su17020420

Xu, Y., & Bradley, J. (2022). Regional merger review integration: ASEAN vs. EU. *Asian Journal of Comparative Law*, *17*(2), 280–305. DOI: 10.1017/asjcl.2022.10

Yang, M., & Ai, Q. (2025). Completion of high-tech M&As by Chinese firms: Knowledge distance, industry attractiveness and government involvement. *Asia Pacific Journal of Management*, *42*(1), 427–454. DOI: 10.1007/s10490-023-09923-3

Young, S. D., & O'Byrne, S. F. (2001). *EVA and value-based management: A practical guide to implementation*. McGraw-Hill Education.

Yukl, G. (2010). *Leadership in organizations* (7th ed.). Pearson.

Yu, S., Liu, Z., Xiong, C., & Liu, Z. (2023, July). Openmatch-v2: An all-in-one multi-modality plm-based information retrieval toolkit. In *Proceedings of the 46th International ACM SIGIR Conference on Research and Development in Information Retrieval* (pp. 3160-3164). DOI: 10.1145/3539618.3591813

Yu, X., Fan, L., & Yu, Y. (2025). Artificial intelligence and corporate ESG performance: A mechanism analysis based on corporate efficiency and external environment. *Sustainability (Basel)*, *17*(9), 3819. DOI: 10.3390/su17093819

Zakaria, N., & Ab Rahman Muton, N. (2022). Cultural code-switching in high context global virtual team members: A qualitative study. *International Journal of Cross Cultural Management*, *22*(3), 487–515. DOI: 10.1177/14705958221137256

Zanon, P. H. (2024). Análise de dados e inovação no marketing digital para a área de saúde.

Zhang, M., & Wei, X. (2024). Resource efficiency, cultural industry, and green economic growth: A synergistic approach. *Resources Policy*, *90*, 104769. DOI: 10.1016/j.resourpol.2024.104769

Zhang, Q. (2025). Functions of PESTEL analysis in the assessment of enterprise environmental adaptability. In *Proceedings of the 2024 2nd International Conference on Economic Management, Financial Innovation and Public Service (EMFIPS 2024)* (pp. 340-349). Atlantis Press. https://doi.org/DOI: 10.2991/978-94-6463-706-9_31

Zhang, X., & Zhu, G. Y. (2024). A literature review of reinforcement learning methods applied to job-shop scheduling problems. *Computers & Operations Research, 106929*. Advance online publication. DOI: 10.1016/j.cor.2024.106929

Zhao, H. (2022). Management team cultural alignment and mergers and acquisitions. *Finance Research Letters, 46*(Part B). *Finance Research Letters*, *102448*, 102448. Advance online publication. DOI: 10.1016/j.frl.2021.102448

Zheng, Z., Wang, P., Liu, J., & Sun, S. (2015). Real-time big data processing framework: Challenges and solutions. *Applied Mathematics & Information Sciences*, *9*(6), 3169. DOI: 10.12785/amis/090646

Zhou, X., Li, G., Wang, Q., Li, Y., & Zhou, D. (2025). Artificial intelligence, corporate information governance and ESG performance: Quasi-experimental evidence from China. *International Review of Financial Analysis*, *102*, 104087. DOI: 10.1016/j.irfa.2025.104087

About the Contributors

Ricardo Marcão, PhD, MBA, PMP, is a globally recognized expert in Project Management, Finance, Strategy, Grand Strategy, and Healthcare Innovation, with extensive experience in Pharma, MedTech, Medical Devices, IT, and Professional Services. Beyond corporate strategy, Ricardo's expertise extends into Grand Strategy, Democracy, and International Relations, with a particular focus on how geopolitics, economic strategy, and competitive intelligence shape global business dynamics. His knowledge in policy frameworks and transatlantic relations positions him as a thought leader in aligning business growth, technological innovation, and governance for long-term impact. Throughout his career, he has led major transformations, implementing gamification strategies to enhance engagement and sales, redefining Pharma and MedTech consulting through digital innovation, and introducing a risk control framework that improved project margins by 20%. From 2022 to 2023, he spearheaded global CRM projects for top pharmaceutical firms, optimizing commercial operations across international markets. An accomplished academic, editor, and international speaker, Ricardo has authored and edited multiple books on strategy, innovation, and performance evaluation. As a coordinator of MBA, Post-Graduate, Master's and Higher Technical programs at ISLA Santarém, he plays a key role in developing future business leaders at the intersection of business, technology, and governance. Actively engaged in SCIP Portugal, APMP NYC, and PMI, he continues to contribute to strategic intelligence, business consultancy, and global policy discourse.

Vasco Ribeiro Santos is an Adjunct Professor at the Polytechnic University of Tomar (IPT) and member of the Research and Innovation Support Office (GAII). He has a Habilitation in Management (European University, Lisbon), a PhD in Business Sciences (Fernando Pessoa University, Porto), a PhD in Tourism (University of Seville, Spain) and a Post-Doctorate in Innovation Management (University of Aveiro). Specialises in Hotel and Restaurant Management. Integrated researcher at

NECE-UI and collaborating researcher at GOVCOPP (University of Aveiro), TECHN&ART (Polytechnic University of Tomar) and CITUR (Polytechnic of Leiria). Editor-in-Chief of the scientific journal 'International Journal of Digital Marketing, Management, and Innovation (IJDMMI)'. Author and reviewer for indexed scientific journals. Author of Book Chapters in IGI Global. Editor of Books in IGI Global.

***

Afef Amdouni is an Assistant Professor of Finance at the Department of Finance and Economics, College of Business Administration, Taibah University, Medina, Saudi Arabia. Her research focuses on financial markets, artificial intelligence applications in finance, behavioral finance, and financial risk modeling. Before joining Taibah University, she was affiliated with the Faculty of Economic Sciences and Management at the University of Tunis El Manar, Tunisia. Dr. Amdouni earned her Ph.D. in Finance from the same university, where she also completed her Master's and Bachelor's degrees. She is actively involved in academic publishing and peer review processes and has taken leadership roles in coordinating editorial activities related to interdisciplinary research at the intersection of finance and artificial intelligence.

Christo George is associated with the Department of Civil Engineering at the Dayananda Sagar College of Engineering, Bengaluru, India. His academic and research interests primarily focus on civil engineering technologies, sustainable infrastructure, and innovative engineering practices that contribute to modern urban development. Dr. George is actively involved in teaching, research, and mentoring students in various areas of civil engineering, while also contributing to scholarly publications and academic collaborations. His work emphasizes the integration of engineering principles with emerging technologies to address real-world challenges in construction, structural design, and infrastructure management.

Pranjal Khare is a distinguished corporate lawyer and is currently working as a law faculty at O.P. Jindal Global University, India. He specializes in Property Law, Corporate laws, Intellectual Property Rights, and International law. Mr. Pranjal is a highly regarded scholar and has published on numerous issues related to international affairs, economy, politics, data & privacy, artificial intelligence and IP disputes. He is also a frequent speaker at legal conferences and has served as a consultant to numerous law firms and corporations.

Lucas Lacerda is an undergraduate student in Computer Engineering at ISLA Santarém – Polytechnic Institute, Portugal.

Filipa Martinho is a researcher and academic with interests in sustainability, innovation, and organizational management. Her work focuses on the intersection between business strategy, environmental and social responsibility, and performance in organizational contexts. She has contributed to academic publications and collaborative research projects addressing contemporary challenges in sustainable management, digital transformation, and corporate governance. Filipa Martinho is engaged in applied and theoretical research aimed at supporting evidence-based decision-making and long-term value creation in organizations.

Vijaishree Pandey is a distinguished academician and legal professional, serves as the President of the Artificial Intelligence for Women's Empowerment and Representation Council, spearheading initiatives at the intersection of law, technology, and gender equality. Experienced and accomplished academician with a demonstrated history of working in the legal services industry and a passion for research and publication. Her expertise in Human Rights and IPRs and had undergone trainings related to Artificial Intelligence. She has worked in collaboration with jails, orphanages, schools, and RWAs, aiming to provide legal aid and basic legal rights. Her leadership skills, coupled with her dedication to professional ethics and academic excellence, have earned her the respect of her peers and students alike. Her dedication to social causes is evident through her involvement in legal aid programs, advocacy efforts, and community outreach initiatives. Beyond academia, Dr. Pandey is a sought-after resource person and guest speaker, lending her expertise to various institutions and organizations. Her expertise spans across various domains, coupled with her leadership acumen and commitment to women's empowerment. As the President of the Artificial Intelligence for Women's Empowerment and Representation Council, Dr. Pandey spearheads initiatives aimed at bridging the gender gap in AI and fostering inclusivity. Her research prowess is evidenced by a prolific publication record, comprising numerous papers, chapters, and books on diverse legal topics. She has also been an active participant in conferences, seminars, and webinars, contributing to the advancement of legal scholarship and continuously expanding her knowledge and professional network. With an extensive portfolio including multiple paper publications in reputed national and international journals, workshops, book chapters in edited books, and conference presentations, she has established a strong presence in the academic community. Experienced Legal Professional with a strong background in Web 4.0 and Artificial Intelligence. She is skilled in analysing complex legal cases and providing innovative solutions. Proficient in applying cutting-edge technology to the legal field, effectively utilizing

AI tools to streamline processes and enhance efficiency. She has developed a deep understanding of the intersection between technology and law, with a focus on leveraging AI advancements to improve access to justice. Looking ahead, her goal is to continue making significant contributions to the legal field and to establish myself as a leading expert and thought leader in the field of law while also mentoring and inspiring the next generation of scholars. She is driven, meticulous, and committed to fostering academic excellence.

Mukhriddin Pulatov is affiliated with the Department of Economics at Termez University of Economics and Service, Termez, Uzbekistan. Her academic interests focus on economic development, entrepreneurship, and the application of modern technologies in economic systems and education. She is actively involved in teaching and research activities that address contemporary economic challenges, including innovation-driven growth, digital transformation, and the development of entrepreneurial competencies among students. Through her academic work, she contributes to the advancement of economic education and promotes interdisciplinary approaches that integrate economic theory with emerging technological trends. Her research and teaching efforts aim to support sustainable economic development and strengthen the role of higher education institutions in fostering entrepreneurial thinking and innovation in the regional and global context.

Ravikumar R. N. is currently a Postdoctoral researcher at Universiti Malaysia Perlis, Malaysia. Also, working as an Assistant Professor in the Department of Computer Engineering at Marwadi University, Rajkot, Gujarat. He has 14 years of national and international teaching experience. He completed his PhD at Amity University, Rajasthan, M.E at VMRF Deemed University, B.E at Anna University, Chennai. He is the co-founder of the Research Activities Club at Marwadi University and trains students on research activities, which leads to the various publications. He has published numerous research articles in Scopus, SCI journals, Book chapters, and Conference papers. Also, he hold several patents and authored books. His specialization is ML, DL, Federated Learning, Recommendation Systems, and Optimization Techniques.

Aarthi S is a dedicated Assistant Professor in Computer Science with over six years of teaching experience. She is currently pursuing her Ph.D. at Marwadi University, Gujarat, and holds an M.Phil. and MCA from Bharathiar University, Tamil Nadu. Throughout her academic career, Aarthi has specialized in programming languages such as C++, Java, and C, and contributed to research in recommender systems and AI-related data privacy. She has published journal articles, contributed to book chapters, and actively participated in technical workshops. Known for her student mentorship and engagement in academic events, Aarthi remains committed to fostering innovation and excellence in computer science education.

Agatha Saber is a university instructor and researcher at the Business School of the Holy Spirit University of Kaslik (USEK). Her work centers on business administration and managerial finance, with a specialized focus on financial transparency, governance, institutional capacity, and sustainable development goals. Dr. Saber is dedicated to bridging academic knowledge with real-world practice through her teaching and research.

Valisher Sapayev is a faculty member in the Department of General Professional Subjects at Mamun University, Khiva, Uzbekistan. He is engaged in teaching and academic activities that support the development of professional and interdisciplinary competencies among university students. His academic interests include modern teaching methodologies, professional education, and the integration of innovative approaches in higher education. Through his teaching and scholarly contributions, he focuses on enhancing students' practical knowledge, critical thinking, and professional skills required for contemporary academic and professional environments. His work contributes to strengthening the quality of higher education and promoting the development of skilled graduates who can effectively respond to the evolving demands of the global workforce.

Suruchi Satsangi is an Assistant Professor, Gitarattan International Business School, Rohini, Delhi. She holds a Doctorate Degree in Accountancy & Law, M.Com. (Specialization in International Business) & B.Com. (Honours) from Dayalbagh Educational Institute. She is the author of 7 papers published in National & International Journals, Springer, Emerald & UGC Care etc. and presented 21 research papers in reputed conferences. Her area of interest is Accounting & Finance, Statistical Analysis, Research related issues in Companies. She has 3 years of experience in teaching and conducted various International E- Conferences, International Webinar, National Seminar and FDP.

Rajeev Shah is an Assistant Professor at IPEM College, Ghaziabad, with a strong academic and professional background in Commerce, Management and Economics. He holds a degree of M.Com, MBA and CMA Inter and has 7+ years of teaching and academic experience at the undergraduate and postgraduate levels. His areas of interest include Financial Management and Economics.

Ruben Silva Pinhal is a management and technology professional with interests in digital transformation, organizational performance, and applied innovation. His work focuses on the integration of technology into business processes, supporting decision-making, efficiency, and competitiveness in organizational contexts. Ruben is also engaged in academic and applied research, contributing to studies that bridge management theory and real-world business practice.

Sheetal Singh is a seasoned legal academic with over 15 years of experience in teaching, research, and academic administration. Currently serving as Assistant Professor at the School of Law, CHRIST (Deemed to be University), Delhi NCR Campus, she previously held senior faculty roles at Amity Law School, Noida, where she also founded the Amity Legal Aid Cell. She holds a Ph.D. in Law from Amity University and is UGC-NET qualified, with expertise spanning Family Law, Criminal Law, Constitutional Law, Property Law, and Human Rights. Dr. Singh has guided more than 150 LLB and LLM dissertations and supervises Ph.D. research on gender justice and victimology. Her scholarly contributions include chapters in edited volumes published by Thomson Reuters, CRC Press, Springer, and Cambridge Scholars Publishing, covering topics such as media law, reproductive rights, cybersecurity, and comparative constitutional analysis. She has presented papers at national and international conferences, delivered guest lectures, and organized seminars and workshops on legal education, gender sensitization, and human rights. Her administrative roles include serving as Head of Department, Program Coordinator, and member of various university committees such as IQAC, Moot Court, and Placement. Widely recognized for her commitment to legal education and interdisciplinary research, Dr. Singh continues to contribute meaningfully to academia and social justice initiatives.

Rituraj Sinha is an Assistant Professor at the School of Law, CHRIST (Deemed to be University), Delhi NCR. He holds a Ph.D. from Guru Gobind Singh Indraprastha University and an LL.M. from NALSAR. With prior teaching experience at Amity Law School and IMS Unison University, he also practiced as an advocate in Delhi. His academic interests include Corporate Law, gender justice, intellectual property rights, and the legal dimensions of emerging technologies. He has contributed to reputed journals and international conference volumes and actively mentors students in research and legal scholarship.

Shashank Solanki is a B.B.A. LL.B (Hons.) student at CHRIST (Deemed to be University), Delhi NCR. With a strong academic foundation and a keen interest in Arbitration, Securities, Corporate Law, and Banking & Finance, Shashank has actively contributed to legal scholarship. His research works have been accepted for publication in esteemed Scopus-indexed platforms, addressing critical areas such as medical big data, digital healthcare ethics, and the Metaverse. Beyond academics, he has demonstrated excellence through multiple internships, gaining hands on experience in dispute resolution, corporate law, and judicial research. Shashank's dedication to academic pursuits and practical legal applications reflects his commitment to contributing meaningfully to the legal domain.

Bruno Sousa is Dean of the School of Hospitality and Tourism (ESHT) at the Polytechnic University of Cávado and Ave (IPCA), Portugal and Coordinating Professor (IPCA). He holds a PhD in Marketing and Strategy from the University of Minho, Portugal. He is Director of the Master's Program in Tourism Marketing (IPCA). He is a research member of UNIAG (Applied Management Research Unit) and CiTUR (Centre for Tourism Research, Development and Innovation). Bruno Sousa has edited several books and published several chapters in IGI Global over the last ten years on topics related to marketing, strategy, tourism, and management. He has published in the Journal of Enterprising Communities, EuroMed Journal of Business, Tourism Management Perspectives, Current Issues in Tourism, Journal of Organizational Change Management, Journal of Hospitality and Tourism Insights, Management Decision, World Review of Entrepreneurship, Journal of Global Marketing, Management and Sustainable Development, among others.

Satya Subrahmanyam is a distinguished academic leader, researcher, and institutional strategist with over 27 years of experience in higher education, leadership, and research management. He holds two PhDs and a Postdoctoral qualification from the Polytechnic Institute of Leiria, Portugal. Currently serving as Professor and Dean (Research) at Holy Spirit University of Kaslik (USEK), Lebanon, he spearheads research initiatives that enhance academic excellence and institutional reputation. He played a pivotal role in the development of the Catholic University in Erbil, Kurdistan, where he established new departments, led research programs, and collaborated on international educational projects. As a founding member and Managing Partner of Vignan Institute of Technology and Management, India, he contributed to its transformation into a premier institution. With expertise in AI-driven business strategies, HR analytics, and leadership in technology adoption, he has published extensively, guided PhD research, and led training programs in corporate and academic settings.

Muhammad Usman Tariq is a strategic higher education leader and scholar with more than 17 years of international experience across academia, research, and industry. He holds dual doctorates, a PhD in Artificial Intelligence and a Doctorate in Business Administration and has published extensively as the author of research articles, case studies, book chapters, and academic texts. His contributions also include several patents, reflecting his applied research in technology, business, and education. He is the Founder and CEO of TheCaseHQ.com, a global hub for professional certification programmes, narrative and video case studies, and digital learning innovation. In addition, he serves as President of the Gulf Higher Education Network (Gulf HE), an initiative dedicated to advancing academic practice, faculty development, and institutional collaboration across the region. He is a Principal Fellow of Advance HE (UK), Chartered Fellow of the CIPD (UK), Senior Fellow of SEDA (UK), and a Senior Member of IEEE, reflecting his standing as both an academic innovator and a global professional leader.

Khayrulla Urozboev is associated with the Department of International Scientific Journals and Ratings at Alfraganus University, Tashkent, Uzbekistan. His academic and professional work focuses on scholarly publishing, research evaluation, and the advancement of international scientific visibility for academic institutions. He is actively involved in activities related to journal indexing, academic rankings, and the promotion of high-quality research publications in global databases. His interests include research management, bibliometric analysis, and strategies for improving the impact and quality of scientific journals. Through his work, he contributes to strengthening research standards and enhancing the international recognition of academic research produced by universities and scholars.

Vijeta Verma is an Assistant Professor at the School of Law, CHRIST (Deemed to be University), Delhi NCR. She holds a Ph.D. in Law from Mewar University and an LL.M. from Amity University, Noida. With over a decade of academic experience, she has previously served as an Assistant Professor at JIMS Engineering Management & Technical Campus and Ideal Institute of Management & Technology. Her research interests lie in Constitutional Law, Human Rights, and Gender Justice. At CHRIST, she actively contributes as the Faculty Convenor for various academic committees and has been a key organizer of national and international legal conferences.

Index

Symbols

A

B

C

D

E

F

R

S

T